THE NEW
PALGRAVE

CAPITAL THEORY

THE NEW PALGRAVE

CAPITAL THEORY

EDITED BY

JOHN EATWELL · MURRAY MILGATE · PETER NEWMAN

W. W. NORTON & COMPANY

NEW YORK · LONDON

© The Macmillan Press Limited, 1990

First published in
The New Palgrave: A Dictionary of Economics
Edited by John Eatwell, Murray Milgate and Peter Newman
in four volumes, 1987

The New Palgrave is a trademark of
The Macmillan Press Limited

First American Edition, 1990
All rights reserved.

ISBN 0-393-02730-9
ISBN 0-393-95855-8 PBK.

W. W. Norton & Company, Inc.
500 Fifth Avenue
New York, NY 10110

W. W. Norton & Company, Ltd.
37 Great Russell Street
London WC1B 3NU

Printed in Hong Kong

1   2   3   4   5   6   7   8   9   0

Contents

Contents

General Preface

The books in this series are the offspring of *The New Palgrave: A Dictionary of Economics*. Published in late 1987, the *Dictionary* has rapidly become a standard reference work in economics. However, its four heavy tomes containing over four million words on the whole range of economic thought is not a form convenient to every potential user. For many students and teachers it is simply too bulky, too comprehensive and too expensive for everyday use.

By developing the present series of compact volumes of reprints from the original work, we hope that some of the intellectual wealth of *The New Palgrave* will become accessible to much wider groups of readers. Each of the volumes is devoted to a particular branch of economics, such as econometrics or general equilibrium or money, with a scope corresponding roughly to a university course on that subject. Apart from correction of misprints, etc. the content of each of its reprinted articles is exactly the same as that of the original. In addition, a few brand new entries have been commissioned especially for the series, either to fill an apparent gap or more commonly to include topics that have risen to prominence since the dictionary was originally commissioned.

As *The New Palgrave* is the sole parent of the present series, it may be helpful to explain that it is the modern successor to the excellent *Dictionary of Political Economy* edited by R.H. Inglis Palgrave and published in three volumes in 1894, 1896 and 1899. A second and slightly modified version, edited by Henry Higgs, appeared during the mid-1920s. These two editions each contained almost 4,000 entries, but many of those were simply brief definitions and many of the others were devoted to peripheral topics such as foreign coinage, maritime commerce, and Scottish law. To make room for the spectacular growth in economics over the last 60 years while keeping still to a manageable length, *The New Palgrave* concentrated instead on economic theory, its originators, and its closely cognate disciplines. Its nearly 2,000 entries (commissioned from over 900 scholars) are all self-contained essays, sometimes brief but never mere definitions.

Apart from its biographical entries, *The New Palgrave* is concerned chiefly with theory rather than fact, doctrine rather than data; and it is not at all clear how theory and doctrine, as distinct from facts and figures, *should* be treated in an encyclopaedia. One way is to treat everything from a particular point of view. Broadly speaking, that was the way of Diderot's classic *Encyclopédie raisonée* (1751–1772), as it was also of Léon Say's *Nouveau dictionnaire d'économie politique* (1891–2). Sometimes, as in articles by Quesnay and Turgot in the *Encyclopédie*, this approach has yielded entries of surpassing brilliance. Too often, however, both the range of subjects covered and the quality of the coverage itself are seriously reduced by such a self-limiting perspective. Thus the entry called '*Méthode*' in the first edition of Say's *Dictionnaire* asserted that the use of mathematics in economics 'will only ever be in the hands of a few', and the dictionary backed up that claim by choosing not to have any entry on Cournot.

Another approach is to have each entry take care to reflect within itself varying points of view. This may help the student temporarily, as when preparing for an examination. But in a subject like economics, the Olympian detachment which this approach requires often places a heavy burden on the author, asking for a scrupulous account of doctrines he or she believes to be at best wrong-headed. Even when an especially able author does produce a judicious survey article, it is surely too much to ask that it also convey just as much enthusiasm for those theories thought misguided as for those found congenial. Lacking an enthusiastic exposition, however, the disfavoured theories may then be studied less closely than they deserve.

The New Palgrave did not ask its authors to treat economic theory from any particular point of view, except in one respect to be discussed below. Nor did it call for surveys. Instead, each author was asked to make clear his or her own views of the subject under discussion, and for the rest to be as fair and accurate as possible, without striving to be 'judicious'. A balanced perspective on each topic was always the aim, the ideal. But it was to be sought not *internally*, within each article, but *externally*, between articles, with the reader rather than the writer handed the task of achieving a personal balance between differing views.

For a controversial topic, a set of several more or less synonymous headwords, matched by a broad diversity of contributors, was designed to produce enough variety of opinion to help form the reader's own synthesis; indeed, such diversity will be found in most of the individual volumes in this series.

This approach was not without its problems. Thus, the prevalence of uncertainty in the process of commissioning entries sometimes produced a less diverse outcome than we had planned. 'I can call spirits from the vasty deep,' said Owen Glendower. 'Why, so can I,' replied Hotspur, 'or so can any man;/ But will they come when you do call for them?' In our experience, not quite as often as we would have liked.

The one point of view we did urge upon every one of *Palgrave*'s authors was to write from an historical perspective. For each subject its contributor was asked to discuss not only present problems but also past growth and future prospects. This request was made in the belief that knowledge of the historical development of any theory enriches our present understanding of it, and so helps to construct better theories for the future. The authors' response to the request was generally so positive that, as the reader of any of these volumes will discover, the resulting contributions amply justified that belief.

John Eatwell
Murray Milgate
Peter Newman

Preface

To some extent the very existence of this collection compounds a common error in economics. It suggests that 'capital theory' is an *application* of economic theory, rather like the theory of finance, or the theory of the firm. But capital theory is not a 'branch' of economics. It is about the determination of prices in an economy in which some of the means of production are reproducible. Leaving aside a few exotic examples (see, for example, R.A. Radford, The Economic Organisation of a P.O.W. Camp, *Economica*, 1945) it is difficult to imagine any actual economy which does not possess this characteristic. Certainly none of the market economies with which economics as a discipline is predominantly concerned lacks reproducible means of production. So capital theory is simply the price theory of the economies in which we actually live.

There is, of course, a good deal of price theory for economies which do not contain reproducible means of production – models of pure exchange, for example, or models of production and exchange using only non-reproducible means of production. But as Wicksell pointed out, these bear

> no possible resemblance to actual production and, strictly speaking, cannot exist in fact. In all these cases the results are, of course, not even approximately correct, but are purely hypothetical, though the enquiry is not, on that account, valueless. They constitute rather a necessary element in the full and correct solution of the problem ... even if it should sometimes prove impossible to complete the reasoning ... (Wicksell, *Lectures in Political Economy*, vol. 1, p. 10).

Capital theory has been one of the most contentious areas of debate in economic analysis. One reason for this is that it is the point at which the classical theory of value and distribution, and the neoclassical theory of price meet, so to speak, on the same ground. Classical theory was devoted to explaining the determination of the rate of profit and associated 'natural prices' in an economy using reproducible means of production. In so far as neoclassical theory attempts to determine the rate of profit and associated 'long-run prices' it is offering an alternative explanation of exactly the same things.

That an analytical issue should prove contentious appears, at first sight, rather odd. Surely, once the specification of the problem is agreed upon, a careful formal examination will determine which argument is correct, and which is false. This has not proved to be the case in capital theory, because neither classical nor neoclassical theory can produce an entirely satisfactory answer to the question posed.

The classical answer is that the rate of profit and associated prices are determined by the conditions of reproduction of a particular size and composition of output once the real wage is taken as exogenously given. It can be demonstrated that this answer is formally correct. But it leaves in the air the question of what determines that size and composition of output, and what determines the real wage.

The neoclassical answer is that the rate of profit and long-run normal prices are determined by supply and demand; or, more accurately, by the competitive resolution of individual attempts to maximize utility subject to constraints, where some of those constraints consist of endowments of reproducible means of production.

Here a serious difficulty arises – a difficulty first outlined with remarkable clarity by Walras.

In models of production and exchange involving only non-reproducible means of production (land and labour) commodities fall into two distinct groups. Either, as in the case of the rentals paid for the services of factor endowments, their prices are determined simply by market clearing, or, as in the case of 'final' goods (consumer goods) their prices must be equal, in equilibrium, to the sum of the rentals of the factor services required for their production (their cost of production). Since, by definition, no factors are reproducible, their prices are not subject to this 'cost of production' condition.

Once reproducible means of production are introduced into this picture, its clarity is obscured. For in this case, the rentals on the endowments of reproducible factors should be determined by market clearing, and yet, in equilibrium, the prices of reproducible factors, like the prices of all reproducible commodities, should be equal to their cost of production. Since the prices of reproducible factors are simply the capitalized values of the rentals paid for their services, two sets of conditions ('market clearing' and 'cost of production') are being applied to the determination of the same prices. The analysis is over-determined.

The difficulty of extending the analysis of supply and demand to models including reproducible means of production impressed itself upon the earliest neoclassical writers (notably Walras, Böhm-Bawerk and Wicksell) and, being unsolved, has been returned to again and again.

One attempted solution involved expressing the endowment of capital goods as a single quantity – either as a fungible amount of value, or within the context of a single commodity world. The former approach permits the composition of the endowment of capital goods to be adjusted to the demand for it (so 'cost of production prices' are market clearing). The latter approach first eschews prices altogether, and then suggests that results obtained within the confines of the one-commodity world (on the relationship between the rate of profit and the 'capital' intensity of production, for example) may be generalized to an economy which contains many different 'capital goods'. The results which fall under the general headings of 'paradoxes' in the theory of capital and 'reswitching' demonstrate that neither of these solutions is viable. Indeed, these results invalidate any attempt to determine the rate of interest by a single market, be it the market for 'capital', or the market for savings and investment.

Alternatively, the problem of reproducible means of production may be approached via many markets – the endowment of capital goods being expressed as a vector, each capital good measured in its own 'technical units'. The problem then is that, as Walras discovered, the analysis of the determination of the 'general rate of net income' (the rate of profit) is overdetermined.

The persistent problem of overdetermination may be evaded if the condition that the prices of all reproducible means of production should be equal to their costs of reproduction is abandoned.

Instead, an equilibrium is defined as a situation in which the price of each capital good is either equal to or less than its cost of production. Those capital goods for which the demand price is below the cost of production are not produced. The rate of return on the non-reproduced capital goods is lower than the rate of return on reproduced goods. This is the case in a wide range of formally correct models of 'intertemporal' equilibria, including the Arrow–Debreu model.

The issue then to be faced is: what is the significance of the change in the notion of competitive equilibrium from the traditional long-run (with the associated rate of profit, long-run prices and short-run deviations from equilibrium) to that of intertemporal models, in which there is, even in equilibrium, no general rate of profit and the distinction between long-run and short-run has no meaning?

(Another reason why capital theory is often so contentious is that it seeks to explain the determination of the distribution of income between wages and profits. It therefore treads close to the boundaries of the most sensitive political debates. Such debates are not considered in this volume, which is devoted to elucidating the analytical issues at stake.)

The fact that the analytical issues in capital theory are unresolved raises difficult questions for other areas of economic theory and for the formulation of economic policy. The theory of employment for example, and much of the content of employment policy, rests on the assumptions made concerning the role of the price mechanism in the determination of the level of economic activity. This then has further ramifications for monetary theory and policy, fiscal policy, and the analysis of inflation. Similarly, much of the theory of the public sector – project appraisal, public sector pricing, and so on – rests on the presumed characteristics of competitive prices.

Price theory stands at the core of any interpretation of the operations of a market economy. Any application of price theory from which practical conclusions are to be drawn must confront the analytical difficulties of capital theory.

The Editors

Quantity of capital

PIERANGELO GAREGNANI

INTRODUCTION. 1. The concept of capital, and therefore that of the 'quantity of capital', is intimately bound up with the question of the distribution of the social product among the classes constituting the community. In order to discuss the role played in economic theory by this concept it is therefore necessary to begin by distinguishing the two broad approaches to a theory of distribution and relative prices which can be traced in the history of economic analysis.

The first approach to appear had its centre in a concept of social surplus. The remuneration of labour was taken to be determined by economic and broader social factors, which could be studied separately from those affecting the social product. Accordingly the shares of the product other than wages were determined as the difference between the social product (net of the replacement of means of production) and the share of labourers, that is, as the 'surplus' of the product over the wages, where the latter were often viewed by those authors as the consumption 'necessary' for production to occur. This approach was first used in a systematic way by the French Physiocrats and was then adopted by the English classical economists from Adam Smith to David Ricardo.

The second approach is that which, in its several versions, has been dominant since the end of the last century. It aims to explain distribution in terms of forces of demand and supply, founded on the 'substitutability' of factors of production. This substitutability would in turn result from (a) the existence of alternative methods of production of each commodity and (b) the choice made by consumers between different goods (below par. 3–5). It is this approach which today is most often referred to as 'neoclassical', though, given its basic differences from the classical approach, 'marginal' or 'marginalist' would seem more appropriate adjectives and will be adopted in this essay. (However, the meaning of the text will not be affected if one reads 'neoclassical' wherever 'marginal' or 'marginalist' appears.)

In fact, in both approaches the same difficulty has arisen. The difficulty is that of 'measuring' capital independently of distribution – that is, of expressing a

1

given set of capital goods as the same magnitude 'capital' whatever the distribution of the social product between productive agents. Within the first approach, the difficulty arose in the attempts made to measure the product independently of distribution, in order to determine by difference the shares of the product other than wages. Thus, the difficulty underlies Ricardo's search for an 'invariable' standard of value, and was inherited by Marx in the form of the determination of a link between 'values' and 'prices of production' (cf. Garegnani, 1960, pp. 42–50). Within the second approach, the difficulty arose, in the forms we shall examine below, in the course of the attempt to give meaning to substitutability between labour and means of production.

Though both approaches require a measurement of 'capital' independent of distribution, the conditions for this measurement differ in one fundamental respect in the two cases. In the classical approach, capital can ultimately be measured as a *set of magnitudes* (physical quantities of the several means of production, or quantities of 'dated labour'), thus allowing for a solution of the problem. As we shall see that same measurement raises basic difficulties in the marginal theories. It is because of this difference in the conditions for its solution that the problem of an independent measurement of capital acquires a central importance for the debate on the validity of the above two competing approaches for an explanation of distribution and relative prices, and, therefore, a central importance for present-day theoretical discussion.

In this essay, we shall concentrate on the marginal theories where the measurement of capital in terms of a single magnitude and therefore the concept of 'quantity of capital' plays an essential role. (For the way in which the analogous problem arises in the classical theories, see Garegnani, 1960, Part I.)

2. The present essay consists of three parts. In Part I, we shall be concerned with exposing the contradiction in marginal theory between, on the one hand, the requirement of expressing the capital endowment in terms independent of distribution, and, on the other hand, the condition of a capital stock adjusted to the outputs produced by the methods of production used.

We shall begin in Part I, section I, by using a simple scheme of marginal theory in order to show the requirements which the theory imposes on the measurement of factors of production. We shall then proceed, in section II, to an examination of the contradiction mentioned above. This will be done by referring to Walras's original general equilibrium system, where the contradiction shows in an inconsistency of the system of equations and therefore in the non-existence, in general, of an economically meaningful solution for it. In fact, Walras differed from most of his contemporaries because of his attempt to deal with the heterogeneity of capital goods in the same way as with the heterogeneity of labour and land, that is, by treating the different kinds of capital goods as separate factors of production. However, that treatment entailed taking the physical composition of the initial capital endowment as a datum. This can be shown to contradict the condition of an equilibrium physical composition of the capital stock, expressed under free competition by the equality in the effective rates of return over the supply prices of the capital goods, and included in Walras's equations (for the concept of 'effective' rate of return, cf. par. 47 below). Hence the non-existence of economically meaningful solutions of those equations.

The nature of the above inconsistency in Walras's original system implies that only one of the two ways out of the inconsistency can be conceived. The first is a *different conception of capital*, by which the latter appears as a *single factor*, which can change 'form' without changing in 'quantity' (for this phrasing, cf. the quotations given in par. 22 and 37 below), and can therefore assume the physical composition appropriate to the equilibrium. The second is a *different conception of the equilibrium* itself, which will not constrain the rates of return on the supply prices of the capital goods. The first way out – that generally taken until recent decades – will be discussed in Part II of this essay, leaving the second for Part III.

Accordingly, in Part II we shall begin (section III) by examining the most serious attempt at a consistent measurement of capital by means of a single quantity, that by Knut Wicksell ([1893] 1954), building on Böhm-Bawerk's (1891) concept of 'average period of production'. We shall see how Wicksell's attempt failed, and how in ([1901] 1934) he had to fall back on a value measurement of capital. Section IV will then examine more closely the deficiencies of that measurement, with respect to the ideas of 'subsistence fund', and of 'real capital' by which it has been justified. The phenomena of 'reverse capital deepening' and 'reswitching' will also be approached in Part II. The implications of those phenomena will however be examined more fully in Part III, section VII, where we shall see why they appear to affect the second conceivable way out of Walras's contradiction, no less than they do the first.

Part III will proceed to that second way out. We shall begin in section V by examining why the traditional concept of equilibrium, and the associated condition of a uniform effective rate of return, appear important in providing for a 'correspondence' between theoretical and observable variables. This will explain why the concept of equilibrium based on that condition has been universally taken for granted until recent decades, and it will lead us to discuss the methodological difficulties raised by the new concepts of equilibrium which have come to replace the older one, by way of a change which seems to have passed almost unnoticed, in spite of its radical implications. Then, in section VI we shall see a further methodological reason for the traditional concept of capital as a single factor of production. The necessity of assuming a sufficient 'substitutability' between factors leads to the conception of the differences between processes of production in terms of differences in the *proportions* rather than in the *kinds* of factors of production. It leads therefore to a view of the capital goods as quantities of a single homogeneous factor 'capital'.

The above methodological difficulties can therefore be seen to result from the attempt to do away with the concept of a 'quantity of capital' and its inconsistencies. However, in the final section of Part III (section VII), we shall contend that the attempt cannot be successful, so long as we keep within the

3

framework of the dominant demand and supply explanation of distribution. We shall argue there that the concept of a 'quantity of capital', while disappearing from the market for a single factor of production called 'capital' (the stock), has to reappear in what was in any case always understood to be its concrete manifestation, namely the market for savings and investment (the flow). The argument will accordingly be that the second conceivable way out of Walras's contradiction is as much affected as the first is by the difficulties of the concept of 'quantity of capital', brought to light by the phenomena of 'reswitching' and 'reverse capital deepening'. The implications of these phenomena will then be examined together with some of the reactions to them from the marginalist side. The conclusion will be that this second way out is no more viable than the first was – indeed it is less viable, once the additional methodological difficulties discussed in sections V and VI are taken into account. What appears to be in question therefore, is the 'neoclassical' explanation of distribution as such, and not simply some specific versions of it.

PART I.
WALRAS'S INCONSISTENCY

I. MARGINAL THEORY AND THE MEASUREMENT OF CAPITAL. 3. Let us start from the simplest possible scheme of marginal theory. Let us suppose an economy where 'corn' is produced in yearly cycles by labour and a capital consisting exclusively of 'corn', the two being susceptible to combination in continuously variable proportions. Land is free and the capitalists are the entrepreneurs. We also assume that all transactions occur in terms of corn.

Each capitalist is faced with a curve of the 'marginal product' of labour, which results when the variable quantity of labour he may hire is applied with the given quantity of 'corn-capital' he possesses. For well-known reasons, the competitive capitalist will maximize his profits when hiring the number of labourers for which the marginal product, a quantity of corn, is equal to the corn-wage he finds ruling in the market. The curve of the marginal product of labour therefore becomes what we might give the neutral name of the 'employment curve' for labour (not yet the 'demand curve' for labour) of that individual capitalist, indicating how many labourers it would be profitable for him to employ with his capital at any given real wage w. These individual 'labour employment curves' could then be added up to obtain a similar 'labour employment' schedule or function $LE-LE'$ for the whole economy, like that indicated in Figure 1a below.

Let us now introduce a second consumer good, call it 'cloth', also produced with labour and 'corn-capital', and assume now, for a moment, that only one method of production exists for each of the two goods, with 'cloth' requiring the higher proportion of 'corn-capital' to labour. Consumer choice can then be seen to play a role similar to producer choice and marginal products in providing the basis for a decreasing 'labour-employment schedule' $LE-LE'$. In fact, any fall in the wage rate w will make the price of labour-intensive 'corn' fall relative to

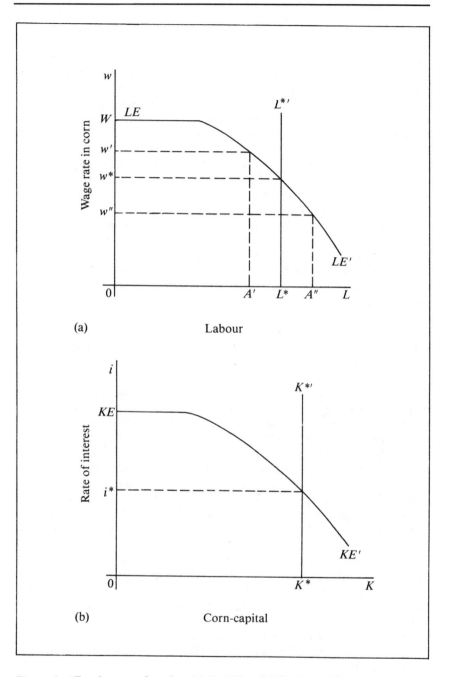

Figure 1 'Employment functions' *LE–LE'* and *KE–KE'* which may constitute acceptable 'demand functions' for labour and for 'corn-capital'.

capital-intensive 'cloth': by the well-known analysis of consumer choice it will generally follow that more 'corn' will be consumed relative to 'cloth'. Given the quantity of 'corn-capital' employed in the economy, a higher proportion of it will generally be employed in producing 'corn', with a consequent increase in the quantity of labour employed in the economy as a whole.

If we reintroduce the alternative of methods of production, applicable to 'cloth' as well as 'corn', it can be seen that the twin concepts of marginal utility and marginal productivity (or the equivalent marginal rates of substitution) will reinforce each other in ensuring the downward sloping labour-employment schedule $LE-LE'$ of Figure 1. As w falls, the quantity of labour employed with the given corn capital will increase as a result *both* of the increased proportions of corn in final output *and* of the more labour-intensive methods used in the production of corn and cloth.

The function $LE-LE'$ has here been given the neutral name of 'employment function' in order to stress the fact that, so far, we have no reason to give the name of 'demand function' to a relation like $LE-LE'$. In order to use $LE-LE'$ as the basis of a 'demand function', we need in fact to establish, e.g., that the amount of 'corn-capital' employed tends to remain the same even when the capitalists are not the entrepreneurs, as is assumed in $LE-LE'$, or, more generally, we need to establish that the amount of 'corn-capital' employed tends to vary in accordance with its 'supply function' as w, and therefore the interest rate r, vary. We also need to assume the kind of flexibility of the wage and of the rate of interest required to ensure their tendency towards the level for which the quantity of labour (or 'corn-capital') 'demanded' and 'supplied' are equal, whatever that level might be. More generally, we need to ascertain that the shape of those 'employment functions' will validate that conception of free competition and ensure that their use as 'demand functions' will not lead to conclusions in conflict with observable phenomena.

4. Indeed, let us now introduce the *additional* assumption that workers will always bid down the corn wage so long as some are unemployed, whereas capitalists unable to hire the workers they want will always bid it up (as we shall mention in the next paragraph, this assumption does not appear to be entailed in the more general concept of free competition, as used e.g. by the classical economists). What we must now see is how *the negative slope of the employment curves* will cause this assumption (i) to become an acceptable part of the concept of free competition; and (ii) to transform the employment function $LE-LE'$ into a 'demand function' for labour and 'corn-capital' – to establish, that is, the familiar demand-and-supply determination of wages and interest, as understood in marginal theory.

Let us start from (i), and suppose that the wage in Figure 1a is w' and the number of labourers employed is OA', less than OL^*, the number of those seeking employment.

In this case, the assumed fall in the real wage will not lead to the absurd conclusion of an indefinite fall towards zero, because it will *come to a stop* at a possible wage w^*, at which everyone will find employment. Similarly, with the initial wage w'', the assumed tendency of capitalist entrepreneurs to bid the wage up indefinitely will not lead to the absurd conclusion of a rise in the wage to its maximum W (where net returns to capital are zero) because the rise will stop at w^*.

However, by thus establishing the plausibility of that specific concept of free competition, we have also established a theory of distribution between wages and profits by the 'demand and supply' forces. Indeed, on our hypotheses, the economy would gravitate around the wage w^* and the corresponding interest (profit) rate i^*. And it is this gravitation about w^* and i^* which allows us to assert that the two functions together determine the 'equilibrium' wage w^* and interest rate i^* and, therefore, to describe the schedule $LE-LE'$ as a 'demand schedule' for labour, with $L^*-L^{*'}$ as the corresponding 'supply schedule'. (It may be noted how the demand and supply functions in question are 'general equilibrium' functions, in that each point on $LE-LE'$ implies equilibrium in the markets for cloth, corn-output, and the hire of corn-capital. For a more general definition of such demand functions, cf. e.g. Garegnani, 1978, p. 346n.)

However, our scheme of marginal theory is not yet complete. We assumed that the quantity of corn-capital employed does not change with the wage or, more generally, that it changes in the way expressed by the supply function of capital, which is both predeterminable and generally compatible with a downward-sloping shape of the labour–demand function. This assumption – rendered immediately plausible here by supposing that the entrepreneurs are capitalists – can now be supported also for the case in which workers, or a third party, are the entrepreneurs, since a mechanism similar to that just described for the labour market will also be at work in the corn-capital market (cf. Figure 1b). As is also well known, under constant returns to scale in the corn industry, the equilibrium wage and rate of interest will not be affected by which person acts as the entrepreneur.

It is equally well known that the two-factor scheme described here can be generalized to any number of factors.

5. We have said that the negative slope of the 'employment functions' plays a key role in establishing the above definition of competition, and the connected demand-and-supply explanation of distribution. Indeed, if the 'employment curves' were like those of Figure 2 (derived on the basis of the value measurement of capital from the 'continuum' of methods of production $k^{(2)}$ to be described in par. 36, Table 2b below), it would no longer be plausible to make the assumption we stressed above that unemployed labourers would bid wages down indefinitely so long as they remain unemployed. The long dominance of demand-and-supply theories of distribution may at first make the assumption of an indefinite flexibility in the wage and rate of interest appear to be an integral part of the general concept of competition, but that assumption does not seem to be entailed in the most general concept of free competition, as the tendency to 'the equalization of returns in various directions opens to an entrepreneur, or investor, or labourer' (Stigler, 1957, p. 3). In particular it does not appear to be

part of the concept of free competition in Adam Smith and David Ricardo, who admitted the possibility of persistent labour unemployment, and saw no contradiction between unemployment, free competition and non-zero natural wages. The idea of these authors seems rather that labour unemployment would exert a pressure on wages towards some minimum below which they cannot fall (cf. Garegnani, 1985, pp. 23–30; for the possibility of persistent unemployment, see e.g. Ricardo's chapter 'On Machinery' in his *Principles*, Ricardo, 1951, p. 390; or Smith, 1776, p. 64).

Indeed, as we shall argue in the last section of this essay, if the employment functions were like those of Figure 2 below, it would seem reasonable to look in a completely different direction for the determinants of the division of the product between wages and profits – in the direction, for example, of the kind of economic and social determination of the wage that we find in those classical authors.

6. We have used here the simplest possible assumptions allowing, for example, for smooth marginal product curves, and for no distinction between present and future prices (see, however, par. 45 and 47 below). In fact the present scheme is only intended to express the basic 'principle of substitution' (Marshall, [1890] 1961, V, III, 3, p. 341), on which the demand and supply determination of prices relies in all its versions, both those founded on the traditional long-period equilibrium, and those of contemporary literature, based on the 'intertemporal' or 'temporary' equilibria (cf. par. 45–46).

The simple scheme above may now be used to approach the problems which arise when capital does not consist of a single product, homogeneous as between alternative processes of production. For this purpose it is convenient to start by distinguishing between the independent and the dependent variables of the theory. As is evident from our scheme, the price of the service of each factor (labour and corn-capital) is determined simultaneously with the relative price of the two commodities, on the basis of three groups of data:

(a) consumer preferences;

(b) the methods of production available at the given state of technical knowledge (in this essay we refer to them in terms of the production function just as we refer to preferences in terms of utility or indifference functions, but of course the conclusions of our argument would not be affected if we referred to production and consumption sets);

(c) the quantities of factors of production available in the economy in the given situation.

It is in connection with the data of groups (b) and (c), that a question of measurement of the factors of production arises. In group (b) the quantities of the factors define the methods of production. In group (c) they appear in the role, peculiar to marginal theory, of a factor endowment, on which the supply functions of the factors are then based.

Now, in both these roles the factors should be measured so that the quantities of them corresponding to any given method of production, and therefore to any given physical output, are known *before* distribution is known (the factors must

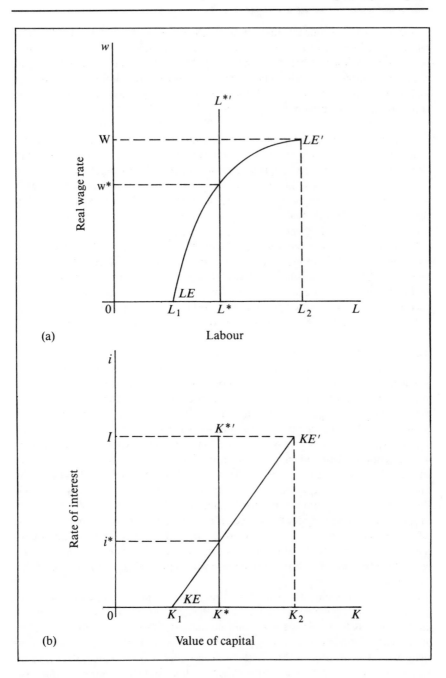

(a)

(b)

Figure 2 'Employment functions' *LE–LE'*, *KE–KE'* would not give rise to acceptable 'demand functions' for labour and capital.

be measured in 'technical units', as Wicksell put it ([1901] 1934, p. 149). The requirement is due to the need to avoid circular reasoning: if we cannot define the quantity of a factor before knowing distribution and relative prices, we shall clearly be unable to use the theory, which allows us to determine distribution and relative prices only when we know the methods of production and the factor endowment of the economy in question.

7. This requirement of independence of distribution can be thought to be easily satisfied by the factors of production traditionally grouped as 'labour' and 'land'. (When the ratios between, say, the wages for different kinds of labour cannot be taken as constants, those kinds of labour can in principle always be dealt with without resorting to value magnitudes, by treating each as a factor to which there correspond separate demand and supply functions.) It is when we come to 'capital' that difficulties appear.

What we have, under the heading of 'capital', is a collection of heterogeneous goods with three common characteristics: that of being products, that of being used for further production, and that of wearing out within a sufficiently short period of time (existing capital goods of longer duration are best treated as natural resources: see e.g. Wicksell, 1954, p. 118 on 'rent goods').

Now, these characteristics in turn entail two consequences. The first is that capital goods, being products of sufficiently short duration, have a price which will always tend towards equality with their costs of production or supply price (we shall generally prefer here the second, less ambiguous, expression).

The second consequence is that, in conditions of free competition, there is a tendency towards equality in the effective rates of return over costs, which the different kinds of capital goods will yield. This is true under conditions of free competition, but the conditions holding for such rates of return under other assumptions (e.g., higher rates of return on the capital goods employed in a monopolistic firm or industry) would not affect the conclusions of this essay, which only depend on the existence of *some* equilibrium conditions linking those rates of return, and requiring that the physical composition of the capital stock should adjust to the outputs and to the methods of production profitable in the situation. Therefore in order to avoid cumbersome expressions, we shall generally refer to the conditions in their competitive forms, but it must be understood that the argument is not confined to that hypothesis (and that the divergence in rates of return here referred to, has nothing to do with that resulting from monopolistic structures).

It is in fact in value terms that capital is reckoned in economic practice, and it is from that commonsensical idea that the concept of capital as a factor of production has been derived in traditional marginal theory. However, the value of the capital goods does not satisfy the requirement of independence from changes in distribution. Whatever the unit in which it is measured, the value of a given physical capital will change when nothing but distribution changes (if that value were made constant by using the capital good in question as its own unit value, the problem would evidently be there for all other capital goods).

One might then think that the way out of the difficulty is to renounce a unitary conception of capital and deal with the heterogeneity of the capital goods in a way analogous to that which we saw for land or labour, that is by treating each kind of capital good as the argument of independent demand and supply functions. However, the case of capital is different from that of labour and land and this is so because of the second consequence of the peculiarities of capital mentioned above: the tendency of all kinds of capital goods towards a uniform rate of return on their supply price. And, as we shall see in section II below, the treatment of capital as a set of factors is in conflict with that tendency. We here find the contradiction, which we mentioned in the introduction.

8. Before examining that contradiction it may however be useful to render explicit a second requirement which must be satisfied by the measurement of factors, besides the independence from distribution. This requirement is that, in any given price situation, the expenditure on the factor should increase as the 'quantity' of it employed increases. This requirement, which is obviously satisfied when the price of the service refers to a physical unit of the factor (and the expenditure on it is *proportional* to its 'quantity'), needs attention when we attempt to measure capital as a single quantity *other than value*, as we must in order to avoid dependence on distribution. Under the condition of a uniform rate of return the net expenditure on capital services is proportional to the value of that capital, and the requirement takes the form that, given the price situation, the value of capital should be an increasing function of the 'quantity' measuring it (cf. below par. 23, for the case of Böhm-Bawerk's average period of production). It is because of this second requirement that, say, 'tons of steel' or the volume of the capital goods, which would obviously satisfy the requirement of independence of distribution, will not do: no reason evidently exists why the heavier, or the bulkier of any two sets of capital goods, should have a higher value and be costlier, other things being equal.

To see the reason for this second requirement it is sufficient to think of a production function. This function only gives the *minimum* quantity of each factor x compatible with a given output and given quantities of the other factors: it excludes, that is, all methods requiring more of x for the same quantities of factors y, z, etc. ... Now, this is only justified if more units of x always cost the entrepreneur more than fewer units, and therefore methods requiring more units of x with no reduction in any other factor can be excluded a priori.

II. THE INCONSISTENCY IN WALRAS'S THEORY OF CAPITALIZATION. 9. While mathematical inquiries have been conducted to ascertain the existence of economically meaningful solutions for the equations of exchange and production as formulated in Walras's *Eléments* (Wald, 1951; Arrow and Debreu, 1951; Dorfman, Samuelson and Solow, 1958, pp. 351–75), the analysis has not been extended, to the writer's knowledge, to Walras's complete system, including the equations of 'capitalization' in their original formulation of Part V of the *Eléments* (for Morishima, 1964, cf. below par. 16). It can however be shown here that Walras's conception of capital as a set of heterogeneous factors of production is inconsistent with his equilibrium condition regarding the rates of return on the different kinds of capital goods and, accordingly, his equations of general equilibrium will not generally admit an economically meaningful solution (the argument that follows is based on that in Garegnani, 1958, Part II, chs II and III, reproduced in Garegnani 1960, chs II and III).

We may begin by restating Walras's equations of exchange and production as they appear in the *Eléments*. We adopt the symbols used by Walras himself to facilitate consultation of the original text.

D_a, D_b, ... D_m: the quantities of the m consumer goods A, B, ... M, produced and demanded in the economy during one year.

O_p, $O_{p'}$, ...; O_t, $O_{t'}$, ...; O_k, $O_{k'}$, ...: the quantities supplied for productive use of yearly services of the n resources distinguished into the several kinds of 'land capital' T, T' ...; of 'personal capital', P, P', ...: and of producible capital goods K, K', ...

P_b, P_c, ... P_p, ...: the prices of consumer goods and yearly productive services, expressed in terms of commodity A, taken as the *numéraire*.

$$\left.\begin{array}{l} a_t, a_{t'}, \ldots a_p, \ldots a_k \ldots \\ b_t, b_{t'}, \ldots b_p, \ldots b_k \ldots \end{array}\right\} \begin{array}{l}\text{the } (m, n) \text{ production coefficients for respectively,} \\ \text{consumer goods } A, B, M, \text{ which we shall at first} \\ \text{assume to be fixed following Walras, who conducted} \\ \text{most of his arguments in the } Eléments \text{ on the basis} \\ \text{of fixed production coefficients.}\end{array}$$

We then have the following equations expressing the conditions of competitive equilibrium in exchange and production, distinguished in four sets:

$$\left.\begin{array}{l} D_a = F_a(p_b p_c, \ldots, p_t, \ldots, p_p, \ldots, p_k, \ldots) \\ D_b = F_b(p_b p_c, \ldots, p_t, \ldots, p_p, \ldots, p_k, \ldots) \\ \qquad\qquad \vdots \\ D_m = F_m(p_b p_c, \ldots, p_m, \ldots, p_t, \ldots, p_p, \ldots, p_k, \ldots) \end{array}\right\} \quad \text{(II.1)}$$

$$\left.\begin{array}{l} 1 = a_t p_t + \cdots + a_p a_p + \cdots + a_k p_k + \cdots \\ p_b = b_t p_t + \cdots + b_p p_p + \cdots + b_k p_k + \cdots \\ \qquad\qquad \vdots \\ p_m = m_t p_t + \cdots + m_p p_p + \cdots + m_k p_k + \cdots \end{array}\right\} \quad \text{(II.2)}$$

$$\left.\begin{array}{l} O_t = a_t D_a + b_t D_b + \cdots \\ \qquad\qquad \vdots \\ O_p = a_p D_a + b_p D_b + \cdots \\ \qquad\qquad \vdots \\ O_k = a_k D_a + b_k D_b + \cdots \\ \qquad\qquad \vdots \end{array}\right\} \quad \text{(II.3)}$$

$$O_t = F_t(p_b p_c, \ldots, p_t, \ldots, p_p, \ldots, p_k, \ldots)$$
$$\vdots$$
$$O_p = F_p(p_b p_c, \ldots, p_t, \ldots, p_p, \ldots, p_k, \ldots) \tag{II.4}$$
$$\vdots$$
$$O_k = F_k(p_b p_c, \ldots, p_t, \ldots, p_p, \ldots, p_k, \ldots)$$
$$\vdots$$

Equations (II.1) give the quantities of consumer goods demanded and produced during the year as the functions of the system of relative prices obtainable from the conditions of consumer equilibrium. Equations (II.2) express the equality between prices and costs of production of consumer goods. Equations (II.3) express the equality between the quantities of productive services supplied and demanded for productive use. Finally, equations (II.4) give the quantities of productive services supplied for productive use as the functions of the system of relative prices obtainable, like functions (II.4), from the conditions of consumer equilibrium. (For equations (II.1), (II.2), (II.3), (II.4) cf., respectively, equations (2), (4), (3), (1), in Walras, [1874–7] 1954, pp. 239–40).

There are $(2m + 2n - 1)$ unknowns appearing in equations (II.1) – (II.4), namely the $(m + n - 1)$ prices, and the $(m + n)$ quantities of consumer goods and productive services demanded and supplied. System (II.1) – (II.4), on the other hand, includes $(2m + 2n - 1)$ independent equations since, as is well known, one of the equations can be obtained from the remainder of the system. It has been demonstrated that these equations will generally admit economically meaningful solutions when some modifications that we shall mention in par. 16 below are introduced into equations (II.2) and (II.3). This result will be assumed in what follows. We shall also ignore the possibility of multiple economically meaningful solutions of these equations since it would complicate the discussion without affecting our conclusions.

10. As a representation of the economic system, equations (II.1) – (II.4) are clearly incomplete, unless we intend to refer to an economy without capital, where all productive services come from personal or natural resources, and cannot be produced like commodities. In order to deal with produced means of production Walras introduced, from the very earliest version of his theory (Walras, 1877), the equations of 'capital formation' that determine the outputs of capital goods and the 'rate of net income'.

The first step in Walras's argument is to draw a distinction between the 'gross' price p_k of the yearly service of a capital good K, and the corresponding 'net' price, obtained from p_k by subtracting a given fraction c_k of the price P_k of the capital good, for yearly amortization. The yearly rate of net income obtained from K is then given by:

$$i = \frac{p_k - c_k P_k}{P_k} \tag{II.5}$$

13

(We may notice here how Walras's way of calculating amortization as a fraction c_k independent of i, is incorrect since even assuming constant efficiency of the capital good, the relations between p_k, i and P_k would be the following, where t is the life of the capital good

$$P_k = \frac{p_k}{(1+i)} + \frac{p_k}{(1+i)^2} + \cdots + \frac{p_k}{(1+i)^t}$$

$$= p_k \frac{(1+i)^t - 1}{i(1+i)^t} \tag{II.5$'$}$$

However our discussion would need no substantial modification if we replaced equation (II.5) with (II.5$'$). We may also note how up to the third edition of the *Eléments*, Walras assumed that raw materials are consumed as soon as they are produced and are not stocked in advance. When, however, that assumption is abandoned in the fourth edition, and a 'theory of circulation' appears as Part VI, circulating capital goods are treated in a way strictly analogous to fixed capital, by simply assuming $c_k = 1$.)

At this point, Walras introduces the competitive condition of a uniform rate of return on all kinds of capital goods. If there are l kinds of such goods, indicated by K, K', ..., of price P_k, $P_{k'}$, ..., with given coefficients c_k, c'_k, ... for amortization and insurance, this condition gives the following l equations (Walras, 1954, pp. 271–2):

$$\left.\begin{array}{c} \dfrac{p_k}{i + c_k} = P_k \\[2mm] \dfrac{p_{k'}}{i + c_{k'}} = P'_k \\ \vdots \end{array}\right\} \tag{II.6}$$

(The already noted fact that Walras ignores changes over time in the relative prices of commodities entails that the competitive uniform *effective* rate of return becomes the uniform rate i *independent* of the numéraire chosen: cf. par. 46 below).

The condition that in equilibrium, the prices of the capital goods should all be equal to their supply prices, gives l more equations (Walras, 1954, p. 271):

$$\left.\begin{array}{c} P_k = k_t p_t + \ldots + k_p p_p + \ldots + k_k p_k + \ldots \\[2mm] P_{k'} = k'_t p_t + \ldots + k'_p p_p + \ldots + k'_k p_k + \ldots \\ \vdots \end{array}\right\} \tag{II.7}$$

Equations (II.7), taken together with (II.6) entail that the condition of a uniform rate of return stated by the latter equations is a uniform rate of return *on the supply prices* of the capital goods.

Let us now come to the production of capital goods implied in equations (II.7). Let the yearly outputs of the capital goods of types K, K', ... be indicated by D_k, $D_{k'}$, ... The total value of these outputs must be equal to the yearly gross savings in the economy, given by the excess of yearly gross income over the expenditure on consumption goods A, B, ... That excess can be obtained from the conditions of consumer equilibrium as a function F_e of the system of prices (Walras, [1874–7] 1954, pp. 272–6):

$$F_e(p_t, p_c, p_m, p_t \cdots p_p \cdots p_k \cdots i) = D_k P_k + D_{k'} P_{k'} + \dots \qquad \text{(II.8)}$$

The introduction of current outputs of capital goods D_k, $D_{k'}$, ..., requires, of course, some modifications in equations (II.3) of exchange and production where the terms $(k_t D_k + k'_t D_{k'} + \dots)$, $(k_{t'} D_k + k'_{t'} D_{k'} + \dots)$, etc., must now appear on the right-hand side.

$$\left.
\begin{aligned}
O_t &= a_t D_a + b_t D_b + \dots + m_t D_m + (k_t D_k + k'_t D_{k'}, + \dots) \\
&\vdots \\
O_p &= a_p D_a + b_p D_b + \dots + m_p D_m + (k_p D_k + k'_p D_{k'}, + \dots) \\
&\vdots \\
O_k &= a_k D_a + b_k D_b + \dots + m_k D_k + (k_k D_k + k'_k D_{k'}, + \dots) \\
&\vdots
\end{aligned}
\right\} \qquad \text{(II.3')}$$

The l unknowns $P_k, P_{k'}, \dots$, can now be eliminated from the system by substituting for them in (II.6) and (II.8) the expressions given by (II.7). Walras's equations of 'capital formation' can then be more compactly written as follows:

$$F(p_b, \dots, p_t, \dots, i) = D_k(k_t p_t + \dots) + D_{k'}(k'_t p_t + \dots) + \dots \qquad \text{(II.A)}$$

$$\left.
\begin{aligned}
\frac{p_k}{i + c_k} &= k_t p_t + \dots + k_p p_p + \dots + k_k p_k + \dots \\
\frac{p_{k'}}{i + c_{k'}} &= k'_t p_t + \dots + k'_p p_p + \dots + k'_k p_k + \dots \\
&\vdots
\end{aligned}
\right\} \qquad \text{(II.B)}$$

Expressed in this form, Walras's theory of capital formation introduces into the system $(1 + l)$ additional unknowns (namely, the current outputs of capital goods D_k, $D_{k'} \dots$ and the rate of net income i) while adding the $(1 + l)$ new independent equations (II.A) and (II.B). Walras claimed that the system so completed will determine those additional unknowns, together with the previous ones (Walras, [1874–7] 1954; p. 276). We shall argue that this conclusion is incorrect.

11. The difficulty lies with equations (II.B). The unknowns appearing in (II.B) are the rate of net income and the prices of the productive services used in producing the capital goods.

To understand the role which service prices play in these equations, let us assume for a moment that individual tastes happen to be such that gross savings in the system are zero. It follows from equation (II.A) that all the D_k's must also be zero (none of the *gross* outputs D_k's can ever be negative). With the elimination from equations (II.3') of any demand for services arising from the production of capital goods, we return to equation (II.3), and system (II.1) − (II.4) is again sufficient to determine the $(2m + 2n − 1)$ unknowns appearing in them, *including the prices of all productive services*. We are then left with the l equations (II.B), where one unknown only remains to be determined: the rate of net income.

12. Thus, if consumer tastes happened to entail zero gross savings, the system would be inconsistent. In fact the demand conditions for consumer goods and the supply conditions of productive services would be sufficient to determine the *prices of the services of the capital goods* together with the prices of all other services and also, therefore, the *supply prices* of those same capital goods. It could only be by a fluke that the two sets of prices would be compatible with a single uniform rate of return over costs, as required by equations (II.B).

The economic meaning of this inconsistency should be clear. To determine prices and outputs, Walras takes as data the heterogeneous capital stocks available in the economy. We cannot expect that configuration of capital stocks to be the one most 'appropriate' to the production of the outputs required by the preferences of the consumers. If, for example, 'cloth' and 'corn' are the only consumer goods in the economy, it will be a fluke if the proportion in which 'looms' and 'tractors' happen to be available in the given capital stock are those corresponding to the relative intensity of consumer demand for the two consumptions goods. The equality between demand and supply of the two capital-goods services will then require that the price of the service of the comparatively abundant capital goods should fall below the level compatible with the rate of return on the supply price obtainable instead on the other capital good (or, equally, that the demand price on the right-hand side of the respective equation (II.B) of the abundant capital good should fall below the supply prices on the left-hand side of the same equation).

However, the only difference between the case of zero gross savings just assumed and the general one is that in the latter, the D_k's need not be zero. Will this make it possible to satisfy equations (II.B), together with the remainder of the system? It is now clear that the answer can be affirmative if, and only if, the degrees of freedom we acquire in the equations of production and exchange because of the relative capital-good outputs D_k make it possible to determine prices of the productive services compatible with equations (II.B). The dependence of the prices of the productive services on the current outputs of capital goods is therefore the only element on which the consistency (existence of economically significant solutions) of the complete system depends.

13. To analyze that dependence, and therefore the general case with non-zero gross savings, let us begin by defining a subsystem (P) including besides the equations of exchange and production (II.1), (II.2), (II.3), (II.4) and the equation (II.A), only one of the equations (II.B), say the first, for capital good K. Also,

we include in (P) an arbitrary 'initial' set of the $(l-1)$ ratios R', R'', ..., of the capital-good outputs, defined as follows

$$R' = \frac{D_{k'}}{D_k}$$

$$R'' = \frac{D_{k''}}{D_k}$$

$$\vdots$$

(II.9)

(Each of the D_k's may take here any positive value between zero and the one which would absorb total gross saving for the period. An infinite value for one of the ratios R', R'', etc. would imply $D_k = 0$, and would therefore involve infinite values of all other ratios with a non-zero numerator; it will then be convenient to replace D_k in the denominator of all the ratios with one of the D_k's which remain above zero.)

Finally we may re-write the last $(l-1)$ equations (II.B') excluded from sub-system (P) as follows, allowing for as many rates of return over costs as there are kinds of capital good involved:

$$\frac{p_{k'}}{i' + c'} = k'_t p_t + \ldots + k'_p p_p + \ldots + k'_k p_k + \ldots$$

$$\frac{p_{k''}}{i'' + c''} = k''_t p_t + \ldots + k''_p p_p + \ldots + k''_k p_k + \ldots$$

$$\vdots$$

(II.B')

Once the $(l-1)$ relations (II.9) are included, sub-system (P) will consist of a straightforward extension of the equations of exchange and production. It will contain $(2m + 2n - 1)$ independent equations, which will determine $(m + n - 1)$ prices and the rate of net income i together with $(m + n)$ outputs. (The possibility of multiple, economically meaningful solutions of (P), which is the same as that for the equations of production and exchange, is here ignored: see par 9 above.)

If we then insert the 'initial' service prices thus determined by (P), in the $(l-1)$ equations (II.B') we shall obtain $(l-1)$ rates of return i', i'' ..., over the supply prices for capital goods K', K'',.... These rates will generally differ from each other and from the rate of return i determined in (P) for capital good K. The question is now whether by appropriate changes in the 'initial' values of R', R'', ... the prices of the productive services determined by (P) can be so modified as to equalize the rates of return i', i'', ... which have been defined above. If, and only if, that result can be achieved, will the complete system admit an economically meaningful solution: that which corresponds to the R's for which the result is obtained.

14. The effects of changes in R', R'', ... on the prices of services determined in subsystem (P) will depend on the proportions in which the services are used in

producing the several kinds of capital goods. If these proportions happened to be the same for all capital goods, no change in R', R'', ... could affect the prices of the services, and therefore the 'initial' disparities between i, i', i'', ... In fact, the same composite unit of factors taken in the absolute size appearing in equation (II.A) would then be employed to produce the new capital goods, irrespective of the ratios R', R'', ..., and the solution of (P) could not be modified by modifying these ratios (that solution would indeed be independent of equations II.9). The complete system would be inconsistent.

However, if the proportions in which the services are used for the capital goods differ, as will generally be the case, then changes in the values of R', R'', ... will affect the prices of services. The prices of the services used in a higher proportion for the capital goods whose output has increased will generally rise *relatively* to the prices of the services used in a higher proportion for the capital goods whose output has decreased (e.g., if we increased $R' = D_{k'}/D_k$ while keeping constant R'', R''', etc., we should compare the ratios between each production coefficient of K' and that of the composite output X, consisting of K'', K''', ... etc., taken in the proportions R'', R''', etc. The increase of R' will generally result in a rise of the prices of any service, say T, relative to the price of any service say T', when $k'_t/x_t > k'_{t'}/x_{t'}$).

Let us then modify the 'initial' values of R', R'', ... in the same direction in which a competitive market would tend to modify them: in favour of the kinds of capital goods that have the highest 'initial' rate of return. The l rates of return i, i', ... will be affected in two ways. One effect will be through the prices of the yearly service of the respective capital goods and, therefore, through the 'demand prices of the capital goods appearing on the left-hand side of equations (II.B). This effect is as likely to widen as it is to narrow the 'initial' disparities between the rates of return: broadly speaking, the disparities will tend to widen if the kinds of capital goods with higher 'initial' rates of return are used more for producing capital goods of their own group, than for producing capital goods of the other group. (It should be remembered here that current production of capital goods can affect the *stocks* only in a subsequent period, and that price changes over time are not considered by Walras, par. 10 above: cf, however, par. 46 below.)

The second effect will be through the supply prices of the capital goods, appearing on the right-hand side of equations (II.B). The supply price of the capital goods with higher 'initial' rates of return, whose relative outputs have increased, will generally rise relatively to the supply price of the other group of capital goods (since, as we saw, the rise in their output will tend to raise the relative price of the services used in a higher proportion for the production of such capital goods). This will evidently tend to narrow the 'initial' disparities between rates of return.

We may now leave aside as unlikely the extreme cases in which the effect on supply prices would not be present (zero gross saving, or equal proportions of the inputs required by the several capital goods) or would be outweighed for at least one capital good by a stronger opposite effect on the price of its service.

The question we must ask ourselves is whether, in the generality of the remaining cases, changes of relative capital outputs can so affect their relative costs as to equalize the rates of net income.

The answer to that question must be negative. If the productive services are not highly specific, the supply prices of the capital goods will hardly be sensitive to changes in their relative outputs. However, the decisive consideration is that the 'initial' disparities between the rates of return can be of any width whatsoever, depending on the data relating to the capital stocks, whereas the change in the relative supply prices of a capital good reaches a limit as soon as its output has fallen to zero. No further narrowing of the 'initial' disparity of its rate of return is then possible, and the complete system has no solution.

So far, our discussion has been conducted on the assumption of fixed coefficients of production on which equations (II.1)–(II.4) and (II.A)–(II.B) rest. However, its results can be easily generalized to the case of production coefficients to be determined within the system by the additional conditions of minimum costs (examined by Walras in Lesson 36 at the end of his *Eléments*). Variable production coefficients would tend to *increase* the difficulty of achieving a solution of the system to the extent that the substitutability in the system between the services used in producing the capital goods is increased, and their prices become therefore less sensitive to changes in the relative outputs of the capital goods.

15. The meaning of this result is the same as that we saw earlier in par. 12 above. Walras takes as data the heterogeneous capital stocks available in the economy and we cannot expect that configuration of capital stocks to be the one most 'appropriate' to the production, in the given technical situation, of the outputs required by the preferences of the consumers. Were it not for Walras's introduction of relative capital outputs as unknowns the inconsistency would assume the obvious form of an excess of independent equations. A striking proof of the deficiency of Walras's procedure would be provided by the case in which the economy happened to be potentially stationary, with gross savings that are just sufficient to allow for the replacement of existing capital goods. Then, even if Walras's equations had a solution, the resulting $D_{k'}$, $D'_{k''}$ ... would not generally be the physical replacements. This may indeed explain why Walras shied away from the case of a stationary economy, with the unconvincing argument that

> to have a supply and demand of capital goods, it is necessary to substitute for the conception of a stationary economy that of a progressive economy (Walras, [1874–7] 1954, collation note (*n*); pp. 586–7).

We could indeed ask, what about the demand for capital goods for replacement? (On this point cf. Barone, 1958, p. 538; Hicks, 1939, p. 396; Stigler, 1949, p. 259; Jaffé, 1942, p. 42; cf. also Garegnani, 1960, pp. 94–5.)

16. Walras did not limit himself to setting forth his equations of capital formation and making sure that their number was equal to that of the unknowns. In

Lesson 25 of the *Eléments* he purported by the device of the *tâtonnements* to show how the complete system is 'in practice solved by the mechanism of free competition'. Here, however, we cannot deal with some of the errors which crept into that discussion by Walras and which favoured his incorrect conclusions (for these matters cf. Garegnani, 1960, pp. 103–12, and Appendix G, to find a discussion of what happened to Walras's theory of capital formation in the work of Vilfredo Pareto). All we need notice is how, by the fourth edition of the *Eléments*, Walras had come close to realizing the inconsistency which vitiated his system. In an unobtrusive passage first introduced into that edition, in Lesson 28, Walras writes:

> it is not at all certain that the amount of savings ... will be adequate for the manufacture of new fixed capital goods proper in just such quantities as will satisfy the last *l* equations [our equations II.B] (Walras, [1874–7] 1954, p. 308).

Here the inconsistency between equations (II.B) and the remainder of the system is in fact admitted, and we have what amounts to a retraction. The next question then becomes inevitable: what can we make of a theory whose equations are thus admitted to be inconsistent?

A comprehensive answer cannot be found in the *Eléments*, or in the work of the younger Pareto, who later in the general equilibrium equations of the *Manuel* (1909) avoided the problem by dropping altogether the equations of capital formation he had retained in the *Cours* of 1896–7 (cf. Garegnani, 1960, Appendix G, pp 241–4). However, Walras provides an indication of what his answer might have been, in a second unobtrusive passage, which also appears only in the fourth edition, in Lesson 25. It is there stated that, after the *tâtonnements*,

> all the equations of system (B) will be satisfied *after the exclusion* of those new capital goods which it was not worthwhile to produce (Walras, [1874–7] 1954, p. 294, our italics).

Nothing more is said, but the capital goods '*qu'il n'y a pas lieu de produire*' are clearly those whose outputs would fall to zero in the course of the *tâtonnements*, without the rates of return over their supply prices having risen to the level obtainable on one or more of the other kinds of capital goods.

In other words, Walras suggests here that we should 'include' in the system only the one or more of equations (II.B) which give the solution with the highest possible rate of net income (cf. our discussion of system (*P*) in par. 13 above). Returning for a moment to equations (II.6) (II.7), from which (II.B) were obtained: Walras's suggestion is that we should drop the equations corresponding to the capital goods in question from system (II.7). Walras also suggests that we should let the outputs of the kinds of capital goods whose equations (II.7) have thus been 'excluded' from the system, fall to zero. It is implied that the demand prices of these capital goods could then be obtained by capitalizing the prices of their services at the rate of net income determined by the system in accordance with equations (II.6). This procedure can be formalized by replacing the signs = with the signs ≤ in (II.7) and, therefore, in (II.B), while adding the conditions of zero output of the capital goods for which the sign < holds. (This formalization has in fact been carried out, e.g. in Morishima, 1974, pp. 83–92, which attempts to demonstrate the existence of solutions of Walras's complete system. But no mention is made of the change in the concept of equilibrium entailed by that formal change.)

17. The above modification of equations (II.B) has, however, some important implications for the meaning of the resulting general equilibrium system.

At first one might be tempted to associate this modification of (II.B) with a use of inequalities in relations (II.2) and (II.3), which have however a quite different meaning. With respect to equation (II.2) the question is that, in order to ensure the existence of solutions to a system of pure exchange and production, we should allow the (notional) prices of certain consumer goods to be less than their cost of production when, even for supplies tending to zero, these demand prices are insufficient to cover costs. With respect to equations (II.3), Walras himself had noted ([1874–7] 1954, p. 250) how the possibility exists that the supply of some productive services might exceed demand even at zero prices. This possibility can be taken care of by replacing the signs = with the signs ≥ in equations (II.3), and adding the condition that when the sign > holds, the price of the corresponding productive service should be zero (cf., e.g., Dorfman, Samuelson and Solow, 1958, p. 360).

In the case of equations (II.2), therefore, the inequality between demand price and supply price at zero outputs simply means letting the system define which consumption goods will be produced by the economy. Similarly, the modification of equations (II.3) only entails allowing the system to define which will be the scarce productive services in the economy. Both these kinds of inequalities are compatible with the equilibrium postulated by Walras's original system, since they do not imply that the maximizing behaviour of the individuals would modify prevailing prices and quantities. The inequality between price and costs referred to in the capital good of relations (II.B) is an entirely different matter, as should be clear from the fact that it merely reflects the fact that the composition of the capital stock is not adjusted to the equilibrium outputs and methods of production. The existence in the economy of stocks of such goods, held for the net income obtainable from them, does imply a tendency in the economy to modify the physical composition of capital and with it, necessarily, the equilibrium prices and quantities.

The modification of equations (II.7) or (II.8) therefore involves a departure from Walras's original notion of equilibrium, and can be accepted or rejected only after an analysis of the *new* conception of equilibrium, which is being implicitly introduced. For brevity this new conception might be referred to as a 'short-period general equilibrium', by analogy with Marshall's partial equilibrium concept which relates to a situation where 'plant' has no time to adjust to prevailing conditions. (It should however be stressed that in the present case the excluded adjustment applies to *all* capital goods, including the circulating capital goods, and not only to the fixed capital goods constituting 'plant' for Marshall. A second, even more important difference is that we are dealing here with a *general* equilibrium concept, unlike in Marshall, where it is true that conditions of long period equilibrium are assumed to hold on an average for the rest of the economy.)

The new conception of equilibrium would in fact relate to a situation where all the forces for maximizing behaviour are at rest, except for those which tend to adjust the existing physical composition of capital to the prevailing conditions, and are therefore at work to modify the *data* of the equilibrium to which the remaining forces would tend. And this modification of the data will generally be rapid, as is evident if we think of circulating capital goods or, more generally, of the fact that only comparatively short-lived, produced, means of production can be properly included under 'capital' (par. 7 above).

The implications of the impermanence of the forces determining this equilibrium will be discussed in detail in Part III below (section V). We may notice that the 'short period' qualification, used here as a shorthand for the new equilibria, and the corresponding reformulations of the theory will thus be taken to cover both the so-called 'temporary equilibria', based on price expectations, and the equilibria forming that sequence of them which constitutes an 'intertemporal equilibrium' (in at least the early components of such a sequence the physical composition of the capital stock, taken initially as a datum, will be unadjusted to the equilibrium outputs and methods of production): these are the two conceptions which we shall discuss in par 45–6 below.

18. Thus, the inconsistency of Walras's original general equilibrium reveals the contradiction inherent in the attempt to treat the heterogeneity of capital like that of labour and land, and treating each kind of heterogeneous resource as a separate factor. This treatment contradicts the search on the part of the investor for the highest rate of return which is in turn only an expression of the fact that the composition of capital tends to adjust both to the outputs and to the methods of production in use.

Our discussion allows us to see why these are the only two conceivable ways out of this contradiction as long as we keep within the general neoclassical (marginalist) demand-and-supply framework, described in section I. The first conceivable way out is to attempt to consider capital as a single factor so that its physical composition can be left to be determined by the equilibrium conditions, and therefore as a *single* factor of production which can change in 'form' without changing in 'quantity' (par. 22 or 37 below). The second conceivable way out is to abandon the traditional concept of equilibrium in favour of the concept of equilibrium above, which would allow for an arbitrary initial physical condition of the capital stock.

In Part III we shall argue that this second way out does not in fact do away with the concept of capital as a single quantity, which reappears in the market for savings and investment. We shall also argue that, in addition, that same way out raises basic methodological difficulties concerning the correspondence between theoretical and observable magnitudes and, more generally, the explanatory capacity of the theory. These difficulties are of course the ones which accounted for the unanimous adherence to the traditional concept of equilibrium, up to the time in which the inconsistencies of the associated concept of a 'quantity of capital' began to emerge in all their implications.

In Part II, which follows, we shall instead consider the first way out of Walras's contradiction, starting in section III, with the failure of Wicksell's attempt to develop the concept of an average period of production, and then proceeding, in section IV, to an examination of the value measurement on which he finally had to fall back. The reader more specifically interested in the contemporary attempts at a solution along the second route, may accordingly proceed directly to sections V–VII, in Part III, and return to Part II later.

PART II
CAPITAL AS A SINGLE FACTOR AND THE TRADITIONAL CONCEPT OF EQUILIBRIUM

III. BÖHM-BAWERK'S AVERAGE PERIOD OF PRODUCTION AND WICKSELL'S THEORY OF CAPITAL. 19. Böhm-Bawerk's average period of production, or 'investment period of the capital' as Wicksell prefers to call it (Wicksell, [1893] 1954, p. 125), is the basis on which an explanation of distribution is advanced in Wicksell's *Value, Capital and Rent*, first published in 1893. For reasons to which we will refer in par. 24 below, three assumptions are needed in order to use that measure of capital: (a) that profits are distributed among the owners of capital goods according to the rules of the simple rate of interest, so that profits which have matured, but have not yet been paid out of the sale of the final consumption good, do not give rise to further profits; (b) that all capital goods are circulating capital (and are therefore entirely consumed in the yearly production cycle that we assume here) and that there is no joint production; (c) that there is only one 'original' factor of production (a factor, that is, other than capital), homogeneous labour.

20. Given these assumptions the concept of capital as periods of time over which labour has remained invested can be expounded very simply. Let us assume that wages are advanced at the beginning of the yearly process of production. The price equation of commodity a, one of the m existing commodities $a, b, \ldots, m$, may be expressed as follows

$$p_a = (1 + i)[wl_{1a} + (p_a a_a + p_b b_a + \ldots + p_m m_a)] \qquad \text{(III.1)}$$

where w is the wage measured like p_a in terms of one of the commodities, e.g. m so that $p_m = 1$; i is the rate of interest (which here, as in Walras, is taken to coincide with the rate of return on capital or rate of profits) and $a, b, c, \ldots, m, l$, are respectively the quantities of commodities a, b, ..., m, and labour, l, required as means of production for a unit of commodity a, so defining the 'method of production' of a.

We can now carry out the reduction to dated quantities of labour of the price of the commodity, an operation by which the different means of production are replaced in the equation with a series of quantities of labour, each with its appropriate date. We begin by substituting for the prices p_a, p_b, ..., p_m applied to the means of production on the right-hand side of (III.1), the expressions given by the respective price equations. In this way the means of production are replaced with their own means of production and quantities of labour, which, having been expended one year earlier, will be multiplied by a profit factor for two years. Next, by substituting for their price, we proceed also to replace this second layer of means of production with their own means of production and labour and to these a profit factor for three years will be applied.

We can carry this operation on as far as we like, and next to the direct labour (which we denote l_{1a} because of its date) we place the successive aggregate quantities of labour which we collect at each step and which we shall call respectively l_{2a}, l_{3a}, ..., l_{na} .... In the general case when at least one of the direct or indirect means at production of a requires itself for its direct or indirect production we shall obtain the production equation in the form:

$$p_a = wl_{1a}(1 + i) + wl_{2a}(1 + i)^2 + \ldots wl_{na}(l + 1)^n \ldots \tag{III.2}$$

Besides the labour terms, there will generally be a commodity residue consisting of minute fractions of the different means of production. It can however be demonstrated that for viable methods of production (capable, that is, of producing a surplus above the mere replacement of means of production) and for a rate of interest less than the maximum admissible in the system (and corresponding to a zero wage) the series on the right-hand side of equation (III.2), will converge, whichever the commodity in terms of which we express the wage and the price.

The same will be all the more true for the infinite series:

$$L_a = l_{1a} + l_{2a} + \ldots l_{na} + \ldots \tag{III.3}$$

independent of i, where L_a defines the quantity of direct and indirect labour necessary to produce a unit of a.

In order to use the average period of production we have now to switch to the simple rate of interest, rewriting the reduction equations as

$$p_a = wl_{1a}(1 + i) + wl_{2a}(1 + 2i) + wl_{3a}(1 + 3i) + \ldots \tag{III.2'}$$

obtaining then

$$p_a = w\{(l_{1a} + l_{2a} + l_{3a}\ldots) + i(l_{1a} + 2l_{2a} + 3l_{3a}\ldots)\}$$

$$= wL_a + iwL_a \frac{l_{1a} + 2l_{2a} + 3l_{3a} + \ldots}{L_a}, \tag{III.4}$$

that is

$$p_a = wL_a + i(wL_a T_a), \tag{III.5}$$

where

$$T_a = \frac{l_{1a} + 2l_{2a} + 3l_{3a} + \cdots}{L_a} \qquad \text{(III.6)}$$

is Böhm-Bawerk's 'average period of production' for commodity a (Böhm-Bawerk, 1891, pp. 88–9): that is the weighted average of the periods of time over which the quantities of labour $l_{1a}, l_{2a}, \ldots, l_{na}, \ldots$ have remained invested in order to produce a, where the weights are given by the respective quantities of labour.

In equation (III.5), the wages for the set of dated quantities of labour, to which capital had been reduced in equation (III.2'), is thus replaced by the wages for the *single* quantity of direct and indirect labour required for its production, L_a, advanced for the average period of production T_a, which is independent of the interest rate i.

21. Some remarks about the concept of capital involved in equation (III.5) may now be useful. We have seen that the term $(iwL_a T_a)$ expressed the amount of profit (interest) included in the price p_a. This may be accounted for in two alternative but equivalent ways of looking at the capital used to produce commodity a.

This expression for profits has emerged above by considering commodity a as if it had been produced by labour which began production without the assistance of any capital goods. That view of the production of a is a logical device used in order to overcome the physical heterogeneity of the commodities constituting capital. By that device we project back in time the several processes of production, which are in fact generally carried out simultaneously in the economy and supply each other with their products.

However, a second view may be taken of T_a as a measure of the capital employed in the direct and indirect production of commodity a. The quantity T_a is also the quantity of labour which is required to produce the set of capital goods which must assist on average one worker *in order to achieve simultaneity between the application of labour to the integrated production of the commodity and the emergence of a corresponding amount of net output.* Let us in fact imagine an integrated process of production of a, that is a process where all the stages of the production of a are carried out simultaneously and side by side, in such a way that the application of a quantity of labour L_a (that is, the payment for such a quantity of labour) at the beginning of the year, becomes simultaneous with the emergence of an output containing the same quantity of labour, while the physical capital used up in that integrated process of production of a is being exactly replaced. Then of course wages need not be advanced, and can be paid out of the sale of the product, but their place in capital is taken by means of production embodying an average T_a labour years for each worker employed in the integrated production of the commodity.

The reason for this necessary correspondence between average period of production and the quantity of labour embodied in the capital goods may perhaps be made intuitively clear by an analogy. Imagine a water reservoir where we let some water in, and an equal amount out, at the beginning of each year. To say that the water remains in that reservoir for an average of T years, and to say that the reservoir contains T gallons of water for each gallon which is being let in (and simultaneously out) is one and the same thing. If L gallons of water are being let in and out at the beginning of each year the amount of water in the reservoir will be LT.

Returning now to labour, T_a is the average period of production. Labour L_a is applied (paid for) at the beginning of each year, at the same moment at which a net output containing L_a labour years flows out as a result of the production cycle just completed. T_a is therefore the period of time over which L_a remains in the reservoir constituted by the capital stock; it follows that the stock must 'contain' $L_a T_a$ labour years.

The profits on the means of production to be paid out of the price p_a will therefore be $(iwL_a T_a)$. Because of the simple rate of interest, the means of production will in fact bear profits for the year in proportion only to their wage costs $[wL_a(T_a-1)]$ (should the profit component of price yield a profit, we would clearly have the case of a compound rate of profits).

The quantity of labour embodied in the stock of capital goods assisting, on average, one labourer in the integrated production of one unit of a commodity, and the average period of production of that commodity, are thus but two ways of visualizing and describing one and the same magnitude for measuring capital. (The conception of capital as a stock of goods such as to make inputs and outputs simultaneous was stressed by J.B. Clark, e.g., 1895, pp. 267–81, though he appeared to view it incorrectly as exclusive of the period-of-production conception: on this and those two equivalent conceptions of capital cf. Garegnani, 1960, pp. 26–8.)

It may be noted finally how, under the hypotheses necessary for the use of the average period of production, the value of the physical capital in any given price situation is a (proportionally) rising function of the 'quantity' of capital employed, as measured by the average period of production or by the labour embodied in the means of production. This measurement of capital satisfies, therefore, the second requirement set forth in par. 8 above.

22. We are now able to return to Wicksell's theory in *Value, Capital and Rent*. We shall assume, as Wicksell does at first, that land is free ([1893] 1954, p. 146) and that only one consumption good is produced in the economy (*ibid.* pp. 126–7; Wicksell's assumption is that the proportional increase in the physical productivity of labour, as the average period is lengthened, is the same in all sectors, so that the relative value of the commodities is constant and they can be treated as one commodity). Further, we assume circulating capital and a simple rate of interest, i (*ibid.*, pp. 120–1).

It will then be possible to calculate the average period of production corresponding to each of the alternative 'systems available for the production' of the consumption good, in the given state of technical knowledge – where by 'system of production' of a commodity we shall mean the set of methods of production consisting of one method for the commodity and one for each of its direct and indirect means of production. We can thus obtain a production function expressing the physical quantity q of the consumption good obtainable from a labour year (yearly output per worker) as a differentiable function of the average period T expressed in years

$$q = f(T) \qquad (III.7)$$

where $f''(T) \leqslant 0$ since if $f(T) > 0$, then, whatever the w and i the entrepreneur may find on the market, he would always prefer some appropriate combination of two adjacent techniques, which would give a higher q for that value of T.

We have then the following equation asserting the equilibrium equality between the product of a labour year and the real wage w paid for it, plus the interest at the (simple) rate i over the average period of production:

$$q = w(1 + iT). \qquad (III.8)$$

Another equation is obtained by Wicksell from the conditions of maximum profits. The reasoning is: assuming that the capitalists are the entrepreneurs, they will choose, for any given rate of wages w, that average period T which will maximize the rate of interest i. The corresponding mathematical condition is (*ibid*. p. 122):

$$dq/dT = wi. \qquad (III.9)$$

(Equation (III.9) could also be obtained by assuming that the workers are the entrepreneurs and that for any given rate of interest, they choose the T which maximizes the wage rate: *ibid*., p. 123.)

A fourth equation is then supplied by the condition regarding the equality between the demand for capital and the supply of it, assumed by Wicksell to be independent of the rate of interest and equal to the value of the capital in existence in the economy, K, expressed in terms of the consumption goods. Wicksell assumes simultaneous production and, therefore, for the reasons seen above (par. 21), the labour embodied in the physical capital assisting on an average one worker will be T and its value will be (wT) in terms of the final product (zero net accumulation is assumed here for simplicity, so that T, the average period of production of the consumption good, is also the average period of the net social product and will measure social capital: see also par. 28 below). The number of workers available in the economy is A and the amount of labour supplied is therefore A labour years (Wicksell assumes the labour time supplied for productive use by each worker to be independent of its rate of remuneration). The value of social capital in terms of the consumption good is therefore given by (wAT). We have then the following equation (cf. eqn (15), *ibid*., p. 126):

$$K = wAT \qquad (III.10)$$

with respect to which Wicksell asserts that, in the process of achieving equilibrium, though 'the forms of capital change, its total value remains unchanged, since, in

27

place of the consumed capital goods, new ones of equivalent value enter successively' (Wicksell, [1893] 1954, p. 103; cf. also *ibid.* p. 119), a statement which is characteristic of the view of capital which has to be taken for continuity with the traditional concept of equilibrium.

We have now four independent equations for determining the four unknowns w, i, T and q.

23. The inconsistency of the value measurement of capital in (III.10) will be examined in detail in section IV below, when we shall also consider the subsistence fund conception of capital, on which Wicksell relied in *Value, Capital and Rent*. All we need for the time being is to point out that if social capital could in fact be measured by the average period of production T, then the value measurement of the quantities demanded and supplied of capital in equation (III.10) would not be essential. That measurement could be replaced by the measurement of capital used in the production function, where the ratio of capital to labour is expressed by T: the number of labour years embodied in the capital stock assisting, on the average, one worker in the economy. If we then take as given the capital K' existing in the economy, measured in terms of the labour years which have been necessary for its production, we shall have the following equation:

$$K' = AT. \qquad \text{(III.10')}$$

If now we replace equation (III.10) with equation (III.10'), the four unknowns p, w, i, T can be determined without resorting to Wicksell's value measurement of capital. The quantity K' of capital appearing there would be independent of distribution. An inverse relation between the rate of interest and the ratio T of capital to labour would on the other hand follow from equation (III.9) – where any fall in i will necessarily lower wi on the right-hand side and render profitable a lengthening of the average period T (Wicksell, [1893] 1954, p. 127–8) – similarly to what we saw in par. 3 above for the quantity employed of a factor when its remuneration falls. (A similar inverse relation could therefore be shown to hold also with respect to the value K of capital in equation (III.10) above: the increase in T as i falls is associated with an increase in w, and therefore, necessarily, in AwT).

24. This discussion has shown how the average period of production could be used as a consistent measure of capital in marginal theory. But the three assumptions of simple rate of interest, absence of fixed capital and a single original factor of production necessary for a correct use of the average period of production (par. 19 above) are drastic enough to prevent its adoption. For reasons of space we can show here neither why these assumptions are necessary for the validity of the average period, nor how, in *Value, Capital and Rent* ([1893], 1954), Wicksell dealt with these three assumptions (for these questions see Garegnani, 1960, Part I, ch. IV, V, and Part II, ch. IV). It is sufficient here to notice the conclusion which Wicksell drew when, in his *Lectures*, he dropped those assumptions and the average period of production together with them.

With this, we see in fact the end of the most serious attempt to arrive at a 'quantity of capital' as the single magnitude independent of distribution, required by 'marginal' theory – an attempt which the phenomenon of reswitching (par. 36 below) shows to have been doomed to failure from the start (Sraffa, 1960, p. 50). And we see the end also of the most serious attempt to reconcile the condition of the independence of distribution, with that of an adjusted physical composition of the capital stock – the two conditions whose conflict generated the inconsistency in Walras's system.

We may now summarize the theory Wicksell proposed in his *Lectures* ([1901] 1934), which he kept revising until his death, in order to show how the value measurement becomes essential there just when his doubts about the conception of a 'fund of subsistence', by which he had justified that value measurement in ([1893] 1954), were increasing. The shortcomings of that measurement of capital will then be discussed in section IV, and also in Part III, section VII.

25. Of the three assumptions necessary for the validity of the average period of production, only the exclusion of fixed capital is retained in the *Lectures on Political Economy* ([1901] 1934) (however Wicksell makes it clear in (1923) how this assumption could also be dropped). Wicksell's procedure now consists of considering the entire set of periods of time over which labour and the other 'original' factors remain invested and not just any average of them.

We may simplify our exposition by assuming that a single consumption good is produced in the economy (Wicksell does the same initially, and only later in the book does he proceed to the case of more than one consumption good).

Then let:

Q be the yearly output of the consumption good;
K be the value in terms of the consumption good of the capital stock available in the economy;
A be the number of labourers available;
B be the acres of land available;
$A_0, A_1, \ldots, A_{(n-1)}$ be the quantities of labour (labour-years) applied $0, 1, 2, \ldots (n-1)$ years before the consumption good emerges (Wicksell assumes here that wages are paid at the end of the production cycle, so that the labour used directly for the production of the consumption good is taken to be applied at the moment in which the final output becomes available);
$B_0, B_1, \ldots, B_{(n-1)}$ be the analogous quantities of land;
w be the yearly wage rate in terms of the consumption good, paid at the *end* of the yearly production cycle,
r be the yearly rent of an acre of land also in terms of the consumption good;
i be the yearly rate of interest.

Wicksell takes the quantities A, B, K as given and as in *Value, Capital and Rent*, he assumes the quantities of factors supplied for productive use to be independent of their rates of remuneration. With labour and land distributed over any number n of dates from 0 to $(n-1)$, the number of unknowns will be

$(2n + 4)$, namely the $2n$ dated quantities of labour and land $A_0, A_1, \ldots, A_{n-1}$; $B_0, B_1, \ldots, B_{n-1}$; besides Q, i, w and r. (The fact that labour works nowhere unassisted by capital goods would make n tend to infinity. It can however be demonstrated that there will always be a value of n large enough to make the quantities A_n, A_{n+1}, etc.; B_n, B_{n+1}, etc., corresponding to any given system of production, small enough to be ignored for all rates of interest below the maximum admissible in that system of production: cf. par. 20 above).

For that determination we have first the production function:

$$Q = f(A_0, A_1, A_2, \ldots, A_{n-1}; B_0, B_1, B_2, \ldots, B_{n-1}). \qquad \text{(III.11)}$$

We then have the $2n$ equations giving the equilibrium equality between the marginal products of the dated quantities of labour and land, and the respective remunerations – which consist of the wage and rent rates plus the interest for the period for which they have been advanced:

$$\left.\begin{aligned}
\frac{\partial Q}{\partial A_0} &= w & \frac{\partial Q}{\partial B_0} &= r \\[2ex]
\frac{\partial Q}{\partial A_1} &= w(1 + i) & \frac{\partial Q}{\partial B_1} &= r(1 + i) \\[1ex]
&\ \ \vdots & &\ \ \vdots \\[1ex]
\frac{\partial Q}{\partial A_{n-1}} &= w(1 + i)^{n-1} & \frac{\partial Q}{\partial B_{n-1}} &= r(1 + i)^{n-1}.
\end{aligned}\right\} \qquad \text{(III.12)}$$

Two equations are then given by the simplifying condition of zero net accumulation. This condition entails that the quantities of labour and land applied at the various dates in the past and embodied in the existing means of production must be equal to the quantities of labour which are being currently employed in order to replace them and must be therefore added to the total quantities A and B of current labour and land entering the production of the net consumption output Q of the year (see in Wicksell, [1901] 1934, the first two equations on p. 204).

$$\left.\begin{aligned}
A_0 + A_1 + \ldots + A_{n-1} &= A \\
B_0 + B_1 + \ldots + B_{n-1} &= B
\end{aligned}\right\} \qquad \text{(III.13)}$$

(It should be noted that the assumption of a zero net accumulation appears to be intended only to simplify the exposition by avoiding the reference to future equilibria which would be required in order to determine the allocation of savings. No difference of principle would in fact be involved if we allowed for the non-zero net accumulation which will be generally dictated by the individual preferences in any equilibrium determined on the basis of given factor endowments and technical conditions of production: cf. also par. 44 below.)

Finally, we have the condition that the value of the capital stock in existence in the economy at the beginning of the yearly production cycle, expressed in terms of the consumption good, should be equal to a given 'quantity of capital' K available in the economy. The expression for K is obtained by remembering that, under the simplifying conditions of zero net accumulation mentioned above, to each A_j for $j = 1, 2, \ldots, (n-1)$, there will correspond j elements of capital, each embodying A_j labour years, applied over each of the years which have elapsed between the moment $(-n)$ and the moment (-1), when the current production cycle begins and the value of capital is being reckoned. (E.g. if A_2 were labour producing iron for ploughs of one-year duration, used in turn in order to produce corn, the consumption good, then we would have, besides the quantity A_2 of labour embodied in the ploughs, and applied one year before the moment of our reckoning of capital, a second quantity A_2 of labour paid for at the time of reckoning and embodied in the iron which is about to be worked upon by the smiths.) We then have the following equation (which Wicksell introduces somewhat reluctantly in [1901] 1934, p. 204):

$$K = \{wA_1 + wA_2[1 + (1+i)] + \ldots + wA_{n-1}[1 + (1+i)^2 + \ldots + (1+i)^{n-2}]\}$$
$$+ \{rB_1 + rB_2[1 + (1+i)] + \ldots + rB_{n-1}[1 + (1+i) + (1+i)^2 \quad \text{(III.14)}$$
$$+ \ldots (1+i)^{n-2}]\}.$$

26. The value measurement of capital in equation (III.14) is now essential to the theory (contrary to what was true in *Value, Capital and Rent*, [1893] 1954). But paradoxically, unlike in that earlier work (cf. the passage quoted in par. 22 above), in the *Lectures* Wicksell is clearly unhappy about the dependence of his system on such a measurement (cf. in this respect Garegnani, 1960, pp. 136 n., 143 n.). Thus despite equation (III.14), he states 'capital is saved-up labour and saved-up land' ([1901] 1934, p. 154). However, suppose he had been consistent with this definition, and had therefore taken as given the capital endowment of the economy in terms of the physical quantities $A_1, A_2, \ldots, A_{n-1}; B_1, \ldots, B_{n-1}$. In accordance with equation (III.13) A_0 and B_0 will result after subtracting from the total current labour and land A and B the quantities needed to replace the saved-up labour and land as they are being used up. Then, the number of unknowns would have fallen below the number of independent equations with the unknowns decreasing by $(2n-2)$ but one equation only, equation (III.21), disappearing. The resulting overdeterminacy would of course have expressed the conflict between the conception of capital Wicksell advances in that passage and his equations (III.12), establishing the uniformity in the effective rate of return i on the wages and rents advanced for the several periods of time and, therefore, on the supply price of the capital goods. We would be faced, that is, by the same problem we saw in Walras, which is indivisible from any attempt to represent capital as a set of distinct factors.

IV. CAPITAL AS A VALUE QUANTITY. 27. We saw how in the *Lectures* ([1901] 1934) Wicksell abandoned the 'average period of production' of *Value, Capital and Rent* ([1893] 1954) because of the unacceptable assumptions necessary for its use. We also saw how he had then to fall back on a value measurement of the existing social capital, in order to fulfil the condition of a uniform rate of return on the supply price of the capital goods. The consideration of capital as a single factor – the way in which Walras's inconsistency had been generally avoided – leads thus to a measurement in value terms, which is clearly not independent of distribution (par. 7 above).

What we must now do is to examine more closely the deficiencies of that measurement and discuss the arguments which have been used to support it, in particular by Böhm-Bawerk and by Wicksell. To simplify the discussion in this section and in section VII, where the argument will be taken up again, we shall assume most of the time only one 'original' factor of production, homogeneous labour. To consider more than one 'original' factor would only corroborate the negative conclusions we shall reach.

28. In order to be clear about the matter it is necessary to start off by returning to the two roles we distinguished in par. 6 above, in which the quantity of each factor, in particular that of capital, has to appear in the equations of the theory. The first role is to express the produced means of production required by the alternative 'systems of production' possible for each commodity (for a definition of the latter see par.22 above). The second is to express the endowment of those means of production in the economy, and therefore the quantity of them in the appropriate demand and supply functions which determine the equilibrium.

In the case of the 'corn-capital' of our introductory scheme (par. 3 above), the units in which the factors were expressed were the same in both roles. That is what the underlying conception of the theory would imply, based as it is on the derivation of decreasing demand functions for the factors from their marginal products in the production function of each commodity, and from the technical conditions of production of the goods among which consumers choose. However, the need to treat capital as a single magnitude, and therefore as a value magnitude, together with the attempt to avoid introducing a value magnitude into the production functions, brings about the separation between the two roles we saw in Wicksell's *Lectures* ([1901] 1934), where the factors of production appear, so to speak, in two separate 'layers'. Those of the first 'layer' appear in the production function (III.11), and are the 'dated' quantities of labour and land, $A_0, A_1, \ldots, A_{n-1}$; $B_0, B_1, \ldots, B_{n-1}$. Those of the second 'layer' appear in the demand and supply functions, whose intersection is expressed by equations (III.13) and (III.14), and are homogeneous labour A, homogeneous land B, and the 'capital' K, a sum of value.

Now, the deficiencies affecting a value measurement of capital, confined to the demand and supply functions, are not the same as those which affect that measurement when it is also used in the production functions. In par. 29–32, we shall consider the latter use, to proceed then in par. 33–6 to the former.

29. So far we have not considered the shortcomings of a value measurement of capital in the role it plays when used in the production function. This was because

that role was not there in either Walras or Wicksell, who were clearly aware of its inconsistency (cf. e.g. Wicksell, 1934, p. 147), which is particularly transparent when the exposition is framed in mathematical terms.

Other theorists were, however, less clear on this point, and a value measurement of capital is used in the definition of the alternative systems of production in J.B. Clark (1911), Wicksteed (1933), and numerous other theorists, including Marshall (1890) and Pigou (1932). (It is however not always clear how far these authors actually envisaged production functions where capital appeared as *physical* quantities of the various capital goods and only the demand and supply functions determining the rates of remuneration were based on capital as a value magnitude: in this case the criticism applicable to those authors is the one that will be examined in pars. 33–6 below. It should in any case be stressed that, contrary to what is sometimes stated (e.g. Samuelson, 1962, p. 193), these authors were in no sense responsible for attempting to represent the conditions of production in the economy in terms of a single 'aggregate production function'. As they were all interested in the determination of relative prices, they distinguished the separate industries just as Walras and Wicksell did. Indeed, after what we saw in par. 18 about the contradiction in Walras's general equilibrium system, it should be clear that the question of measuring capital in terms of a single quantity – of 'aggregate capital', as it is often somewhat misleadingly put – has in principle nothing whatsoever to do with using 'aggregate production functions'.)

On this first use of capital as a value magnitude, the essential point can be expressed very briefly; the definition of the system of production of a commodity (par. 22) requires that a single level of output be ascribed to any given technical combination of resources. Now, no such unique relation between output and quantities of inputs can be established when the capital inputs appear in terms of the *value* of that capital. Leaving aside the special hypotheses which would validate the labour theory of value and therefore ensure relative values independent of distribution, the value of the several physical capital goods will change with distribution, whichever value unit is used. The same system (technique) of production of the commodity would then appear to require different 'quantities of capital' depending on distribution. A production function which has the value of capital as one of its variables is therefore illusory, in the sense that it could never be reckoned from technical data alone, as it should in order to deduce from it the propositions which the theory requires (par. 3–5 above).

30. It might however be objected that when a production function with the value of capital as one of its arguments is put forward for a productive sector, what is in fact meant thereby is the value of the appropriate set of capital goods estimated at the particular prices ruling at the interest rate (real wage rate) for which the system of production is profitable (under the hypothesis made in par. 27 above, relative prices are determined once the rate of interest is given).

In answer to this objection the following three observations can be made:
(i) No unique relationship between output and quantities of factors could be

established in that way, because the same system will generally be in use over an *interval* of values of the rate of interest, with a corresponding range of values of the capital stock in terms of any numéraire (this consideration is independent of the phenomena of reswitching and reverse capital deepening: par. 36 below).

(ii) The difficulty, however is more fundamental. Thus if the highly abstract assumption of continuity in the change of system were made, allowing for a system to be in use only for a single level of the rate of interest (see e.g. Garegnani, 1970, pp. 412, 420 n.), the resulting 'marginal products' would be an entirely different construction from the traditional marginal products of the theory, assuming a physical measurement of all the factors. This is shown in the first place by the fact that they would generally not be equal to the rates of remuneration of the corresponding factors.

(iii) The different nature of those constructs is revealed even more clearly by the fact that even when, under further, more restrictive hypotheses, these 'marginal products' happened to coincide with factor remunerations, they would not possess the property of being inversely related to the quantity of the factor which, as was argued in par. 15 above, is what is analytically relevant about 'marginal products'. (For propositions (ii) and (iii), cf. Garegnani, 1984, in particular, p. 148.) Because of (i), therefore, the production functions discussed here could not generally be defined even if capital were to be evaluated at equilibrium prices. And when the assumption of a 'continuum' of methods made such a definition possible, (ii) and (iii) above would prevent the function from providing the basis of demand functions for the factors.

(Our point (ii) can be used to explain the shortcomings of the idea of 'surrogate capital' in Samuelson (1962). Given the continuum of alternative systems to be described below (par. 36), involving heterogeneous capital goods in the production of a consumption good, the attempt is made to argue that the relation between the wage and the rate of interest would be the same obtainable from an appropriately ·defined (surrogate) production function involving (surrogate) capital as a single factor. However, for such a function to give the correct product – that is the correct sum of wages and profits – the 'surrogate capital' would evidently have to coincide with the value in terms of consumption of the capital in use. But then because of point (ii) above, the resulting production function could give no marginal products equal to the correct rates of remuneration. A 'surrogate production function' cannot therefore be generally defined, since no such function can exist, giving both the correct rates of remuneration and the correct product: Samuelson, 1962; Garegnani, 1970, pp. 414–16.)

31. A device has sometimes been suggested which avoids shortcoming (i), without necessarily resorting to the hypothesis of a continuum of methods of production, while at the same time avoiding also shortcoming (ii). The device is that of a 'chain index of capital', with which to register, so to speak, the equilibrium value of the physical capital per worker, when the system of production in question, say *I*, first becomes profitable in the course of a monotonic change of the interest rate, and then to keep constant that value for the interval of *i* over which *I*

remains profitable. It will then allow that value to change in proportion to the relative value of the capital goods of the new system at the prices of the switch point, as the economy switches to the adjacent system *II* and so on and so forth as the monotonic change of the rate of interest makes the economy switch to the appropriate systems (cf. Champernowne, 1953; Swann, 1956). However, as Champernowne freely recognized (1953, p. 118), the key difficulty – (iii) above – remains, and no inverse relation between the rates of remuneration of the factors and the quantities of them employed can be established, when capital is measured as the usual value magnitude in terms of any commodity. The difficulties that we shall discuss in pars 35–36 below would therefore remain when attempting to base a determination of distribution on such a production function.

Indeed, not even a one-to-one correspondence between physical capital and level of the 'chain index' would hold. When, with 'reswitching', the same system of production is profitable over more than one interval of the rate of interest (below par. 36), the chain index method would indicate a different amount of capital in each of these intervals (Champernowne, 1953). Perhaps, even more strikingly, when more than one switch point occurs different 'marginal products' would be found, at each of the switch points between the same two systems of production.

It would also be difficult to see how the arbitrarily given capital stock of the economy could ever be reckoned in terms of such a chain-index, so as to provide the argument of a supply function matching a demand function drawn on this basis. The device of a 'chain-index' measurement of capital appears in fact to have been designed only in order to analyze a process of capital accumulation, by reconstructing its path through a sequence of equilibria. It does not therefore seem to address the basic question on which the discussion about the 'measurement of capital' turns, whether or not the 'neoclassical' demand-and-supply apparatus provides a valid explanation of distribution and relative prices. This is so because it *assumes* that the explanation is valid – and only attempts to represent the process of accumulation by abstracting from the value changes of the capital goods which, it is held, should not be counted as 'savings'.

32. One may therefore conclude on the use of a value measurement for capital in the production function, by returning to what was said in par. 29. That measurement assumes distribution and relative prices to be known when defining the parameters of the very functions which should determine them, and no valid argument can be based on such an illusory basis. We have seen accordingly that even when the assumption of a 'continuum' of methods is made in order to be able to define a 'production function' in those terms, that function will not yield the key analytical proposition which the theory derived from it – the inverse relation between quantity employed and the rate of remuneration of a factor. A 'chain index of capital' does not seem to improve matters, since while it eliminates the price changes of the capital goods over the interval of *i* for which the respective system is in use, it cannot eliminate the really damaging effects of those price

changes, which are those on the sequence with which the systems become profitable as i changes monotonically.

The criticism of any attempt to treat capital as a value magnitude in the definition of the production possibilities open to the economy appears however to be widely accepted, even to the point of being incorrectly identified with the criticism of the traditional conception of capital as such. In effect, it only impinges upon some less careful, less exactly specified, versions of marginal theory.

33. In approaching that use of a value measurement of capital, as an argument in the demand-and-supply functions for factors, it seems important to make a preliminary distinction between two groups of difficulties we meet there. The first group regards the difficulties we meet in expressing the capital stock in existence of the economy as a value magnitude: they are those which touch, so to speak, on the supply aspect of capital. These difficulties appear to impinge directly only on the traditional versions of the theory, which treat the capital endowment as a single quantity. The second group of difficulties pertains instead to the demand aspect of capital and in particular to the shape of the 'demand functions' for the factors and bears on all versions of the theory. This paragraph and the next will deal with the 'supply' aspect of the question, whereas pars. 35 and 36 will treat the demand aspect.

Böhm-Bawerk and Wicksell were perhaps, among their contemporaries, the authors who showed the greatest awareness of the deficiencies of a value measurement of capital. It is therefore not surprising that to them we must turn for what are perhaps the most serious attempts to justify the value measurement of capital in its supply aspect – beyond the mere popular plausibility of using a measurement long used in business practice for purposes of theory. (For a fuller discussion of Böhm-Bawerk's and Wicksell's arguments cf. Garegnani, 1960, Part II, ch. V.)

It is to Böhm-Bawerk's (1891) conception of a 'subsistence fund' that Wicksell refers when supporting in ([1893] 1954) his value measurement of the capital endowment. Böhm-Bawerk held that:

> all goods which appear today as the stock or parent wealth of society ... will, in the more or less distant future ... ripen into consumption goods, and will consequently cover, for a more or less lengthy time to come, the people's demand for consumption (Böhm-Bawerk, 1891, p. 322),

and he went on to specify that:

> in any economical community the supply of subsistence available for advances of subsistence, is ... represented by the total sum of its wealth (p. 319),

where by 'sum' he clearly meant the *value* of the stock in question in terms of subsistence (that is, of some composite unit of consumption goods).

Böhm-Bawerk's idea is therefore that the value of the existing stock of capital in terms of consumption represents a fund of consumption goods which will, so to speak, be there at the disposal of the community in a sufficiently definite amount, independently both of the methods of production to be used, and of the ruling rates of wages and interest (though of course, it is admitted that this 'fund' will 'ripen' only progressively). The fund will thus allow the community to undertake those processes of production of consumption goods which, as we saw in section III, while taking up longer periods of production, will increase the productivity of the 'original factors' (labour and land).

However, this idea of Böhm-Bawerk's seems not to stand up to close examination. It is true that the value of a capital good in terms of some composite consumption commodity will tend to bear some definite relationship to the output of subsistence goods, on whose production it is directly or indirectly employed. This relationship is, however, such that the value of such a capital good, far from being independent of the system of production according to which it will be employed and of the ruling rates of wages and interest, will in most relevant situations be the *outcome* of those very factors. Let us consider, e.g., a circulating capital good. The amount of the consumption good which will be finally obtained from it, and the moment in the future at which it will be obtained, will depend on the methods of production adopted in the remaining stages of the production process. On the other hand the value of the capital good in terms of consumption goods will at any moment tend to be equal to that amount of consumption goods, minus the sum of (a) the wages for the labour required in the stages of that production yet to come; (b) the value of the replacement of the capital goods used in those stages; and, finally, (c) the interest on both the wages and the capital goods (including the capital good whose value we are ascertaining) for the time between the present and the moment at which the consumption goods will emerge from production.

Nor would any greater independence of Böhm-Bawerk's 'subsistence fund' from the variables to be determined emerge if we considered the equilibrium equality between the price and the costs of production of the capital good. These costs will clearly depend on the same variables. Above all, that equilibrium price will not obtain when the capital good has to be 'transformed' into some other capital good (if that price held the capital good would be replaced as it stands and not be changed in 'form': par. 22 above): precisely the situation in which the 'subsistence' assumed by Böhm-Bawerk and Wicksell would have to come into existence to provide for the original factors producing the new capital goods.

34. Indeed, there are signs that, by the time of his *Lectures*, Wicksell had come to doubt the validity of Böhm-Bawerk's conception (par. 26 above). Wicksell seems then to have fallen back on the idea that the value measurement of capital could be taken as a workable *approximation* to something he was searching for, and to which he referred as 'real' capital. As he put it:

It may be difficult – if not impossible – to define this concept of [real] social capital with *absolute precision* as a definite quantity. In reality it is rather a complex of quantities (Wicksell, [1901] 1934, p, 165, our italics).

What such a justification of a value measurement ignores is the fact that, in order to speak of one magnitude as a workable approximation to another, we should first be able to define the second magnitude exactly: and the 'real capital' magnitude is precisely what, in most relevant cases, cannot be defined. All that we can say is that in those special cases where we can use a 'real capital' magnitude – as in comparing two situations in which the physical capital stock is the same, but distribution has varied – the value magnitude of capital can vary to almost any degree, even though 'real capital' has remained constant.

35. We can now proceed to the difficulties which beset the demand aspect of conceiving capital as a value magnitude. It may be useful to begin from the reasoning we saw in par. 3, above, for an inverse relation between the quantity of a factor employed and its rate of remuneration, and restate it in a way that will make it clear why it no longer applies when one of the factors is measured in value terms.

Two factors only, x and y may be assumed without loss of generality. If both x and y are measured in physical terms, a fall in the price p_x of the service of x relative to that of y will necessarily entail a cheapening of the productive processes which use x in a higher proportion. In fact if p_a is the 'price' of a process of production a which requires quantities x_a, y_a of the factors, and p_b is the analogous 'price' of a process b, then:

$$\frac{p_a}{p_b} = \frac{x_a p_x + y_a p_y}{x_b p_x + y_b p_y} = \frac{\dfrac{x_a p_x}{y_a p_y} + 1}{\dfrac{x_b p_x}{y_b p_y} + 1} \frac{y_a}{y_b}. \tag{IV.1}$$

It is evident (from IV.1) that if, say, process a uses x in a higher proportion, so that $x_a/y_a > x_b/y_b$; then p_a/p_b will have to fall as p_x/p_x falls. This cheapening of the x-intensive process a is what will set in motion *both* the technical substitution of x for y (with a and b as two alternative systems for the production of the same commodity, equation (IV.1) shows that the system becoming more profitable must be the more x-intensive one), and the consumer substitution between the two factors (a and b can be interpreted as the production of two different consumer goods), with the consequences we saw in par. 3–5 above. However, the above argument clearly ceases to hold as soon as we interpret x in equation (IV.1) as the *value* of the capital goods required in the two processes. Then x_a/y_a and x_b/y_b will generally *change* merely as a result of the fall in p_x/p_y and it is conceivable, e.g., that the relative value x_a/x_b of the two sets of capital goods required by processes a and b respectively, might *rise*, and rise in such a way as to make p_a/p_b rise rather than fall. Then the quantity of x employed with a given quantity of y would fall, and not rise, as p_x/p_y falls.

In fact to the writer's knowledge the only attempts to demonstrate an inverse relation between the quantity of the factor employed and its rate of remuneration, when capital, the value magnitude, is among the factors, were those by Böhm-Bawerk and Wicksell indicated above, based on the average period of production (par. 23 above), and dependent on the unacceptable hypotheses we saw in par. 19. In spite of this it apparently continued to be assumed that the dependence of the value of capital goods on distribution would not affect the inverse relation between the price of the service and the quantity of the factors employed.

36. This may explain why in more recent years, when in the wake of Sraffa's book (1960), and of earlier work inspired by Sraffa (Robinson, 1953: for her debt to Sraffa see Robinson 1972, pp. 144–5), the problem was again analysed, the proposition was found to be false. Once capital, the value magnitude, is introduced among the factors, the principle of a cheapening of the more capital-intensive process ceases to hold. As a result the inverse relation between the remuneration of the factor and the proportion in which it is employed is no longer entailed by the existence of alternative systems of production, and of the choice of consumers.

The, by now, well-known phenomenon of 'reswitching' was also shown to be possible: the system of production *I* becomes less profitable than *II* as, say, the real wage falls, but may again become more profitable than *II* when the wage falls still further and this may occur one or more times (cf., e.g. Pasinetti *et al.*, 1966). What this phenomenon – whose possibility also follows from the variability of x_a/x_b in equation IV.1 – immediately reveals, is the impossibility of asserting that as the interest rate (wage rate) changes *monotonically*, the alternative systems of production of the commodity become profitable in succession and can be ordered according to a capital intensity ascertainable independently of distribution (Sraffa, 1960, p. 50).

In Fig. 3 below, these phenomena are illustrated for a simple model where a consumption good *a* is produced by means of alternative methods each requiring a single (circulating) capital good which *differs* from system to system and is produced by means of quantities l_c of labour and c_c of itself, l_a and c_a being the analogous quantities used to produce the consumption good. A *continuum* of systems is assumed there by expressing the coefficients of production defining them as continuous functions of a parameter *u*, so that, in the given interval, each value of *u* defines one *type* of capital good and, therefore, one possible system of production (the example is taken from Garegnani, 1970, where it is analysed on pp. 428–31; for the concept of a 'continuum' of systems see *ibid.*, p. 412). In particular, Fig. 3a shows the wage interest relationship for one such a continuum, where each system, with the exception of that for $u = 1.505$ is in use at *two* distinct levels of the rate of interest *i*. These are the levels for which the wage-curve of the system lies above all the others and is therefore tangent to the external 'envelope' curve *EE*. Then, Fig. 3c shows the resulting relation between *i* and the value *k* of capital per worker in terms of good *a*, in the 'integrated production' of that good, with Fig. 3b giving the analogous relation between *w* and the quantity of labour per unit of consumption-good value of capital. Finally

39

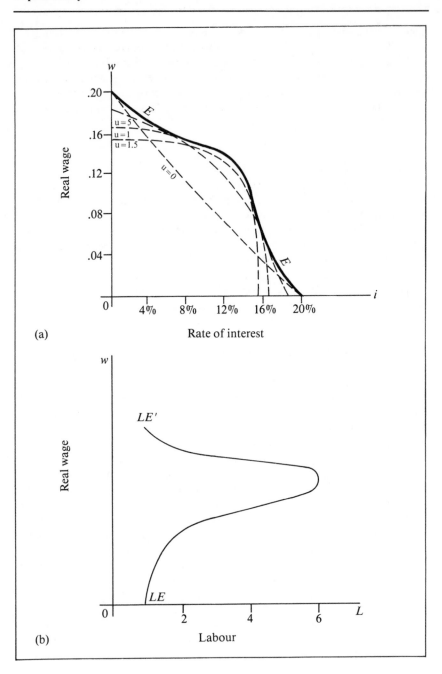

(a)

(b)

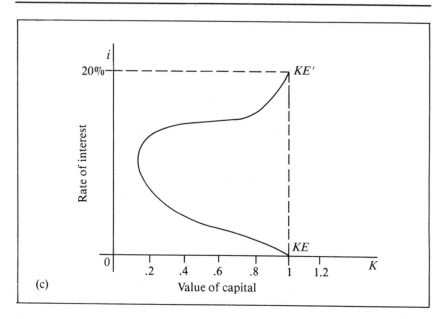

Figure 3 Relations between i, w, L and K.

Table 1 gives the coefficients of production of the 'continuum' of systems of production giving rise to those curves in which, as the wage falls monotonically from $w = 0.200$ to $w = 0.129$, all systems come into use in the order from $u = 0$ to $u = 1.505$, and all become profitable again in the reverse order, as w falls further from $w = 0.129$ to $w = 0$. Table 1 also gives the two rates of interest at which each system is in use and the corresponding two consumption-good values of the unchanged physical capital per worker required by the system.

(The example just described incidentally shows the fallacy of the impression sometimes created that a continuum of alternative systems for the production of

TABLE 1

Parameter u	Production of a Unit of the Consumer Good		Production of a Unit of the Capital Good		System in use at			
	Labour l_c	Physical Capital c_c	Labour l_c	Physical Capital c_c	i %	K	i %	K
0.000	0.500	0.750	1	0.833	0.00	1.080	20.0	0.000
0.250	2.584	0.424	1	0.839	2.6	0.635	17.5	0.997
0.500	3.930	0.237	1	0.845	4.1	0.393	16.9	0.850
0.750	4.834	0.133	1	0.851	8.1	0.237	15.3	0.715
1.000	5.478	0.075	1	0.857	8.3	0.184	15.1	0.534
1.250	5.974	0.042	1	0.863	10.5	0.148	14.4	0.379
1.505	6.391	0.023	1	0.868	12.9	0.179	—	—

a commodity is incompatible with the phenomenon of 'reswitching': cf. e.g. Burmeister and Dobell, 1970; S. Marglin, 1984, pp. 285 and 541. The impossibility of reswitching to which those authors refer is in fact not related to the *continuity* in the change of system, which as the example of Fig. 3 shows is perfectly compatible with it. It is instead the result of the assumption that the alternative methods only differ by the proportions of the *same* physical factors, whether these proportions are continuously variable or not; an assumption which obviously is difficult to accept, once each kind of capital good is treated as a separate factor.)

The freedom with which the value of capital may vary with i, even in this very simple two-commodity, circulating-capital example, is then illustrated further in Fig. 4 below where *any curve lying in the shaded area* OSTQ can be shown to correspond to a family of possible systems of production (for a demonstration of this and the following examples cf. Garegnani, 1970, pp. 431–5). Three such relationships are then chosen and drawn in the diagram. They are $k^{(1)}$, where the value of the capital employed does not change at all as i changes, though the system of production changes continuously; $k^{(2)}$ where the value of capital increases in a straight line with i; and finally $k^{(3)}$, where it increases and then decreases as i rises. The production coefficients and the other relevant variables

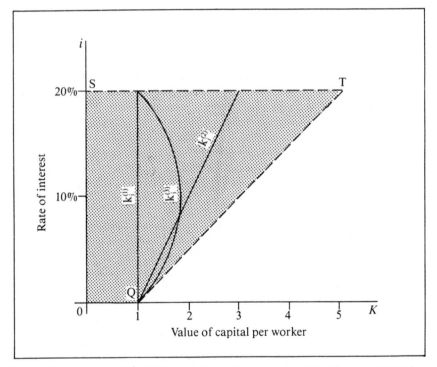

Figure 4 Any curve $k_i^{(j)}$ which starts from Q and stays within the area $STQO$ is a possible relation between the value of capital per worker k_i and the rate of interest.

TABLE 2

(a) *The case $k_i^{(1)} = 1$*

| Parameter | Systems of Production | | | | Net Phys. Prod. per Worker | In use at | | Value of Capital per Worker |
| | Input-Coefficients (*) | | | | | | | |
u	l_a	c_a	l_c	c_c	q_i	i	w	$k_i^{(1)}$
0	0.076	0.0006	1	0.976	1	0	1	1
0.00	1.027	0.0017	1	0.932	0.95	0.05	0.9	1
0.10	1.216	0.0037	1	0.892	0.80	0.10	0.7	1
0.15	1.750	0.0097	1	0.857	0.55	0.15	0.4	1
0.20	4.537	0.0772	1	0.833	0.20	0.20	0	1

(b) *The case $k_i^{(2)} = 1 + 10i$*

| Parameter | Systems of Production | | | | Net Phys. Prod. per Worker | In use at | | Value of Capital per Worker |
| | Input-Coefficients (*) | | | | | | | |
u	l_a	c_a	l_c	c_c	q_i	i	w	$k_i^{(1)}$
0	0.968	0.0010	1	0.969	1	0	1	1
0.05	0.959	0.0006	1	0.915	0.975	0.05	0.9	1.5
0.10	0.986	0.0156	1	0.873	0.9	0.10	0.7	2
0.15	2.978	0.0359	1	0.845	0.775	0.15	0.4	2.5
0.20	1.204	0.0772	1	0.834	0.6	0.20	0	3

(c) *The case $k_i^{(3)} = 1 + 18i - 90i^2$*

| Parameter | Systems of Production | | | | Net Phys. Prod. per Worker | In use at | | Value of Capital per Worker |
| | Input-Coefficients (*) | | | | | | | |
u	l_a	c_a	l_c	c_c	q_i	i	w	$k_i^{(1)}$
0	0.958	0.0017	1	0.958	1	0	1	1
0.00	0.928	0.0083	1	0.907	0.984	0.05	0.9	1.675
0.10	1.010	0.0142	1	0.875	0.890	0.10	0.7	1.900
0.15	1.394	0.0211	1	0.850	0.850	0.15	0.4	1.675
0.20	4.537	0.0772	1	0.833	0.200	0.20	0	1

of those three families of systems of production are given in Table 2, whereas the 'employment curves' for labour and capital corresponding to each of those three relations are drawn in Fig. 6 (par. 54 below).

The destructive implications of the phenomena illustrated by Fig. 3 and 4 with respect to marginal theory may be gathered by referring to what we saw in par. 3–5 above regarding the role played by the inverse relation between rate of remuneration and quantity of a factor employed in providing a plausible basis for the theory. The question must however be postponed until section VII, where it will be possible to specify its relevance with reference also to the second conceivable way out of Walras's inconsistency and the corresponding 'short-period' versions of the theory.

PART III
CAPITAL AS A SET OF FACTORS:
THE NEW CONCEPT OF EQUILIBRIUM

V. THEORETICAL VARIABLES AND OBSERVABLE MAGNITUDES. 37. In Part II, we saw the attempts made to conceive of capital as a single factor of production, as required by the equilibrium condition of a uniform effective rate of return over costs for the different kinds of capital goods (or any equivalent condition under assumptions other than free competition, par. 7 above). These attempts clashed with the impossibility of relating capital to an 'average period of production' independent of distribution. As a result they had to fall back on a conception of capital as a value magnitude and on the related inconsistencies (whether due to using that magnitude directly in the production function, or only in the demand and supply functions for factors, as exemplified in Wicksell, 1934).

The experience of these difficulties and of their implications, which first culminated in the discovery of the phenomena of 'reswitching' and 'reverse capital deepening', would seem to have left little choice to theorists, except to attempt the second of the two conceivable ways out of Walras's contradiction. This second way out, it will be recalled from par. 17 above, consists of dropping the equilibrium condition relating to the rates of return and attempting a new conception of equilibrium, independent of it. This has in fact been the line increasingly taken in pure theory in recent decades.

Our discussion will start in this section by examining the reasons why previous theoreticians, including Walras and Pareto, before they realized the inconsistency that vitiated their systems, had been so unanimous in implicitly rejecting it. Even Sir John Hicks, who after his *Value and Capital* (1946) was to become perhaps the single most influential author in establishing the new conception of equilibrium, had ruled it out as late as 1932, in his *Theory of Wages*. He had rejected there the concept of a 'short-period' marginal product of labour where 'not only the *quantity*, but also the *form* of cooperating capital is supposed unchanged' on the ground that 'it is very doubtful if [this marginal product] can be given any precise meaning which is capable of useful application' (Hicks, 1932, pp. 21–22, our italics).

We shall argue in this section that this is indeed so, and that we do not have to look far to explain this unanimous reference in the general theory of distribution to a position of the economy where the equilibrium condition relating to the rates of return are fulfilled. The reasons for that unanimity lie in the first place in the 'correspondence' between theoretical and observable variables, which is basic for any science. They also lie, as we shall see in the next section (section VI), in the necessity to allow for a sufficient degree of factor substitutability in the system and, therefore, in the need to conceive the alternative processes of production as differing by the *proportions*, and not by the *kinds*, of factors, as has been chiefly the case when each kind of capital good is treated as a distinct factor.

However, in section VII we shall see how the above methodological difficulties are in effect *additional* to the basic one of conceiving capital as a single quantity independent of distribution. That conception underlies, we shall argue, the new formulations of the theory no less than it does the traditional ones, and it vitiates the former no less than the latter.

38. Our argument in this section regarding the importance of the uniform rates-of-return condition for a 'correspondence' between theoretical and observable variables will proceed by three successive steps. We shall first consider how in economics that correspondence has been traditionally founded on the conception of the theoretical variables as centres about which the corresponding observable magnitudes would gravitate, and, therefore, as corresponding to some average of the latter (par. 39–40 below). In our second step we shall see how that conception of the theoretical variables rests on the persistence of the forces which determine them, when compared with that of the forces causing deviations of the observable levels from their theoretical levels (par. 41 below). Finally, in our third step, we shall see why, in a general theory of distribution and relative prices, persistence appears to entail the condition of the equality of the effective rates of return. The conclusion will be that the abandonment of that condition in the new equilibria undermines the possibility of conceiving these equilibria as centres of gravitation of the economic system and, therefore, their correspondence with observable phenomena.

This three-step argument will then be buttressed by two further arguments which also bear on the importance of the condition of a uniform rate of return for the explanatory force of the theory. The first of these elements will be that the persistence of the determining forces makes it possible to define the traditional equilibrium independently of the changes it will undergo over time. This avoided the dilemma between, on the one hand, the absurd assumption of complete future markets and perfect foresight of future conditions, necessary for the constructs of the 'intertemporal equilibrium', and, on the other hand, the indefiniteness of results implied by the reliance on the subjective price expectations of the 'temporary equilibria' (par. 44–6 below). The second additional argument relates to the impossibility of treating the individual capital stocks as independent variables which, while explaining the insufficient persistence of these equilibria, prevents the analysis of changes in the economy in the way this was traditionally carried out in economic theory: that is, by means of the comparison between equilibria (par. 47 below). We shall argue that a capital endowment of adjusted composition can be treated as the independent variable required for such comparisons, but this is not true for the several capital stocks of the new equilibria. The latter equilibria, therefore, impose an analysis of changes based on a sequence of equilibria, the fruitfulness and significance of which appears to have been greatly overestimated in recent theory.

39. The prices and quantities which economic theory determines cannot be the actual magnitudes observable moment by moment in the market. These actual magnitudes, influenced as they are by accidental factors, could not be known in advance and would also be uninteresting when our concern is for the generality of the phenomena. As Pareto puts it with reference to Fig. 5 below:

> the concrete economic phenomenon is represented by the line *ab*, but by means of the theory we can only come to a knowledge of the general form of this phenomenon represented by line *mn*, so as to explain the phenomena as general and average facts (Pareto, 1896–97, pars 36–7).

Pareto then proceeded to argue that a scientific theory can indeed only deal with such 'general and average facts' (*ibid.*, par. 36).

Now, it appears that the way in which economics can arrive, and had traditionally arrived, at such 'general and average facts' is that exemplified in Adam Smith's analysis of the tendency of the actual or 'market' price (the 'concrete economic phenomenon' of line *ab*) towards the natural price (the *general*

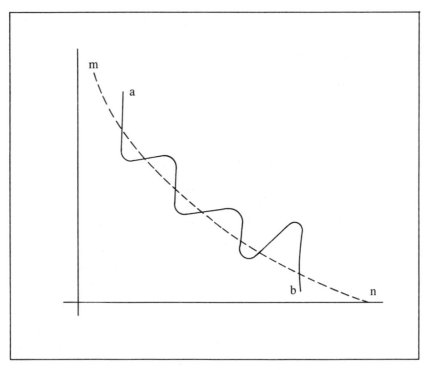

Figure 5   The 'concrete phenomenon' is represented by line *ab*; its 'general form' by *mn* (from Pareto, 1909, par. 37).

form of the phenomenon represented by line *mn*), and which led Smith to conclude that:

> the natural price ... is ... the central price to which the prices of all commodities are continually gravitating (Smith, [1776] 1960, Bk I, Ch. VII, pp. 48–51),

where the analogy with gravity arises from the fact that these forces are automatically activated by the distance from a centre to which they tend.

These concepts of 'normal' prices and of the associated 'normal' outputs as centres of gravitation of the corresponding observable variables are in their essence those to which theory has uniformly continued to refer until recent decades, whether in the classical theories of Ricardo and Marx, or in the later marginal theories, or in the period of transition between the two. (In order to cover the concept in both kinds of theory we shall use the adjective 'normal' and apply it to price, output or more generally to the corresponding position of the economy, reserving the adjective 'equilibrium' for those concepts when used in their marginalist specification.) Thus, for example, J.S. Mill ([1848] 1909, pp. 451–3) related his concept of 'necessary value' to that of the 'natural price' of Smith and Ricardo, which he then proceeded to describe as follows:

> the centre value towards which ... the market value of a thing is constantly gravitating, and any deviation from which is but a temporary irregularity, which the moment it exists sets forces in motion tending to correct it (Mill, [1848] 1909, pp. 451–53).

In the later marginal theory, we find, e.g., in Wicksell, that

> the relative prices of commodities will more or less rapidly approach a certain equilibrium position or else oscillate about it (Wicksell, 1950, p. 53),

and in Walras:

> Equilibrium is the normal state in the sense that it is the state towards which things spontaneously tend under a regime of free competition (Walras, 1954, p. 224),

and

> the market is like a lake agitated by the wind where the water is incessantly seeking its level without ever reaching it (*ibid.*, p. 380).

40. This concept of the theoretical level of the variable being the one which the actual level of the variable tends towards and gravitates about, is basic for relating theory to observable phenomena. This is so because it allows one to suppose that over a sufficient interval of time, the deviations of the actual values from their theoretical counterparts will tend to compensate each other. The theoretical level can then emerge as a sufficiently accurate guide to some average of the actual

47

levels. To illustrate this specific conception, let us see how economists as diverse as J.S. Mill, Marx, and J.B. Clark put it:

> On some average of years sufficient to enable the oscillations on one side of the central line to be compensated by those on the other, the market value agrees with the natural value, but it very seldom coincides with it at any particular time (J.S. Mill, [1848] 1909, p. 453).

> These deviations of market prices from prices of production mutually balance one another, so that in the course of certain longer periods the average market prices equal the prices of production (Marx, [1894] 1974, p. 356).

> This tendency towards costs of production ... fixes the level at which, in the long run, the market values ... tend to conform (J.B. Clark, 1907, ch. VII, pp. 85–6).

For his part, Pareto described in the following way the relationship between theoretical and observable variables which he found in Walras, and which he evidently shared:

> Walras has shown how the competition of entrepreneurs and traders is a way to solve by groping the equations of the equilibrium of production (Pareto, 1896–7, par. 101).

where the strict relation that Pareto sees between theory and observable phenomena gives rise to the strong metaphor for which reality ('the competition of entrepreneurs') solves the equations of the theory, the same metaphor which we find in Walras himself ([1894–7] 1954, e.g. p. 106).

41. As is implied in the passages quoted, this way that economics has of aiming at its 'general and average facts' requires that the forces considered for determining the normal level of the variable should be *persistent*, when compared with the forces which at any moment of time will make the actual level deviate from the normal one (Garegnani, 1976, p. 28). It is only if these forces are persistent in that sense, that they can last long enough to allow for a repetition of the relevant activities (e.g. markets) sufficient to compensate for the deviations of the 'actual' from the normal levels of the variables. In Marshall's words these deviations are due to 'causes whose action is fitful and short lived', and which, therefore, will not persist over a repetition of activities, thus allowing for the 'compensation' we mentioned above:

> The actual value at any time, the market value as it is often called, is more influenced by passing events, and by causes whose action is fitful and short-lived, than by those which work persistently. But in long periods these fitful and irregular causes in large measure efface one another's influence so that in the long run *persistent causes* dominate value completely (Marshall, [1890] 1961, V, III, 7, our italics).

We find here the same principle we had when Ricardo wrote:

Having fully acknowledged the *temporary* effects which in particular employ-
ments of capital, may be produced on the prices of commodities, as well as on
the wages of labour and the profits of stock, by accidental causes, without
influencing the general price of commodities, wages or profits, since these effects
are equally operative in all stages of society, we will leave them entirely out
of our consideration when we are treating of the laws which regulate natural
prices, natural wages, and natural profits (Ricardo, [1821] 1951–73, I, ch. IV,
pp. 91–2, our italics),

where the argument for leaving the deviations of 'market' from 'natural' values
of the variables entirely out of consideration rests ultimately on the 'temporary'
nature of these deviations in contrast with our concern with lasting changes.

42. Now, it is precisely this necessity for a sufficient persistence of the forces
analysed that apparently led all theorists until recent decades to refer the general
theory of distribution and prices to a position of the economy where the tendency
of investors to maximize the returns from their capital would be at rest. It therefore
led them, under the assumption of free competition in all products and financial
markets, to the condition of a uniform effective rate of return on the supply prices
of the various capital goods (cf. e.g. equations (II.6), par. 10 above for Walras;
or (III.5) and (III.12) for Wicksell).

In fact if those conditions are not satisfied, changes will occur in the *composition*
of the capital stock. It was evidently felt by theorists at the time that those changes
in the composition of the capital stock would deprive prices and distributive
variables determined in the absence of such a condition of a persistence
sufficient to ensure their correspondence with the observable variables.

43. The reasons which determined the unanimous adoption of the traditional
normal position may perhaps be seen better by contrast in terms of their mirror
image: the methodological difficulties raised by the new 'short-period' general
equilibria, where the conditions relating to the rates of returns is dropped in
order to avoid Walras's inconsistency (on the specification of these equilibria as
'inter-temporal' and 'temporary' cf. par. 46–7 below).

The main point here is that the tendency to a uniform rate of return on the
capital goods would be rapid in modifying the physical composition of the capital
stock, as is evident from the fact that the stock includes circulating capital (more
generally, an essential characteristic of the goods to be treated as capital is that
their life should be short: par. 6 above). As a result, some of the data of these
equilibria – the capital stocks – are likely to change *before* a sufficient repetition
of activities has allowed the deviations of the actual magnitudes from their
equilibrium levels to be corrected (compensated).

To the extent to which this is true, a purely methodological reason, quite
independent of the content of the theory, arises for questioning the capacity of
these equilibria to offer sufficient guidance to the behaviour of the economy. On

the one hand, the levels of the prices and of the distributive variables determined in these equilibria clearly cannot correspond to the *actual* levels of those variables, as they are at any one moment of time (or over a period of time short enough for no appreciable changes to occur in the composition of the capital stock). This will be so because of those 'fitful and short-lived causes' (par. 41 above) that will keep the economy out of these equilibria, just as they kept it out of the traditional normal positions, at any one particular moment of time. On the other hand, these same equilibrium levels cannot correspond to any average of the observable levels taken over a period of time long enough for those 'fitful and short-lived causes' to efface one another's influence through the repetition of the activities. This is so because, over such a period, considerable changes are bound to occur in the composition of capital, and therefore in the equilibrium itself. (The empirical relevance generally attributed to quasi-rents, Marshall's short period equilibria, appears to be due to two elements that are absent here. The first is that Marshall takes as given only the size of long-lived, slowly adjusting plant, and not that of all capital stocks. The second is that his short-period equilibrium is a 'partial' equilibrium, and he can therefore make it rest on prices of other factors that are largely determined by long-period forces: on this, cf. Garegnani, 1976, p. 37n.)

That such appreciable changes in the composition of the capital stock are *likely* to occur, or even are *bound* to occur, may become clearer when we reflect that the conditions assumed to be satisfied in the new equilibria are the same as those of the traditional long-period equilibria, with the single exception of the condition regarding the physical composition of the capital stock. Under free competition these conditions imply a uniform price for the same productive service whichever the industry in which it is employed. They imply therefore that all productive services should be in conditions to move in and out of firms and industries, and that the number of firms should change in the course of the oscillations and of the associated compensation of deviations, through which alone the equilibrium becomes observable. It seems evident that the time required to realize this degree of mobility of all productive services is such that the composition of the capital stock has to change considerably under the impact of the tendency to a maximization of the returns on them and the consequent concentration of investment on the capital goods with the highest rate of return.

This is obvious in the case of circulating capital. On the other hand, fixed capital may even be seen to give rise to a contradiction between the condition of a uniform rental rate across the industries in which the capital good is employed and the treatment of the initial physical composition of the capital stock as a datum. The mobility of fixed capital goods between industries exists, in fact, in a large majority of cases, only in so far as the capital goods wear out and need replacement. Now, this replacement will occur if, and only if, the capital goods in question yield a rate of return over their supply price, which is no less than that obtainable by investing in other directions. The mobility *included* in the new concept of equilibrium is then inextricably linked with the adjustment in the physical composition of the capital stock, which is instead excluded from that concept. (The way out which would consist in treating the immobile fixed capital goods as so many separate factors would on the other hand seem to be no less damaging to the theory, in that it would drastically reduce any substitutability left in the system: cf. par. 49 below.)

It seems possible therefore to conclude that the insufficient persistence of the forces assumed to determine these new general equilibria, where the composition of the initial capital stock is arbitrary, undermines the 'correspondence' between theoretical and observable variables which is to be expected from economic theory, as from any science. An admission of this central methodological weakness of the new concept of equilibrium may in fact be read when Hicks recognized (1965, p. 73) the doubtful legitimacy of his assumption that prices remain unchanged throughout the period to which they refer, and that these prices are the equilibrium prices. The fact is that the analogous condition in traditional theory was not based on any such clearly unacceptable assumption. It was based on the plausible assumption of the *compensation* of the deviations of actual from equilibrium prices through repetition which, as we saw in par. 40 above, was assumed by all authors until recent decades, and which Hicks implicitly admits here to be absent from his equilibria (on the general topic of the 'correspondence' between theoretical variables and observable phenomena in science, cf., e.g., Nagel, 1961, p. 105).

44. However, what we said about the need to conceive the theoretical variables as a centre to which the actual variables tend, does not appear to exhaust the reasons that had led theorists to refer their theory of prices and distribution to a normal position, characterized, under free competition, by uniform effective rates of return over the costs of the capital goods. Other reasons for the choice of the traditional normal position can be traced to the need to avoid referring to changes of normal prices over time in the definition of the normal position itself. They can also be traced to the need to analyse changes by the *comparison* of such positions, and not by a *sequence* of them (par. 48 below).

With respect to the first point, the persistence of the forces determining the traditional normal position made it natural to determine that position *as if* normal prices were to remain constant during the time elapsing between the buying of the inputs and the selling of the outputs by the firm. That persistence ensured in fact that the changes in the normal prices over such a period would be small enough to be safely ignored.

(The possibility of ignoring price changes in the definition of the normal position might seem questionable in marginal theory, because price changes are there necessary to activate the substitutability between means of production and other factors, and would therefore need consideration for the determination of the current outputs of the capital goods, together with all prices and outputs. However it appears that a strict treatment of the question was generally thought unnecessary, on the assumption that the allocation of savings among capital goods could not appreciably influence the equilibrium position: cf. e.g., par. 25 above for Wicksell's treatment; but see par. 15 for Walras's use of the allocation of savings to allay the over-determinacy entailed by his conception of capital. In this connection, and in order to avoid a frequent misunderstanding, it may perhaps be stressed that changes in normal prices over time were ignored in traditional theory because they were considered sufficiently *small*, and not because of any assumption of stationary or steady growth of the economy. To take just the two marginalist authors to whom we referred most in this essay, see Walras, 1954, e.g., Lesson 36; Wicksell, [1901] 1934, Part III. For the origin of this frequent surprising misinterpretation, cf. Garegnani, 1976, pp. 26–7 and p. 33, n. 11. That no such assumption was made should be clear already from the fact that the normal positions were meant to be centres of gravitation of the actual economy, and this could not have been the case for a stationary or steady-state position of the economy. In fact the temptation felt by some contemporary authors to consider a steady-state economy as a centre of gravitation – Marglin, 1984, e.g. p. 55 – seems to be seriously misleading. This may be illustrated by remembering e.g. that, as Pasinetti (1962) has shown, in a steady-state economy, workers' propensity to save would not affect the economy's average propensity to save – which is surely something we cannot expect to be verified as an average over any number of years whatever.)

45. This possibility of ignoring price changes in the definition of the equilibrium disappears when conditions change as fast as they are bound to do in the 'short-period' general equilibria we are discussing. The same (potentially) rapid change of the equilibrium position, which does not allow for a compensation of the deviations of the actual magnitudes from their equilibrium levels, renders illegitimate the assumption that that change will not affect the behaviour of the individuals and therefore the equilibrium conditions themselves. The investment, concentrated as we must assume it to be, on the few capital goods that give the highest rate of return over their supply price, is bound to alter quickly the relative scarcity of the several capital goods. The relative prices of their services are accordingly likely to change drastically and quickly (say, to rise from zero to comparatively high positive values) and the error of assuming constant prices in defining the equilibrium can no longer be ignored.

However, when future conditions have to be taken into account, a number of difficulties arise. We may leave aside here the formal complications that arise from considering, in the definition of equilibrium, those changes which equilibrium will undergo over time, and the loss of transparency consequent upon those complications. The main methodological difficulty is different. The influence of future normal positions on the present normal position presents us with a dilemma. This is that between, on the one hand, attributing an independent determining role to subjective price expectations, as is done in the literature on the 'temporary equilibrium', from Hicks (1946) onwards; and, on the other hand, assuming complete 'futures' markets, as is done in the contemporary literature on the general 'intertemporal' equilibrium (e.g., Debreu, 1954: for the seeming paradox of classifying among our 'short-period' equilibria the 'intertemporal' equilibrium, which aims at determining the path of the economy into the infinite future, cf. par. 16 above).

The influence of future prices would in fact be susceptible to an objective treatment, if we could assume the existence of complete markets for future commodities. However, such complete 'futures' markets not only do not exist, but cannot ever be thought to exist. It is impossible to imagine that we can now make all contracts relating to production and consumption over the entire future, and expect them to be fulfilled. The necessary foresight regarding the tastes of the individuals of future generations, future endowments of original factors, and the future technical conditions cannot evidently be assumed.

Moreover, complete 'futures' markets appear to raise a second methodological difficulty. The concept of a 'dated' commodity used there seems difficult to reconcile, even in principle, with that repetition of transactions which, as we saw, is necessary to ensure a sufficient 'correspondence' between theoretical and observable variables. Indeed, it is not clear *which* observable prices could conceivably correspond to the distinct prices which the theory attributes to the same commodity taken as an input and then as an output. Any repetition required to give rise to a mutual compensation of the deviations of actual prices from equilibrium prices seems to be excluded by definition since it would relate to different dates and therefore to different equilibrium prices. And even if a 'date' could be taken to cover a period long enough to allow for some repetition, the difference between the input and the output price of the commodity over each cycle is likely to be *less* than the difference between its two prices as the inputs (or as the outputs) of a repeated production cycle: it would then be difficult to see the significance of distinguishing between an (average) input price and an (average) output price, while failing to distinguish between two subsequent input or output prices. (The difficulty does not seem to arise to the same extent for the price changes relevant for the determination of long-term investment: there the time interval between input and output allows each 'date' to cover a period long enough for repetition.)

46. If complete 'futures' markets cannot be assumed, there remains the alternative of introducing price expectations concerning the future commodities for which no present market exists – as is done with 'temporary equilibria'. While this does not do away with the conflict between the dating of equilibrium prices and the repetition of activities required for 'correspondence' between theoretical and observable magnitudes, introducing these purely subjective expectations among the determinants of the system raises the problem of the determinateness of the theory. In fact that introduction renders the equilibrium position corresponding to a given objective situation almost indefinitely variable, depending on the hypothesis we wish to make about such expectations, and thus, it seems, deprives the theory of sufficiently definite results. We may here refer again to Hicks who wrote in his review of Keynes's *General Theory*:

> the method of [of expectations] is thus an admirable one for analyzing the impact effects of disturbing causes, but is less reliable for studying the further

effects [since] it is probable that the change in actual production during the first period will influence the expectations ruling at the end of that period, and there is no means of telling what the influences will be. The more we go into the future the greater the danger, when it is applied to long periods, of the whole method [of expectations] petering out (Hicks, 1936, p. 241).

The unreliability and danger described here are, of course, precisely the ones which seem to have led all authors, up to the theoretical crisis of the last few decades, to exclude autonomous expectations from a general theory of distribution and prices (as distinct from excluding them from the treatment of specific short-run problems, where they may of course play an important or even an essential role) and refer instead to the traditional normal positions of the system where price expectations played no autonomous role.

47. A question raised at the beginning of this essay, when we referred to 'effective' rates of return on capital goods (par. 2), can now be finally dealt with.

The introduction of changes in relative prices over time introduces a kind of 'nominal' divergence between rates of return over the supply prices of the capital goods, which should be sharply distinguished from that 'effective' divergence between those same rates of return, which has played the key role in the distinction, drawn in this essay, between the traditional normal position, which did not admit it, and the new 'short period' equilibria, designed to come to terms with just that divergence.

This distinction between 'nominal' and 'effective' rates may be clarified by referring first to rates of interest on loans, rather than to rates of return on capital goods. The 'nominal' difference in rates of interest becomes an integral part of the *definition* of the uniform 'effective' rate of interest, brought about by competitive arbitrage, as soon as *changes in relative prices* over time are allowed for. It is in fact obvious that if the price of commodity a rises 10% during the year relative to that of commodity b, the uniform 'effective' rate of interest brought about by the arbitrage on a loan in terms of a (or 'own rate of interest' of a) will have to be smaller by 0.10 with respect to the rate on a loan denominated in b (or 'own rate of interest' of b) so that if the latter were e.g., 0.20 the former would have to be approximately 0.10. As a result the *numerical expression* of the uniform effective rate of interest brought about by arbitrage will depend on the numéraire in which we express the prices, and will be equal to the 'own rate of interest' of the numéraire chosen.

Now this divergence in *nominal* rates of interest, an expression of the uniformity of the *effective* rate of interest, will evidently carry over from rates of interest on loans, to rates of return on the supply prices of capital goods. Indeed this divergence would be part of the *definition* of such a uniform 'effective' rate of return, as soon as changes in relative prices were to be allowed for in the traditional normal position. We saw that the persistence of the forces considered there allowed such changes to be ignored: however, in principle, those changes *could* be considered (as resulting, say, from capital accumulation or from changes in labour supply), without affecting the characteristic feature of that normal position, namely the adjusted physical composition of the capital stock, and its sharp distinction from the short-period equilibria we are discussing, with their unadjusted capital stock.

In fact, within marginal theory, the condition of a uniform effective rate of return requires an adjusted capital stock whether or not changes in relative prices are allowed for. With an arbitrary composition of the initial capital stock, the condition will *not* be fulfilled, whether price changes over time are allowed or not. The existence of economically meaningful solutions will therefore require in this case no less than it did in Walras's, that such a condition be dropped from the system of equations, thus giving rise to the 'short-period' equilibria we have been discussing. In those equilibria, just as in Walras's modified system, it will be true that the prices of some capital goods will have to be *below* their costs in order to allow for the uniform effective rate of return which is brought about by competitive arbitrage (cf. par. 16 above).

Naturally the equality between 'costs' and prices of the capital goods would be satisfied irrespective of the composition of the initial capital stock if we re-defined the mere transferral over time from t to $t + 1$ of a capital good C, as 'production' of a capital good $C^{(t+1)}$ by an equal amount of C^t. But, of course, this would only change the matter verbally, where that *kind* of 'production', contrary to production as commonly understood, would signal an unadjusted composition of the capital stock. In particular that re-definition of production would of course not affect in the least the methodological difficulties discussed in this section.

48. What in fact the insufficient persistence of the forces that determine these short-period equilibria brings to light is the artificiality of treating the initial stocks of the several capital goods in the economy as independent variables of the system. The continuous rapid tendency to adapt the physical composition of capital to the prevailing outputs and methods of production disqualifies the initial stock of each kind of capital good from playing the role of an independent variable in any general explanation of distribution and relative prices. This point comes fully to light when we proceed to a third methodological difficulty raised by the new concept of equilibrium, besides the impossibility of considering it as a centre of gravitation for the economy, and the dilemma it opens up with respect to future prices.

In classical or marginal theories, the traditional normal position was used in order to analyze changes chiefly by means of a comparison between the normal positions before and after the change being examined. Now, this ceases to be possible when in the new versions of marginal theory we treat the several capital stocks as data of the equilibrium. This is so because it would be economically meaningless to treat those stocks as independent variables, as would be required by that kind of analysis.

It would in fact be arbitrary, or in any case uninteresting for a general theory of distribution and relative prices, to analyze the effect of, say, a change in population, in tastes, or in technical knowledge, by comparing the two equilibria before and after the change, on the assumption that the stocks of each of the myriad capital goods have all remained unchanged. Clearly, the physical composition of the capital stock which, as we argued, would have quickly adapted to the previous methods of production and outputs, would quickly adapt to the assumed different conditions. It would be even more arbitrary to examine the effect of, say, capital accumulation by considering a set of independently specified increments of the several stocks.

In effect, in a marginal theory, the analysis of changes in distribution and prices by means of comparisons appears to be only conceivable when the comparison is effected between traditional equilibria, where what is given is, to paraphrase Wicksell, or Hicks, the 'quantity' of the cooperating capital, but not its 'form' (par. 22 and 37 above). That 'quantity of capital' can be assumed to undergo only slow changes (cf. e.g. Marshall, 1890, VI, ii, 4, p. 534) and it would therefore not be arbitrary to assume that it remains approximately constant during the adjustment to the new conditions, or that it undergoes changes which can be treated as independent when analyzing a process of accumulation.

A confirmation of this comes paradoxically from Walras, who did attempt to analyse changes by comparing equilibria defined on the basis of capital stocks taken as data or independent variables. In fact, as revealed by expressions such as 'rise in the quantities of capital goods proper' (Walras, 1954, e.g. p. 387) which he used in those comparisons, Walras treated the several stocks of capital as if they constituted a *single* composite physical quantity of capital. Thus, for example, he concluded that in a progressive economy, where such 'quantities' would increase relative to labour and land services 'the price of capital services will fall appreciably' and that 'if we assume prices [of capital goods] to remain constant, the rate of net income will fall appreciably' (Walras, 1954, pp. 390–91). Here, the independent variables are not in fact the individual capital stocks, but rather, a single composite capital stock, or even the value of that stock. However, the possibility of assuming that in the different equilibria the absolute amount of capital stocks may differ, but that their proportions will remain the same, or that the value in terms of any given numeraire of each capital good will remain only approximately the same, is clearly inconsistent with Walras's own equations. There, as the rate of net income falls, there is no reason why the quantities of capital goods should all rise or all fall, not to mention any reason why they should all rise or fall in the same proportion. It will generally happen, on the contrary, that some will rise and some will fall, while the values of the capital goods relative to any numeraire may change in any way whatsoever.

Thus, the 'short-period' general equilibria of contemporary theory appear to leave us with no choice but to analyse changes by means of the *sequence* of equilibria, whether the sequence is that implicit in an *intertemporal equilibrium*, or is one of *temporary equilibria*. That is, we have to study the sequence of equilibria initiated by the assumed independent change in data, comparing it, if necessary, with the sequence as it would have been in the absence of those independent changes. It seems then inevitable to recall what Alfred Marshall wrote:

dynamical solutions, in the physical sense of economic problems, are unattainable and statical solutions, afford starting points for such rude and imperfect approaches to an analysis of changes as we may be able to attain to (Marshall, 1898; e.g., pp. 38–9).

Thus, for example, the consideration of any such sequence of equilibria raises the danger of an accumulation of errors. This will be because the uncompensated deviations from equilibrium in each of the preceding stages of the sequence, will make the capital stocks in subsequent actual situations of the economy deviate from the levels assigned to them in the theory. The data themselves will therefore deviate from their theoretical values in those subsequent situations, thus adding a second cumulative reason for deviations of the observable variables from the theoretical ones.

VI. ON AN INSUFFICIENT SUBSTITUTABILITY BETWEEN FACTORS OF PRODUCTION AS DEFINED FOR THE NEW EQUILIBRIA. 49. So far the reasons for the traditional conception of capital as a single factor (and for the shortcomings of the alternative conception of capital as a set of distinct factors) have been examined from the point of view of the need to satisfy the equilibrium conditions pertaining to the effective rates of return over costs on capital goods. Looking at the question, as we shall do from now on, from the side of the shortcomings of the new concepts of equilibrium, our results can be summarized as follows: the impossibility of satisfying the rates of return condition drastically reduces our capacity to apply the theory to the analysis of reality by:
(i)   generally undermining the 'correspondence' between theoretical variables and observable magnitudes;
(ii) imposing a consideration of price-changes over time in the very definition of equilibrium, with the consequent alternative between either a 'general intertemporal equilibrium', with its arbitrary assumption of complete 'futures' markets, or a 'temporary equilibrium', with its indefinite results following from the introduction of price expectations;
(iii) preventing an analysis of changes by means of a comparison of equilibria in favour of one by a 'dynamic' sequence of equilibria, which appears to be of doubtful significance.

However, a second methodological shortcoming appears to be associated with the conception of capital as a set of separate productive factors. The shortcoming is that this conception of capital fails to allow for a sufficient degree of substitutability in the system.

In section I, we argued that marginal theories rest essentially on an inverse relation between the price of a factor service and the quantity of it employed in the system with given quantities of the other factors (where the distinction we traced in par. 28 between two 'layers' of factors is relevant, the factors here referred to are clearly those of the second 'layer', as they appear in the demand-and-supply equations). This inverse relation is in fact embedded in a general equilibrium system to the extent that the processes of production represented there differ by the *proportions* in which the *same factors* are used, and not by the *kind* of factors.

Now, with respect to capital goods, this representation of the processes of production as differing by the proportions of factors is only plausible if the individual capital goods can be envisaged as different 'quantities' of a single factor, 'capital', which can change in 'form' without changing in 'quantity'. This was in fact the conception from which the idea of a general substitutability between labour and 'capital' derived in the first place.

However, this representation ceases to be plausible if we conceive each kind of capital good as an independent factor. The alternative methods available for the production of a commodity, or the methods for alternative commodities, will generally differ in the quality, rather than the proportions, of the capital goods required. As a result, when each kind of capital good is conceived as a separate 'factor', the general equilibrium 'demand' functions for such factors will tend to be rigid. The rentals of the capital goods determined by 'demand' and 'supply' will therefore tend to be either zero or, alternatively, such as to absorb the entire excess of the commodity price over the part of it going to factors, like those grouped under labour and land, the specification of which can be wide enough to allow for their employment in more than one industry or method of production (so that the price of their service will not depend only on conditions within one industry).

50. Thus, prima facie, marginal theories seem to present us with an alternative in this respect. Either the definition of the factors allows for that 'substitutability' among them on which the potential significance of the theory ultimately rests, in which case we fall into the inconsistencies of conceiving capital as a single factor, as we saw in Part II. Or, alternatively, we attempt to avoid those inconsistencies by resolving capital into a set of heterogeneous factors, and then there is the risk that the theory will become an empty shell. This alternative is independent of the other, also turning on the two alternative conceptions of capital, between, on the one hand, a concept of equilibrium that allows for a potential 'correspondence' between theory and observable phenomena and, on the other, the new concepts of equilibrium dictated by an attempt at a consistent measurement of capital. However, in the next and final section of this essay, we shall contend that the second alternative is illusory. The alternative of logical consistency (of correctly deducing the propositions on which the theory was built) does not exist. The concept of capital as a single factor and its difficulties, we shall claim, are present in the short-period equilibria, where capital is seemingly resolved into a set of physical factors, just as they are present in the traditional equilibria where capital appears as a single factor.

VII. THE NEW CONCEPT OF EQUILIBRIUM AND THE 'QUANTITY OF CAPITAL'. 51. To realize why the second conceivable way out of Walras's contradiction is no more viable than the first was – with the additional disadvantage of the methodological difficulties we have seen in the last two sections – it is necessary to start by taking a closer look at the meaning of the demand and supply functions for 'capital', which we find in the traditional versions of the theory (cf. equation (III.14), par. 25 above) and which are apparently dispensed with in the new versions.

In any given instant of time the available 'capital' is not, of course, the 'fluid' assumed in those versions, which may quickly assume the physical form compatible with the corresponding point of its demand function. On the contrary, at any given instant, 'capital' is embodied in a certain set of capital goods. It can only assume the required physical form over a period of time as, each year, a part of the capital goods in existence wears out and a corresponding proportion of the labour force becomes, so to speak, 'free' to be re-equipped, by appropriately investing the gross 'savings' of the year. (For the general concept of 'free capital' and its use in Wicksell, cf. Garegnani, 1978–9, II, p. 625 n, in which it is considered how the savings-investment market involves the decisions of three groups of people: savers, investors and producers of capital goods. Cf. also *ibid.*, I, p. 343 n, for the distinction between, on the one hand, the decisions to save or invest relevant for the functions discussed here, and on the other, the realized savings or investment.)

Accordingly, the demand and supply functions for capital (the stock) envisaged in those theories were supposed to operate over time through a sequence of demand functions for gross investment, and supply functions for gross savings (the flows). To see this ultimate intended equivalence between demand and supply for 'capital' on the one hand, and demand and supply for savings on the other, it is sufficient to assume that production takes place in annual cycles and that all capital is circulating capital. If the wage-rate and product-prices are assumed to adjust without appreciable delay to the equilibrium compatible with the new rate of interest (cf. par. 53 below), the demand function for investment at the end of each year will simply be the demand function for 'capital' as a stock. When there is fixed capital, the analogous relation between demand for investment and demand for capital would be less simple but, in principle, it would be no less strict (see Garegnani, 1978–9, I, Appendix, p. 352, where the relation is examined in its connection with the turnover period of fixed capital).

The traditional theory implies that the delayed adjustments in the wages, rents, and prices of products do not fundamentally alter the terms of the question. The theory also implies that the other circumstances which influence the demand for investment moment by moment (such as the effects of technical progress, the continuous reproportioning of the various industries, the differences in the age structure of fixed capital or the cyclical oscillations engendered by them) will similarly leave unaltered the terms of the question. The interest elasticity of the sequence of demand functions for investment would continue to reflect, on an average, the elasticity of the demand for capital as a stock. Hence the significance of the demand and supply functions for capital as a stock, which would exhibit the basic tendencies destined to emerge from the multiplicity of forces acting at any given moment in the savings investment market.

Of course the fact that the demand and supply functions for 'capital' were in effect supposed to operate through a sequence of demand and supply functions for savings, meant that the market for 'capital' was indissoluble from that for money loans and that its analysis was bound to meet the additional problems of aggregate monetary demand and the price level. We find here, therefore, questions like that of credit creation on the part of the banks, or of the fact, of which we know much more since Keynes, that savings ('free capital') tend to disappear when they are not used, unlike what happens with other unused resources like labour, land, or already 'crystallized' capital (the capital goods in existence). However the attempts to deal with these questions, among which the foremost before Keynes is that by Wicksell (e.g. 1934, II, pp. 190–208), seemed to confirm the belief that, so long as the demand functions for capital and other factors had the shapes of Figure 1 (par. 3 above), and accordingly investment had a sufficient elasticity relative to the rate of interest, the assimilation of capital to other factors was not misleading. Thus, e.g., if the savings forthcoming under conditions of full employment of labour and other resources exceed the decisions to invest, and if this excess fails to act on the rate of interest directly, through an increased supply of money loans, it could be plausibly argued that the ensuing cumulative deflationary process would make it inevitable that the interest rate would ultimately adjust investment to full employment savings – since we would be sure that some realistic level of the rate of interest would exist for which that could occur.

52. When it is understood that the traditional analyses of the demand and supply for capital were in effect intended to be an analysis of the demand and supply for savings, abstracting from the complications likely to operate at each particular moment of time in the savings-investment market, it also becomes clear that the difficulties associated with the demand for 'capital' in the traditional long-period versions have to be present also in the contemporary short-period versions of the theory. (In what follows we shall have chiefly in mind the formulations in terms of intertemporal equilibrium, but the same phenomena are bound to affect any plausible sequence of temporary equilibria, provided the price expectations of each period are affected by the experience of the previous periods.)

These short-period versions do of course encompass the production of means of production in each period, and, therefore, the magnitudes constituting the aggregate gross investment and the aggregate gross savings of the period. These magnitudes will depend on the entire intertemporal price system and, in particular, on the system of 'effective' rates of interest of the relevant periods, expressed in terms of the chosen numéraire.

Now these demand and supply functions will refer to 'capital' in its 'free' form, and will ultimately have as their argument a 'quantity' which can be in the form of any particular capital good just like the demand and supply functions of 'capital' in the traditional versions. Different capital goods can and will in fact be produced in the period in question, depending on the intertemporal system of prices and in particular on the effective rates of interest over the relevant time periods. As we saw in par. 35 above, the phenomena of 'reverse capital deepening' and 'reswitching' have their root in the way the relative prices of capital goods change as the prices of factor services change, and there appears to be no reason why the consideration of price changes over time characteristic of intertemporal equilibria should make those prices any less responsive to changes in the prices of factor services.

Accordingly there appears to be no reason why these phenomena, with the resulting 'perverse' reactions of the demand for means of production to changes in the effective rates of interest for the relevant dates, should here be any less relevant for the stability of the equilibria and, therefore, for the plausibility of the results, than they were in the traditional versions of the theory. Indeed by looking at the savings–investment market, we are potentially dealing with the problems emerging in the traditional versions in a more *direct* form.

The form which the savings–investment functions of the several periods are likely to take in the 'short-period' equilibria of the new versions of the theory, and in particular in the intertemporal equilibria, do not seem as yet to have been analyzed in the detail which would be required from the point of view that interests us there. Further work will therefore be required before the effects of the phenomena underlying the 'capital employment curves' of Figures 2, 6 and 7 acquire the same degree of transparency here as they by now have in the traditional versions. But for the reasons stated above, some of the lines of this necessary work, and even some of its broad conclusions may be tentatively gathered by referring to the savings investment market implicit in the demand and supply of capital (the stock) of the traditional versions of the theory. Let us therefore take up the thread at the point where we left it in par. 36 at the end of Part II, where those functions were introduced.

53. To see the significance of the phenomena of 'reswitching' and 'reverse capital deepening' stated in par. 36, it may be convenient to begin by recalling how in section I we argued that the basic scheme of marginal theory is founded on the deduction of decreasing 'employment functions' for productive resources from (i) the existence of alternative methods of production of the same commodity, and (ii) the choice of consumers between different goods. We then saw in section II how the capital goods have to be treated as constituents of a single factor of production 'capital', if the conditions of an adjusted capital stock, and the corresponding conditions of a uniform rate of return over costs, are to be fulfilled in the theory. Finally, it resulted from our argument in section III that the attempt to conceive capital as a single factor inevitably leads to its measurement in value terms.

Now what we saw in par. 36 was in fact how the deduction of decreasing 'employment functions' on which that whole complex structure rests, proves to be wrong when capital, as the value magnitude to which we had thus arrived is included among the factors. There arises then the possibility of 'employment functions' like those of Figures 2, 6 and 7 – and we have already indicated in par. 5 above how these 'employment functions' would make it difficult to explain distribution by a demand-and-supply apparatus. This question is what must now be examined in some detail.

61

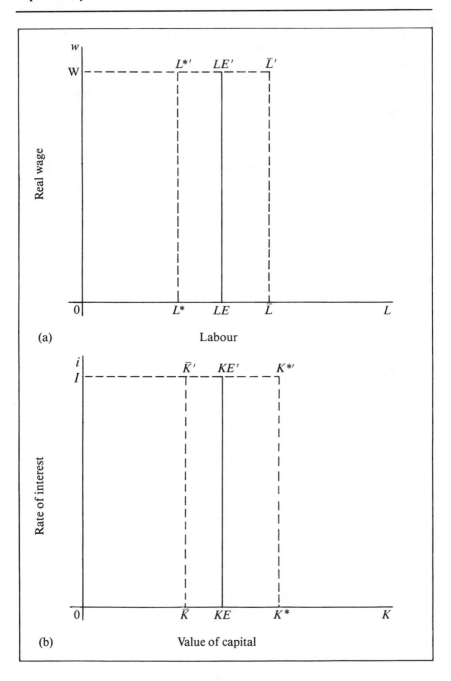

Figure 6 The 'labour employment' and 'capital employment' curves for cases $k_i^{(1)}$, $k_i^{(2)}$ and $k_i^{(3)}$ of Figure 4, and Table 2 of par. 36.

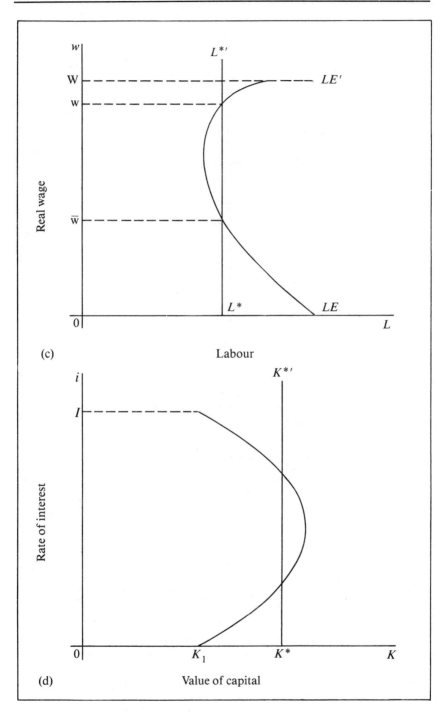

(c)

Labour

(d)

Value of capital

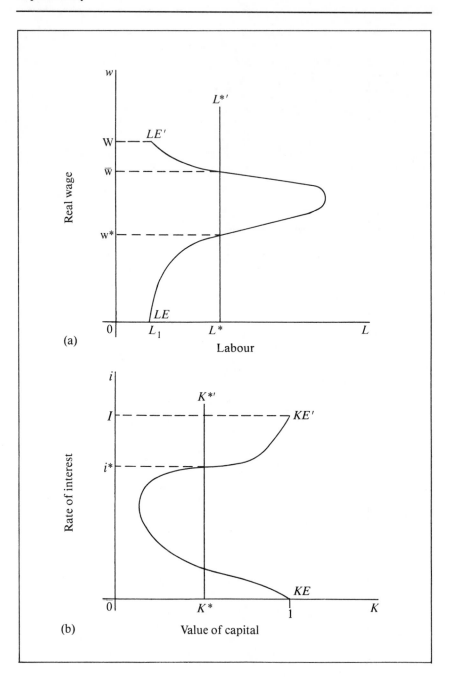

Figure 7 Relations between i, w, L and K, and the family of systems represented in Figure 3.

Our argument will be developed in three stages. We will begin in par. 54 by examining the implications for the labour market, of labour-employment curves like those in Figures 2, 6 and 7, while assuming at first that the whole of the 'capital' supplied (treated as a single factor) is employed. This first stage of the argument will therefore refer to the traditional versions of the theory. Its additional relevance for the labour market envisaged in short-period versions will be tentatively indicated only later (par. 60).

In the second stage of our argument (par. 55–8) we shall proceed to the capital market. We shall distinguish between two meanings of the equality between demand and supply of 'capital' assumed in the preceding stage of the argument: one meaning relates to the physical capital stocks, and the other to the savings–investment market (par. 55). The latter equality will be found to be that on which the possibilities depicted by the 'capital employment functions' in Figures 2, 6 and 7 impinge directly (par. 57), and will be discussed there. In this second stage of the argument we shall also consider the influence of disequilibrium in the savings–investment market on aggregate monetary demand (par. 58).

In the third and final stage of the argument we shall return to the markets for labour and the capital stocks in order to gather together the threads of the previous two stages of the argument and conclude it (par. 59–61).

After an attempt to use the vantage point reached by the previous argument in order to bring the significance of the phenomena of 'reswitching' and 'reverse capital deepening' into better focus (par. 62), the present section – and the essay as a whole – will conclude by discussing some reactions in the literature to the emergence of those phenomena (par. 63–6).

54. Let us take then the 'labour-employment functions' represented in Figures 2a, 6a, 6c and 7a as relating to economies in which a single consumption good is produced by the systems of production summarized in Tables 1 and 2. We already know that the introduction of more than one consumption good and therefore of 'consumer substitution', far from modifying the negative results obtained by deriving those functions on the basis of alternative systems of production for a single consumption good, would provide an additional independent reason for those negative results (cf. our discussion of eq. (IV.1) in par. 35). In the same way, our negative conclusions will not be affected by the assumption that the net product of those economies consists entirely of the consumption good.

We may therefore take those 'employment functions' as the 'demand functions' which marginal theory interprets them to be. Correspondingly we may assume that so long as it persists, labour unemployment will cause wages to fall. These 'labour employment functions' are drawn up on the assumption that the capital employed is of a constant value in terms of the consumption good. In order, to interpret them as the (general equilibrium) demand functions we want to discuss, we may therefore assume that the supplies of 'capital' and labour, are absolutely rigid, and are depicted by the vertical lines $L^*L^{*\prime}$ and $K^*K^{*\prime}$ in the respective figures.

Let us begin from the demand function for labour of Figure 2a – that we would have in the case of the continuum of systems of production which gives $k_i^{(2)}$ in Figure 4. If the wage w happened to be initially below w^* we would be forced to conclude that w will have to fall towards zero, without succeeding in equalizing the demand and supply of labour (see point L_1 in Figure 2a indicating labour employment at zero wages). If, instead, w happened to be initially above w^* we should conclude that w would have to rise to its maximum W – and the interest rate i fall to zero – with an increase, instead of a decrease, in the excess demand for labour (see point L_2 in Figure 2a). Nor could a resting point for positive levels of both w and i be found at w^* as it would be an 'unstable equilibrium', indicating the boundary between the region of gravitation towards a zero wage and that of gravitation towards a zero interest rate.

Analogous conclusions would have to be reached in the case of the 'demand function' in Figure 7a, which results from the 'continuum' of systems of production of Figure 3 and Table 1, and in that of Figure 6e which results from the continuum $k_i^{(3)}$ in Figure 4 and Table 2. The difference between these two cases, and that of Figure 2a is that, in moving away from w^*, the wage w would find a resting point at $\bar{w}$ before reaching its maximum (Figure 7a) or its zero level (Figure 6c), respectively. No less striking is the case of the 'demand function' in Figure 6a, which results from the continuum $k_i^{(1)}$ in Figure 4 and Table 2, in which the wage would have to fall to zero if the supply happened to be lower than LE (e.g. $\bar{L}$), or rise to its maximum, if the supply happened to be greater than LE (e.g. $L^* L^{*'}$).

This potential contradiction between the results of the theory and anything ever observed in the actual economy becomes even more striking as we proceed now to the capital market in order to discuss the assumption we have made so far that the capital employed remains equal to its supply.

55. The first question which we meet here is the meaning we must attribute to that equality. There seem in fact to be two distinct and complementary meanings which we must attribute to it. The first meaning is that of an equality between the demand and supply of the physical stocks of capital goods. It is the kind of demand and supply equality of 'capital' which is in the foreground in the short-period versions of the theory. The same condition must however be satisfied in the traditional versions where each point of the labour-demand function implies a full utilization of the capital stocks (which will be of the physical form most appropriate to the outputs and production methods of that point).

There is however a second kind of equality between demand and supply of 'capital', which had to be assumed in our argument about the labour market: it is the equality that relates to the flows of savings and investment. As we argued in par. 51, this equality is implied in the equality between the demand and supply of 'capital' as a value fund analyzed in the traditional versions of the theory. But, as we also argued there, the same savings and investment equality is present in the contemporary short-period versions, which imply equality in each period between the aggregate demand and supply of the outputs of means of production.

We shall in fact have to assume this equality when in par. 60 below we shall discuss the labour market within the short-period versions.

56. The second preliminary observation about the equality between demand and supply of 'capital' assumed in par. 54 is that a failure of that equality, in its savings–investment sense, will generally entail changes in aggregate monetary demand, as soon as money is introduced in its role as a store of value. It should however be noted that from a purely logical point of view a failure of that equality appears conceivable also in the absence of money, and in strict symmetry with a similar failure in the labour market. This is so when, as is done here, investment is interpreted in the stricter sense of the aggregate of products used for further production. What the absence of money appears to imply is in fact only an equality between decisions to save and decisions to accept goods which are *not* used for consumption, whether these are then used for further production, or just stored, or wasted. Accordingly our discussion of the savings–investment market will at first be conducted under the assumption that there is no money as a store of value, in order to leave the implications of that market for aggregate monetary demand for later (par. 58 below).

57. The capacity of the (effective) rate of interest to equalize the demand for investment and the supply of savings forthcoming in conditions of full utilization of the factors, is however precisely what the emergence of the possibility of 'capital–employment functions' like those of Figures 2, 6 and 7 makes it difficult to accept. The falsification of the traditional deduction about a fall in the interest rate resulting in a higher proportion of capital to labour in the economy, renders questionable the postulate that a fall in the rate of interest will generally result in a higher level of investment.

In fact, those 'capital employment functions' would mean that, assuming, as we are doing here, a quantity of labour employed which remains constant, a fall in the rate of interest, far from increasing the level of investment, may tend to decrease it. Then, if we were to insist that the rate of interest is determined by the demand for investment and the supply of savings, we would have to conclude that it may have to fall to zero without eliminating excess savings (cf. points K_1 in Figures 2a and 6d, for $i < i^*$); or rise to its maximum, making the wage fall to zero, without eliminating excess investment (cf. points K_2 in Figures 2a and 7b, for $i > i^*$); or even switch from the one movement to the other after accidentally crossing the boundary line of an interest rate of unstable equilibrium (cf. the point for $i = i^*$ in Figure 2b). In even greater conflict with experience would be a demand-and-supply determination of the rate of interest in the case of Figure 6b. There the rigidity of investment with respect to the rate of interest, in spite of the assumed continuous change in methods of production, would only leave room for the zero rate of interest, or alternatively a zero wage rate, depending on whether the supply of 'capital' (and therefore the flow of gross, full-employment savings) happens to exceed or to fall short of the demand for gross investment on the assumption of full employment of labour.

(A possible objection to what we have just argued may perhaps be considered before proceeding. It is sometimes claimed that an interest-elastic demand function can be derived on an alternative basis, independent of the phenomena to which 'reswitching' and 'reverse capital deepening' relate. This basis would be that, as the interest rate falls, more investment projects would have to become profitable, *given their expected future returns*. It would then seem that, in spite of capital–employment functions like those of our examples, decreasing invest-ment functions could somehow be postulated and no difficulties therefore would arise from the side of the capital market. Only the difficulties in the labour market could be admitted. What is not clear about this argument, when applied to investment within marginal theory and therefore under conditions of full employment of labour and the other 'original' factors, is what is supposed to occur with the investment motivated in this way. Only two alternatives would seem possible: either it goes to capital waste due to erroneous expectations, or, alternatively, it coincides with the investment we have been examining, in which case of course the kind of functional dependence upon the rate of interest can only be that entailed by our 'capital–employment functions'. In fact the difficulty with such a basis for an investment–demand function lies in ignoring the price adjustments which would necessarily be associated with the relevant persistent changes in the interest rate: cf. Garegnani, 1978–79, II, p. 78 n. The mechanism by which the interest rate is assumed to adjust investment to savings as the interest rate falls – not unlike the mechanism by which technical innovations come to be applied – would have to operate chiefly through the competitive coercion of the changes in wages and prices, consequent upon the change in interest rate.)

58. We have so far seen the difficulty raised by the failure of the inverse relation between interest rate and amount of capital employed in the savings–investment market, and we have seen it in terms which were strictly symmetrical with those of the labour market. This required abstracting from money as a store of value. Without money in that role, the decisions to save unaccompanied by decisions to invest would take the form of commodities which are neither consumed nor used for further production (par. 56 above). The excess supply in the savings–investment market would therefore always take a tangible form, just as in the market for any particular commodity, or for labour, with no consequences on aggregate output.

However as we proceed to taking money into account the demand-and-supply mechanism in the savings–investment market, an expression of the market for 'capital', acquires strong asymmetric effects on the market for other factors. Inequality between decisions to save and decisions to invest then undermines the equality between aggregate monetary demand and aggregate supply which are postulated in those other markets. Thus the determination of the rate of interest on the basis of the investment demand functions implied by the 'capital–employment functions' of Figures 2, 6 and 7, would not only entail the tendency of the interest rate to fall to zero when i falls below i^*. By the received concept of competition in the market of the factors, that excess supply of full employment savings would entail an indefinite fall in aggregate monetary demand (except for any effects of the fall in the price level in lowering the tendency to save). Similarly the excess demand for investment which would be entailed by the interest mechanism in the examples in Figures 2b and 7b for $i > i^*$), or in that in Figure 6b, for a supply $K > K^*$, would not only entail a tendency of the interest rate to its maximum (of the wage to zero), but also an indefinite inflationary process, which would present us with a similar dilemma between observation and theory.

The discussion of the saving–investment market has been carried out here within the long-period versions of the theory, where we can assume the direct correspondence between 'capital–employment function' and investment–demand function for which we argued in par. 51 above. But for the reasons we then saw in par. 52, there appears to be no reason why the difficulties we have seen above should not be equally present in the savings–investment market envisaged by the short-period versions of the theory.

59. Keeping in mind the above two negative results, flowing from the savings–investment market (that concerning the difficulty of envisaging the rate of interest as the equilibrator of savings and investment even in a non-monetary economy, and that concerning aggregate monetary demand), let us return to the market for labour (or, more generally, for labour and other physical factors), and now consider both the short-period versions of the theory as well as the traditional long-period ones.

With respect to the traditional versions, the conclusion is straightforward. We saw in par. 54 that there would have been no reason to expect a tendency to a full employment equilibrium, even if the equality between investment and full employment savings were always satisfied. However, we can now see that because of the analogous phenomena affecting the savings–investment market, we have two effects which are likely to add to the instability of the division of the product between wages and profits. The first and most important is that, when money is considered, the failure of a tendency towards an equilibrium between the demand and supply for savings will undermine the aggregate demand condition postulated for the adjustment mechanism in the market for labour as well as for the individual physical capital stocks. It will then prevent the translation of any assumed flexibility of the money wage and rentals into the required flexibility in the real wage and rentals. The second effect is that, to the extent that the equality between savings and investment is not realized, the competitive interplay need not continue to occur around the same labour-employment functions, as we assumed in par. 54. Any excess of gross savings over gross investment would involve a progressive shift leftwards in those functions, as a result of the fall over time in the physical capital that would otherwise have been employed.

The theory would therefore seem to force us to admit the possibility of meaningless continued monetary inflation or deflation, while at the same time presenting us with the phenomena in the labour market we saw in par. 54 above, enhanced by the shifts in the demand function for labour resulting from the non-monetary effects of the failures of the equilibrating mechanism in the capital market.

60. As we proceed now to the form which these phenomena are likely to assume in the contemporary short-period versions of the theory, the first question that arises is that upward-sloping labour-employment functions, like those in Figures 2a, 6a and 7a, are not possible when all factors are measured in physical terms (cf. par. 35 above), as is the case in those versions. Reflection will however reveal that the phenomena shown by those functions cannot have disappeared. They can only have changed form, in that they are now bound to emerge from the *sequence* of equilibria over which the existing physical capital will be replaced. Assuming as we did for those functions in Figures 2, 6 and 7, that the equilibrium between investment and full employment savings is preserved over the relevant period of time, we should admit that, as the real wage falls over those periods, the existing capital goods will tend to be replaced by other ones, which will employ less (and not more) labour at the new, lower, real wage. There will therefore be a *shift* to the left of the relevant part of the short-period demand for *labour*. Through the sequence of such equilibria this will tend to cause the fall in wages towards zero which we saw, e.g., in our long-period analysis of the cases depicted in Figures 2a or 7a for $w < w^*$.

Once this form which the phenomena of 'reswitching' and 'reverse capital deepening' are likely to take in the market for labour of the contemporary short-period versions of the theory is made clear, it should also be clear that the effects that this version would force us to admit are likely to be strictly similar with those we saw would follow from the traditional long-period versions. In particular we are equally likely to find there the increased instability and the tendency to either zero or indefinitely high *money* wages which results from the effects on aggregate monetary demand of disequilibria in the savings–investment market.

61. In marginal theory those results concerning the labour market and its interaction with the savings–investment market in the presence of the phenomena of 'reverse capital deepening' and 'reswitching', would tend to be described in terms of the instability of the equilibria, or of their multiplicity, or of equilibria with excess supplies and, therefore, with zero prices. Those phenomena might then be seen as pointing to causes of instability inherent in reality. The difficulty of that interpretation is, of course, that nothing approaching that kind of instability has ever been observed in economic reality.

It would, on the other hand, be begging the question to argue that this conflict between observation and theory shows that in actual fact the employment functions of labour or capital do not have shapes like those of our examples in Figures 2, 6 and 7. That claim would indeed *assume* the validity of the demand and supply theory of distribution, which is precisely what is in dispute. Thus, if the forces determining distribution were those envisaged by the old classical economists (cf. par 1, above), then the technical conditions underlying those employment functions could hardly result in any instability of distribution and the price system.

The natural way to approach that conflict between theory and observable facts would seem therefore to lie in a different direction. The explanation of distribution in terms of demand and supply forces was built and accepted in the belief that the existence of consumer choice and alternative methods of production made it possible to deduce that a fall in w (rise in i) would always raise the amount of labour employed in a regular determinable way. It seems inevitable then that that explanation should be become questionable when that key deduction has proved false. We shall return to this point in our concluding remarks.

VIII. ON SOME POSITIONS IN THE LITERATURE ON THE DIFFICULTIES CONCERNING CAPITAL. 62. Before proceeding to consider some reactions to the difficulties exhibited in Figures 2, 6 and 7, it may be useful to pause here for some considerations concerning the nature of those difficulties. 'Reverse capital deepening', and the parallel phenomenon of the 'reswitching' of systems of production, seem to have been viewed at times as something of a purely logical interest, of no great consequence for the key propositions of the theory of distribution and relative prices. It should however be clear now that on the contrary those phenomena reflect the absence of a *factual basis* for the theory.

Indeed, after reflection, few would probably claim that the factual evidence on which the theory was erected has been the observation of demand and supply *functions* for labour and other factors. In particular it would not be claimed that those theories were founded on the observation of spontaneous tendencies of the quantity of a factor of production employed, say labour, to adjust to an independently given supply through changes in the price of its service, and irrespective of the quantities of the other factors available.

The factual basis of the theory has in fact been entirely different. It has been provided by the existence of alternative methods of production, and by the possibilities of choice open to consumers. These were the *facts* held to be self-evident, which allowed theorists to obtain plausible 'demand functions' for factors by *logical deduction alone* (par. 3–5 above). Now, the phenomena of 'reswitching' and 'reverse capital deepening' have shown that those deductions were incorrect. They have thereby shown that the factual basis which was thought to support the edifice was not there to support it.

63. We may now consider some *specific* reactions to the contemporary emergence of these phenomena. (At a more *general* level we have already seen one kind of reaction, namely the increasing adoption of the new concept of equilibrium discussed in this third part of our essay.)

We may leave aside here the reactions which have consisted purely of assuming away the phenomena in order to proceed as before. We may also deal briefly with those which have consisted of asserting or implying that the 'probabilities' of such phenomena are slender, in some sense (e.g. Malinvaud, 1986). The possibilities indicated by Figures 2, 6 and 7 under hypotheses as simple as those of such two-commodity systems with circulating capital only, seem significant for the potential generality of those phenomena. The essential point appears however to be different.

As we have just stressed, the principle of decreasing demand functions for productive resources was basically a logical deduction from self-evident facts. Therefore, the attempt to ascertain the 'probabilities' of a decreasing demand function, relative to a non-decreasing one, would by itself imply a drastic change in the *nature* of the theory. The theory would be shifted from its former basis of a deduction from *self-evident facts* to a new, intentionally empirical one. Of course that shift of basis is a matter of consequence. A purely empirical regularity is liable to exceptions. Therefore, even if it could somehow be shown to exist in this field, such a regularity would seem hardly sufficient for a premise as basic as that of a decreasing demand relation for factors, on which the whole of a general theory of distribution and relative prices has been made to rest. And this shift of basis is made even more perilous by the fact that it would occur in a field like economics, where experiment is impossible and, besides, the material of the science is so highly complex and variable as generally to limit considerably the weight one can attribute to any observed, purely empirical regularity.

64. Less incongruous perhaps with respect to the nature of the theory which is being defended is a reaction like the one we find in Hicks (1965, p. 154), according to which the failure of the principle concerning capital intensity leaves us in a position which, though not satisfactory, 'has parallels in other parts of economic theory'. Hicks seems here to suggest that the possible fall in the value of capital per worker as the interest rate falls does not affect traditional theory any more than do the well-known anomalies of the demand functions due to 'income effects', in particular those in the case of 'inferior goods'; or, perhaps, the anomalies of equilibria in industries subject to increasing returns, which had much preoccupied Marshall.

With respect to the case of inferior goods, Hicks's position seems however to overlook the fact that that case did not call into question the general demand-and-supply analysis of prices simply because it could be plausibly argued (a) that should those anomalies give rise to a multiplicity of equilibria, the equilibrium with the highest price would be stable, while that with the lowest price would be likely to be stable too; and (b) that if the latter equilibrium were unstable, the rest of the economic system would not be affected, since all we would have is that the commodity would not be produced due to a lack of demand willing to pay the supply price. We shall mention below Marshall's similar argument with respect to the case of an increasing return industry. However, to the writer's knowledge, no analogous arguments have been advanced so far, with respect to the fall in capital intensity as the interest rate falls.

65. A different position from that of Hicks is F. Hahn's, where a separation is drawn between an 'equilibrium theory' and the theories relating to the 'adjust-

ments' towards the equilibrium. According to Hahn, the critics of marginal theory:

> have continued to believe that [reswitching] is damaging to neo-classical *equilibrium theory* which it is not, and have neglected various neo-classical *adjustment theories* which are certainly at risk (Hahn, 1982, p. 373 our italics).

The first difficulty encountered in this passage is that it is difficult to see how 'equilibrium theory' may be left untouched by whether the equilibrium wage or the equilibrium interest rate are at positive levels as in Figure 1, with a corresponding *equality* between the quantities of the factor demanded and supplied, or at a zero level with an excess supply of the factor – a possibility which, as we saw, might well be entailed by the phenomena of reswitching and reverse capital deepening.

However the main difficulty in Hahn's position is that, contrary to what is implied in Hicks's passage above, Hahn seems to overlook the essential link that exists between the analysis of an equilibrium and that of the 'manner in which such an equilibrium is supposed to come about' (*ibid.* p. 373). It is the link which (as exemplified in par. 38–41) had long been taken for granted, between the relevance of the variables determined by the theory, and their nature as centres towards which the actual variables would tend. (An even more extreme position in this matter may be noted in Bliss, 1975, p. 117 n., where the author seems to assert that the premise about an inverse relation between the amount of capital employed and the interest rate is irrelevant to the explanation of distribution in contemporary general equilibrium theory. Even Hahn's view, according to which 'various neo-classical adjustment theories are certainly at risk' when that premise is not satisfied, would seem sufficient to counter that position by Bliss.)

The link between equilibrium and stability is of course that for which Alfred Marshall would qualify only a 'stable' equilibrium as a 'real' equilibrium, and admit an unstable equilibrium merely as a 'dividing boundary' between two stable equilibria (Marshall, 1890, Appendix H, 2, p. 806 n.; cf. also Pigou, 1932, p. 795). By thus qualifying the equilibrium Marshall showed his awareness of the fact that 'unstable' equilibria, and therefore the possibility of 'equilibria' with zero prices for commodities or productive services known to have a price, would call into question the validity of a demand-and-supply explanation of those prices. They would, that is, call that validity into question, unless it could be convincingly argued that should such unstable equilibria arise, they would not lead to results too greatly at variance with experience (cf., e.g., how, in the case of unstable equilibria for 'commodities obeying the law of increasing return', Marshall carefully went on to show that its consequences would remain confined to the possibility that the commodity might not be produced; Marshall, 1890, Appendix H, 2, p. 806 n.).

The point made here by Marshall may also make clear why the authors to whom Professor Hahn refers as 'Neo-Ricardian' have focused their criticism on theory as such, and not only on what he describes as 'adjustment theories'. The reason is essentially that in the view of those critics, anything which affects in that way 'adjustment theories', affects thereby the theory, and therefore what Hahn calls 'equilibrium theory' (cf. e.g. Garegnani, 1970, pp. 425–6).

66. One should however recognize that Professor Hahn's position is not isolated. Since the late 1930s the formerly indissoluble link between a normal position and the tendency to it, has become progressively looser in the theory. This striking development seems not to have been unconnected with the impact of Keynes on the theoretical situation of his time.

The dominant theory of distribution and relative prices rested on a tendency to the full utilization of productive resources, in particular labour, and that was just what Keynes aimed to deny. However, in the absence of an equally comprehensive alternative, the rejection of received theory as a whole was hardly conceivable. Equally impossible, at the time, was a rejection of the Keynesian conclusions, buttressed as they were by the massive unemployment of the 1930s and by the important applications they were having in the field of economic policy. A way of reconciling or, at least, of making less glaring the resulting contradictions, was to envisage the absence of the tendency to the full employment equilibrium postulated by the theory (due, it was believed, to uncertainty and incorrect expectation) as pertaining to a separate field of analysis, Hahn's 'theory of adjustments'. That allowed for the main body of the theory of distribution and prices to be insulated, to some extent, from the implications of Keynes's criticism.

Hahn's passage reveals how this position, which might be seen to be merely a question of a classification of topics, or of a specialization in the profession, might in fact help to render more opaque the difficulty in which the theory finds itself. The difficulty however is there, and overcoming it would seem to require *either* showing that the 'adjustments' are not in fact 'at risk', and the 'equilibrium theory' can rest secure on its necessary basis of 'adjustment theories' – or, alternatively, to work towards the determination of new normal positions for the economy, the adjustment to which *can* be postulated. In either case it would seem that 'equilibrium theory' can hardly continue to be separated from 'adjustment theories'. (Marglin, 1984, p. 538, appears close to the position taken here on the necessary link between 'equilibrium' and 'adjustments' towards it. However, he does not seem to be correct when at p. 283, he describes our argument about 'perversely shaped factor-demand functions' as a denial of the 'existence' of equilibrium: using his terminology, the argument would clearly have to be described as a denial of 'stability'.)

67. We have followed throughout this essay the contradiction which appears to affect the marginal theory of distribution on the question of the measurement of capital. The contradiction is that between (i) a measurement of capital independent of distribution (but related to value in the way we saw in par. 8); and (ii) the assumption of an adjusted composition of the capital stock expressed under the hypothesis of free competition by the equilibrium condition of a uniform effective rate of return over the supply price of the capital goods. Condition (i)

is required for consistency in expressing the data of the theory and deducing the relations postulated there between the prices of factor services and the quantities of them employed. Condition (ii), on the other hand, had been taken for granted until recent decades as necessary to ensure that the theoretical variables of a general theory of distribution and prices should constitute plausible centres of gravitation of the corresponding observable magnitudes, and should therefore supply the required guidance to the behaviour of the economy.

In section II we have seen this contradiction in its most striking expression: the logical inconsistency of Walras's original general equilibrium system, which prevents it from generally admitting an economically meaningful solution. Condition (i) had in fact led Walras to treat heterogeneous capital goods as so many independent factors of production, like labour or land of different qualities. Then, however, equilibrium condition (ii), assumed by Walras no less than by all other theorists at the time, could not be satisfied.

We proceeded then, in Parts II and III, respectively, to an examination of the only two ways out of that contradiction which are conceivable: a measurement of capital in terms of a single factor which can change 'form' without changing in 'quantity', and would thus allow equilibrium condition (ii) to be satisfied; or, alternatively, the abandonment of condition (ii) in favour of a new concept of equilibrium which would allow for an attempt to treat capital as a set of independent factors, along the lines of Walras. We concluded that both these conceivable ways out meet one and the same difficulty.

Along the first route the impossibility of measuring capital as a single quantity independent of distribution was exhibited in the failure of Wicksell's attempts at a measurement in terms of Böhm-Bawerk's average period of production. Wicksell had then to fall back on a value measurement of capital (section III). This measurement, we argued in section IV, dependent as it is on distribution, is inconsistent when it is used in defining the technical conditions of production, and, it is no less inconsistent when it is used only in order to define the argument in the demand and supply functions determining the system, as is done by Wicksell. The inconsistency shows in taking the existing capital as a datum. It shows above all in the invalidity, then, of the deduction of an inverse relation between the prices of factor services and the quantities of them employed, on which the theory ultimately rests for its demand functions for factors.

Along the second route, on the other hand, the market for capital (the stock), characterizing the first route, is resolved into as many markets as there are heterogeneous capital stocks, where the upward-sloping employment functions of Figures 2, 6 and 7 are not possible. However, capital as the single factor which can change 'form' without changing in 'quantity' reappears there in the savings–investment market (that is, in the demand-and-supply of that part of the yearly output which consists of the aggregate of means of production). Thus, despite the basic methodological difficulties which it raises (sections V and VI), the abandonment of equilibrium condition (ii) does not appear to do away with the essential difficulties of conceiving capital as a single quantity. Thus, the relations depicted in Figures 2, 6 and 7 appear to be as damaging along this route –

where they are bound to underlie the investment demand functions, and the behaviour of the labour market, over a succession of periods – as they are by now generally admitted to do along the first route.

Along both routes, therefore, we arrive at the conclusion that marginal theory would force us to admit the possibility of phenomena of instability in the division of the product between wages and interest, which would affect the entire economic system. But the actual economic system has never experienced, or come close to experiencing, that kind of instability.

The specific reactions to this from the marginalist side seems, on the other hand, not to have so far been in keeping with the nature and implications of these phenomena (par. 61–6). As we noted in par. 61, the essential phenomena emerge if we start from the fact that the dominant explanation of distribution was built on deducing from consumer choice, and from the existence of alternative systems of production, the idea that a fall in w (rise in i) would always raise in a regular determinable way the amount of labour employed with an amount of capital in some sense given. This provided what appeared to be a firm theoretical basis for the idea of 'demand and supply' as forces determining distribution, and therefore prices. That key logical deduction is what has been proved false by 'reswitching' and 'reverse capital deepening'. The instabilities or tendencies to zero of wages, or of the net returns on capital is what would follow from the theory once that error is corrected. It is therefore not surprising that nothing should correspond to them in reality. Had theoreticians realized earlier that the deduction in question was invalid, we would probably not be thinking today in terms of demand and supply functions for labour (as in fact theoreticians did not do up to Ricardo and then, again, in the interregnum between the fall of the wage-fund theories and the rise of the marginal ones: cf. e.g. Samuelson, 1956). We would then see no reason why the 'employment functions' should entail instability in wages, since wages would be seen to be determined by altogether different factors.

The natural way to face the above conflict between theory and observation would therefore seem to pick up the thread of the theory of distribution where it was left by Ricardo, following upon Adam Smith and his predecessors from Petty to the Physiocrats, at the beginning of the period of increased social struggle heralded by the British Chartist movement.

Much further work will be needed to clarify and carry further the view of distribution which those authors had been developing for over a century. And much work will be required to analyse further the difficulties besetting the conception of a 'quantity of capital' in the contemporary reformulations of the dominant theory, in order to see what has to be abandoned and what may preserve validity. However, the general lines of this work may perhaps be discerned already. It is in this sense that we can view the current debate on capital theory as a focal point for the theory of distribution as a whole: a centre around which there turns the issue of whether the distribution of the social product has to do with a balance between demand and supply forces originating from factors substitution, and conceived on a mechanical analogy, or has instead to do with more complex economic and social forces like those envisaged by the old classical economists.

BIBLIOGRAPHY

Arrow, K.J. and Debreu, G. 1951. Existence of an equilibrium for a competitive economy. *Econometrica*, 22 July, 265–90.

Arrow, K.J. and Hahn, F.H. 1971. *General Competitive Analysis*. San Francisco: Holden Day.

Barone, E. 1958. Sopra un libro del Wicksell. *Giornale degli economisti* 11, November, 524–39.

Bliss, C.J. 1975. *Capital Theory and the Distribution of Income*. Amsterdam: North-Holland.

Böhm-Bawerk, E. von. 1891. *Positive Theory of Capital*. London: Macmillan.

Burmeister, E. and Dobell, A.R. 1970. *Mathematical Theories of Economic Growth*. New York: Macmillan.

Champernowne, D.G. 1953. The production function and the theory of capital. *Review of Economic Studies* 21(2), 112–35.

Clark, J.B. 1895. The origin of interest. *Quarterly Journal of Economics* 9, April, 257–78.

Clark, J.B. 1907. *The Essentials of Economic Theory: As Applied to Modern Problems of Industry and Public Policy*. New York: The Macmillan Co.

Debreu, G. 1954. *Theory of Value, An Axiomatic Approach to Economic Equilibrium*. New Haven: Yale University Press.

Dorfman, R., Samuelson, P.A., Solow, R.M. 1958. *Linear Programming and Economic Analysis*. New York: McGraw-Hill.

Garegnani, P. 1960. *Il capitale nelle teorie della distribuzione*. Milan: Giuffrè.

Garegnani, P. 1970. Heterogeneous capital, the production function and the theory of distribution. *Review of Economic Studies* 37, June, 407–36.

Garegnani, P. 1976. On a change in the notion of equilibrium in recent work on value and distribution. In *Essays in Modern Capital Theory*, ed. M. Brown, K. Sato and P. Zarembka, Amsterdam: North-Holland.

Garegnani, P. 1978–9. Notes on consumption, investment and effective demand, I and II, *Cambridge Journal of Economics* pt. I. 2(4), December 1978, 335–53; pt. II, 3(1), March 1979, 63–82.

Garegnani, P. 1983. The classical theory of wages and the role of demand schedule in the determination of relative prices. *American Economic Review, Papers and Proceedings* 73, May, 309–13.

Garegnani, P. 1984. On some illusory instances of 'marginal products'. *Metroeconomica* 36, June–October, 456–68.

Garegnani, P. 1985. Sraffa: classical versus marginalist analysis. Paper delivered at conference on Sraffa's *Production of Commodities* after 25 years'; forthcoming in Acts of the Conference.

Garegnani, P. 1988. Reply to Hahn. *Cambridge Journal of Economics*, forthcoming.

Hahn, F. 1982. The neo-Ricardians. *Cambridge Journal of Economics* 6(4), December, 353–714.

Harcourt, G. 1972. *Some Cambridge Controversies on the Theory of Capital*. Cambridge: Cambridge University Press.

Hicks, J.R. 1935. Wages and interest: the dynamic problem. *Economic Journal* 45, September, 456–68.

Hicks, J.R. 1936. Mr. Keynes' theory of employment. *Economic Journal* 46, June, 238–58.

Hicks, J.R. 1939. Leon Walras. *Econometrica* 2, October. 338–48.

Hicks, J.R. 1946. *Value and Capital*. 2nd edn, Oxford: Clarendon Press.

Hicks, J.R. 1965. *Capital and Growth*. New York: Oxford University Press.

Jaffé, W. 1942. Leon Walras's theory of capital accumulation. In *Studies in Mathematical Economics*, ed. O. Lange et al., Chicago: Chicago University Press.

Malinvaud, E. 1986. Pure profits as forced saving. *Scandinavian Journal of Economics* 88(1), 109–30.

Marglin, S.A. 1984. *Growth, Distribution and Prices.* Cambridge, Mass.: Harvard University Press.

Marshall, A. 1890. *Principles of Economics.* 9th (variorum) edn, London: Macmillan, 1961.

Marshall, A. 1898. Distribution and exchange. *Economic Journal* 8, March, 37–59.

Marx, K. 1894. *Capital,* Vol. III. London: Lawrence & Wishart, 1974.

Mill, J.S. 1848. *Principles of Political Economy.* London: Longman Green, 1909.

Morishima, M. 1964. *Equilibrium, Stability and Growth: a Multi-sectoral Analysis.* Oxford: Clarendon Press.

Nagel, E. 1961. *The Structure of Science.* New York: Harcourt Brace.

Pareto, V. 1896–7. *Cours d'économie politique,* 2 vols. Lausanne: Libraire de l'Université.

Pareto, V. 1909. *Manuel d'économie politique.* 2nd edn, reprinted, Paris: R. Picon et R. Durand Auzias, 1963.

Pasinetti, L.L. et al. 1966. Paradoxes in capital theory: a symposium. *Quarterly Journal of Economics* 80, 503–83.

Pigou, A.C. 1932. *The Economics of Welfare.* London: Macmillan.

Ricardo, D. 1951–73. *Collected Works,* ed. P. Sraffa, Cambridge: Cambridge University Press.

Robinson, J. 1953. The production function and the theory of capital. *Review of Economic Studies* 21(2); Winter, 81–106.

Robinson, J. 1972. Capital theory up to date. *Canadian Journal of Economics,* May 1970, as reprinted in J. Robinson, *Collected Economic Papers,* Vol. IV, Oxford: Blackwell.

Samuelson, P.A. 1956. Social indifference curves. *Quarterly Journal of Economics* 70(1), February, 1–22.

Samuelson, P.A. 1962. Parable and realism in capital theory: the surrogate production function. *Review of Economic Studies* 29, June, 193–206.

Smith, A. 1776. *The Wealth of Nations.* 2 vols, London: Dent, 1960.

Sraffa, P. 1960. *Production of Commodities by Means of Commodities.* Cambridge: Cambridge University Press.

Stigler, G.J. 1949. *Production and Distribution Theories.* New York: Macmillan.

Stigler, G.J. 1957. Perfect competition, historically contemplated. *Journal of Political Economy* 65(1), February, 1–17.

Swann, T.W. 1956. Economic growth and capital accumulation. *Economic Record* 32, November, 334–61.

Wald, A. 1951. Some systems of equations in mathematical economics. *Econometrica* 19, October, 368–403.

Walras, L. 1877. *Théorie mathématique de la richesse sociale.* Paris, later reprinted with the same title in Lausanne, 1883.

Walras, L. 1874–7. *Éléments d'économie politique pure.* Lausanne: Cobaz. Trans. by W. Jaffé as *Elements of Pure Economics.* London: George Allen & Unwin, from the 1926 definitive edition, 1954.

Wicksell, K. 1923. Real capital and interest. *Economisk Tidskrift* 21 (5–6), reprinted in Wicksell (1934), 258–99.

Wicksell, K. 1934. *Lectures on Political Economy.* Vol. I, London: Routledge and Kegan Paul. First published 1901.

Wicksell, K. 1954. *Value, Capital and Rent.* London: Allen & Unwin. First published 1893.

Wicksteed, P.H. 1933. *The Common Sense of Political Economy, etc.* 2 vols, ed. L. Robbins, London: Routledge.

Debates in capital theory

HEINZ D. KURZ

Capital theory is notorious for being perhaps the most controversial area in economics. This has been so ever since the very inception of systematic economic analysis. Much of the interest in the theory of capital lies in the fact that it holds the key to the explanation of profits. Since the notion of 'capital' is at the centre of an inquiry into the laws of production and distribution in a capitalist economy, controversies in the theory of capital are reflected in virtually all other parts of economic analysis.

We can distinguish between debates *within* different traditions of economic analysis and debates *between* them. In what follows our concern will be mainly with the latter. At the cost of severe simplification, the various traditions in the theory of capital and distribution may be divided into two principal groups, one rooted in the surplus approach of the classical economists from Adam Smith to Ricardo and the other in the demand and supply approach of the early marginalist economists. The so-called 'Cambridge controversies' (cf. Harcourt, 1969), triggered off by a seminal paper by Joan Robinson (1953), consisted essentially in a confrontation of these two radically different traditions. The debate is still continuing. Currently, the discussion focuses on some of the neoclassical authors' claim that the classical theory, as it was reformulated by Sraffa (1960), is a 'special case' of modern general equilibrium theory. We shall come back to this questionable proposition towards the end of the entry.

THE SURPLUS APPROACH. The general method underlying the classical economists' approach to the theory of capital and distribution was that of 'normal' or 'long-period' positions. These were conceived as centres around which the economy is assumed to gravitate, given the competitive tendency towards a uniform rate of profit. Because of the assumed gravitation of 'market values' to the 'normal' levels of the distributive and price variables, the former were given little attention only, being governed by temporary and accidental causes, a proper scientific analysis of which was considered neither necessary nor possible.

Emphasis was on the persistent or non-temporary causes shaping the economy. Accordingly, the investigation of the permanent effects of changes in the dominant causes was carried out by means of comparisons between 'normal' positions of the economic system.

The development of a satisfactory theory to determine the general rate of profit was thus the main concern of the classical economists. As regards the content of this theory, profits were explained in terms of the *surplus product* left after making allowance for the requirements of reproduction, which were conceived inclusive of the wages of labour (Ricardo, 1817, vol. 1, p. 95). As Sraffa (1951, 1960) emphasized, the determination of the social surplus implied taking as data (i) the system of production in use, characterized, as it is, by the dominant technical conditions of production of the various commodities and the size and composition of the social product; and (ii) the ruling real wage rate(s). In accordance with the underlying 'normal' position the capital stock was assumed to be so adjusted to 'effectual demand' (Adam Smith) that a normal rate of utilization of its component parts would be realized and a uniform rate of return on its supply price obtained. Thus the classical authors separated the determination of profits and prices from that of quantities. The latter were considered as determined in another part of the theory, i.e. the analysis of accumulation and economic and social development.

The rate of profit was defined by the ratio between social surplus and social capital, i.e. two aggregates of heterogeneous commodities. Thus the classical theory had to face the problem of value. Ricardo's ingenious device to solve the problem consisted in relating the exchange values of the commodities to the quantities of labour directly and indirectly necessary to produce them. This led to the first formulation of one of the key concepts in the theory of capital ever since – the inverse relationship between the real wage and the rate of profit (Ricardo, vol. 8, p. 194).

It was not until Marx that additional important steps in the development of the surplus approach were taken. In particular, in Marx the analytical role of the 'labour theory of value' in the determination of the general rate of profit was brought into sharp relief. According to him the explanation of profits in terms of the surplus approach would have been trapped in circular reasoning if the value expression of either aggregate (surplus and capital) were to depend on the rate of profit. The measurement of both aggregates in terms of labour values, which themselves were seen to be independent of distribution, was considered a device to circumvent this danger and provide a non-circular determination of the rate of profit, $r = s/(c + v)$, where r is the general rate of profit, s the 'surplus value', c the value of the means of production or 'constant capital', and v the wages advanced or 'variable capital'. A central message of Marx's *Capital* reads that the rate of profit is positive if and only if there is 'exploitation of workers', i.e. there is a positive 'surplus value'.

In Marx's opinion it was only after the rate of profit had been determined that the problem of normal prices, or 'prices of production' as he called them, could be tackled. Marx dealt with it in terms of a multisectoral analysis of the production of commodities by means of commodities; the deviations of relative prices from labour values are systematically traced back to sectoral differences in the 'organic composition of capital', i.e. the proportion of 'constant' to 'variable' capital (cf. the so-called 'transformation' of values into prices of production; Marx, 1894, Part II).

Yet Marx did not fully succeed in overcoming the analytical difficulties encountered by the classical economists in the theory of capital and distribution. He was particularly wrong in assuming that the determination of the rate of profit is logically prior to that of normal prices. Given the system of production and the real wage, the rate of profit and prices can be determined only simultaneously. This was first demonstrated by Bortkiewicz (1907). For a rigorous and comprehensive formulation of the classical surplus approach see Sraffa (1960), whose contribution will be dealt with in more detail below.

THE NEOCLASSICAL APPROACH. The abandonment of the classical approach and the development of a radically different theory, which came to predominance in the wake of the so-called 'marginalist revolution' in the latter part of the 19th century, was motivated (apart from ideological reasons ever present in debates in capital theory) by the deficiencies of the received (labour) theory of value. Since the new theory was to be an alternative to the classical theory, it had to be an alternative theory about the same thing, in particular the normal rate of profit. Consequently, the early neoclassical economists, including, for example, Jevons (1871), Walras (1874), Böhm-Bawerk (1889), Wicksell (1893, 1901) and J.B. Clark (1899), adopted fundamentally the same method of analysis: the concept of 'long-period equilibrium' is the neoclassical adaptation of the classical concept of normal positions.

The basic novelty of the new theory consisted in the following. While the surplus approach conceived the real wage as determined *prior* to profits (and rent), in the neoclassical approach all kinds of incomes were explained simultaneously and *symmetrically* in terms of the 'opposing forces' of supply and demand in regard to the services of the respective 'factors of production', labour and 'capital' (and land). It was the seemingly coherent foundation of these notions in terms of *functional* relationships between the price of a service (or good) and the quantity supplied or demanded elaborated by the neoclassical theory that greatly contributed to the latter's success.

As regards the supply side of the neoclassical treatment of capital, careful scrutiny shows that its advocates, with the notable exception of Walras (at least until the fourth edition of the *Eléments*), were well aware of the fact that in order to be consistent with the concept of a long-period equilibrium the capital equipment of the economy could not be conceived as a set of given physical amounts of produced means of production. The 'quantity of capital' in given supply rather had to be expressed in *value* terms, allowing it to assume the physical 'form' best suited to the other data of the theory, i.e. the technical conditions of production and the preferences of agents. For, if the capital endowment is given in kind only a short-period equilibrium, characterized by

81

differential rates of return on the supply prices of the various capital goods, could be established by the forces constituting demand and supply. However, under conditions of free competition, which would enforce a tendency towards a uniform rate of profit, such an equilibrium could not be considered a 'full equilibrium' (Hicks, 1932, p.20).

Thus the formidable problem for the neoclassical approach in attempting the determination of the general rate of profit consisted in the necessity of establishing the notion of a market for 'capital', the quantity of which could be expressed *independently* of the 'price of its service', i.e. the rate of profit. If such a market could be shown to exist, profits could be explained analogously to wages (and other distributive variables) and a theoretical edifice erected on the universal applicability of the principle of demand and supply.

Now, the plausibility of the supply and demand approach to the problem of distribution was felt to hinge upon the demonstration of the existence of a unique and stable equilibrium in the market for 'capital'. (On the importance of uniqueness and stability see, for example, Marshall, 8th edn, 1920, p. 665n.) With the 'quantity of capital' in given supply, this, in term, implied that a monotonically *decreasing* demand function for capital in terms of the rate of profit had to be established (see Figure 1). This inverse relationship was arrived at by the neoclassical theorists through the introduction of two kinds of substitutability between 'capital' and labour: substitutability in consumption and in production. According to the former concept a rise in the rate of profit relatively to the wage rate would increase the price of those commodities, whose production is relatively 'capital-intensive', compared to those in which relatively little 'capital' per worker is employed. This would generally prompt consumers to shift their demand in favour of a higher proportion of the cheapened commodities, i.e. the 'labour-intensive' ones. According to the latter concept a rise in the rate of interest (and thus profits) relatively to wages would make cost-minimizing entrepreneurs in the different industries of the economy employ more of the relatively cheapened

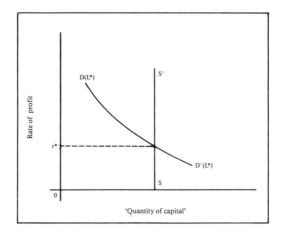

Figure 1

factor of production, i.e. labour. Hence, through both routes 'capital' would become substitutable for labour and for any given quantity of labour employed a decreasing demand schedule for capital would obtain. In Figure 1 the demand schedule DD' corresponding to the *full-employment* level of labour $L*$ (determined simultaneously in the labour market) together with the supply schedule SS' would then ensure a unique and stable equilibrium E with an equilibrium rate of profit $r*$. Accordingly, the division of the product between wages and profits is expressed in terms of the 'scarcity of factors of production', including 'capital' conceived as a value magnitude that is considered independent of the rate of profit.

Let us now briefly look more closely at some of the characteristic features of neoclassical capital theory and point out differences between the main versions in which it was presented.

To define 'capital' as an amount of value requires the specification of the standard of value in which it was to be measured. A rather common procedure was to express capital in terms of consumption goods or, more precisely, to conceive of it as a 'subsistence fund' in support of the 'original' factors of production, labour and land, during the period of production extending from the initial expenditure of the services of these factors to the completion of consumption goods. This notion corresponded to the view that capital resulted from the investment of past savings, which, in turn, implied 'abstention' from consumption. Thus it appeared to be natural to measure 'capital' in terms of some composite unit of consumption goods. However, there was a second dimension of capital contemplated by these authors: the *time* for which capital is invested in a process of production. The idea was that capital can be increased either by using more of it or by lengthening the period of time for which it is invested.

The first author to use time as a single measure of capital was Jevons (1871). The gist of his argument consisted in the concept of a 'production function' $y = f(T)$, where output per unit of labour, y, is 'some continuous function of the time elapsing between the expenditure of labour and the enjoyment of results, T; this function is assumed to exhibit diminishing returns (1871, pp. 240–41). Jevons showed that in equilibrium $r = f'(T)/f(T)$.

Jevons's contribution was the starting point of the Austrian theory of capital and interest with Böhm-Bawerk and Wicksell as its main representatives. Böhm-Bawerk's concern was with establishing a temporal version of the demand and supply approach. This involved the appropriate reformulation of the data of the theory. The central elements of his analysis were the concepts of 'time preference' and the 'average period of production', used in describing consumer preferences and technical alternatives, respectively. As in Jevons social capital was conceived as a subsistence fund and was seen to permit the adoption of more productive but also more 'roundabout', i.e. time-consuming, methods of production. It was to the concept of the 'average period of production' that the marginal productivity condition was applied in the determination of the rate of interest.

Among the older neoclassical economists it was perhaps Wicksell who understood best the difficulties related to the problem of a unified treatment of capital in terms of the demand and supply approach. In particular, Wicksell was critical of attempts to work with the value of capital as a factor of production alongside the physically specified factors of labour and land in the production function of single commodities. This implied 'arguing in a circle' ([1901] 1934, p. 149), since capital and the rate of interest enter as a cost in the production of capital goods themselves. Hence the value of the capital goods inserted in the production function depends on the rate of interest and will change with it. Moreover, Wicksell expressed doubts as to the possibility of providing a sufficiently general definition of the 'average period of production' that could be used to represent capital in a way that is not threatened by this kind of circularity. In the *Lectures* he tried to overcome these difficulties by introducing production functions in terms of *dated* services of the 'original' factors labour and land.

While Wicksell shared Böhn-Bawerk's procedure of conceiving the 'capital endowment' of the economy as a value magnitude, he became increasingly sceptical whether it was admissible to identify it with some unspecified stock of subsistence goods, which, in turn, was seen to provide some measure of 'real' capital. With capital as a value magnitude Wicksell showed that the rate of interest is generally not equal to the marginal productivity of 'capital'. This discrepancy is due to the revaluation of the capital stock entailed by a change in distribution. The phenomenon is known as the 'Wicksell effect' and was regarded by Joan Robinson as the key to a criticism of the marginal productivity theory of income distribution.

Authors like J.B. Clark and Marshall appear to have been less aware of the fact that the conditions of production of single commodities cannot be defined in terms of production functions that include 'capital' among the factors of production. Obviously, the criticism levelled against these versions applies also to the concept of the 'aggregate production function', which boomed in the late 1950s and throughout the 1960s in conjunction with neoclassical growth theory.

Alternative views of the fundamentals of capital theory were expressed in a controversy between Böhm-Bawerk and J.B. Clark around the turn of this century (cf. in particular Böhm-Bawerk, 1907, and Clark, 1907). Böhm-Bawerk criticized Clark's attempt to differentiate between 'true capital', a permanent abiding fund of productive wealth, and 'concrete capital goods', each of which is destructible and has to be destroyed in order to serve its productive purpose; in Böhm-Bawerk's view this is 'dark, mystical rhetoric'. Furthermore, Böhm-Bawerk refuted Clark's claim that no concept of 'waiting' or 'abstinence' is needed to explain interest in stationary equilibrium. Without some concept of time preference, and thus a theory of saving, the determination of the rate of interest is left hanging in the air.

Irving Fisher (1930) extended general equilibrium theory to intertemporal choices. However, he proceeded as if there were a single composite commodity to be produced and consumed at different dates. In his discussion of the theory of interest all prices, wages and rents are assumed to be fixed. Hence the interrelationship between the rate of interest, prices and the remaining distribution variables is set aside. The 'investment opportunities' available to an individual and to society as a whole are summarized in intertemporal production possibility frontiers. Due to the assumption of diminishing returns Fisher arrived at a decreasing demand function for saving with respect to the rate of interest. As Keynes noted, this is equivalent to his 'marginal efficiency of capital' schedule (Keynes, 1936, p.140). Because of 'impatience' the supply of saving is considered to be positively related to the rate of interest. The market equilibrium between the supply of, and the demand for, saving gives the rate of interest, which is equal to the marginal rate of return over the cost of the marginal increase in the capital stock. (For an attempt to generalize Fisher's rate of return approach see Solow, 1967. For a critique of Fisher and Solow see Pasinetti, 1969, and Eatwell, 1976.)

The 1930s brought a further controversy on the theory of capital (cf. Kaldor, 1937). This was triggered off by a series of articles by F.H. Knight (e.g. Knight, 1934), in which he launched an attack on the concept of the 'period of production' revived a few years earlier by Hayek, among others. In particular, Knight argued that there is no need to refer to a 'quantity of capital' and that therefore the 'vicious circle' disappears. The rate of interest could be ascertained with reference to the instantaneous rate of investment and the present value of the additional stream of future income generated by it. However, Knight's proposed solution to the problem of circularity in terms of a 'theory of capital without capital' is illusory, since if the accusation of circularity applies at all (because the value of capital goods cannot be ascertained independently of the rate of interest), it applies both to the stock variable 'capital' and the corresponding flow variable 'investment'.

Finally, some recent attempts to revive and reformulate basic elements of the doctrines of the older neoclassical and Austrian authors should be noted, in particular: Weizsäcker (1971), Hicks (1973) and Faber (1979) on the Austrian theory, Morishima (1977) on Walras, and Hirshleifer (1970) and Dougherty (1980) on Fisher. (For a critical assessment of the older theories see especially Garegnani, 1960.)

THE RECENT CRITIQUE OF NEOCLASSICAL THEORY. Sraffa (1960) deserves the credit for having elaborated a consistent formulation of the classical surplus approach to the problem of capital and distribution. His analysis provided the fundamental basis for a critique of the prevalent neoclassical theory during the so-called 'Cambridge controversies in the theory of capital' (see Harcourt, 1969; Kurz, 1985).

Sraffa starts from a given system of production in use in which commodities are produced by means of commodities. If wages are assumed to be paid at the end of the uniform production period, then, in the case of single-product industries (i.e. circulating capital only) and with gross outputs of the different products all measured in physical terms and made equal to unity by choice of units, we have the price system

$$p = (1 + r)Ap + wl,$$

where p is the column vector of normal prices, r is the profit rate, A is the square matrix of material inputs, l is the vector of direct labour inputs and w is the wage rate. Under certain economically meaningful conditions, for any given feasible wage rate in terms of a given standard, the above equation yields a unique and strictly positive price vector in terms of the standard and a unique and non-negative value of the rate of profit. The investigation of the 'effects' of variations in one of the distribution variables on the other one and on the prices of commodities, assuming that the methods of production remain unchanged, yields the following results. First, the system possesses a finite maximum rate of profits $R > 0$ corresponding to a zero wage rate. Second, the vector of prices in terms of the wage rate p/w (prices in terms of quantities of *labour commanded*) is positive and rises monotonically for $0 \leqslant r < R$, tending to infinity as r approaches R. Third, at the maximum level of wages corresponding to $r = 0$ relative prices are in proportion to their labour costs, while at $r > 0$ relative prices generally deviate from relative labour costs and vary with changes in r (or w); it is only in the special case of uniform 'proportions' of labour to means of production in all industries that prices are proportional to 'labour values' for all levels of r (w). (For a discussion of joint production, fixed capital and land, see Pasinetti, 1980.)

While earlier authors were of the opinion that the capital–labour or capital–output ratios of the different industries could be brought into a ranking that is independent of distribution, this is generally not possible: 'the price of a product ... may rise or it may fall, or it may even alternate in rising and falling, relative to its means of production' (Sraffa, 1960, p. 15). This result destroys the foundation of those versions of the traditional theory that attempted to define the conditions of production in terms of production functions with 'capital' as a factor. Moreover, as regards the concept of the 'capital endowment' of the economy conceived as a value magnitude, the same 'real' capital may assume different values depending on the level of r. Sraffa concludes that these findings 'cannot be reconciled with *any* notion of capital as a measurable quantity independent of distribution and prices' (1960, p. 38).

Samuelson (1962), in an attempt to counter Joan Robinson's (1953) attack on the aggregate production function, claimed that even in cases with heterogeneous capital goods some rationalization can be provided for the validity of simple neoclassical 'parables' which assume there is a single homogeneous factor called 'capital', the marginal product of which equals the rate of interest. But, alas, Samuelson based his defence of traditional theory in terms of the construction of a 'surrogate production function' on the assumption of equal input proportions (cf. 1962, pp. 196–7). By this token the 'real' economy with heterogeneous goods was turned into the 'imaginary' economy with a homogeneous output, i.e. the 'surrogate production function' was nothing more than the infamous aggregate production function. (For a critique of Samuelson's approach see particularly Garegnani, 1970.)

Implicit in the above system of price equations is the inverse relationship between the wage and the rate of profit, or *wage curve*, of the given system of production, $w = w(r)$. We may now turn to the hypothesis that for one or several industries alternative technical methods are available for the production of the

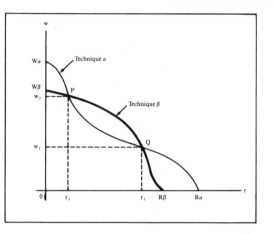

Figure 2

corresponding commodity. The technology of the economic system as a whole will then be represented by a series of alternative techniques obtained from all the possible combinations of methods of production for the various commodities. Expressing w and p in terms of a commodity produced in all the alternative systems, we obtain as many different wage curves as there are alternative techniques. In Figure 2 it is assumed that only two techniques, α and β exist. Clearly, at any level of the wage rate (or rate of profit), entrepreneurs will choose the *cost-minimizing* system of production. It can be shown that, whichever the system initially in use, the tendency of producers to switch to the cheaper system will bring them to the one giving the highest rate of profit (wage rate), whereas systems giving the same r for the same w will be indifferent and can coexist. Thus, in the example of Figure 2, in the two intervals $0 < w < w_1$ and $w_2 < w \leqslant W_\alpha$ technique α will be chosen, while in the interval $w_1 < w < w_2$ technique β turns out to be superior; at the two switch points P and Q both techniques are equiprofitable. It follows that with a choice of technique the relationship between w and r, or wage *frontier*, will be represented by the outermost segments or envelope of the intersecting wage curves.

Figure 2 shows that the same technique (α) may be the most profitable of a number of techniques at more than one level of the wage rate even though other techniques (here β) are more profitable at wage rates in between. The implication of this possibility of the *reswitching* of techniques is that the direction of change of the input proportions cannot be related unambiguously to changes of the so-called 'factor prices'. The central element of the neoclassical explanation of distribution in terms of supply and demand is thus revealed as defective. This element consisted in the proposition that a rise of r must decrease the 'quantity of capital' relative to labour in the production of a commodity because of the assumed substitutability in production and consumption. The demonstration that a rise in r may lead to the adoption of the more 'capital-intensive' of two

87

techniques clearly destroys the neoclassical concept of substitution in production. Moreover, since a rise in r may cheapen some of the commodities, the production of which at a lower level of r was characterized by a relatively high 'capital intensity', the substitution among consumption goods contemplated by the traditional theory of consumer demand may result in a higher, as well as in a lower, 'capital intensity'. It follows that the principle of substitution in consumption cannot offset the breakdown of the principle of substitution in production. Finally, it is worth mentioning that reswitching is not necessary for *capital reversing* (cf. Symposium, 1966, p. 516).

The negative implication of reverse capital deepening for traditional theory can be illustrated by means of the example of Figure 3, in which the value of capital corresponding to the full employment level of labour is plotted against the rate of profit. Obviously, if with traditional analysis we conceived the curve KK' as the 'demand curve' for capital, which, together with the corresponding 'supply curve' SS', is taken to determine the 'equilibrium' level of r, we would have to conclude that this equilibrium, although unique, is unstable. With free competition and perfectly flexible distributive variables a deviation of r from r^* would lead to the complete extinction of one of the two income categories. According to the critics of traditional theory, the finding that the quantity of a factor demanded need not be related to the price of the factor service in the conventional, inverse manner demonstrates the failure of the supply and demand approach to the explanation of normal distribution, prices and quantities.

NEOCLASSICAL RESPONSES. Neoclassical economists tried to counter the attack in various ways. At first it was claimed that reswitching is impossible. When this claim was shown conclusively to be false (cf. Symposium, 1966), doubts were raised as to its empirical importance (see, for example, Ferguson, 1969), thereby insinuating that neoclassical theory was a simplified picture of reality, the basic

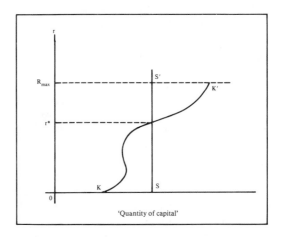

Figure 3

correctness of which would not be endangered by 'exceptions' of the kind analysed in the capital debate. Other advocates of the neoclassical approach were conscious of how defective the attempt was to play down the importance of reswitching and capital reversing using the 'empirical' route. Since the phenomenon was irrefutable it had to be absorbed and shown to be compatible with the more sophisticated versions of the dominant theory.

Perhaps the first move in this direction was made by Bruno, Burmeister and Sheshinski (1966), who drew an analogy between reswitching and the long-known possibility of the existence of multiple internal rates of return. However, whereas the latter phenomenon is a discovery within the partial, 'fixed-price' framework of microeconomic theory of investment, reswitching presupposes a total, general framework. Moreover, we are not told how traditional theory was both able to cope with reswitching and yet preserve its basic structure.

A more interesting challenge came from authors such as Bliss (1975) and Hahn (1982). They contended that because of its concern with a uniform rate of profit Sraffa's analysis can be considered a 'special case' of general equilibrium theory. According to these authors the criticism of traditional neoclassical capital theory implicit in Sraffa is correct but has no bearing upon modern general equilibrium theory. Since in the latter the distribution of income is explained in terms of given *physical* endowments of agents, there is no need to find a scalar representation of the capital stock. The uniformity of profit rates is taken to be 'a very special state of the economy' (Hahn, 1982, p. 363) which, for given preferences and production sets, presupposes a particular composition of initial endowments. In general, there will be as many own rates of return as there are different assets in the endowment set.

The first thing to be noticed is that the preservation of the basic supply and demand approach to the explanation of prices, distribution and quantities in modern general equilibrium theory is effectuated at the cost of the abandonment of the traditional long-period method. As we have seen, this method was shared by all 'forerunners' of this theory, including, most notably, Walras and von Neumann (1936). Indeed, the change in the notion of equilibrium involved expresses a fundamental break with the analytical method used by all economic theory up to the 1930s, when, partly because of a growing perception among neoclassical economists that the whole approach was threatened by the difficulties concerning the notion of capital, a drastic methodological reorientation was advocated (cf. Garegnani, 1976; Milgate, 1979). Most influential in this move away from the traditional method was apparently Hicks's *Value and Capital* (1939; second edition 1946). Interestingly enough, Hicks himself appears to have become increasingly sceptical as to the usefulness of the 'temporary equilibrium method' then suggested by him (see, for example, Hicks, 1965, pp. 73–4).

The second observation concerns Hahn's attempt to interpret Sraffa's analysis as a special case of general equilibrium theory. Since the latter takes as data (i) the preferences of consumers, (ii) the technical conditions of production, and (iii) the physical endowments, Hahn's view necessarily leads to the question of which constellation of these data is compatible with a uniform rate of profits. Clearly, to superimpose the latter specification on an ordinary general equilibrium system would render it overdetermined, as some of the older neoclassical authors were well aware of. Hence, following the interpretation under consideration, (i), (ii) or (iii) cannot be taken as independent variables. Now it is Hahn's contention that at the basis of Sraffa's price equations there must be a special proportion between the initial endowments; i.e. (iii) is tacitly assumed to be specified accordingly. However, as we have seen there is no evidence in support of this presupposition. The surplus approach does not require given endowments of produced means of production in order to determine distribution and normal prices. In fact, looking at classical analysis as a whole the quantities of the capital goods available may be considered as dependent rather than independent variables. In analysing the problem of value, capital and distribution the classical economists took the capital stocks installed in the different industries as exactly adjusted to *given outputs*, such that the latter could be produced at minimum costs. The tendency towards normal capital utilization and a uniform rate of profit was seen to be the outcome of the working of the persistent forces of the system reflected in the competitive decisions of producers.

Since the opinion entertained by Hahn that Sraffa's analysis can be subsumed as a 'special case' under modern neoclassical theory has to be rejected, the question remains, which of the two is the more powerful instrument of analysis. There does not seem to exist a ready-made answer at present. The following remarks on the dominant neoclassical theory must suffice.

Obviously, to take the capital endowment as given in kind implies that only 'short-period' equilibria can be determined. Because firms 'prefer more profit to less' (Hahn, 1982, p. 354) the size and composition of the capital stock will rapidly change. Thus, major factors which general equilibrium theory envisages as determining prices and quantities are themselves subject to quick changes. This, in turn, makes it difficult to distinguish them from those accidental and temporary factors, which, at any given moment of time, prevent the economy from settling in the position of equilibrium. More important, the fast variation in relative prices necessitates the consideration of the influence of future states of the world on the present situation.

This can be approached in two different ways. First, if there were complete future markets the analysis could be carried out in terms of the concept of *intertemporal equilibrium*. However, the assumption that all intertemporal and all contingent markets exist, which has the effect of collapsing the future into the present, can be rejected on grounds of realism and economic reasoning (see, for example, Bliss, 1975, pp. 48 and 61). Moreover, there is the following conceptual problem (see Schefold, 1985). If in equilibrium some of the capital stocks turn out to be in excess supply these stocks assume zero prices. This possibility appears to indicate that the expectations entrepreneurs held in the past when deciding to build up the present capital stocks are not realized. Hence, strictly speaking we are faced with a disequilibrium situation because otherwise the wrong stocks could not have accumulated. Therefore, the problem arises how the past or, more exactly, possible discrepancies between expectations and facts influence the future.

Since the notion of intertemporal equilibrium cannot be sustained the theory is ultimately referred back to the introduction of individual price expectations concerning future deliveries of commodities for which no present markets exist. This leads to the *temporary equilibrium* version of modern neoclassical theory. The basic weakness of the theories of temporary equilibrium concerns the necessarily arbitrary choice of hypotheses about individual price expectations. Indeed, as Burmeister stresses, 'all too often "nearly anything can happen" is the only possible unqualified conclusion' (Burmeister, 1980, p. 215). Moreover, the stability properties of this kind of equilibrium are unclear, since small perturbations caused by accidental factors may entail changes in expectations, which define that very equilibrium.

The danger of lapsing into empty formalism and of depriving the theory of clear-cut results was of course recognized by several supply and demand theorists and considered a fundamental weakness. In view of it some of them were prepared to dispense with the alleged generality of general equilibrium theory and return to some version of traditional neoclassical analysis. After the recent debate in capital theory this involved ruling out reswitching and other 'perverse', i.e. non-conventional, phenomena in terms of sufficiently bold assumptions about available techniques. It comes as no surprise that given these assumptions the central neoclassical postulate of the inverse relation between the capital–labour ratio and the rate of profit should re-emerge as 'one of the most powerful theorems in economic theory' (Sato, 1974, p. 355). However, in order to be clear about this move it deserves to be stressed that it was motivated, as one author expressly admits, by the fact that 'regular economies' have 'desirable properties' (Burmeister, 1980, p. 124).

BIBLIOGRAPHY

Bliss, C.J. 1975. *Capital Theory and the Distribution of Income*. Amsterdam: North-Holland.

Böhm-Bawerk, E. von. 1889. *Positive Theorie des Kapitales*. Jena: Gustav Fischer. Trans. as *Positive Theory of Capital*, London: Smart, 1891.

Böhm-Bawerk, E. von. 1906–7. Capital and interest once more. *Quarterly Journal of Economics* 21, Pt. I, November 1906, 1–21; Pt. II, April 1907, 247–82.

Bortkiewicz, L. von. 1907. Zur Berichtigung der grundlegenden theoretischen Konstruktion von Marx im dritten Bande des 'Kapital'. *Jahrbücher für Nationalökonomie und Statistik*, July. English trans. in Appendix to E. von. Böhm-Bawerk, *Karl Marx and the Close of his System*, ed. P. Sweezy, New York, 1949.

Bruno, M., Burmeister, E. and Sheshinski, E. 1966. The nature and implications of the reswitching of techniques. *Quarterly Journal of Economics* 80(4), November, 526–53.

Burmeister, E. 1980. *Capital Theory and Dynamics*. Cambridge and New York: Cambridge University Press.

Clark, J.B. 1899. *The Distribution of Wealth*. London: Macmillan.

Clark, J.B. 1907. Concerning the nature of capital: a reply. *Quarterly Journal of Economics* 21, May, 351–70.

Dougherty, C. 1980. *Interest and Profit*. London: Methuen; Columbia University Press.

Eatwell, J. 1976. Irving Fisher's 'Rate of return over cost' and the rate of profit in a capitalistic economy. In *Essays in Modern Capital Theory*, ed. M. Brown, K. Sato and P. Zarembka, Amsterdam: North-Holland.

Faber, M. 1979. *Introduction to Modern Austrian Capital Theory*. Berlin: Springer-Verlag.

Ferguson, C.E. 1969. *The Neoclassical Theory of Production and Distribution*. Cambridge: Cambridge University Press.

Fisher, I. 1930. *The Theory of Interest*. London: Macmillan; New York: A.M. Kelley, 1961.

Garegnani, P. 1960. *Il capitale nelle teorie della distribuzione*. Milan: Giuffrè.

Garegnani, P. 1970. Heterogeneous capital, the production function and the theory of distribution. *Review of Economic Studies* 37(3), July, 407–36.

Garegnani, P. 1976. On a change in the notion of equilibrium in recent work on value.In *Essays in Modern Capital Theory*, ed. M. Brown, K. Sato and P. Zarembka, Amsterdam: North-Holland.

Hahn, F.H. 1982. The neo-Ricardians. *Cambridge Journal of Economics* 6(4), December, 353–74.

Harcourt, G.C. 1969. Some Cambridge controversies in the theory of capital. *Journal of Economic Literature* 7(2), June, 369–405.

Hicks, J.R. 1932. *The Theory of Wages*. London: Macmillan; 2nd American edn., New York: St. Martin's Press, 1963.

Hicks, J.R. 1939. *Value and Capital*. 2nd edn, Oxford: Clarendon Press, 1946.

Hicks, J.R. 1965. *Capital and Growth*. Oxford and New York: Oxford University Press.

Hicks, J.R. 1973. *Capital and Time – a Neo-Austrian Theory*. Oxford: Oxford University Press.

Hirshleifer, J. 1970. *Investment, Interest and Capital*. Englewood Cliffs: Prentice-Hall.

Jevons, W.S. 1871. *The Theory of Political Economy*. Reprint, New York: Kelley, 1970.

Kaldor, N. 1937. The recent controversy on the theory of capital. *Econometrica* 5, July, 201–33.

Keynes, J.M. 1936. *The General Theory of Employment, Interest and Money*. London: Macmillan; New York: Harcourt, Brace.

Knight, F.H. 1921. *Risk, Uncertainty and Profit*. Chicago: University of Chicago Press.

Knight, F.H. 1934. Capital, time and the interest rate. *Economica* 1, August, 257–86.

Kurz, H.D. 1985. Sraffa's contribution to the debate in capital theory. *Contributions to Political Economy* 4, 3–24.

Marshall, A. 1890. *Principles of Economics*. 8th edn (1920). Reprint, reset, London: Macmillan, 1977.

Marx, K. 1894. *Capital*. Vol. III. Moscow: Progress Publishers; Harmondsworth: Penguin, 1959.

Milgate, M. 1979. On the origin of the notion of 'intertemporal equilibrium'. *Economica* 46, February, 1–10.

Morishima, M. 1977. *Walras' Economics: a Pure Theory of Capital and Money*. Cambridge and New York: Cambridge University Press.

Neumann, J. von. 1936. Über ein ökonomisches Gleichungssystem und eine Verallgemeinerung des Browerschen Fixpunktsatzes. In *Ergebnisse eines Mathematischen Kolloquiums*, ed. K. Menger, Vienna: F. Deuticke. Trans. as 'A Model of General Economic Equilibrium', *Review of Economic Studies* 13(1), (1945–6), Winter, 1–9.

Pasinetti, L.L. 1969. Switches of technique and the 'rate of return' in capital theory. *Economic Journal* 79, September, 508–31.

Pasinetti, L.L. (ed.) 1980. *Essays on the Theory of Joint Production*. London: Macmillan; Columbia University Press.

Ricardo, D. 1951–73. *The Works and Correspondence of David Ricardo*. 11 vols, ed. P. Sraffa in collaboration with M.H. Dobb, Cambridge and New York: Cambridge University Press.

Robinson, J. 1953. The production function and the theory of capital. *Review of Economic Studies* 21(2), Winter, 81–106.

Samuelson, P.A. 1962. Parable and realism in capital theory: the surrogate production function. *Review of Economic Studies* 29, June, 193–206.

Sato, K. 1974. The neoclassical postulate and the technology frontier in capital theory. *Quarterly Journal of Economics* 88(3), August, 353–84.

Schefold, B. 1985. Cambridge price theory: special model or general theory of value? *American Economic Review, Papers and Proceedings* 75(2), May, 140–45.

Smith, A. 1776. *An Inquiry into the Nature and Causes of the Wealth of Nations.* Ed. E. Cannan, introduced by G.J. Stigler, Chicago: Chicago University Press, 1976.

Solow, R.M. 1967. The interest rate and the transition between techniques. In *Socialism, Capitalism and Economic Growth, Essays presented to Maurice Dobb*, ed. C.H. Feinstein, Cambridge: Cambridge University Press.

Sraffa, P. 1951. Introduction. In D. Ricardo, *The Works and Correspondence of David Ricardo*, Vol. 1.

Sraffa, P. 1960. *Production of Commodities by Means of Commodities.* Cambridge: Cambridge University Press.

Symposium. 1966. On paradoxes in capital theory: a symposium. *Quarterly Journal of Economics* 80(4), November, 526–83.

Walras, L. 1874–7. *Eléments d'économie politique pure.* Lausanne: Corbaz. 4th edn 1900. Trans. by W. Jaffé of definitive edn (1926) as *Elements of Pure Economics*, London: Allen & Unwin, 1954; Homewood, Ill.: R.D. Irwin.

Weizsäcker, C.Ch. von. 1971. *Steady State Capital Theory.* Berlin, Heidelberg, New York: Springer-Verlag.

Wicksell, K. 1893. *Über Wert, Kapital und Rente.* Jena: Gustav Fischer. Trans. as *Value, Capital and Rent*, New York: Kelley, 1954.

Wicksell, K. 1901. *Föreläsingar i Nationalekonomi*, Vol. 1. Lund: Berlingska Boktryckeriet. Trans. as *Lectures on Political Economy*, Vol. 1, London: Routledge & Kegan Paul, 1934; New York: A.M. Kelley, 1967.

Amortization

CHARLES R. HULTEN

Amortization is an accounting term meaning to allocate a cost to several time periods. The term is derived from the Latin word for death and literally means to 'kill off' the liability. Debts which are paid off gradually are said to be amortized, and the term is also applied to the depreciation costs of certain assets which are used up in producing income.

Amortization in the second sense is illustrated by the following example (Table 1). A firm spends $10,000 to invent and patent a new product which is expected to yield revenue (net of operating expenses) of $5000 in the first year of production, $2000 in each of the next three years, and $1500 in the fifth year (see column (3) of Table 1). The product is assumed to become obsolete at the end of five years and to generate no additional revenue. The patent thus becomes valueless at that time.

Table 1 Amortization of Hypothetical Asset

(1) End of:	(2) Outlay ($)	(3) Net Revenue ($)	(4) Present Value* ($)	(5) Amortization ($)	(6) Profit ($)
yr 0	10 000	0	10 000	0	0
yr 1	0	5 000	6 000	4 000	1 000
yr 2	0	2 000	4 599	1 401	599
yr 3	0	2 000	3 058	1 541	459
yr 4	0	2 000	1 364	1 694	306
yr 5	0	1 500	0	1 364	136

*Present value of remaining net revenue calculated using discount rate of 9.992%.

The present value of the net revenue stream associated with the invention is initially $10,000 at an approximate 10 per cent rate of discount. However, the present value of the remaining net revenue falls to $6000 at the end of the first year, to $4599 at the end of the second year, to $3058 and $1364 at the end of the third and fourth years, and to zero at the end of the product's useful life (see column (4)). This implies that the original $10,000 investment has been eroded by $4000 at the end of the first year, $1401 in the second year, and so on (see column (5)). In considering how much profit was earned in the first year, the loss in the value of the investment must be subtracted from revenue in order to keep the original value of the investment intact. Thus, profit in the first year is $1000, or 10 per cent of the original investment. Inpection of columns (4) and (6) reveals that the ratio of profit to remaining present value in the previous year is always 10 per cent.

If, on the other hand, the reduction in value is not recognized as a cost, one would erroneously conclude that the investment yielded $12,500 over the life of the asset (the sum of column (3)) rather than $2500 (the sum of column (6)). However, the value of the investment would have fallen from $10,000 to zero.

The year-to-year loss of asset value is termed 'amortization'. In this context, amortization is analogous to depreciation, although the former typically (but not always) refers to intangible assets while the latter typically (but not always) refers to tangible capital like plant and equipment. The concept of depreciation is, however, more intuitive since it is associated with physical deterioration and ultimate retirement from service. Intangible assets, on the other hand, are invisible and are difficult to measure or even value, so it is harder to believe that they are being used up in the production of income. For this reason, the term 'amortization' carries the connotation of an arbitrary and gradual killing off of asset value. This is unfortunate, since the true depreciation of tangible capital is hard to measure and arbitrary 'amortization' rules are typically used in tax and financial accounting.

The graduation write-off of a debt is another context in which the term 'amortization' is frequently used. The level-payment home mortgage is, for example, a common type of amortized loan. In the level-payment mortgage, the sum of the interest and principal payments is constant. During the early life of the loan, the bulk of this constant (or 'level') payment is for interest on the outstanding balance of the loan. The proportion of the level-payment allocated to the repayment of principal gradually increases as time goes by, since interest is paid on the outstanding balance of the loan. In the fully amortized loan, the sum of the period-by-period repayments of principal over the life of the loan is equal to the original value of the debt.

This type of arrangement may be contrasted with the case of the 'balloon' loan, in which the entire principal is repaid at the termination date of the loan. Loans may be a mixture of the two types: amortization of part of the principal with a balloon payment equal to the unamortized balance.

95

The amortization of a loan is conceptually related to the amortization of an intangible asset. Table 1 could, for example, be reinterpreted as the payoff schedule for a $10,000 debt. Column (5) could be interpreted as annual return of principal (a non-level payment schedule), and column (6) as interest paid on the outstanding balance of the debt. However, the amortization of a loan involves the gradual write-off of a liability while the amortization of an intangible involves the gradual write-off of an asset. Both cases involve allocating a cost over several time periods.

Eugen von Böhm-Bawerk

K.H. HENNINGS

As civil servant and economic theorist, Böhm-Bawerk was one of the most influential economists of his generation. A leading member of the Austrian School, he was one of the main propagators of neoclassical economic theory and did much to help it attain its dominance over classical economic theory. His name is primarily associated with the Austrian theory of capital and a particular theory of interest. But his prime achievement is the formulation of an intertemporal theory of value which, when applied to an exchange economy with production using durable capital goods, yields a theory of capital, a theory of interest, and indeed a theory of distribution in which the time element plays a critical role. Both this construction and his equally famous critique of Marx's economics strongly influenced the development of economic theory from the 1880s until well into the 1930s.

Eugen Böhm Ritter von Bawerk was born in Brünn (now Brno) in Moravia on 12 February 1851, the youngest son of a distinguished civil servant who had been ennobled for his part in quelling unrest in Galicia in 1848, and who died in 1856 as deputy governor and head of the Imperial Austrian administration in Moravia. After reading law at the University of Vienna, Böhm-Bawerk entered the prestigious fiscal administration in 1872. In 1875, however, after taking his doctorate in law, Böhm-Bawerk obtained a government grant to do graduate work abroad and prepare himself for a teaching position in economics at an Austrian university, as did his class-mate and future brother-in-law Friedrich von Wieser. He worked for a year at Heidelberg with Karl Knies, and spent a term each at Leipzig, where Roscher taught, and at Jena, where Hildebrand taught. After working for another three years in the fiscal administration and the ministry of finance, he obtained his *Habilitation* (licence to teach) in 1880, and was immediately afterwards appointed to a professorship in economics at the University of Innsbruck which he held until 1889. From a scholarly point of view, Böhm-Bawerk's years in Innsbruck were the most fruitful of his life. A book on the theory of goods, based on his *Habilitation* thesis, appeared in 1881, the first volume of *Kapital und Kapitalzins* in 1884. In 1886 he published a monograph on the theory of value in the most influential German language journal in economics, and in 1889 the second volume of *Kapital und Kapitalzins*. These publications established his as one of the leading members of the group of economists around Carl Menger who came to be known as the 'Austrian School'. In 1889 Böhm-Bawerk preferred an appointment in the Austrian ministry of finance to a chair at the University of Vienna because it carried the assignment to work out a reform of the Austrian income tax. He distinguished himself in the execution of this task, and rapidly rose in rank, obtaining the position of a permanent secretary in 1891, and in 1892 also the vice-presidency of a commission to assess the proposal of a return to the gold standard. Having been appointed minister of finance in a caretaker government in 1893, Böhm-Bawerk was considered to have risen too high to return to his former position when it was replaced by a parliamentary post after a few months, and he was made president of one of the three senates of the Verwaltungsgerichtshof, the highest court of appeal in administrative matters. In 1896 he was again made minister of finance in a caretaker government, but returned once more to the Verwaltungsgerichtshof in 1897. He was yet again appointed minister of finance in 1900, this time in a civil servants' government which fell when he resigned in 1904 after large increases in military expenditure had been voted which he deemed threatened financial stability. This time he was offered, among other positions, the post of governor of the central bank, the most lucrative position in the monarchy. Yet he turned it down in favour of a chair at the University of Vienna which was especially created for him. Alongside Friedrich von Wieser (who had succeeded Menger in 1902) and Eugen von Philippovich, Böhm-Bawerk lectured on economic theory and conducted a seminar that soon attracted many able students, among them Joseph Schumpeter, Rudolf Hilferding, Otto Bauer, Ludwig von Mises, Emil Lederer and Richard von Strigl. He did not, however, return to the quiet life of a scholar. Having been elected a member of the Austrian Academy of Sciences in 1902, he was elected its vice president in 1907, and its president in 1911. He had also been made a Geheimrat (privy councillor) in 1895, had been appointed to a seat in the upper house of the Austrian parliament in 1899, and was from time to time given various other official assignments. Böhm-Bawerk died on 27 August 1914 at Rattenberg-Kramsach in Tyrol where he had tried to restore his health after having fallen ill on his way to a congress of the Carnegie Foundation in Switzerland as the official Austrian representative.

Böhm-Bawerk was as much a civil servant as a scholar, and in his later years an elder statesman in academic affairs as much as in the public realm of what was still a Great Power. He was extremely successful as an administrator and economic policy maker. But it is for his contributions to economic theory that he is chiefly remembered today. *Kapital und Kapitalzins* has become an economic classic even though it is defective both in construction and exposition. The first edition was written in great haste, and although Böhm-Bawerk responded over-conscientiously and meticulously to almost every criticism in the two further editions which appeared in his lifetime, adding so much material that two slim volumes grew into three massive tomes, he never found the time to rethink the structure as a whole. This absorptive attention to criticism was due to temperament as well as to circumstances. Böhm-Bawerk had a lawyer's mind and found it difficult to think in terms other than disjunct categories or 'cases' which needed to be distinguished sharply and did not fit into a continuum in which things shade into one another. Moreover, writing in a thoroughly anti-theoretical environment dominated by the German Historical School, he felt obliged to take issue and to sharpen differences for the sake of discussion. As a result, Böhm-Bawerk acquired an undeserved reputation as a casuistic and ungenerous controversialist which did much to place his (admittedly in some respects imperfect) contributions in a more critical light than they merit.

The core of Böhm-Bawerk's theoretical endeavours is the development of an intertemporal theory of value, capital and interest. This attempt owes much to his teachers in economics. A.E.F. Schäffle, Menger's predecessor in Vienna, seems to have convinced him that it was necessary to respond on a theoretical plane to the social question, the most pressing economic policy problem of the day, by developing a satisfactory theory of distribution (see Schäffle, 1870). Karl Knies (1873–79) drew his attention to the problems of capital theory and the work of Marx. Carl Menger, finally, provided the starting point for his own theory.

In his *Grundsätze der Volkswirthschaftslehre* (1871), Menger had developed an atemporal theory of value, allocation and exchange. In his exposition and elaboration of that theory, Böhm-Bawerk (1886) strongly emphasized two of its aspects. Firstly, consumer behaviour is sharply distinguished from producer behaviour because only the former can evaluate goods directly; producers can do so only indirectly on the basis of their expectations of consumers' evaluations because production, being roundabout production, is necessarily time-consuming. Secondly, in both cases the evaluation of a commodity involves both the marginal utility of the commodity to the evaluating agent, and the marginal utility of the income available to him. In Böhm-Bawerk's usage, therefore, evaluations are shadow prices, or inverse demand schedules which imply an optimal allocation of commodities in the light of an agent's preferences as well as his income.

On the basis of such inverse demand schedules it was easy to show that the market price of a commodity could not be lower than the lowest price the 'last' buyer is prepared to offer, nor higher than the highest price the 'last' seller demands; here the 'last' seller is defined as the seller whose asking price is low enough to prevent any other seller from selling to the 'last' buyer: and the 'last' buyer as that buyer whose price offer is high enough to prevent any other buyer from buying from the 'last' seller. This definition, complicated as it is, is adapted to include the case of indivisible commodities which Böhm-Bawerk for one reason or another considered relevant.

Böhm-Bawerk also elaborated on Menger's seminal contribution by refining the analysis of distribution: he showed how inputs are evaluated by imputation, i.e. by imputing to them their proper share of the value of the output they help to produce. In essence this amounted to a marginal productivity theory along lines laid down by J.H. von Thünen, but again adapted to his peculiarly Austrian assumptions of limited substitutability and finite divisibility of inputs.

Böhm-Bawerk generalized (in 1889) this theory of price formation in atemporal exchange to include intertemporal exchange by assuming that agents evaluate and trade not only currently available commodities, but also subjectively certain prospects of commodities available in the future. In this theory of goods, Böhm-Bawerk (1881) had shown in a surprisingly modern manner that such prospects exist, and how they can be evaluated. Assuming further that a market exists on which currently available commodities can be exchanged for subjectively certain prospects of commodities available in the future, the same argument can be applied to intertemporal exchange as was applied to atemporal exchange. Böhm-Bawerk did so in two stages, first considering a pure exchange economy without production, and then analysing an exchange economy with production.

In a pure exchange economy, all agents are consumers. Their inverse demand schedules, Böhm-Bawerk argued, involve for each agent a subjective rate of interest at which he is prepared, given his preferences over time and his (expected) income over time, to exchange subjectively certain prospects of commodities available in the future for the same amount of commodities available in the present. They also, Böhm-Bawerk maintained, typically exhibit positive time preference: commodities available in the present are typically evaluated at higher prices than subjectively certain prospects of the same commodities available in the future. This assertion is contained in the first two of Three Reasons he adduced for the positivity of the rate of interest. The first Reason postulates that the marginal utility of income will decline over the planning horizon because of higher expected incomes in the future. The second Reason postulates that for psychological reasons such as the finiteness of life, the marginal utility of a commodity declines as a rule with the length of time that elapses before it becomes available. As both these postulates have been much disputed it should be added immediately that Böhm-Bawerk regarded them as no more than testable assumptions which he deemed realistic but which admit exceptions. If these postulates are granted for all agents, their subjective rates of interest will always be positive, so that the market rate of interest will always be positive. The same will hold true if only a majority of agents behave according to these postulates. Böhm-Bawerk admitted that not all agents will always behave as postulated by him: but argued that as an empirical regularity they almost always did, and that his theory was applicable also when they did not. All that follows in the latter case is that the rate of interest is not positive. Note, therefore, that Böhm-Bawerk's argument establishes at one and the same time the existence of a (market) rate of interest in a pure intertemporal exchange economy, and identifies as the determinants of its height the relative intensities of the demand for, and supply of, commodities in the present and in the future, as expressed in agents' inverse demand schedules. Of course, these are commodity rates of interest which do not necessarily exhibit any particular term structure, nor uniformity across different types of commodities. Both these properties need the further assumption that intertemporal markets exist for all commodities, and that at least some agents are prepared to engage in arbitrage operations (see Nuti, 1974). Böhm-Bawerk did not explicitly make these assumptions, but he argued as if these properties were assured. Note also that Böhm-Bawerk conceived in this model of a pure exchange economy of the rate of interest as a property of an intertemporal price structure, and not as the specific price of something, be it abstinence, the productivity of money, waiting, or whatever.

In order to extend the model just considered to include production Böhm-Bawerk argued that producers can be shown to have intertemporal inverse demand schedules like consumers, and postulated in his third Reason that producers under-evaluate commodities available in the future on technical grounds. These assertions he derived from his analysis of the nature of production, and the role of capital in it. Production is assumed to be roundabout. It transforms non-produced or 'original' factors of production into consumable output with the help of capital goods which are internal to the production process. Because some capital goods are durable, production takes time, Böhm-Bawerk emphasized strongly the heterogeneity and specificity of capital goods. He also denied that they can be aggregated into some physical measure for the capital stock; aggregation is in his view possible only by valuing capital goods. He employed a forward-looking measure of capital value in which durable capital goods are valued by the present value of their services, and indeed generalized this procedure to all durable goods by showing that their valuation involves a subjective rate of interest which is equalized when durable goods are traded on markets.

The view of production as roundabout led Böhm-Bawerk to postulate a correspondence between the amounts of different capital goods used in production and the time which elapses before a particular dose of non-produced inputs has matured in the form of consumable output. This correspondence he formalized in the concept of a period of production which is defined, as the average period for which the various doses of non-produced inputs required for the production of a unit output remain 'locked up' in the production process. This definition was a mistake which got him into more than one difficulty, and provided material for heated debates. To get round all the difficulties raised in these debates, assume that it is possible to define a period of production as a technical property of a particular production system which does not depend on factor prices; and assume further (with Böhm-Bawerk) that it can be used to order difficult methods of production in such a way that methods with a longer period of production can be said to be more capital intensive. More specifically, assume a temporal production function which (for a unit output) has only the period of production as argument, and which exhibits diminishing returns but is not homogeneous.

On this basis Böhm-Bawerk formulated a theory of producer behaviour in which competition forces producers to choose production methods that generate just enough output to pay the costs of production. As Böhm-Bawerk showed, this implied a discounted marginal productivity doctrine of (original) factor pricing, and hence the existence of positive quasi-rents at the margin. He also showed that this construction involved inverse demand schedules for capital goods which for each period of production define a profit maximizing rate of interest for given factor prices. At this point in his analysis, Böhm-Bawerk assumed the capital stock of an economy as given, and argued that the profit maximizing rate of profit can be determined with the help of that assumption. While that is correct it was another mistake which was duly seized upon (see e.g. Garegnani, 1960) and which led to many debates. For the value of the capital stock associated with any method of production is an endogenous variable in his construction, as Böhm-Bawerk realized in other contexts. Nor was it necessary to make this assumption. It is sufficient to note that a single producer is forced by competition to pay neither less nor more than the discounted marginal value for the inputs he uses, if a time-consuming roundabout method of production is in operation. Translated into output prices this implies that he under-evaluates output available in the future. This is what Böhm-Bawerk asserted in the third Reason; the technical ground being the method of production in operation. Note that this is not so much a postulate or empirical regularity as it is an equilibrium condition.

Having thus established that producer behaviour can be characterized by derived inverse demand schedules for output which involve positive time preference, Böhm-Bawerk goes on to determine the market rate of interest in what is in effect a macroeconomic general equilibrium model. Attention is centred on the market for output available in the present, and the markets for claims to output available in the future. Supply on the market for output available in the present is fixed by decisions taken in the past; so is the supply available at all future dates whose production has already begun. Demand for output available in the present comes from consumers but will not exhaust supply if they save. Part of these savings will be taken up by other consumers in exchange for claims to output available in the future; transactions are consumption loans, and are likely, on Böhm-Bawerk's assumptions, to imply a positive rate of interest. Another part of savings will be taken up by producers, again in exchange for claims of future output, who use it to bid for more non-produced inputs in an attempt to expand the scale of production. As Böhm-Bawerk assumed that the amount of non-produced original factors is fixed, this results in higher factor prices and a change in the method of production (because higher factor prices can only be sustained if more output is produced). Net savings in the form of loans for productive purposes therefore imply a change in the method of production which, on Böhm-Bawerk's assumptions, implies capital deepening. Both kinds of transactions together determine the market rate of interest, which is thus seen to be determined by intertemporal consumer behaviour as summarized in the notion of positive time preference, and based on intertemporal preferences and the (expected) intertemporal distribution of incomes, on the one hand; and intertemporal producer behaviour as summarized in the period of production and the marginal product of extending it, and based on the intertemporal structure of roundabout methods of production on the other hand. Or, as Böhm-Bawerk put it, the rate of interest is determined by the relative evaluation of (output available in) the present and the future on the part of both, consumers and producers. On his assumptions, this rate of interest is positive.

In some passages Böhm-Bawerk suggested that the rate of interest determined in his model is equal to the marginal product of an extension of the period of production. That created the impression that he had done no more than to establish, in a more roundabout way, what Jevons (1871, ch. vii) had already demonstrated. In other passages, however, Böhm-Bawerk seems to be aware that a change in the method of production involves a change in the value of the capital goods it requires, and that these Wicksell (or revaluation) effects imply that the rate of interest is less than the marginal product of an extension of the period of production. Böhm-Bawerk also obscured his argument by introducing the concept of a subsistence fund, thereby suggesting that his theory was no more than a revamped wages fund theory. Neither these nor other infelicities in his exposition should obscure the fact, however, that the hard core of his argument is the determination of the rate of interest as the property of an intertemporal price structure which in turn is determined by an intertemporal theory of value and allocation in consumption and production.

Böhm-Bawerk's model consciously referred to a stationary state as he wished to show that the rate of interest has something to do with the efficient allocation of resources in stationary as well as in non-stationary states. This comes out most clearly when he considers a socialist economy and demonstrates that it would require a positive rate of interest as does a capitalist economy. He did, however, consider non-stationary states in an interesting comparative static analysis of the effects of an increase in savings, and of technical progress. That he obtained a positive rate of interest in a stationary state is of course due to his assumptions, and no contradiction to Schumpeter's argument (1912) which is based on a somewhat different model (see Böhm-Bawerk (1913) for a discussion of these differences).

The argument sketched on the preceding pages is expounded in Böhm-Bawerk's *Positive Theory* (1889) which he prefaced by a 'History and Critique of Interest Theories' (1884) in which he critically examined earlier (and in later editions also contemporary) attempts to explain the rate of interest. The purpose of this volume has often been misunderstood. It is not a history of the subject which generously corrects mistakes, nor an attempt to differentiate his own product. Rather it is a 'negative theory' (Edgeworth): an attempt to survey the building blocks for his own theory and to pinpoint the pitfalls a satisfactory theory should avoid. Yet it cannot be denied that it is often over-critical. Thus Böhm-Bawerk shows again and again that the rate of interest cannot be said to be *determined by* marginal productivity considerations, but does not add that these nevertheless have a role to play in a more complete explanation. A similar omission occurs when he discusses abstinence or more generally intertemporal preferences.

One of the conclusions Böhm-Bawerk drew from his demonstration is that the existence of the rate of interest is not due to exploitation. It is obvious that on his argument workers can get the whole product of labour only if production were instantaneous. As long as production is roundabout, the present value of the workers' share in the value of the output they have helped to produce is necessarily less than what it would be if production were instantaneous. This is due, of course, to the existence of capital; but Böhm-Bawerk argued that interest would have to be paid irrespective of who owns such capital goods. That was also the gist of his critique of Marx's economics (1896), in which he singled out the labour theory of value as the basis of all errors. Böhm-Bawerk was (apart from Schäffle and Knies) one of the first economists to discuss Marx's economics on a scholarly plane; but he remained curiously blind to Marx's critique of the social institutions of a capitalist society. Although his critique drew a long reply from one of his students (Hilferding, 1904) it was very influential and remained the best analytical performance of its kind until well into the 1950s (see Sweezy, 1949).

Böhm-Bawerk's single-minded concentration on economic phenomena is also evident in his discussion of the role of economic power in markets (1914): in the short run, he argued, economic power may cause deviations from the state of affairs as defined by economic forces; in the long run, however, the latter will prevail. Again he was blind to any changes economic power may cause to the environment in which economic forces operate.

The impact of Böhm-Bawerk's work was immense, but its reception was made difficult by its prolixity and its technical defects, which offered many openings to critics. In essence, Böhm-Bawerk combined elements of neoclassical economic theory with elements of classical economic theory. He was neoclassical in his concern with rational economic behaviour and its consequences for the demand and supply of commodities, their pricing on markets, the forces which bring about equilibrium on markets, and the interaction of different markets. By contrast, classical lines of thought predominate in Böhm-Bawerk's analysis of production. However much he denied any adherence to classical cost theories of value, his view of production and the role of capital and time in it bear the mark of the Ricardian tradition.

The neoclassical part of his argument, in particular his analysis of intertemporal consumer behaviour, was taken up by Irving Fisher (1907, 1930) and developed into a theory of interest which is based on the notion of time preference (which Fisher transformed into a property of utility functions) and the concept of investment opportunities; these Fisher assumed rather than derived, thus cutting away Böhm-Bawerk's analysis of production and the role of capital in it. In this form, which admittedly offers insights into the problem of intertemporal allocation Böhm-Bawerk did not offer, Böhm-Bawerk's intertemporal theory of exchange became part of the heritage of orthodox neo-neoclassical economic theory.

The more classical part of Böhm-Bawerk's model was taken up and elaborated by Wicksell (1893, 1901). In an attempt to free it of its classical garb, Wicksell turned it into a marginal productivity theory of the rate of interest. He ran into difficulties, however, not only over the proper definition of the period of production, but also because his neglect of what Böhm-Bawerk had to say about intertemporal consumer behaviour forced him to assume a given capital stock in order to close his model. Wicksell used what had by then become the standard neoclassical concept of capital as a value sum, as proposed by J.B. Clark (1899), and (with good reason) combatted by Böhm-Bawerk (see Hennings, 1986b). The shortcomings of such an argument, which was before long imputed to Böhm-Bawerk himself, were soon pointed out (see Cassel, 1903, and Garegnani, 1960). Nevertheless Wicksell's interpretation became the standard portrayal of the 'Austrian' theory of capital and interest (see e.g. Lutz, 1956; Dorfman, 1959a, 1959b; Hirshleifer, 1967).

In the 1930s various attempts were made to reformulate Böhm-Bawerk's theory in such a way that it could be used as the basis of a theory of the short-run behaviour of an economy, particularly by Hayek (1931, 1939; and see Hicks, 1967) but also by Hicks (1939, parts iii and iv). This led to an intensive debate in which especially the capital theoretic foundations of his argument were examined, and found wanting (see Kaldor, 1937, and Reetz, 1971, for a survey). There were some attempts at reconstruction (Eucken, 1934; and Strigl, 1934), but the definition of the period of production provided a major stumbling-block. At the same time, Hayek and Knight repeated the debate between Böhm-Bawerk and Clark about the concept of capital on a somewhat different level. Finally Hayek (1941) made a major attempt to get round the difficulties the debate had shown up, and achieved some advances: but in the end his contribution turned out to be the final word that did not persuade anybody. The major difficulty which he did not manage to overcome was the fact that Böhm-Bawerk's construction does not lend itself to dynamic analysis precisely because his classical, macroeconomic approach to production and the role of capital requires an equilibrium approach, and does not provide a suitable basis for a discussion of producer behaviour out of equilibrium, and its dynamics.

More recent restatements of Böhm-Bawerk's argument consequently emphasize its static nature (Weizäcker, 1971; Faber, 1979), but do not really go beyond an exact formulation, in terms of modern capital theory, of some aspects of his theory. By contrast, Hicks (1973) is an innovative attempt to salvage some of the salient features of Böhm-Bawerk's view of production and capital, especially his emphasis on the role of time in production processes, in a modern framework which once more attempts to formulate a dynamic analysis (see also Belloc, 1980; or Magnan de Bornier, 1980). It centres on the concept of a 'transition' from one steady state to another, i.e. a more long-term kind of economic dynamics than was considered in the 1930s; this is a promising approach which proves the vitality of Böhm-Bawerk's ideas.

Böhm-Bawerk posed a problem which had not been seen before in its full importance: the role of the rate of interest in the choice of an optimal method of production when production is roundabout, and its determination in a theory which takes seriously the impossibility to aggregate capital goods in physical terms. The solution he proposed is not without problems. But however much economic theory has progressed, some parts of his argument stand out as landmarks in the development of economic thought. Among them are his discussion of price formation on markets, especially those on which indivisible or finitely divisible commodities are traded, his analysis of time preferences, his analysis of intertemporal exchange, and his demonstration that the rate of interest is no more than a property of intertemporal price structures. His definition of the period of production turned out to be a cul-de-sac, but the possibilities his analysis of the role of time in production offers do not yet seem to have been exhausted.

Finally, the importance of his emphasis on the value aspect of the notion of aggregate capital and its implications has only recently been recognized as a seminal contribution. He can perhaps no longer be accorded the stature of a Ricardo or Marx. But the vitality of his ideas still ranks him among the great economists.

SELECTED WORKS

1881. *Rechte und Verhältnisse vom Standpunkte der volkswirtschaftlichen Güterlehre.* Innsbruck: Wagner. Trans. as 'Whether legal rights and relationships are economic goods' in Böhm-Bawerk (1962).

1884. *Kapital und Kapitalzins. Erste Abteilung: Geschichte und Kritik der Kapitalzins-Theorien.* Innsbruck: Wagner. 2nd edn, 1900; 3rd edn, 1914; 4th edn, Jena: Fischer, 1921. Translation of 1st edn as *Capital and Interest,* London: Macmillan, 1890. Translation of 4th edn as *Capital and Interest,* vol. 1. South Holland, Ill.: Libertarian Press, 1959.

1886. Grundzüge der Theorie des wirthschaftlichen Güterwerthes. *Jahrbücher für Nationalökonomie und Statistik* 13, 1–82 and 477–541. Reprinted separately, London: London School of Economics, 1932.

1889. *Kapital und Kapitalzins. Zweite Abteilung: Positive Theorie des Kapitales.* Innsbruck: Wagner. 2nd edn, 1902; 3rd edn in two volumes 1909 and 1912; 4th edn in two volumes, 1921, Jena: Fischer. Translation of 1st edn as *The Positive Theory of Capital,* London: Macmillan 1891. Translation of 4th edn by G.D. Huncke as *Capital and Interest,* vols 2 and 3, South Holland, Ill.: Libertarian Press, 1959.

1896. Zum Abschluss des Marxschen Systems. In *Staatswissenschaftliche Arbeiten, Festgaben für Karl Knies.* ed. O. von Boenigk, Berlin: Haering. Trans. as *Karl Marx and the Close of his System,* London: Fisher Unwin, 1898. Reprinted in Sweezy (1949). Also trans. as 'Unresolved contradictions in the Marxian economic system' in Böhm-Bawerk (1962).

1913. Eine 'dynamische' Theorie des Kapitalzinses. *Zeitschrift für Volkswirtschaft, Socialpolitik und Verwaltung* 22, 520–85 and 640–57.

1914. Macht oder ökonomisches Gesetz? *Zeitschrift für Volkswirtschaft, Socialpolitik und Verwaltung* 23, 205–271.

1924. *Gesammelte Schriften,* ed. F.X. Weisz, Vienna and Leipzig: Hölder-Pichler-Tempsky.

1926. *Kleinere Abhandlungen über Kapital und Zins.* Vienna and Leipzig: Hölder-Pichler-Tempsky.

1962. *Shorter Classics.* South Holland, Ill.: Libertarian Press.

BIBLIOGRAPHY

Belloc, B. 1980. *Croissance économique et adaption du capital productif.* Paris: Economica.

Cassel, G. 1903. *The Nature and Necessity of Interest.* London: Macmillan.

Clark, J.B. 1899. *The Distribution of Wealth.* New York: Macmillan.

Dorfman, R. 1959a. A graphical exposition of Böhm-Bawerk's interest theory. *Review of Economic Studies* 26, 153–8.

Dorfman, R. 1959b. Waiting and the period of production. *Quarterly Journal of Economics* 73, 351–72.

Eucken, W. 1934. *Kapitaltheoretische Untersuchungen.* 2nd edn, Tübingen: Mohr.

Faber, M. 1979. *Introduction to Modern Austrian Capital Theory.* Berlin: Springer.

Fisher, I. 1907. *The Rate of Interest.* New York: Macmillan.

Fisher, I. 1930. *The Theory of Interest.* New York: Macmillan.

Garegnani, P. 1960. *Il capitale nelle teorie della distribuzione.* Milan: Giuffrè.

Hayek, F.A. von. 1931. *Preise und Produktion*. Vienna: Springer. Trans. as *Prices and Production*, London: Routledge; 2nd edn., New York: A.M. Kelley, 1967.
Hayek, F.A. von. 1939. *Profits, Interest and Investment*. London: Routledge; New York: A.M. Kelley, 1969.
Hayek, F.A. von. 1941. *The Pure Theory of Capital*. London: Routledge; New York: University of Chicago Press, 1962.
Hicks, J.R. 1939. *Value and Capital*. Oxford: Clarendon Press.
Hicks, J.R. 1967. The Hayek story. In J.R. Hicks, *Critical Essays in Monetary Theory*, Oxford: Clarendon Press.
Hicks, J.R. 1973. *Capital and Time*. Oxford: Clarendon Press.
Hilferding, R. 1904. Böhm-Bawerk's Marx-Kritik. In *Marx Studien* 1, ed. M. Adler and R. Hilferding, 1–61. Trans. as 'Böhm-Bawerk's criticism of Marx' in Sweezy (1949).
Hirshleifer, J. 1967. A note on the Böhm-Bawerk/Wicksell theory of interest. *Review of Economic Studies* 34, 191–9.
Jevons, W.S. 1871. *The Theory of Political Economy*. London: Macmillan; New York: Kelley & Millman, 1957.
Kaldor, N. 1937. Annual survey of economic theory: the recent controversies on the theory of capital. *Econometrica* 5, 201–33.
Knies, K. 1873–9. *Geld und Kredit*. 3 vols, Berlin: Weidemann'sche Buchhandlung.
Kuenne, R.E. 1971. *Eugen von Böhm-Bawerk*. New York and London: Columbia University Press.
Lutz, F.A. 1956. *Zinstheorie*. Tübingen: Mohr. Trans. as *The Theory of Interest*. Dordrecht: Reidel, 1967.
Magnan de Bornier, J. 1980. *Economie de la traverse*. Paris: Economica.
Menger, C. 1871. *Grundsätze der Volkswirthschaftslehre*. Vienna: Braumüller. Trans. as *Principles of Economics*, Glencoe, Ill.: Free Press, 1951.
Nuti, D.M. 1974. On the rates of return of investment. *Kyklos* 27, 345–69.
Reetz, N. 1971. *Produktionsfunktion und Produktionsperiode*. Göttingen: Schwartz.
Schäffle, A.E.F. 1870. *Kapitalismus und Sozialismus*. Tübingen: Laupp.
Schumpeter, J.A. 1912. *Theorie der wirtschaftlichen Entwicklung*. Leipzig: Duncker & Humblot. Trans. as *The Theory of Economic Development*, Cambridge, Mass.: Harvard University Press, 1934.
Schumpeter, J.A. 1914. Das wissenschaftliche Lebenswerk Eugen von Böhm-Bawerks. *Zeitschrift für Volkswirtschaft, Socialpolitik und Verwaltung* 23, 454–528. Trans. as ch. 6 in *Ten Great Economists*, ed. J.A. Schumpeter, London: Allen & Unwin, 1952.
Schumpeter, J.A. 1925. Eugen von Böhm-Bawerk. *Neue österreichische Biographie 1815–1918*, 2, 63–80.
Stigler, G.J. 1941. *Production and Distribution Theories*. New York: Macmillan.
Strigl, R. von. 1934. *Kapital und Producktion*. Vienna: Springer.
Sweezy, P.M. (ed.) 1949. *Karl Marx and the Close of his System by Eugen von Böhm-Bawerk and Böhm-Bawerk's Criticism of Marx*. New York: Kelley.
Weizsäcker, C.C. von. 1971. *Steady State Capital Theory*. Berlin: Springer.
Wicksell, K. 1893. *Über Wert Kapital und Rente nach neueren nationalökonomischen Theorien*. Jena: Fischer. Trans. as *Value, Capital and Rent*, London: Allen & Unwin, 1954; New York: Rinehart, 1954.
Wicksell, K. 1901. *Föreläsningar i Nationalekonomi. Vol. I: Teoretisk Nationalekonomi*. Lund: Berlinska Boktryckeriet. Trans. as *Lectures on Political Economy*, Vol. 1, *General Theory*, London: Routledge, 1934; New York: A.M. Kelley, 1967.
Wicksell, K. 1911. Böhm-Bawerks kapitalteori och kritiken därav. *Ekonomisk Tidskrift* 13, 39–49. Trans. in K. Wicksell, *Selected Papers on Economic Theory*, London: Allen & Unwin, 1958; Cambridge, Mass.: Harvard University Press.
Wicksell, K. 1914. Lexis och Böhm-Bawerk. *Ekonomisk Tidskrift* 16, 294–300, 322–34.

Capital as a factor of production

K.H. HENNINGS

The role played by capital in production has frequently been in dispute: 'When economists reach agreement on the theory of capital they will shortly reach agreement on everything else' (Bliss, 1975, p. vii). Disagreements are due as much to divergent definitions, or uses, of the term 'capital' as to different views about what should be considered a factor of production. But above all there have been differing views about whether, and in what sense, capital can be said to be productive. In particular, there has been disagreement about whether it can be said that a more capital-intensive production method is more productive than a less capital-intensive one. Preclassical, classical, neoclassical and neo-neoclassical economic theory have given different answers to these questions. These will be considered below, but the discussion will be confined to the role of capital as a factor of production. It should be noted in particular that the problem of why capital earns its owner an income depends as much on the social institution of ownership and the institutional organization of production as on the role capital plays in production. It is only the latter, in a sense technical, problem which will be addressed here.

TERMINOLOGY. Capital goods are produced commodities which are required for production no matter how much or how little they are subject to wear and tear. A stock (at a point of time; see Fisher, 1906) of different capital goods is a *capital*; this concept is to be taken in a vector sense. As long as they are required in production, all capital goods can be valued, even when they are not traded on markets, as many of them are. Because of their heterogeneity, different capital goods cannot be aggregated, but their values can. A *capital value* is therefore the sum of the capital values of those capital goods which constitute a capital. Note that this is a book-keeping term, which depends on the valuation of the capital goods involved; the capital value can change although there is no change in the stock of capital goods. The term *money capital* will be used in a similar sense, but with a somewhat different connotation: it denotes the sum of money necessary to buy a specified stock of capital goods. Real counterparts in a scalar sense to a given capital value or money capital can be constructed in principle (Hicks, 1974, p. 151), but not in an unambiguous manner.

PRODUCTION: BASIC NOTIONS. Production is the transformation of inputs into outputs. Inputs are those things which need to be increased in order to obtain more output by the same method of production, where the latter is defined as a blueprint which details what inputs are required when and in which proportions to produce a unit bundle of outputs. As there may be more than one method to produce the same unit bundle of outputs, a production process is defined as a particular method of production to produce a particular unit bundle of outputs. A production process always uses inputs in fixed proportions; variable proportions are represented by different production processes. If there exist various different production processes with which the same unit bundle of outputs can be produced, they will differ in the proportions in which they use various inputs; but in general it will not be possible to compare them from a purely technical point of view. Different production processes are comparable only if their costs are computed and related to the value of the outputs obtained. In general, however, any ordering obtained in this way need not be unique: two different production processes may have the same unit costs. Moreover, if the prices of inputs change a given ordering need not be preserved. Such difficulties affect the choice between different production processes; they do not, however, affect the role of capital in production, or its status as a factor of production.

Production typically is roundabout, i.e. proceeds in stages: what is produced as output in one production process is used as an input (alongside others) in another. If all these intermediate products (outputs which are used as inputs) are specific in the sense that they have only one possible use, all production processes required to produce a particular bundle of outputs can be strung together into a sequence of production processes. Consolidating all stages, one can view the sequence as transforming 'primary' inputs into 'final' outputs. Here primary inputs are those which are not produced within the sequence of production processes, if indeed they can be produced at all; final outputs are those which are not used, or used up, within the sequence.

Not all intermediate products are specific in the sense that they have only one possible use. In this case all interlocking sequences can be combined into a production system which again can be viewed as transforming primary inputs into final outputs. Without loss of generality one can assume that such a production system comprises all production processes in operation in an economy. Consolidating them amounts to adopting a 'black box' view of production. Disregarding the internal structure of the production system and of the production processes which constitute it, one links directly primary inputs to final outputs, and disregards all inputs produced and used, or used up, within the production system. The advantage of this procedure is that it reduces the number of inputs to be considered.

109

The definition of what is a primary input, or a final output, depends on the level of aggregation as well as the nature of the production processes involved. Production on a barren island will require many inputs as primary ones which are intermediate products in a production system comprising all production processes operating in a continent rich in resources. Similarly the final outputs produced by the island economy's production system may be confined to what are intermediate products in the production system of a continent.

By definition, an increase in output can only be obtained by an increase in inputs in fixed proportions. From this one can infer that all required inputs together are productive, and have a non-negative marginal production. This cannot, however, be inferred for any single input. This can only be done if either there are at least two different production processes for the production of the same unit bundle of outputs because then it is possible to calculate the marginal net value product of an input (Bliss, 1975, ch. 5); or if there are alternative uses for all inputs in production processes which produce other unit bundles of outputs (Uzawa, 1958). Only when there exists only one production process for a particular unit bundle of outputs and there are no alternative uses for some of the inputs it requires is it impossible to calculate their marginal contribution to the outputs obtained individually; it is of course still possible to calculate their contribution as a group of inputs.

FACTORS OF PRODUCTION. In modern usage, all primary inputs can be called 'factors of production'. Conventionally, however, primary inputs are considered, following Senior (1836), the services of agents or stocks, and the term 'factor of production' is reserved for the latter. If they are the services of natural agents or human beings, they are called 'original factors of production'; they are called simply 'factors of production' if they also include the services of stocks of durable commodities. Factors of production can therefore be defined as those agents or durable stocks the services of which are primary inputs in production processes.

Factors of production are productive and have a non-negative marginal product if their services are productive and have a non-negative marginal product.

The definition of factors of production just given is reasonably precise as far as natural agents and human beings are concerned. Land and labour have been considered factors of production at least since Petty (1662). Land was often understood, if tacitly, to include all beneficial powers of nature; the term 'natural agents' was introduced by Senior (1836). In preclassical theory durable stocks were called simply 'stocks' (see, e.g., Barbon, 1690), but usage of the term was often confined to trade and commerce. When production came to be seen as the dominant economic activity, produced means of production, considered as a factor of production, came to be called 'capital'. This term had been in use for a long time (see Hohoff, 1818–19; Salin, 1930; Assel, 1953), but now acquired a new meaning, thus inviting confusion and controversy. It will be useful, therefore, to trace historically the use made of that term, and the notions attached to it.

PRECLASSICAL THEORIES OF CAPITAL AND PRODUCTION. There is very little about production and its relation to capital in economic writings before the mid-18th century. Barbon (1690) provides an early, but singular, instance of an analysis in which a surplus is seen to arise from the use of what he calls a 'stock' (of capital goods) in trade as well as in the production of commodities. In a similar vein, Hume used the term 'stock' somewhat indiscriminately to denote both a store of commodities and a sum of money. But he did distinguish, as had Barbon, between profits from 'stock' and interest on money (1752, p. 313), thus separating the investment of money from the productive use of 'stock', e.g. capital goods, although he is none too clear about the latter.

The Physiocrats were probably the first to develop a clear view of production and the role of capital in it. But they did not use the term 'capital'. Cantillon (1755) strongly emphasized the need for accumulated sums of money required to buy stocks of goods in which to trade, or with which to produce. But he called them 'funds' not 'capital'. Thus he speaks of the farmer who needs to have enough funds (*assez de fond*) to conduct his business. Quesnay used the term 'advances' (*avances*) in a similar way in the sense of money capital. Behind his usage is a clearly drawn picture of agricultural production which uses land and labour to produce output, and needs money capital to finance the lag between the expenditure on inputs and the sale of the output obtained. Probably deliberately, Quesnay eschewed the term 'capital'. Where he used it (1766b), he spoke explicitly of money capital (*capital d'argent*), but conceived it as invested in buildings, implements, stores of grain, cattle, and so on (1766a, pp. 172–3). These, however, he clearly conceived as productive. Moreover, his argument centres on the idea that larger advances would permit more productive production methods to be used (see Eltis, 1984, chs. 1 and 2).

Turgot (1770) was the first to develop a specific theory of capital as a factor in production when, possibly under the influence of Hume's ideas, he generalized Quesnay's theory. Quesnay had shown that advances were necessary for agricultural production. Turgot, in an attempt to develop Quesnay's theory of a society dominated by agriculture into a theory of a commercial society, places commerce and manufacture on an equal footing with agricultural production, and emphasized that advances are required in all branches of economic activity. Such advances are paid out of capital, which is defined as 'accumulated values' (1770, § LVIII). If account is taken of the various degrees of risks involved, the rates of return on all possible investments are equalized by competition between the owners of the various capitals (Turgot uses the plural, *capitaux*) such that the rate of interest can 'be regarded as a kind of thermometer of the abundance or scarcity of capitals in a Nation, and of the extent of the enterprises of all kinds in which it may engage' (1770, § LXXXIX). At the same time, Turgot argues emphatically that some return on all these kinds of investment is necessary in order to keep production on the same level; if the rate of return were lowered, capitals would be withdrawn, and production could not be kept on the same level as before (1770, § XCVI). Thus to Turgot 'capitals' are money capital. Money capital is required because production is roundabout and thus needs

111

capital goods as well as original factors of production. Like Quesnay, Turgot assumed that larger amounts of money capital make possible higher levels of production. One might be inclined to argue that therefore money capital, i.e. advances, are productive; but although Turgot is not entirely clear on this point it seems that he considered not so much advances as the capital goods which represent them as productive.

THE CLASSICAL THEORY OF CAPITAL AND PRODUCTION. The classical view of the role of capital in production was worked out by Adam Smith. He began by emphasizing the division of labour, but then switched to a detailed consideration 'Of the Nature, Accumulation, and Employment of Stock' (1776, book II) in which he effectively adopted the theory put forward by Quesnay and Turgot. His attempts to integrate these two approaches were not entirely successful (Bowley, 1976); although the division of labour retained its status as a device which enhances the productivity of labour in classical economic theory, the emphasis was shifted to the accumulation of capital as the prime force making for growth. This was of course linked to the idea that production needs advances, and the proposition that labour was the more productive the larger these advances. Smith also changed the emphasis in another respect: he formally defined 'capital' as that part of a person's stock of commodities which is expected to yield an income. Smith described its function as assisting labour in production: fixed capital (machines, buildings, land improvements, and 'acquired and useful abilities') 'facilitates' labour by increasing its effectiveness; circulating capital (money, raw materials, goods in process and goods in stock) 'abridges' by providing (material) advances.

This distinction is ambiguous, but characteristic for Smith's position. Fixed capital, he argued, yields an income, i.e. is productive, by being used 'without changing masters': while circulating capital needs to be either given up (in trade) or be destroyed (in production) in order to be productive (1776, pp. 279–83). What is considered are capital goods; but only money capital can circulate in the way Smith described. The two approaches can be reconciled; but the way in which Smith expressed himself invited confusion between money capital on the one hand, and capital in the sense of capital goods on the other. In fact, Smith needed both concepts. James Mill (1821), Rae (1834) and other classical writers often used the term 'instrument' when emphasizing that they meant capital goods, and continued to speak of capital in the sense of money capital. Money capital played indeed an important role in classical economic thought for it permitted classical writers to argue, in a rather loose way, that production methods were the more productive, the more money capital they required. It is for this reason that Hicks (1974) called them 'Fundists'. At the same time, however, they also considered the role of capital goods in production processes (Sraffa, 1960) and thus maintained a 'real capital doctrine' (Corry, 1962, p. 18).

The view that capital assists labour was attacked by Lauderdale (1804), who pointed out that capital could, and frequently did, supplant labour when circulating capital was substituted for fixed capital. This initiated the debate on the 'machinery question', and confirmed the role of capital as a factor of production: what can supplant a factor of production surely must be considered as belonging to the same species.

Smith had separated a person's stock of commodities into durable consumer goods and capital by requiring that the latter be expected to earn an income. This led to many attempts to show that not only capital goods used in production are expected to yield an income (i.e. Hermann, 1832, or Menger, 1888). These discussions often confused the role of money capital in investment processes with the role of capital goods in production processes, and contributed to the survival of the concept of money capital as a factor of production referred to above.

The view that production requires advances in the form of capital goods was so dominant that the role of fixed capital was often pushed into the background. Thus Ricardo spoke of production as 'the united application of labour, machinery, and capital' (1817, p. 5), thus equating capital with circulating capital. As Smith had subsumed the consumer goods required for the maintenance of labour under circulating capital stocks, this particular part of the total stock of commodities in an economy acquired, under the name of the 'wages fund', a pivotal role in all discussions of the role of capital in production. Following a precedent set by Smith, the wage fund was seen to be derived from, and increased by, saving, i.e. non-consumption or 'abstinence', as Senior (1836) was to call it. Destined to supply the consumption goods required as advances while production processes continue, the concept was used as a theory of wage determination on the assumption that the wages fund was given at least in the short run and thus determines the wage level when workers compete freely for employment.

In spite of all the attention Smith gave to the accumulation of capital as a factor making for economic growth, he reserved a special role for human labour as the prime factor of production, especially in those passages in which he set out his conjectural history. This emphasis, which is clearly based on the view that production requires advances, remained a feature of the classical theory of capital, and was a mainstay of the labour theory of value as developed by Ricardo and others. It is symptomatic that from this point of view the use of 'machinery and other fixed and durable capital' was considered no more than an (admittedly considerable) modification of the labour theory of value by Ricardo (1818, p. 30). More radical writers, such as Hodgskin (1827) emphasized the notion of capital goods as 'stored-up' labour (i.e. outputs produced by past labour) that had been worked out by James Mill (1821) and Ricardo (1817) and on its basis denied fixed capital the status as a factor of production.

The special role Smith has reserved for labour did not prevent him from juxtaposing labour, stock and land to parallel wages, profits and rent (1776, p. 69). This juxtaposition was elaborated into a strict parallelism between factors of production and their earnings by Say (1814) which became generally accepted by the middle of the 19th century. Thus when J.S. Mill (1848) summarized the classical theory of capital into his four propositions, he still adhered to the view that production required advances in the form of capital goods. But when he comes to discuss the laws of increase of factors of production, he treats them on an equal footing (though in exactly the order Smith had listed them: and not the land–labour–capital order which Say had made familiar). At the same time, however, Mill often gives the impression that he means money capital when he speaks of 'capital', especially in those passages in which he argues that competition will establish a uniform rate of return on capital because capital will be transferred from one industry to another.

In a similar way Marx (1867) used the term capital to mean both a stock of commodities, and a sum of values. In addition, Marx insisted that capital goods are capital only in a capitalistic society, and thus used the term also to describe a particular organization of production in society.

Finally, the view that production requires advances in the form of capital goods which Smith had expounded, and which most classical writers accepted, was developed by a few of them into a theory which strongly emphasized the time element in production. There are some traces of this in Ricardo (1817), especially in his recognition that all the difficulties he encountered in his theory of value are due to the temporal aspect of production processes. The view was worked out in detail by Rae (1834), by Longfield (1834), and also by Senior (1836). Their work foreshadows one aspect of the neoclassical theory of capital.

Classical economic theory considered three factors of production: land, labour, and capital. Each had its own dimension: land was a stock, labour a flow, and capital was money capital in the form of a stock of capital goods. In the original conception their standing was not equal: labour worked on land with the help of capital. Hence the capital intensity of production mattered: the more money capital was invested, the more productive was labour in its efforts to work up the bounty of nature into consumable output. These notions were not, however, made very precise: that was left for neoclassical theorists. Thünen's early discussion of the marginal productivity of capital (1850) remained an exception.

THE NEOCLASSICAL THEORY OF CAPITAL AND PRODUCTION. Neoclassical economic theory was not a coherent construct: up to the 1930s there were different versions of neoclassical theory as far as the treatment of capital as a factor of production is concerned (Stigler, 1941).

Perhaps the most contentious version was the Austrian one as worked out by Böhm-Bawerk (1889). To some extent it had been foreshadowed by Jevons (1871), even though Jevons had little to say about production. But there is a clear picture in Jevons of the necessity of money capital which is 'invested' in the form of advances in time-consuming production processes. What is more, Jevons formulated, very much *ad hoc*, a temporal production function which postulated that there are diminishing marginal returns to the length of investment of such advances: and used it to derive the marginal product of an extension of that length, which clearly is a measure for the capital intensity of production.

Böhm-Bawerk, by contrast, consciously and explicitly developed a theory of production. It very much follows classical lines: production requires time, and hence needs advances in the form of capital goods. Capital goods are seen as produced means of production, and at the same time as stored-up land-and-labour, even though they derive their value not, as the classics had maintained, from the fact that they represent land and labour services spent in the past: but from their prospective usefulness in the production of future output. Nevertheless Böhm-Bawerk emphatically denied that capital goods can be productive, and insisted that only the production processes which they make possible are productive. Although this could have meant that the notion of productiveness was transferred from factors of production to production processes, Böhm-Bawerk did not take this step. He seems to begin by saying that only land and labour should be called productive, and ends by postulating something very much like a productivity of the length of the period of production. As in Jevons (1871), this view is based on a temporal production function in which the degree of roundaboutness of production processes is explicitly taken as a measure for the capital intensity of the production processes in operation. Böhm-Bawerk attempted to overcome in this manner the difficulty of deriving any such measure from diverse sets of capital goods. The roundaboutness of production processes was turned into a variable which was chosen by profit-maximizing entrepreneurs subject to a given amount of money capital.

The relationship of this construction to classical economic thought is obvious. Nevertheless Böhm-Bawerk's attempt to provide a temporal theory of production based on the notion of capital as a derived factor of production, or intermediate good, turned out to be very contentious. The theory of interest which he had been built upon it was turned into what became the standard (neoclassical) theory of interest by Fisher (1907, 1930) – but only after it had been cut loose from its production-theoretic underpinnings: and after Fisher had substituted instead an analysis of investment opportunities based on the concept of money capital. Various attempts to reformulate Böhm-Bawerk's theory of the role of capital in production (Wicksell, 1893; Strigl, 1934; Hayek, 1940) generated much debate, but did not manage to rescue it.

The Austrian theory of capital is much more traditional than other versions of neoclassical theory which gave up the 'advances' view of capital. Thus Wicksteed (1894) placed all factors of production on an equal footing, including all kinds of capital goods, and postulated that 'The Product being a function of the factors of production we have $P = f(a, b, c, ...)$' (1894, p. 4) without even mentioning whether production takes time or not. Being considered akin to any other input in this respect, capital goods are of course productive; but nothing can be said about the capital intensity of production. Marshall (1890) argued in a similar way, although he kept to the classical tradition by reserving a place for money capital alongside the capital goods used in production. Taking up a distinction first made, it seems, by Menger (1888, p. 44), Marshall distinguished between capital goods which earn quasi-rents, and money capital which earns interest. In essence this is the distinction between production and investment: capital goods are used in production, and if used productively, earn quasi-rents; money capital is invested, and if invested successfully, earns interest. Clark (1899) equally rejected the advances view of production. In his view, production did not require advances once production processes were properly set up, or synchronized. As in Wicksteed, capital is a factor of production on an equal footing with land or labour. At the same time, Clark separated clearly between material capital goods or produced means of production, on the one hand, and capital as a 'quantum of productive wealth' (1899, p. 119), measured in money, which is invested in capital goods. Although Clark calls this 'a material entity' (1899, p. 119), his 'capital' is money capital, just as it was in Marshall (or Menger for that matter). Knight (1933) continued in this vein, but emphasized money capital, considered as a 'material entity', so much that capital goods were almost lost sight of. As a result, 'capital' came to be seen more and more as a homogeneous mass which was created by saving decisions, which could be invested in one industry and transferred to another, which was productive in the sense that it has a non-negative marginal product if used properly, and which guaranteed higher productivity if employed in larger amounts in relation to other factors of production. Not surprisingly, this conception was attacked by the heirs to the Austrian tradition in capital theory, especially Hayek (1936, 1940), as a 'mythology of capital'. But their own position was so much bound up with the deprecated notion of a period of production that Knight's conception (1933, 1934, 1935, 1936) became the dominant doctrine.

The notion of capital as a 'material entity' was formulated rigorously by Pigou, who provided a sophisticated definition of a capital stock, consisting of heterogeneous capital goods, which 'is capable of maintaining its quantity while altering its form' (1935, p. 239). This was possible only by making some rather strong assumptions on the way the capital stock was maintained. Thus Pigou assumed, among other things, that any item of a constant capital stock that needs to be replaced is replaced by another capital good yielding equal quasi-rents at the time of replacement. Later changes in quasi-rents are disregarded. While such assumptions may be objected to, they do make it possible in principle to give precise meaning to the notion of a capital stock as a changing 'material entity' without aggregating heterogeneous capital goods, i.e. without negating its quality as a vector.

Walras (1874–7) and Pareto (1909) treated capital very much as Wicksteed had done: as yet another factor of production in a production system which was fully synchronized and which was not in need of advances. As they used production functions and thus assumed, as Wicksteed had done, that there always exist many production processes for the production of the same unit bundle of outputs, the productivity of capital goods was no problem for them. But because they espoused the black box view of production they somewhat lost sight of the internal structure of production, and hence of the character of capital goods as produced means of production: capital goods are in their conceptual scheme simply part of the endowment which economic agents use to maximize their satisfaction. Moreover they could not form a notion of the capital intensity of production as they had no way of aggregating capital goods in an unambiguous manner.

Wicksell, finally, in his later treatment of the matter (1901) attempted to provide a synthesis of neoclassical capital theory by combining the general equilibrium framework of Walras and Pareto with the Austrian view of production as a time-consuming process. This led him to emphasize capital goods and their productivity. But when he came to close his system he took refuge, as Böhm-Bawerk had done, in the idea of a given fund of money capital. The importance of a given fund of money capital which acted as a constraint on entrepreneurial choices between different degrees of roundaboutness of production processes was also emphasized by Schumpeter (1911) and Cassel (1918).

Neoclassical economists have in common that they attempted to formulate a theory of production; but they differed in their conceptions (Hennings, 1985). Böhm-Bawerk and those who followed him made an attempt to formulate more precisely what they saw as the gist of the classical theory of the role of capital in production: but their efforts were not generally accepted. All other neoclassical writers except Wicksell jettisoned the advances view of capital, and were in consequence faced with the necessity of formulating a measure for the capital intensity of production if they wished to uphold the proposition that more capital-intensive methods of production were more productive. Wicksteed as well as Walras and Pareto did not do so, and simply refrained from making such statements. Marshall, Clark, and Knight in one way or another attempted to solve the problem by taking refuge in a concept of capital which is in essence a notion of money capital, and which cannot unambiguously serve for that purpose. Only Pigou formulated an unambiguous concept of capital as a changeable 'material entity'.

THE NEO-NEOCLASSICAL THEORY OF CAPITAL IN PRODUCTION. The neo-neoclassical view of the role of capital in production is based on the work of Viner (1930), Stackelberg (1932), Schneider (1934) and others, who worked out the theory of production as well as a theory of production costs, and the syntheses later provided by Hicks (1939) and Samuelson (1947) of the various neoclassical theories on the basis of the Walras–Pareto theory of general equilibrium (Arrow and Hahn, 1971). Originally strongly microeconomic in nature, capital goods held the stage. But as this theory was essentially static, little thought was given to dynamic considerations (Hicks (1939) was the exception), and hence to the problems that arise if concrete capital goods are shifted from one industry to another. Where such problems came up, refuge was taken in the Clark–Knight conception of capital as a fairly homogeneous and amorphous mass which could take on different forms. With the growth of macroeconomic one-sector thinking – Hicks (1932) is one of the earliest examples in this part of economic theory – this conception was more and more resorted to. It received the seal of approval in Samuelson's textbook (1948), and in numerous empirical studies based on the macroeconomic production function first proposed by Cobb and Douglas (1928). It was of course realized that capital consisted of capital goods: but their aggregation into a more or less homogeneous aggregate was considered an index number problem which could be solved in principle as well as in practice. It was against these notions that opposition arose in the 1950s and 1960s.

RECENT DEBATES. As Joan Robinson (1954, 1956) pointed out, the Clark–Knight concept of capital cannot serve in a macroeconomic production function à la Cobb–Douglas because it is essentially a monetary measure. Surprisingly, this contention engendered a major debate in capital theory. Essentially two answers were given to Robinson's objection. On the one hand it was argued that one should search for appropriate indices that can be used to aggregate heterogeneous capital goods into a scalar measure (Champernowne, 1954).

This created a specialist literature on aggregation problems which demonstrates that in general conditions for consistent aggregation are rather restrictive, although in many cases appropriate indices exist (Green, 1964). On the other hand, it was argued that macroeconomic analyses should be abandoned in favour of microeconomic ones if heterogeneity (which after all exists in land and labour as well as in capital goods) is the issue (Swan, 1962).

In the course of the debates referred to above it was demonstrated that the value paradoxes Joan Robinson had pointed out may invalidate the idea that different production processes can be brought into a continuous ordering which corresponds to their respective capital intensities. While this point was eventually accepted, its importance is still under dispute (see Harcourt (1972) and Blaug (1974) for summaries and evaluations from divergent points of view). To some, such demonstrations completely invalidate neoclassical and in particular neo-neoclassical economic theory, because both are considered to be founded on the idea that marginal products of factors of production need to be calculated on the basis of technical data alone. Others accept such demonstrations as exceptions to a general rule. What is sometimes lost sight of in these assessments is the fact that reswitching of production processes, capital revaluations, Wicksell effects, *et hoc genus omne* do not invalidate all propositions in capital theory (whether neoclassical or not). One can well do without capital in the sense of capital value (i.e. as a scalar magnitude) for some purposes (see, e.g. Nuti, 1970). Moreover, it should be appreciated that Robinson's objections do not apply to Pigou's notion of capital as a changeable 'material entity' even though it is not at all obvious that such a concept would serve well in a macroeconomic production function.

Another attack on neoclassical capital theory was made by Garegnani (1960, 1970, and 1976). The gist of his argument seems to be that the Walrasian model of general equilibrium, if properly extended to include the production of capital goods, cannot generate equilibrium as well as a unique rate of return on all capital goods for all possible initial endowments. As Garegnani has not specified the dynamic adjustment processes he envisages, his claim is difficult to adjudicate. Nor is it clear in what respect, if any, it invalidates received notions of the role of capital in production processes. Recent debates (Hahn, 1982; Duménil and Lévy, 1985) have not thrown much light on these issues.

CONCLUSION. Capital always consists of heterogeneous capital goods; indeed it is useful precisely because goods are heterogeneous and specific in the sense that they cannot be used for all purposes. Attempts to represent them by some kind of aggregate are useful only if they preserve this aspect of capital goods. In classical economic theory the notion of advances was used as such an aggregate, although in a rather loose fashion, with an awareness of the heterogeneity of the capital goods that assisted labour in time-consuming production. Austrian neoclassical economic theory attempted unsuccessfully to make this notion more precise in the form of a temporal theory of production. Non-Austrian neoclassical and neo-neoclassical economic theory sacrificed the heterogeneity capital goods that assisted labour in time-consuming production. Austrian neoclassical economic theory attempted unsuccessfully to make this notion more precise in the form of a temporal theory of production. Non-Austrian goods in terms of prospective output is a 'theoretical anomaly'; it is nevertheless appropriate in view of their character as produced means of production. It is not surprising, therefore, that anomalies result when such concepts are used. The alternative is obviously to analyse the role of capital goods in a framework which admits their heterogeneity and permits them to be used for different purposes, i.e. in a general equilibrium framework. Such analyses have so far been mainly confined to stationary states. Some of the essential characteristics of capital goods, however, such as their specificity, are of importance only in non-stationary states. Much remains to be done, therefore, before the role of capital and of capital goods as factors of production can be said to be completely elucidated.

BIBLIOGRAPHY

Arrow, K.J. and Hahn, F.H. 1971. *General Competitive Analysis*. San Francisco: Holden Day; Edinburgh: Oliver & Boyd.

Assel, H.G. 1953. Der Kapitalbegriff und die Kapitallehre bis zum Beginn der Neuzeit. *Wirtschaft und Gesellung. Festschrift für Hans Proesler zu seinem 65. Geburtstag.* Erlangen.

[Barbon, N.] 1690. *A Discourse on Trade.* By N.B.M.D. London: Milbourn for the Author.

Blaug, M. 1974. *The Cambridge Revolution: Success or Failure?* London: Institute of Economic Affairs.

Bliss, C.J. 1975. *Capital Theory and the Distribution of Income.* Amsterdam and Oxford: North-Holland Publishing Company. Böhm-Bawerk, E. von. 1889. *Kapital und Kapitalzins. Zweite Abteilung: Positive Theorie des Kapitales.* Innsbruck: Wagner. Trans. as *The Positive Theory of Capital,* London: Macmillan, 1891.

Bowley, M. 1975. Some aspects of the treatment of capital in 'The Wealth of Nations'. In *Essays on Adam Smith,* ed. A.S. Skinner and T. Wilson, Oxford: Clarendon Press.

Cantillon, R. 1755. *Essai sur la nature du commerce en général.* Londres: Gyles. Edited with an English translation by Henry Higgs, London: Cass, 1959.

Cassel, G. 1918. *Theoretische Sozialökonomie.* Leipzig: Deichert. Trans. as *Theory of Social Economy,* London: Fischer Unwin, 1923.

Champernowne, D.G. 1954. The production function and the theory of capital: a comment. *Review of Economic Studies* 21, 112–35.

Clark, J.B. 1899. *The Distribution of Wealth.* New York: Macmillan.

Cobb, C.W. and Douglas, P.H. 1928. A theory of production. *American Economic Review* 18, March, 139–65.

Corry, B.A. 1962. *Money, Saving and Investment in English Economics 1800–1850.* London: Macmillan; New York: St. Martin's Press.

Duménil, G. and Lévy, D. 1985. The classicals and the neoclassicals: a rejoinder to Frank Hahn. *Cambridge Journal of Economics* 9, 327–45.

Eltis, W. 1984. *The Classical Theory of Economic Growth*. London: Macmillan; New York: St. Martin's Press.

Fisher, I. 1906. *The Nature of Capital and Income*. New York: Macmillan.

Fisher, I. 1907. *The Rate of Interest*. New York: Macmillan.

Fisher, I. 1930. *The Theory of Interest*. New York: Macmillan.

Garegnani, P. 1960. *Il capitale nelle teorie della distribuzione*. Milano: Guiffrè. Trans. as *Le capital dans les théories de la répartition*, Paris: Presses Universitaires de Grenoble et François Maspero, 1980.

Garegnani, P. 1970. Heterogeneous capital, the production function and the theory of distribution. *Review of Economic Studies* 37, 407–36.

Garegnani, P. 1976. On a change in the notion of equilibrium in recent work on value and distribution. In *Essays in Modern Capital Theory*, ed. M. Brown, K. Sato and P. Zarembka, Amsterdam, New York, Oxford: North-Holland.

Green, H.A.J. 1964. *Aggregation in Economic Analysis*. Princeton: Princeton University Press.

Hahn, F.H. 1982. The neo-Ricardians. *Cambridge Journal of Economics* 6, 353–74.

Harcourt, G.C. 1972. *Some Cambridge Controversies in the Theory of Capital*. Cambridge and New York: Cambridge University Press.

Hayek, F.A. von. 1936. The mythology of capital. *Quarterly Journal of Economics* 50, February, 199–228.

Hayek, F.A. von. 1940. *The Pure Theory of Capital*. London: Routledge & Kegan Paul; New York: University of Chicago Press, 1962.

Hennings, K.H. 1985. The exchange paradigm and the theory of production and distribution. In *Foundations of Economics*, ed. M. Baranzini and R. Scazzieri, Oxford: Blackwell.

Hermann, F.B.W. 1832. *Staatswirthschaftliche Untersuchungen*. Munich: Weber.

Hicks, J.R. 1932. *The Theory of Wages*. London: Macmillan. 1963; New York: St. Martin's Press.

Hicks, J.R. 1939. *Value and Capital*. Oxford: Clarendon Press.

Hicks, J.R. 1974. Capital controversies, ancient and modern. *American Economic Review* 64, May, 307–16. Reprinted in J.R. Hicks, *Economic Perspectives*, Oxford: Clarendon Press, 1977; New York: Oxford University Press.

[Hodgskin, T.] 1827. *Popular Political Economy*. London: Tait and Wait.

Hohoff, W. 1819–19. Zur Geschichte des Wortes und Begriffes 'Kapital'. *Vierteljahrshefte für Sozial- und Wirtschaftsgeschichte* 14, 554–74 and 15, 281–310.

Hume, D. 1752. Of Interest. *Political Discourses*. Edinburgh: Fleming. Reprinted in D. Hume, *Essays Moral, Political and Literary*, Oxford: Oxford University Press, 1963.

Jevons, W.S. 1871. *The Theory of Political Economy*. London: Macmillan; 5th edn, New York: Kelley & Millman, 1957.

Knight, F.H. 1933. Capitalistic production, time and the rate of return. In *Economic Essays in Honour of Gustav Cassel*, London: George Allen & Unwin.

Knight, F.H. 1934. Capital, time, and the interest rate. *Economica*, NS 1, August, 257–86.

Knight, F.H. 1935. Professor Hayek and the theory of investment. *Economic Journal* 45, March, 75–94.

Knight, F.H. 1936. The quantity of capital and the rate of interest. *Journal of Political Economy* 44, August, 433–63, and October, 612–42.

Lauderdale, J. Maitland, 8th Earl of. 1804. *An Inquiry into the Nature and Origin of Public Wealth.* Edinburgh: Constable.

Longfield, M. 1834. *Lectures on Political Economy.* Dublin: Milliken.

Marshall, A. 1890. *Principles of Economics.* London: Macmillan; 8th edn., New York: Macmillan, 1956.

Marx, K. 1867–94. *Das Kapital.* 3 vols, Hamburg: Meisner. Trans. as *Capital*, 3 vols, Chicago: Kerr, 1906–9.

Menger, C. 1888. Zur des Kapitals. *Jahrbücher für Nationalökonomie und Statistik*, NF 17(51), 1–49.

Mill, J. 1821. *Elements of Political Economy.* London: Baldwin, Cradock and Joy.

Mill, J.S. 1848. *Principles of Political Economy.* London: Longmans, Green; New York: A.M. Kelley, 1965.

Nuti, D.M. 1970. Capitalism, socialism, and steady growth. *Economic Journal* 80, March, 32–57.

Pareto, V. 1909. *Manuel d'économie politique.* Paris: Giard & Brière. Trans. as *Manual of Political Economy*, London: Macmillan, 1972.

Petty, W. 1662. *A Treatise of Taxes and Contributions.* London: Brooke. Reprinted in *The Economic Writings of Sir William Petty*, ed. C.H. Hull, Cambridge: Cambridge University Press, 1899, Vol. 1.

Pigou, A.C. 1935. Net income and capital depletion. *Economic Journal* 45, June, 235–41.

[Quesnay, F.] 1766a. (Premier) Dialogue entre Mr. H. et Mr. N. *Journal d'Agriculture, du Commerce et des Finances*, June, 61–109. Reprinted in *Physiocrates*, ed. E. Daire, Paris: Guillaumin, 1846.

[Quesnay, F.] 1766b. Observations sur l'intérêt de l'argent (par M. Niasque). *Journal d'Agriculture, du Commerce et des Finances*, June, 151–71.

Rae, J. 1834. *Statement of Some New Principles of the Subject of Political Economy.* Boston: Hilliard Gray & Co.

Ricardo, D. 1817. *On the Principles of Political Economy and Taxation.* London: Murray. In *The Works and Correspondence of David Ricardo*, ed. P. Sraffa, Cambridge and New York: Cambridge University Press 1951, vol. 1.

Robinson, J. 1954. The production function and the theory of capital. *Review of Economic Studies* 21, 81–106. Reprinted in *Collected Economic Papers of Joan Robinson*, Vol. II, Oxford: Blackwell.

Robinson, J. 1956. *The Accumulation of Capital.* London: Macmillan; Homewood, Ill.: R.D. Irwin.

Salin, E. 1930. Kapitalbegriff und Kapitallehre von der Antike zu den Physiokraten *Vierteljahrsschrift für Sozial- und Wirtschaftsgeschichte* 23, 401–40.

Samuelson, P.A. 1947. *Foundations of Economic Analysis.* Harvard Economic Studies 80, Cambridge, Mass.: Harvard University Press.

Samuelson, P.A. 1948. *Economics: An Introductory Analysis.* New York: McGraw-Hill.

Say, J.B. 1814. *Traité d'économie politique.* 2nd edn, Paris: Deterville.

Schneider, E. 1934. *Theorie der Produktion.* Vienna: Springer.

Schumpeter, J.A. 1911. *Theorie der wirtschaftlichen Entwicklung.* Leipzig: Duncker & Humblot.

Senior, N.W. 1836. (*An Outline of the Science of*) *Political Economy.* London: Griffin.

Smith, A. 1776. *An Inquiry into the Nature and Causes of the Wealth of Nations.* London: Strahan and Cadell. Ed. R.H. Campbell and A.S. Skinner with W.B. Todd, *The Glasgow Edition of the Works and Correspondence of Adam Smith*, Vol. II, Oxford: Clarendon Press, 1976.

Sraffa, P. 1960. *Production of Commodities by Means of Commodities.* Cambridge: Cambridge University Press.

Stackelberg, H. von. 1932. *Grundlagen einer reinen Kostentheorie.* Vienna: Springer.

Stigler, G.J. 1941. *Production and Distribution Theories.* New York: Macmillan.

Strigl, R. von 1934. *Kapital und Produktion.* Vienna: Springer.

Swan, T.W. 1956. Economic growth and capital accumulation. *Economic Record* 32, 334–61.

Thünen, J.H. von 1850. *Der isolierte Staat.* Theil II, 1. Abteilung: *Der naturgemässe Arbeitslohn und dessen Verhältnis zum Zinsfuss und zur Landrente.* Rostock: Leopold. Trans. by B. W. Dempsey as *The Frontier Wage,* Chicago: Loyola University Press, 1960.

Turgot, A.R.J. 1770 Réflexions sur la formation et la distribution des richesses. *Ephémérides du Citoyen,* November and December 1769, January 1770. Trans. as 'Reflections on the Formation and Distribution of Wealth' in *Turgot on Progress, Sociology and Economics,* ed. R.L. Meek, Cambridge and New York: Cambridge University Press, 1973.

Uzawa, H. 1958. A note on the Menger–Wieser theory of imputation. *Zeitschrift für Nationalökonomie* 18, 318–34.

Viner, J. 1930. Cost curves and supply curves. *Zeitschrift für Nationalökonomie* 3, 23–46.

Walras, L. 1874–7: *Eléments d'économie politique pure.* Lausanne: Corbaz. Trans. as *Elements of Pure Economics,* London: George Allen 1954; Homewood, Ill.: R.D. Irwin.

Wicksell, K. 1893. *Über Wert, Kapital und Rente.* Jena: Fischer. Trans. as *Value, Capital and Rent,* London: George Allen & Unwin, 1954; New York: Rinehart.

Wicksell, K. 1901. *Föreläsningar i Nationalekonomi,* Första Delen: *Teoretisk Nationalekonomi.* Lund: Berlingska Boktryckeriet. Trans. as *Lectures on Political Economy,* Vol. 1: General Theory, London: Routledge, 1934; New York: A.M. Kelley, 1967.

Wicksteed, P. H. 1894. *An Essay on the Co-ordination of the Laws of Distribution.* London: Macmillan.

Capital goods

HARALD HAGEMANN

Capital goods are a series of heterogeneous commodities, each having specific technical characteristics. Outside the hypothetical case where real capital consists of a single commodity, it is impossible to express the stock of capital goods as a homogeneous physical entity. As a consequence of capital's heterogeneous nature its measurement has become the source of many controversies in the history of economic thought.

The function of capital goods is production. Unlike labour ('in the raw') and (non-cultivated) land, capital goods are not given, they are themselves produced. Being an output as well as an input, the size and variation of the capital stock are intra-economic phenomena. Because real capital is not an 'original' factor of production but is the result of economic processes in which it participates as one of the determinants, the formation of real capital or investment is the central channel through which all other determinants, be they technical progress, changes in labour supply or the exploitation of natural resources, influence the long-run development of an industrial system.

A distinction is normally made between durable or fixed capital, including not only plant and machinery but also buildings and other essential parts of the industrial infrastructure which are used up only partially during the year, and circulating capital, consisting of stocks of raw materials, semi-finished goods, etc., capital which is fully used up during the production period and must therefore be replaced in full.

Capital has at least two different aspects: capital as goods and capital as value. From a technological point of view, produced means of production are a condition for the operation of any social and economic system, once Smith's early and rude state of society is overcome. It was Marx who emphasized that these necessary physical instruments of production become 'capital' only under the capitalistic rules of the game when the means of production are separated from the labourers and owned by the capitalists. Thus the means of production possess a double aspect in capitalistic societies: on the one hand 'capital' is understood to mean the total of heterogeneous goods and equipment designed for specific uses (productive concept), on the other hand it is regarded as a homogeneous fund of value and source of 'unearned' income in the form of profits (portfolio concept).

The value of the capital goods corresponding to each system of production, even with a constant technique, will change with income distribution in whatever unit they are measured. Current relative prices change when the rate of profits or the real wage rate changes, so that the same physical capital represents a different value whereas different stocks of capital goods can have the same value. Furthermore, only in long-run equilibrium will a given stock of capital goods have the same value whether it be determined as the accumulated sum of past investment expenditures or as the expected future net returns discounted back to the present at the ruling rate of profits.

Another way of measuring capital goods is in terms of labour time directly and indirectly required to produce them, the appropriately dated quantities of labour compounded at the various given rates of profits. As the analyses of Joan Robinson (1956), who called it 'real capital', and Sraffa (1960) show, it is impossible to get any notion of capital as a measurable quantity independent of distribution and prices.

Whereas the individual is concerned with the extent to which he owns capital goods as a store of wealth and a source of income, society as a whole is never faced with problems of buying or selling capital goods against money or credit. Greater output unambiguously requires a greater amount of capital goods, given the degree of capacity utilization and technology. These additional capital goods can be provided only by a process of accumulation or net investment.

Emphasis on the strategic role of the capacity to produce capital goods in the domestic economy plays a decisive role in the analyses of Fel'dman (1928) and Lowe (1955, 1976). Both authors take as their starting point Marx's famous two-departmental scheme of expanded reproduction, modifying it in an adequate way to include all activities that increase the capacity of an economy to produce output in one sector. During the Soviet industrialization debate in the late twenties, Fel'dman formalized the notion that investment priority for the capital-goods sector was a precondition for attaining a higher growth rate. Structural incapacity to supply enough capital goods will prevent a rise in the saving ratio from being fully transformed into the desired level of investment. But it has to be taken into account that a one-sided preoccupation with this 'Fel'dman constraint' on the investment capacity side may bring the 'Pre-obrazhenski constraint' on the consumption side into action. If the initial capacity of the capital goods industry is just sufficient to replace the worn-out machines, growth can only take place as a result of a temporary reduction in the output of consumer goods which may be impossible for subsistence reasons. In this case a *circulus vitiosus* will emerge.

The strategic role of the machine tools sector and the compulsion to enlarge first the equipment in capital goods industries were also dealt with by economists discussing the growth and planning problems of underdeveloped countries in the Fifties and Sixties (see, for example, Dobb, 1960 and Mathur, 1965). Countries like India which lack a self-sufficient machine tools sector can speed up their transformation process by foreign trade. The Fel'dman constraint would be binding only if the domestic output of machine tools could not be supplemented with imports.

The perception that there is a group of fixed capital goods which hold the strategic position in any industrial system like seed corn for agricultural production, led Lowe to the conclusion that it is useful to split up the capital goods sector in the Marxian scheme of reproduction into two subsectors. In his 'tripartite' scheme of three vertically integrated sectors, the first produces primary equipment goods or 'machine tools' which are directly used for production in sectors I and II. Sector II produces the secondary equipment goods which are used as inputs only in sector III producing consumer goods, which means that the capital stock in the latter is not transferable. Thus sector I is the only one capable not only of producing machines for other sectors but also for itself; it is therefore a *self-reproducible sector*. In Sraffa's terminology, sector I represents the 'basic system'.

The sub-division of the capital goods group is relevant for investigating the structural conditions for steady growth and, even more, in addressing questions of 'traverse analysis', when the problem of structural change is moved to the centre of the stage. The decisive problem that the economy faces upon departing from a steady growth path is the inadequacy of the old capital stock. The dynamic traverse from one steady growth path to another necessarily involves a change in the whole quantity structure, especially the rebuilding of the capital stock. The economy cannot change output unless it first changes inputs, i.e. the capital goods group must provide the commodities demanded for changing the inputs to produce the new output pattern. The production of machine tools is the bottle-neck which any process of rapid expansion must overcome. The key to a higher growth rate lies in increasing the shares of sector I. The same logic requiring that the system as a whole first has to change inputs before it can change output makes such an increase dependent on the prior expansion of the capital stock of this sector. Whereas in the two-sectoral Fel'dman model this is only possible by a policy of putting a larger proportion of new machine tools into the production of more machine tools, in the Lowe model an additional *ex post* transfer of machines from sector II to sector I is possible, thereby shortening the time of adjustment. Both models come to the same result, namely that in order to increase the growth rates of total output and consumption output in the long run, at first a temporary fall in the growth rate of consumption output is necessary.

The neo-Austrian theory developed by Hicks is characterized by a completely different treatment of the durable means of production. In his neo-Austrian model, a stream of labour inputs is converted into a stream of final outputs (consumption goods). 'Capital goods are simply stages in the process of production' (Hicks, 1973, p. 5), i.e. they are regarded as intermediate products which do not appear explicitly but are implied and produced within each process of 'maturing' of original inputs into the final product. Thus the intertemporal aspect of production and consumption is placed into the forefront of the analysis; time is the essence of capital in the Austrian view. By treating fixed capital as if it were working capital, Hicks does not recognize the need for a special machine-tools sector. There is no basic product in this model. Hence, the production process is not 'circular'; the neo-Austrian approach turns out to be a further variant of the production theoretic paradigm of marginalist analysis, which conceives of the production process as a 'one-way avenue that leads from "Factors of production" to "Consumption goods"' (Sraffa, 1960, p. 93).

It is precisely the focus on the adjustment problems caused by the impact of technical innovations that has led Hicks to his vertical representation of the productive structure. In contrast to Leontief–Sraffa–Lowe systems, in Hicks neither intersectoral transactions, nor therefore the effects of innovation upon industrial structure, are shown. Hicks sees the decisive advantage of the Austrian method in its ability to cope with the important fact that process innovations nearly always involve the introduction of new capital goods. This would lead to insurmountable difficulties in the traverse analysis if capital goods were physically specified because 'there is no way of establishing a physical relation between the capital goods that are required in the one technique and those that are required in the other' (Hicks, 1977, p. 193). A similar explanation is given by Pasinetti who develops his theory of structural change in terms of vertically integrated sectors. While conceding that the input-output model gives more information on the structure of an economic system at any point in time, he points out that because of the change of input-output coefficients and the 'breaking down' of the inter-industry system over time, the vertically integrated model is superior for dynamic analysis (see Pasinetti, 1981, pp. 109–17). Measuring capital goods in units of vertically integrated productive capacity of the final commodity 'has an unambiguous meaning through time, no matter which type of technical change, and how much of it, may occur' (p. 178).

Whilst it is true that a sectorally disaggregated approach encounters difficulties when the effects of innovations connected with the introduction of new capital goods are studied, the price that Austrian-type models have to pay for their linear 'imperialism' is rather high. Technical change takes place at the industry level, a characteristic which is completely washed out in vertically integrated models. The industry-specific nature of technical change also implies that, contrary to Pasinetti's assumption, rates of productivity growth in the different vertically integrated sectors cannot be thought of as being independent of each other. How could the new capital goods be produced without the old ones existing at the beginning of the traverse? Thus the existence of a basic system remains relevant, even when the basic product(s) is(are) changing its(their) quality. Innovations introducing new consumption goods cannot be dealt with in a satisfactory way. All this does not imply that the concept of vertically integrated sectors is meaningless, on the contrary, it can be very helpful as a complementary perspective. But it illustrates that input-output models emphasizing intersectoral interdependencies retain conceptual priority.

Fixed capital has two other important dimensions: its degree of capacity utilization, and its durability. Thus the choice of cost-minimizing technique involves the choice of the 'planned' degree of capital utilization and the choice of the economic lifetime of a fixed capital good. The latter can best be dealt with on the basis of a von Neumann–Sraffa treatment of fixed capital goods (which contain Hicks's neo-Austrian model as a special case) as a joint part of the gross output, thus identifying machines of different ages as different commodities. To every technically possible lifetime corresponds a specific w-r relation which may slope upwards over some range for a given truncation (in which case the prices of partly worn-out machines become negative and premature truncation is advantageous), whereas the w-r frontier is always downwards sloping. The analysis of the choice of the optimal lifetime or truncation period shows that with constant or increasing efficiency the maximum technical lifetime will always be chosen, independently of income distribution. With decreasing or changing efficiency, however, premature truncation may become profitable (see Hagemann and Kurz, 1976). A change in the wage rate (rate of profits) will generally lead to changes in the optimal economic lifetimes of fixed capital goods. With more complex patterns of the time profile of efficiency, the return of the same truncation period at different intervals of the rate of profits is possible, a phenomenon closely linked to reswitching of techniques (see also Schefold, 1974).

BIBLIOGRAPHY

Dobb, M. 1960. *An Essay on Economic Growth and Planning.* London: Routledge; New York: Monthly Review Press.

Fel'dman, G.A. 1928. On the theory of growth rates of national income, I and II. In ed. N. Spulber, *Foundations of Soviet Strategy for Economic Growth*, Bloomington: Indiana University Press, 1964.

Hagemann, H. and Kurz, H.D. 1976. The return of the same truncation period and reswitching of techniques in neo-Austrian and more general models. *Kyklos* 29(4), 678–708.

Harcourt, G.C. 1972. *Some Cambridge Controversies in the Theory of Capital.* Cambridge and New York: Cambridge University Press.

Hicks, J. 1973. *Capital and Time. A Neo-Austrian Theory.* Oxford: Clarendon Press.

Hicks, J. 1977. *Economic Perspectives. Further Essays on Money and Growth.* Oxford: Clarendon Press; New York: Oxford University Press.

Lowe, A. 1955. Structural analysis of real capital formation. In ed. M. Abramovitz, *Capital Formation and Economic Growth*, Princeton: Princeton University Press.

Lowe, A. 1976. *The Path of Economic Growth.* Cambridge and New York: Cambridge University Press.

Mathur, G. 1965. *Planning for Steady Growth.* Oxford: Blackwell; New York: A.M. Kelley.

Pasinetti, L.L. 1981. *Structural Change and Economic Growth. A theoretical essay on the dynamics of the wealth of nations.* Cambridge and New York: Cambridge University Press.

Robinson, J. 1956. *The Accumulation of Capital.* London: Macmillan; Homewood, Ill.: R.D. Irwin.

Schefold, B. 1974. Fixed capital as a joint product and the analysis of accumulation with different forms of technical progress. In *Essays on the Theory of Joint Production*, ed. L.L. Pasinetti, London: Macmillan; New York: Columbia University Press, 1980.

Sraffa, P. 1960. *Production of Commodities by Means of Commodities. Prelude to a critique of economic theory.* Cambridge: Cambridge University Press.

Capitalistic and acapitalistic production

LIONELLO F. PUNZO

If 'capital' is the set of produced means of production, (almost) all production is capitalistic. Thus, the presence of capital in this sense can at most be (and in the history of economic doctrines was taken to represent) a necessary condition for defining capitalistic production. Differences arose as to the relative emphasis put on the social or techno-economic aspects of such transformation processes.

In Marx's analysis, capitalistic production is the organization of social production specific to a society characterized by private ownership of the means of production and by its separation from 'labour'. This historically given Mode of Production is contrasted with pre- and post-capitalistic forms, where power relationships are regulated according to different principles. By contrast, the distinction between production with and without capital focuses upon the relationship between means and objectives (consumption goods) of production activity. It played a role in the era of the full articulation of neoclassical thought. Its analytical use obviously depended upon the specific conception (and representation) of capital.

According to perhaps the most common theory, Capital is a factor of production, a member of a triad with Labour and Land. This view emphasizes the aspect of capital as a stock of man-produced goods which are at any point of time available in fixed quantities. (A)capitalistic production entails the application of (un)aided labour to natural resources. On the other hand, according to the Austrian (Böhm-Bawerk) definition, capital is the set of intermediate goods (or 'maturing consumption goods') emerging in the transformation of labour services into final goods when indirect methods of production are employed. This conception emphasizes the functional relationship whereby capital is the mode of realization of advanced production activity. Accordingly, acapitalistic production is direct production of consumption goods through application of bare labour to natural resources. Finally, in Wicksell's theoretical compromise, capital is a stock of used-up services of both labour and land. Production without capital is carried on by means of labour and natural resources in a state where capital goods either do not exist or are free goods relative to the available technology. (See Part II of the first volume of Wicksell's Lectures, 1934.) This definition obviously overlooks the fact that capital goods are themselves a byproduct of the advancement of technological knowledge, an idea implicit in Böhm-Bawerk and hinted at by Schumpeter.

At any rate, in all its various interpretations, acapitalistic production was a logical abstraction meant to illustrate, in a simpler analytical context, some basic principles holding for capitalistic production. In Böhm-Bawerk, this is the principle of the higher productivity of indirect (i.e. capitalistic) methods of production. In Wicksell, the distinction is meant to illustrate the marginalistic approach to the distribution of income and to show how it can be extended from the simpler production with labour and land only to production involving capital goods. In the former case, wage rate and rent are regulated by the marginal productivities of the two factors, in a state of full employment of labour and zero entrepreneurial profits. However, the extension of the marginal productivity principle to the theory of interest meets a crucial conceptual difficulty due to the fact that capital, being an aggregate of produced goods, has to be measured in value and the latter depends itself on income distribution. It is to avoid a circular argument that Wicksell proposes to regard capital as 'a single coherent mass of saved up resources'. Hence, interest would be (equal to) the difference between the marginal productivity of saved up labour and land and the marginal productivity of current labour and land. According to Wicksell, 'experience' shows that capital has a higher productivity and this is the reason why its share in the national product is normally positive.

It has been proved, in the debate on capital theory in the 1960s, that Wicksell's attempt at finding a way out of the difficulties of the marginalistic approach to income distribution is unsatisfactory. However, the recurrence of the theme of the distinction between acapitalistic and capitalistic production is interesting for it indicates the neoclassical authors' awareness of the theoretical difficulties they met in the treatment of capital and distribution.

BIBLIOGRAPHY
Böhm-Bawerk, E. von. 1889. *Positive Theorie des Kapitals*. Trans. by G.D. Huncke as Vol. 2 of *Capital and Interest*, South Holland, Ill.: Libertarian Press, 1959.
Schumpeter, J.A. 1954. *History of Economic Analysis*. London: Allen & Unwin; New York: Oxford University Press.
Wicksell, K. 1934. *Lectures on Political Economy*. 1st English edn, ed. L. Robbins, London: George Routledge & Sons; New York: A.M. Kelley, 1967.

Capital perversity

TATSUO HATTA

Neoclassical capital theory regards the interest rate as the market price of the composite factor 'capital'. In this theory the interest rate is equal to the marginal product of the capital, since the demand curve for capital is its marginal productivity schedule. Moreover, the theory assumes that capital obeys the law of diminishing returns just like any other factor, so that its demand curve is downward-sloping. In an economy where labour is the only primary factor and constant returns to scale prevail, this implies the following postulate: *as the interest rate falls, the capital–labour ratio increases*, which plays an important role in neoclassical growth theory and in comparative static analyses of interest rate determination.

Neoclassical capital theory also makes another closely related postulate: *as the interest rate falls, the output–labour ratio increases*. This postulate does not explicitly use the concept of aggregate capital. However, it too implies that 'capital' obeys the law of diminishing returns. For the output–labour ratio can be raised only when some input other than labour is increased behind the scenes, and in this economy capital is the only such input available.

Both postulates necessarily hold if output is produced by labour and a *single* capital input in a linear homogeneous production function, as in the Clark–Ramsey production function. Cambridge economists, led by Robinson (1953–4, 1956), Champernowne (1953–4) and Sraffa (1960), criticized these postulates, however, for economies with heterogeneous capital goods, thus kindling the so-called Cambridge controversies in capital theory as surveyed by von Weizsäcker (1971). Harcourt (1972), Blaug (1974), and Burmeister (1980). Eventually, counter-examples that appeared in Pasinetti et al. (1966) showed irrefutably that both postulates can fail to hold in such economies. These paradoxical phenomena are called *capital perversities*. They showed very clearly that 'capital' is different from other factors in that diminishing returns do not hold for it even in contexts quite free of aggregation problems.

130

In order to examine the first postulate for economies with heterogeneous capital goods, one has to aggregate heterogeneous capital goods into a single dollar value of capital. Such a measure could well be specious, however, due to the index number problem involved in the aggregation, the interest rate affecting the prices of capital goods with different gestation periods differently. Since the second postulate does not depend on a particular aggregate measure of capital, it may appear a more robust characterization of diminishing returns from roundabout processes than the first. In fact, the following proposition due to Burmeister and Dobell (1970, Corollary 7.2) implies that the two postulates are equivalent once a proper price index is chosen for evaluating capital.

Suppose that an exogenous increase in interest rate shifts one stationary-state production equilibrium to another. Then, as long as the interest rate is positive, the ratio of output to labour moves in the same direction as the ratio of 'constant-price capital' to labour, where the 'constant-price capital' is the dollar value of the new capital input vector measured at the initial input price vector.

For this reason we will examine only the failure of the second postulate to hold.

RESWITCHING. Capital perversity was demonstrated via examples of the so-called reswitching phenomenon; the simplest and most illuminating is Samuelson's (1966). He assumes that output this year is produced by applying labour inputs in three preceding years according to the following production function:

$$Y = y(x_1, x_2, x_3), \tag{1}$$

where Y is this year's output level and x_1, x_2, and x_3 are labour inputs one, two, and three years ago, respectively. Let p_t be the present value of the wage rate t periods prior to the production year. Producers chose the cost-minimizing input vector (x_1, x_2, x_3) for the given output level under the input price vector (p_1, p_2, p_3). Samuelson also assumes free entry, so that maximized profit is zero.

Now consider a steady-state economy where Y is produced every year and prices are constant. Then we have

$$p_t = w \cdot r^t, \tag{2}$$

where w is the (constant) wage rate and r is 1 plus the interest rate. Input and output variables for each year may be shown as in Table 1. Each column shows the total amount of labour L applied in the entire production process that year as

$$L = x_1 + x_2 + x_3. \tag{3}$$

As the macroeconomist sees it, this economy as a whole produces Y every year by applying capital inputs in the form of goods-in-process and an amount L of labour.

131

Samuelson considered the case where the technology (1) consists of only two techniques α and β: α's input vector (x_1, x_2, x_3) for producing a unit output is $(0, 7, 0)$ and β's $(6, 0, 2)$. He showed that β minimizes cost when the interest rate lies between 50 and 100 per cent per year, while α does so otherwise. As the interest rate increases from zero, therefore, the cost-minimizing technique switches first from α to β, and then back to α. This phenomenon, that as the interest rate increases, a once-abandoned technique becomes re-employed, is called *the reswitching of techniques*. It is obvious that when it happens capital perversity necessarily occurs. In Samuelson's case, for example, when the interest rate is increased past 100 per cent, technique β with $Y/L = 1/8$ is switched to α with $1/7$, falsifying the second postulate. It can readily be shown that at this switching interest rate the first postulate also fails, even after the index number problem is removed.

Table 1

1986	1985	1984	1983	1982	1981	1980
			Y	x_1	x_2	x_3
		Y	x_1	x_2	x_3	
	Y	x_1	x_2	x_3		
Y	x_1	x_2	x_3			

WHAT CAUSES PERVERSITY? Examples of reswitching had to be given for economies with discrete technologies, since it occurs with probability zero in a smoothly substitutable production function. But neither reswitching nor a discrete technology is necessary for perversity itself. Indeed, Hatta (1976) constructed an example of a smoothly substitutable and linear homogeneous function of type (1) that behaves perversely.

To see how this might work, consider a generalized version of (1):

$$Y = \mathscr{y}(x_1, x_2, \ldots, x_n), \tag{4}$$

where $\mathscr{y}$ is quasi-concave, linear homogeneous, and differentiable. Then we have the following proposition due to Hatta (1976), which was independently hinted at by Solow (1975, p. 52):

For capital perversity to occur in (4) it must have at least one complementary input pair. (A)

Equivalently, if all input pairs in (4) are (Hicksian) substitutes, perversity cannot occur.

According to a standard Hicksian demand rule (1946, ch. 3), (net) complementarity among inputs can occur in (4) only if n is greater than 2. Thus Proposition (A) implies that for perversity to occur in (4), n must be greater than 2. When $n = 2$, on the other hand, the economy has only one capital good, i.e., the one produced by the labour input applied in the previous year. Proposition (A) therefore implies that:

Heterogeneity of capital is necessary for perversity in (4).   (B)

We now prove (A) for the case $n = 3$. The cost-minimizing input vector for output level Y under the input price vector (p_1, p_2, p_3) is given by the following set of input demand functions:

$$x_s = a_s(p_1, p_2, p_3, Y) \qquad s = 1, 2, 3.$$

We assume that the interest rate is positive, i.e.,

$$r > 1. \qquad (5)$$

Noting (2) and the zero-degree homogeneity of a_s in the prices, the following must hold when cost is minimized:

$$x_s = a_s(1, r, r^2, Y) \qquad s = 1, 2, 3.$$

In view of equation (3), therefore, the total labour movement requirement in this stationary economy is

$$L = a_1(1, r, r^2, Y) + a_2(1, r, r^2, Y) + a_3(1, r, r^2, Y).$$

By definition perversity occurs if the L necessary to produce a constant Y every year is lowered when the interest rate is raised, i.e., if

$$\partial L / \partial r < 0. \qquad (6)$$

Carrying out this differentiation, we obtain

$$\frac{\partial L}{\partial r} = (r - 1) \cdot a_{12} + 2(r^2 - 1) \cdot a_{13} + (r^2 - r) \cdot a_{23}. \qquad (7)$$

where

$$a_{st} \equiv \partial a_s / \partial p_t.$$

This and (5) imply that $\partial L / \partial r$ is positive if all a_{st}'s (i.e. Hicksian cross-substitution terms) are positive. This in turn implies that for perversity to occur, there must be at least one complementary input pair.   Q.E.D.

For general n, Proposition (6) is proved similarly, since (7) generalizes to

$$r \cdot \frac{\partial L}{\partial r} = \sum_{s=1}^{n-1} \sum_{t=s+1}^{n} (t - s)(p_t - p_s) \cdot a_{st}.$$

Now look at Samuelson's example in the light of (A). Assume that for given Y and given prices, β is cost-minimizing. Now let p_1 increase, keeping p_2 and p_3 constant. Eventually this will make β more costly than α, so α will be employed. But α uses less x_3 than β in order to produce the same output, so the rise in p_1 has caused a reduction in x_3, i.e. pair $(1, 3)$ is complementary. Thus Samuelson's discrete model is consistent with our Proposition (A), obtained for the neoclassical production function.

Hence perversity is simply one of the many paradoxes caused by complementarity. The reason why the Clark–Ramsey production function always behaves well is now clear: it has only two inputs, which must be substitutes.

WHY COMPLEMENTARITY? Why does complementarity cause perversity? Note first that when $n = 3$ perversity cannot occur if either the input pair $(1, 2)$ or the pair $(2, 3)$ is complementary. Indeed, when $n = 3$ the following stronger version of (A) holds: For perversity to occur in (1), a_{13} must be negative, i.e., the specific input pair $(1, 3)$ must be complementary. (C)

Just as a complementary pair of consumption goods can be regarded as a composite good, a complementary pair of inputs (e.g. truck and garage) may be treated as a composite input. When a neighbouring input pair is complementary in the production function (1), therefore, that function can be regarded as containing just two inputs: one (composite) labour and a (composite) capital. For example, when $(1, 2)$ is complementary, the pair $(1, 2)$ can be regarded as composite labour. In such cases the production function is essentially of Clark–Ramsey form and so behaves well.

When $(1, 3)$ is complementary, on the other hand, the technology's two (composite) inputs $(1, 3)$ and 2 cannot be ranked in terms of their gestation periods. The two inputs can interchange the roles of capital and labour for different levels of interest rate, which explains why perversity can occur in this situation. Observe that $(1, 3)$ is also complementary in Samuelson's model with a discrete technology, and the above explanation is applicable to his model.

Proposition (C) can be extended in various ways to the case where $n > 3$. For example, perversity never occurs if the structure of complementarity is such that the n inputs can be classified into one composite labour and one composite capital. Thus perversity occurs only if complementarity creates a composite input that cannot be unequivocally ranked with another (composite) input vis-à-vis their gestation periods. As Hatta (1976) argues, Bruno, Burmeister and Sheshinski's (1966) non-reswitching condition can be interpreted in this spirit.

The proof of (C) is straightforward. Noting that $a_{11} + ra_{12} + r^2 a_{13} = 0$ and $a_{31} + ra_{32} + r^2 a_{33} = 0$, from the homogeneity property of the input demand functions in prices, we can rewrite (7) as:

$$\frac{r}{w} \cdot \frac{\partial L}{\partial r} = (1 - r) \cdot a_{11} + (r^3 - r) \cdot a_{13} + (r^3 - r^4) \cdot a_{33}.$$

This implies that a_{13} must be negative if perversity occurs, since r is greater than 1 and a_{11} and a_{33} are negative from the Hicksian demand rule. Thus (C) is proved.

CONCLUSION. To construct models of growth and the interest rate in an economy with heterogeneous capital-good inputs, the concept of 'capital' is not at all necessary: microeconomic production functions can be specified directly in terms of the physical units of those inputs. The main focus of the Cambridge controversies in capital theory was rather on the question of how well the simple

Clark–Ramsey production function can approximate the qualitative properties of a production economy with heterogeneous capital-good inputs.

It was established through these controversies that the monotonic relationship between output–labour ratio and interest rate, a basic property of the Clark–Ramsey production function, fails to hold in a world of heterogeneous capital inputs. Since this relation has nothing to do with the index number problem, the fact that it breaks down in a general model clearly contradicted that part of neoclassical capital theory which was based upon the Clark–Ramsey production function. This was a genuinely new finding that came out of the capital controversies. As we have seen, however, it is fully explicable within neoclassical theory, being no more (and no less) than one of the many intractable problems caused by the presence of complementarity.

BIBLIOGRAPHY

Blaug, M. 1974. *The Cambridge Revolution: Success or Failure?* London: The Institute of Economic Affairs.

Bruno, M., Burmeister, E. and Sheshinski, E. 1966. The nature and implications of the reswitching of techniques. *Quarterly Journal of Economics* 80(4), November, 526–53.

Burmeister, E. 1980. *Capital Theory and Dynamics.* Cambridge and New York: Cambridge University Press.

Burmeister, E. and Dobell, R. 1970. *Mathematical Theories of Economic Growth.* New York: Macmillan Co.

Champernowne, D.G. 1953–4. The production function and the theory of capital: a comment. *Review of Economic Studies* 21, 112–35.

Harcourt, G.C. 1972. *Some Cambridge Controversies in the Theory of Capital.* London and New York: Cambridge University Press.

Hatta, T. 1976. The paradox in capital theory and complementarity of inputs. *Review of Economic Studies* 43, 127–42.

Hicks, J. 1946. *Value and Capital.* 2nd edn, London: Oxford University Press.

Pasinetti, L.L. et al. 1966. Paradoxes in capital theory: a symposium. *Quarterly Journal of Economics* 80(4), November, 503–83.

Robinson, J. 1953–4. The production function and the theory of capital. *Review of Economic Studies* 21, 81–106.

Robinson, J. 1956. *The Accumulation of Capital.* London: Macmillan; Homewood, Ill.: R.D. Irwin.

Samuelson, P.A. 1966. A summing up. *Quarterly Journal of Economics* 80, 568–83.

Solow, R. 1975. Brief comments. *Quarterly Journal of Economics* 89, 48–52.

Sraffa, P. 1960. *Production of Commodities by Means of Commodities. Prelude to a Critique of Economic Theory.* Cambridge: Cambridge University Press.

von Weizsäcker, C.C. 1971. *Steady State Capital Theory.* Berlin: Springer-Verlag.

Capital theory: paradoxes

LUIGI L. PASINETTI AND ROBERTO SCAZZIERI

PROLOGUE. The idea that capital theory might lead economists to discover forms of 'paradoxical' behaviour has emerged in the economic literature of the 1960s largely as an outcome of developments in the field of production theory (theory of linear production models). What happened in capital theory is in fact a special instance of a more general phenomenon. Economists sometimes tend to examine a large domain of economic phenomena by adapting theoretical concepts that had originally been devised for a much narrower range of special issues. The discoveries of 'paradoxical' relations derive from the fact that their process of generalization often turns out to be ill-conceived and misleading, if not entirely unwarranted.

For a long time, in capital theory, it had been taken for granted that there is a unique, unambiguous profitability ranking of production techniques in terms of capital intensity, along the scale of variation of the rate of interest. The discovery that this is not necessarily true has induced many economists to speak of 'paradoxes' in the theory of capital. But the roots of apparently paradoxical behaviour are to be found, not in the economic phenomena themselves, but in the economists' tendency to rely on too simple 'parables' of economic behaviour.

Traditional beliefs about capital are deeply rooted in the history of economic analysis, and may be traced back to pre-classical literature. As will be shown in the next section, a long post-classical tradition was then developed on that basis. The length of ancestry might explain the survival of conventional beliefs.

THE EMERGENCE OF THE CONVENTIONAL VIEW. The notion of 'capital' was associated for a long time with investible wealth and its income generating power, and was largely independent of detailed consideration of the function of invested wealth in the production process. The earliest development of capital theory took place within the analytical framework of a pure exchange economy (Petty, Locke). Within this perspective, capital was often associated with purely financial transactions (lending and borrowing) and the relationship between capital and

136

rate of interest came quite naturally to be conceived as the relationship between loanable funds and their price. The origin of the belief in the inverse monotonic relation between the demand for capital and the rate of interest may be traced back to this phase of the literature on capital.

The association of capital with the process of production did not come to the fore until quite late, in spite of certain isolated anticipations. (Hicks (1973, p. 12) even quotes Boccaccio's *Decameron* on the issue.) The description of capital as a stock of means of production became common with the Physiocrats and the Classical Economists. In this period, Cesare Beccaria (1804, ms 1771–72) presented what J.B. Say considered to be the first analysis of 'true functions of productive capitals' (Say, 1817, p. xliii). Soon after him, Adam Smith (1776) built upon the distinction between 'productive' capital and 'unproductive' consumption his theory of structural dynamics and economic growth. Finally, David Ricardo gave a definite shape to classical capital theory by examining the relationship between capital accumulation and diminishing returns and by considering in which way different proportions of capital in different industries might influence the relative exchange values of the corresponding commodities (Ricardo, 1817, ch. I, sections IV and V). Classical capital theory is characterized by lack of interest in the purely financial dimension of investment. As a result, the relation between capital accumulation and the rate of interest recedes into the background and is substituted by the relation between real capital accumulation and the rate of profit. (In Ricardo, the rate of profit is determined by equality with the rate of net output on the least fertile land.)

In this way, the foundations of capital theory shifted from the exchange to the production sphere, and the demand-and-supply mechanism was confined to the process by which the rate of interest is maintained equal to the rate of profit in the long run. However, certain aspects of the pre-classical approach maintained a foothold in economic analysis. In particular, a number of economists (starting with Thünen, Longfield and Senior) continued to be interested in the income-generating function of capital at the level of the individual investor, and tried to combine this approach with the emphasis on the productive function of capital that had emerged in the classical literature. The marginal productivity theory of capital and interest was developed as an answer to this conceptual problem. The essential features of that theory may be clearly seen in Thünen:

The return, which the total amount of capital provides since the moment in which it is lent, is determined by the utility of that portion of capital which is last employed (Thünen [1850], 1857, p. 131).

It must then be known at which point the agriculturist should stop along the ranking of improvements which he might either introduce or give up. The answer is as follows: he would find an advantage in introducing all those improvements that bring him a return which, when compared to the capital employed, is greater than the rate of interest that could be obtained by lending the same amount of capital (Thünen [1850], 1857, p. 186).

Thünen's theory suggests a relationship between the rate of interest (i) and the rate of profit (r) quite different from the one found in Ricardo. The reason for this is that Ricardo had taken r to be fixed for the individual entrepreneur, so that equality between i and r was brought about by adjustment between the supply and demand for loans in the financial markets. Thünen suggested a different adjustment mechanism by taking r to be variable for the individual entrepreneur, so that the attainment of the long run equality between the rate of profit and the rate of interest came to depend on the change in the physical productivity of capital as much as on adjustment in the financial markets.

This view is founded upon a thorough transformation of the Ricardian theory of diminishing returns and provided the logical starting point for the later marginalist theory of diminishing returns from aggregate capital. The analytical and historical process leading to this outcome is a rather complex one, and it is best understood by distinguishing two separate stages. In the first stage, the law of diminishing returns, which Ricardo considered to hold for the economy as a whole in the long-run, was applied to the short-run behaviour of the individual entrepreneur. As a result, the change in input proportions within any given productive unit is associated with the change in the physical productivity of capital. Here the variation of the capital stock is unlikely to influence the system of prices, so that the decrease (or increase) in the return from the last 'increment of capital' could be unambiguously associated with an increase (or decrease) in the physical capital stock. The second stage consisted in extending the above result to the variations in the aggregate quantity of capital available in the economic system as a whole (quantity of 'social capital').

The process which we have described permitted the transformation of the classical conception of diminishing returns from a macro-social law into a microeconomic relation derived from the law of variable proportions. This new type of diminishing returns was then extended to the 'macro-social' sphere once again. As a result, it became possible to think that the rate of interest and the rate of profit (tending to be equal to each other) are associated with the physical marginal productivity of social or aggregate capital: an increase in the relative quantity of capital with respect to the other inputs would be associated with lower marginal productivity of capital and thus with a lower equilibrium rate of interest and rate of profit. This inverse monotonic relation between the rate of interest (or the rate of profit) and the quantity of capital per man eventually became an established proposition of capital theory. Its relevance can be seen from the attempts by Jevons (1871), Böhm-Bawerk (1889) and Clark (1899) to found on the theory of the marginal productivity of factors the explanation of the distribution of the social product among factors of production under competitive conditions.

Further light on the conceptual roots of the marginalist view of capital is shed by the contributions of Jevons and Böhm-Bawerk. In their theories, profit is considered as the remuneration due to the capitalist as a result of the higher productiveness of 'indirect' or 'roundabout' processes of production when compared with processes carried out by 'direct' labour only. The generalization of the marginal principles which they carried out is thus associated with the description of the production process as an essentially 'financial' phenomenon in which final output, like interest in financial transactions, could be considered as 'some continuous function of the time elapsing between the expenditure of the labour and the enjoyment of the result' (Jevons [1871], 1879, p. 266). The subsequent discovery of 'anomalies' in the field of capital accumulation was possible when economists started to question this extension of capital theory from the financial to the productive sphere, and when the technical structure of production was examined on its own grounds independently of the 'financial' aspect which might be considered to be characteristic of 'the typical business man's viewpoint' (Hicks, 1973, p. 12).

ANTICIPATIONS OF DEBATE. It has just been shown that microeconomic diminishing returns provided the foundations for a theory of the diminishing marginal productivity of social capital, which was extended from the microeconomic sphere by way of logical analogy.

The pitfalls of this approach did not take long to emerge, as economic analysis came to grips with the full complexity of the production process. Knut Wicksell, discovered that, in the case of an economic system using heterogeneous capital goods, it might be impossible to describe diminishing returns from aggregate capital. The reason for this is that a variation in the capital stock might be associated with a change in the price system that would make it impossible to compare the quantities of capital before and after the change (see Wicksell [1901-6], 1934, pp. 147 and ff., and p. 180). Wicksell also recognized that this difficulty is characteristic of capital because 'labour and land are measured each in terms of its own *technical* unit ... capital, on the other hand, ... is reckoned, in common parlance, as a sum of *exchange value*' (Wicksell [1901-6], 1934, p. 149).

The special difficulty associated with heterogeneous capital goods is in fact an outcome of a particular procedure by which the fundamental theorems concerning capital and interest had been formulated with reference to the idealized setting of an isolated producer, and then extended by analogy to the case of the 'social economy'. The drawbacks of this methodology were perspicaciously noted by Nicholas Kaldor in the late Thirties:

it is rather unfortunate that, following Böhm-Bawerk and his school, we have been generally accustomed to start with a more specialised set-up, with the picture of Robinson Crusoe engaged in net-making. This Crusoe approach makes it unnecessarily difficult to single out features which are merely the property of a special case from the demonstration of general principles. Had the analysis started with the 'general case' – by imagining a society where *all* resources are produced and the services of all resources co-operate in producing further resources – a great deal of the controversies concerning the theory of capital might not have arisen (Kaldor, 1937, p. 228.)

139

It is remarkable that so many 'paradoxical' results of modern capital theory were subsequently discovered precisely as an outcome of the procedure here described by Kaldor.

The stage of modern controversy was set by the consideration of two distinct problems: (i) the measurement of 'social capital' in models with heterogeneous capital goods; (ii) the discovery that production techniques that had been excluded at lower levels of the rate of profit might 'come back' as the rate of profit is increased (this phenomenon is known as *reswitching of technique*).

Joan Robinson started the discussion by calling attention to the difficulties inherent in any physical measure of social capital (Robinson, 1953–4). She also pointed out the 'curiosum' that the degree of mechanization associated with a higher wage rate and a lower rate of profit might be lower than the degree of mechanization associated with a lower wage rate and a higher rate of profit. (She attributed this 'curiosum' to Miss Ruth Cohen, but later on she attributed it to the reading of Sraffa's Introduction to Ricardo's *Principles.*)

Immediately afterwards, David Champernowne discovered that, in general, we must admit 'the possibility of two stationary states each using the same items of equipment and labour force yet being shown as using different quantities of capital, merely on account of having different rates of interest and of food-wages' (Champernowne, 1953–4, p. 119). Champernowne also admitted that the inverse monotonic relation between the rate of profit and the quantity of capital per man (as well as the inverse monotonic relation between the rate of profit and capital per unit of output) might not be generally true: 'it is logically possible that over certain ranges of the rate of interest, a fall in interest rates and rise in food-wages will be accompanied by a *fall* in output per head and a *fall* in the quantity of capital per head' (Champernowne, 1953–4, p. 118). Champernowne's explanation of what appeared to be perverse behaviour from the point of view of traditional theory was that changes in the interest rate can be associated with changes in the cost of capital equipment even if the capital stock is unchanged. As a result, perverse behaviour was attributed to pure 'financial' variations and a physical measure of capital was still thought to be possible. This Champernowne tried to obtain by introducing a chain index method for measuring capital (Champernowne, 1953–4, p. 125). A few years later, Joan Robinson again took up the same issue in her *Accumulation of Capital* (1956, pp. 109–10). The reason she gave for the 'Ruth Cohen curiosum' is quite different from the one proposed by Champernowne. She explicitly recognized that 'financial' factors such as a higher wage rate and a lower rate of interest would have 'real' consequences by influencing the actual choice of technique. (In the 'perverse' case a lower rate of interest would be associated with the choice of the less mechanized technique.)

When a few years later Michio Morishima attempted a multi-sectoral generalization of Joan Robinson's Simple Model he confirmed the possibility of a positive relationship between the rate of interest and the degree of mechanization of a technique (Morishima, 1964, p. 126). Finally John Hicks came up with the same problem when examining 'the response of technique to price changes' in the framework of a simple economy consisting of a consumption good 'industry' and a net investment good 'industry', and in which the same capital good is used in both industries (see Hicks, 1965, pp. 148–56).

But in spite of all these anticipations, it must be admitted that the issue of technical reswitching was not given an important place in economic theory before the publication of Piero Sraffa's *Production of Commodities by Means of Commodities* (1960). It is with Sraffa's work that the phenomenon becomes prominent. Sraffa's result is in fact remarkable not only for the discovery that the choice of the production technique is not in general a monotonic function of the rate of profit but also for the special route that he followed to obtain that result. Sraffa was able to show that heterogeneity of capital goods and of 'capital structures' (different proportions between labour and intermediate inputs in the various processes of production) would normally give rise, with the variation of the rate of profit and of the unit wage, 'to complicated patterns of price-movement with several ups and downs' (Sraffa, 1960, p. 37). This phenomenon would in turn bring about changes in the 'quantity of capital' that are not generally related to the rate of profit in a monotonic way. Reswitching of technique and reverse capital deepening are thus derived from a general property of production models with heterogeneous capital goods. (See REVERSE CAPITAL DEEPENING.)

NEOCLASSICAL PARABLES AND THE CAPITAL CONTROVERSY. Following the publication of Sraffa's book, a lively debate on capital theory suddenly flared up in the 1960s, and the way it did so is itself an interesting event.

It is known that when propositions derived from individual behaviour are applied to the more complex case of the 'social economy', the extension is admittedly possible on condition that the social economy has a number of special features making it identical, from the analytical point of view, to the case of the isolated individual. To test these features, the social economy is often described in terms of a 'parable' in which those particular conditions are satisfied. This 'parable', though unrealistic, is taken to be useful, from a heuristic or a persuasive point of view.

In this vein Paul Samuelson attempted to construct a 'surrogate production function' by analogy with microeconomic behaviour (Samuelson, 1962). His work can be considered as the first explicit attempt to get rid of the complexities of an economic system with heterogeneous capital goods by constructing a model in which that system is described in terms of an 'aggregate parable' with physically homogeneous capital. After introducing the assumption that 'the same proportion of inputs is used in the consumption-goods and [capital-] goods industries' (Samuelson, 1962, pp. 196–7), Samuelson was able to prove that 'the Surrogate (Homogeneous) Capital ... gives exactly the same result as does the shifting collection of diverse capital goods in our more realistic model' (Samuelson, 1962, p. 201). In particular, 'the relations among w, r, and Q/L that prevail for [the] quasi-realistic complete system of heterogeneous capital goods' could 'be shown to have the same formal properties as does the parable system' (Samuelson, 1962, p. 203). This result was taken to be a justification for using the surrogate

141

production function 'as a useful summarizing device' (ibid.). In fact, Pierangelo Garegnani, who was present at a discussion of a draft of Samuelson's paper, did point out that Samuelson's result is crucially dependent on the assumption of equal proportions of inputs (see Garegnani, 1970). Samuelson acknowledged Garegnani's criticism in a footnote to his paper and admitted that it would be a 'false conjecture' to think that the 'extreme assumption of equi-proportional inputs in the consumption and machine trades could be lightened and still leave one with many of the surrogate propositions' (Samuelson, 1962, p. 202n). But Samuelson and various other economists continued to look for conditions that would ensure a monotonic relation between the rate of profit and the choice of technique even in presence of a non-linear relation between w and r.

The outcome appeared a few years later. David Levhari, a PhD student of Samuelson's, in his dissertation and then in a paper for the *Quarterly Journal of Economics*, claimed he had proved that reswitching of the whole technology matrix would be impossible if this matrix is of the 'irreducible' or 'indecomposable' type (Levhari, 1965). This property – Levhari claimed – would exclude reswitching and thus make it possible to extend the use of a 'surrogate production function' to the non-linear case with production technologies for basic commodities.

However, Levhari's theorem was disproved by Luigi Pasinetti in a paper at the Rome 1st World Congress of the Econometric Society in 1965. Pasinetti's final draft of his paper was published in the November 1966 issue of the *Quarterly Journal of Economics* (Pasinetti, 1966) together with papers written in the meantime by Levhari and Samuelson (1966), Morishima (1966), Bruno, Burmeister and Sheshinski (1966) and Garegnani (1966). This set of papers was called by the journal editor 'Paradoxes in capital theory: a symposium', thereby originating the term. Paul Samuelson concluded the discussion with a 'Summing up' in which he admitted that 'the simple tale told by Jevons, Böhm-Bawerk, Wicksell, and other neoclassical writers', according to which a falling rate of interest is unambiguously associated with the choice of more capital-intensive techniques, 'cannot be universally valid' (Samuelson, 1966, p. 568).

The various contributions to this discussion showed that the reswitching might occur both with 'decomposable' and 'indecomposable' technologies. This result was proved in different ways by Pasinetti (1965 and 1966), Morishima (1966), Bruno, Burmeister and Sheshinski (1966) and Garegnani (1966). Samuelson stated in his summing up that 'reswitching is a logical possibility in any technology, indecomposable or decomposable' (Samuelson, 1966, p. 582). He then called attention to the associated phenomenon of reverse capital deepening and concluded that 'there often turns out to be no unambiguous way of characterizing different processes as more "capital-intensive", more "mechanized", more "roundabout"' (Samuelson, 1966, p. 582).

Although the logical possibility of reswitching was admitted by all participants in the discussion, Bruno, Burmeister and Sheshinski raised doubts as to its empirical relevance: 'there is an open empirical question as to whether or not reswitching is likely to be observed in an actual economy for reasonable changes in the interest rate' (Bruno, Burmeister and Sheshinski, 1966, p. 545n). The same doubt was expressed in Samuelson's summing up (Samuelson, 1966, p. 582). Bruno, Burmeister and Sheshinski also mentioned a theorem, which they attributed to Martin Weitzman and Robert Solow, according to which reswitching of technique may be excluded, in a model with heterogeneous capital goods, provided at least one capital good is produced by 'a smooth neoclassical production function', if 'labour and each good are inputs in one or more of the goods produced neoclassically' (Bruno, Burmeister and Sheshinski, 1966, p. 546). This theorem is based on the idea that 'setting the various marginal productivity conditions and supposing that at two different rates of interest the *same* set of input-output coefficients holds, the proof follows by contradiction' (Bruno, Burmeister and Sheshinski, 1966, p. 546).

It is worth noting that Weitzman–Solow's theorem is simply a consequence of the idea that, in the case of a commodity produced by a neoclassical production function, each set of input–output coefficients ought to be associated in equilibrium with a one-to-one correspondence between marginal productivity ratios and input price ratios. No ratio between marginal productivities would be associated with more than one set of input prices, and this is taken to exclude the possibility that the same technique be chosen at alternative rates of interest, and thus at different price systems. The Weitzman–Solow theorem is at the origin of a line of arguments that has been followed up by a number of other authors, such as Starrett (1969) and Stiglitz (1973). These authors have pursued the idea that 'enough' substitutability, by ensuring the smoothness of the production function, is sufficient to exclude reswitching of technique. However, non-reswitching theorems of this type involve that, for each technique of production, the capital stock may be measurd either in physical terms or at given prices. For in a model with heterogeneous capital goods, if we allow prices to vary when the rate of interest or the unit wage are changed, there is no reason why the same physical set of input–output coefficients might not be associated with different price systems: even in the case of a continuously differentiable production function, the marginal product of 'social' capital cannot be a purely real magnitude independent of prices. Once it is admitted that 'in general marginal products are in terms of net value at constant prices, and hence may well depend upon what those prices happen to be' (Bliss, 1975, p. 195), it is natural to allow for different marginal productivities of the same capital stock at different price systems. It would thus appear that reswitching of technique does not carry with it any logical contradiction even in the case of a smoothly differentiable production function.

Pasinetti also pointed out that the concept of *neoclassical* substitutability is itself a very restrictive concept indeed, as it requires the possibility of infinitesimal variations of each input at a time. In fact, Pasinetti pointed out that it is possible to have a *continuous* variation of techniques (i.e. continuous substitutability) along the w-r relation and yet wide discontinuities in the variation of many inputs between one technique and another, thus making reswitching a quite normal phenomenon (see Pasinetti, 1969). Moreover, a non-monotonic relation between the rate of profit and capital per man may also be obtained in the absence of reswitching (Pasinetti, 1966; Bruno, Burmeister and Sheshinski, 1966). This last possibility calls attention to the phenomenon that lies at the root of the various 'paradoxes' in the theory of capital: the fact that, unless special assumptions are made, a change in the rate of profit and in the unit wage at given technical coefficients is associated with a change of relative prices.

This debate continued for a few years in the late 1960s and early 1970s, with a series of journal articles (see for example Robinson and Naqvi, 1967) and books (see for example Harcourt, 1972). In particular, Hicks presented a 'Neo-Austrian' model in *Capital and Time* (1973), concluding that reswitching of technique can be excluded only in the special case in which all the techniques have the same 'duration parameters', which means the same 'construction period' and 'utilization period' (pp. 41–4).

In the end, therefore, numerous details were added. Yet the essential results remained those that had emerged from Sraffa's book and from the symposium on 'Paradoxes in capital theory'.

SYNTHESIS. The source of most of the difficulties that have emerged in capital theory may be traced back to the fact that 'capital' may be conceived in two fundamentally different ways: (i) capital may be conceived of as a 'free' fund of resources, which can be switched from one use to another without any significant difficulty: this is what may be called the 'financial' conception of capital; (ii) capital may be conceived of as a set of productive factors that are embodied in the production process as it is carried out in a particular productive establishment: this is what may be called the 'technical' conception of capital.

The idea that there exists an inverse monotonic relation between the rate of interest and the demand for capital was born in the financial sphere. The parallel idea of an inverse monotonic relation between the rate of profit and the 'quantity of capital' employed in the production process is the outcome of a long intellectual process of extensions and generalizations. But the recent debate on capital theory has conclusively proved that such extensions and generalizations are devoid of any foundation.

It is logically impossible to make the 'financial' and the 'technical' conceptions of capital coincide, except under very restrictive conditions indeed. There is no unambiguous way in which a decreasing rate of profit may be related to the choice of alternative techniques, in terms of a monotonically increasing capital intensity, or for that matter in terms of monotonically increasing profiles of net production flows over time.

These analytical results are hardly in dispute by now. But their ultimate significance and relevance for economic theory remain highly controversial.

A group of economists now maintain that the new discoveries in capital theory concerning the relations between the rate of profit, capital per man and technical choice call for a reconstruction of economic theory from its foundations. It is stressed that the traditional beliefs are due to mistaken generalizations from the theory of short-run microeconomic behaviour, and it is argued that the economic theory (marginal economic theory) that led to the inconsistencies should be abandoned. It is pointed out that the obvious alternative is a resumption and development of the more comprehensive approach to the classical economists. A characteristic feature of this view is the attention accorded to the 'fully settled' and long-run positions of the economic system, which are made to emerge independently of the forces, such as demand and supply, that determine the level of the economic magnitudes in the short-run (see Garegnani, 1970, and in a different context, Pasinetti, 1981).

A second line of interpretation maintains that economic theorists should be prepared to give up the analytical tools of equilibrium analysis but should concentrate on the actual historical dynamics of the economic system. A characteristic argument associated with this view is that the analysis of the 'capital paradoxes' was carried out through comparison of the virtual positions of the economic system at different levels of the rate of profit and of the unit wage, and that it would be impossible in this way 'to describe an actual process of moving from one equilibrium point to another' (Robinson, 1975, p. 87). A similar argument has been put forward by Hicks (1979, p. 57), according to whom 'nothing can be shown about the *accumulation* of capital' by means of comparison among virtual positions of the economic system. As a result, reswitching of technique is acknowledged as a logical possibility but doubts are expressed on its importance in actual economic history.

A third line of interpretation is taken by more traditionally minded economists. It is argued that the discovery of 'anomalies' in the field of capital theory does point to an important deficiency in traditional economic theory, which leads to the inevitable abandonment of the concept of 'aggregate capital' in neoclassical theory. However it is also argued that there is a way of overcoming this deficiency without giving up the basic premises of traditional theory, and in particular without rejecting the application of the demand-and-supply framework to the study of production. This way leads to concentrating the analysis either on the study of 'short-run' ('temporary') equilibria, in which the physical stocks of technical capital are given, or on the equilibrium of an intertemporal economy, in which goods are described by taking their date of delivery into account. In either case, the logical possibility (or 'existence') of an equilibrium price vector is studied without explicitly considering the movement of 'free' capital from one use to another, and the importance of 'capital paradoxes' is explicitly recognized but the associated difficulties are transferred to the field of stability analysis. In fact the issue of 'stability' of equilibrium is often left open and simply stated in a problematic way (see Hahn, 1982). The traditional 'parables' are thus abandoned in pure economic theory, even if they are still retained to play a role in the fields of applied economics.

Whatever the view that is taken, the major victim of the debate has been the Böhm-Bawerk–Clark–Wicksell theory of capital that was patiently constructed towards the end of the 19th century. This theory relied on a conception of 'aggregate capital' that was taken as measurable independently of the rate of profit and of income distribution. Such a conception of 'capital' has had to be

145

jettisoned. This has on the one hand led to a return to the Walrasian formulation of general equilibrium theory, and on the other hand to the revival of classical political economy. In any case the debate has induced theoretical economists to be much more rigorous about the nature and limits of their assumptions. In many important cases, it has also brought about a change in the main focus of their analyses. Yet it is unlikely that the next generation of economists will leave the issue of capital theory at rest.

BIBLIOGRAPHY

Beccaria, C. 1804. *Elementi di economia pubblica* (ms 1771–72). In *Scrittori Classici Italiani di Economia Politica*, ed. Pietro Custodi, Vol. XVIII, 17–356 and Vol. XIX, 5–166, Milan: Destefanis.

Bliss, C.J. 1975. *Capital Theory and the Distribution of Income*. Amsterdam and Oxford: North–Holland; New York: American Elsevier.

Böhm-Bawerk, E. von. 1889. *Positive Theorie des Kapitales (Kapital und Kapitalzins, Zweite Abteilung)*. Translated as *The Positive Theory of Capital*, London: Macmillan, 1891.

Bruno, M., Burmeister, E. and Sheshinski, E. 1966. The nature and implications of the reswitching of techniques. *Quarterly Journal of Economics* 80(4), November, 526–53.

Burmeister, E. 1980. *Capital Theory and Dynamics*. Cambridge and New York: Cambridge University Press.

Champernowne, D. 1953–4. The production function and the theory of capital: a comment. *Review of Economic Studies* 21(2), 112–35.

Clark, J.B. 1899. *The Distribution of Wealth*. New York: Macmillan.

Garegnani, P. 1966. Switching of techniques. *Quarterly Journal of Economics* 80(4), November, 554–67.

Garegnani, P. 1970. Heterogeneous capital, the production function and the theory of distribution. *Review of Economic Studies* 37(3), July, 407–36.

Hahn, F. 1982. The neo-Ricardians. *Cambridge Journal of Economics* 6(4), December, 353–74.

Harcourt, G.C. 1972. *Some Cambridge Controversies in the Theory of Capital*. Cambridge and New York: Cambridge University Press.

Hicks, J. 1965. *Capital and Growth*. Oxford and New York: Clarendon Press.

Hicks, J. 1973. *Capital and Time. A Neo-Austrian Theory*. Oxford: Clarendon Press.

Hicks, J, 1979. *Causality in Economics*. Oxford: Basil Blackwell.

Jevons, W.S. 1871. *The Theory of Political Economy*. London: Macmillan and Co; 2nd edn, 1879. 5th edn, New York: Kelley & Millman, 1957.

Kaldor, N. 1937. Annual survey of economic theory: the recent controversy on the theory of capital. *Econometrica* 5(3), July, 201–33.

Levhari, D. 1966. A nonsubstitution theorem and switching of techniques. *Quarterly Journal of Economics* 79(1), February, 98–105.

Morishima, M. 1964. *Equilibrium, Stability and Growth. A Multi-Sectoral Analysis*. Oxford: Clarendon Press.

Morishima, M. 1966. Refutation of the nonswitching theorem. *Quarterly Journal of Economics* 80(4), November, 520–25.

Pasinetti, L.L. 1965. Changes in the rate of profit and degree of mechanization: a controversial issue in capital theory. (Unpublished) paper presented at the First World Congress of the Econometric Society, Rome, 1965.

Pasinetti, L.L. 1966. Changes in the rate of profit and switches of techniques. *Quarterly Journal of Economics* 80(4), November, 503–17.

Pasinetti, L.L. 1969. Switches of technique and the 'rate of return' in capital theory. *Economic Journal* 79(3), September, 508–31.

Pasinetti, L.L. 1981. *Structural Change and Economic Growth: A theoretical essay on the dynamics of the wealth of nations.* Cambridge and New York: Cambridge University Press.

Ricardo, D. 1817. *On the Principles of Political Economy and Taxation.* Vol. I of *The Works and Correspondence of David Ricardo,* ed. Piero Sraffa with the collaboration of M.H. Dobb, Cambridge and New York: Cambridge University Press, 1951.

Robinson, J. 1953–4. The production function and the theory of capital. *Review of Economic Studies* 21(2), 81–106.

Robinson, J. 1956. *The Accumulation of Capital.* London: Macmillan; Homewood, Ill.: R.D. Irwin.

Robinson, J. 1975. The unimportance of reswitching. In Joan Robinson, *Collected Economic Papers,* Vol. V, Oxford: Basil Blackwell, 1979, 76–83.

Robinson, J. and Naqvi, K.A. 1967. The badly behaved production function. *Quarterly Journal of Economics* 81(4), November, 579–91.

Samuelson, P. 1962. Parable and realism in capital theory: the surrogate production function. *Review of Economic Studies* 29(3), June, 193–206.

Samuelson, P. 1966. A summing up. *Quarterly Journal of Economics* 80(4), November, 568–83.

Say, J.B. 1817. *Traité d'économie politique.* Paris: Déterville.

Smith, A. 1776. *An Inquiry into the Causes of the Wealth of Nations.* General editors R.H. Campbell and A.S. Skinner; textual editor W.B. Todd, Oxford: Clarendon Press, 1976.

Sraffa, P. 1960. *Production of Commodities by Means of Commodities.* Cambridge: Cambridge University Press.

Starrett, D. 1969. Switching and reswitching in a general production model. *Quarterly Journal of Economics* 83(4), November, 673–87.

Stiglitz, J. 1973. The badly behaved economy with the well-behaved production function. In *Models of Economic Growth,* ed. J.A. Mirrlees and N.H. Stern, London: Macmillan; New York: Wiley.

Thünen, J.-H. 1857. *Le salaire naturel et son rapport aux taux de l'intérêt.* Translated by Mathieu Wolkoff, Paris: Guillaumin et Cie (German original published in 1850).

Wicksell, K. 1901–6. *Lectures on Political Economy.* Vol. I, *General Theory.* London: Routledge, 1934; New York: A.M. Kelley, 1967.

Equal rates of profit

CHRISTOPHER BLISS

The concept of equality, or its opposite inequality, implies a comparison, and a comparison must be based on the consideration of a population of cases. Therefore equality and inequality have different implications according to the definition of that population. This general observation applies in particular to rates of profit.

Three different types of comparison of rates of profit will be examined:

(i) we may compare the rates of profit in terms of a fixed *numéraire*, particularly money, which can be obtained over a certain period of time from investment of funds in different lines of activity. We shall refer to equality in this sense as *sectoral equality* of rates of profit. Or,

(ii) we may compare the rate of profit obtainable over a certain period of time in terms of one *numéraire* with that obtainable over the same period of time in terms of another *numéraire*. In a famous chapter of his *General Theory* (Keynes, 1936, ch. 17), Keynes employs the term 'own rates of interest' to describe these rates of return in terms of different *numéraires,* and we shall borrow the same term and call equality of the rates of return in different numéraires *own rates* equality. Finally,

(iii) we may compare the rate of profit obtainable in terms of the fixed *numéraire,* which may again be money, during one period of time with that obtainable during another later period of time. This comparison includes the historically important question of the long-term trend of the rate of interest: whether it will tend to constancy, to increase, or to decline and, if it is not constant, what will be its eventual limit. We shall refer to equality in this sense as *temporal equality* of rates of profit. (In common with many writers, particularly in the past, we ignore in the present discussion distinctions between the rate of interest and the rate of profit. The main cause of a persistent difference between the two must be sought in the uncertainty from which our analysis abstracts.)

While it is convenient to have discussions of sectoral, own-rate and temporal equality of rates of profit respectively collected together in one article, it will be clear that these are distinct notions and that the investigation of the conditions for one will raise quite different issues from the investigation of the conditions required for another.

THE THEORY OF PROFIT. An argument concerning equality of rates of profit might depend importantly on which theory of the rate of profit is invoked. Such is inescapably the case where temporal equality of rates of profit is concerned. However a good deal of our argument concerning sectoral and own rate equality of rates of profit is independent of the exact theory of the determination of rates of profit in general. This unexpected possibility might be realized because equality of rates of profit depends above all upon arbitrage, the tendency for capital to seek the highest return. Indeed in some cases an arbitrage condition alone suffices to demonstrate that rates of profit must be equal.

We shall refer to a state of the economy in which all possibilities of profitable arbitrage have been put into effects, which is a kind of short-period equilibrium, as an *arbitrage equilibrium*. It has sometimes been claimed that profit (where what is intended is a part of profit distinct from a normal rate of return) is essentially a phenomenon of disequilibrium. On this account an arbitrage equilibrium would not only exhibit equal rates of profit, but all rates of profit would equal zero. Only the normal rate of return would be realized in an arbitrage equilibrium.

To argue about terminology where weighty issues are involved shows poor judgement. Even if profit is defined to be an excess of return to capital above the return generally available, and even if we exclude temporary rents, it remains to show that no sector can enjoy a permanent profit advantage against which arbitrage is for some reason powerless. If, on the other hand, profit is taken to include temporary rents it is evident that there is really no case for equality. Hence the only interesting question to decide is whether rates of profit defined as net returns to capital divided by the values of capital employed (on average or at the margin) are equal in an arbitrage equilibrium.

SECTORAL EQUALITY OF RATES OF PROFIT. Nowhere is the power of arbitrage, together with its limitations, better illustrated than in the case of comparisons of profit rates across sectors. The desire of every investor to obtain the highest possible rate of return may reasonably be assumed to equalize the equivalent rates of return on different bonds. Will not a similar principle ensure the equalization of rates of profit in different activities, be they regions or industries?

The answer depends on two important points. First, we must decide how to compare two rates of return. What are the principles of equivalence? Secondly, arbitrage may encounter obstacles. This is true even where bonds are concerned, and is more important still where we are concerned with different sectors.

Clearly rates of return should be true economic rates including allowances for capital gains, etc. Moreover, two apparently different rates of return may not excite arbitrage if they represent different risks, or different liabilities to taxation, or if the difference is too small to overcome transactions costs. Although they are important in empirical investigations, these detailed considerations may be neglected for our purposess. So we are left with structural obstacles to arbitrage.

When economic theorists assume equal rates of profit in different sectors they are implicitly ignoring questions of industrial structure. (For an excellent treatment of the concept of industrial structure and its implications for profitability, see Hay and Morris, 1979, ch. 7.) It is typically supposed, for example, that capital may be shifted from one sector to another in arbitrarily small quantities. If increasing returns to scale imply that operation at a very small scale will be costly, the putative entrant must choose between staying out of the sector or fighting his way into what must be an oligopolistic market. There is naturally no reason to suppose that the rate of profit enjoyed by those already inside may not exceed that obtainable in a competitive sector of small-scale units.

It would not be necessary to reiterate the foregoing point if it had not apparently been challenged by the late Piero Sraffa in the oft-quoted foreword to his *Production of Commodities by Means of Commodities* (1960). Sraffa's model for the determination of prices is striking for its simplicity and for the fewness of its assumptions. In his foreword the author warned his readers against the temptation to assume that his argument depended upon assuming constant returns to scale. In a sense it does not, as that assumption is never directly employed. However equality of rates of profit, sectoral equality according to our present terminology, is assumed. We cannot of course claim that sectoral equality requires constant returns to scale. However it requires some assumptions about the environment, specifically the market environment, in which firms operate, and constant returns to scale and free entry are obvious sufficient conditions for sectoral equality of profit rates.

EQUALITY OF OWN RATES OF INTEREST. Consider a price system extending through time so that for each period t there is a present price for each of N goods. Such a price system may be represented thus:

$$
\begin{pmatrix}
p_{11} & p_{12} & \cdots & p_{1t} & \cdots & p_{1T} \\
p_{21} & p_{22} & \cdots & p_{2t} & \cdots & p_{2T} \\
\cdots & \cdots & \cdots & \cdots & \cdots & \cdots \\
p_{N1} & p_{N2} & \cdots & p_{Nt} & \cdots & p_{NT}
\end{pmatrix}
\tag{4.1}
$$

As problems raised by infinite price systems need not concern us here, we suppose that the prices only extend forward to period T. If we imagine that good 1 is money, it will be seen that the money rate of interest in period 1 for a t-period loan may be calculated as follows. One unit of present money costs p_{11} and one unit of money bought now for delivery in period t costs p_{1t}. Hence one unit of money surrendered now buys p_{11}/p_{1t} units of money at t. This corresponds to a rate of interest equal to $p_{11}/p_{1t} - 1$, or $(p_{11} - p_{1t})/p_{1t}$. What was denoted above by the term the money rate of interest can equally be designated the *own rate of interest* on money, in this case for a t-period loan.

The money rate of interest measures the extra money obtainable by postponing payment as a proportion of the payment deferred. This notion generalizes to any good. We may for example measure the extra wheat obtainable by postponing delivery as a proportion of the quantity of wheat delivery deferred. Suppose that wheat prices occupy the second row of (4.1). Then the t period own rate of interest for wheat will be equal to $p_{21}/p_{2t} - 1$, or $(p_{21} - p_{2t})/p_{2t}$, which is exactly analogous to the expression of the money rate of interest already derived.

Turning from the rows of (4.1), which correspond to different goods, consider the columns, which correspond to different periods of time. It is easily shown that if the columns are proportional to each other, which is the same as saying that relative prices are the same in all periods, then the own rate of interest for a given duration of loan is the same for all goods. Suppose that the own rate of interest for good 1 for a deferment from period 1 to period t is $r_1 t$. Then, as we have already seen:

$$r_1 t = (p_{11} - p_{1t})/p_{1t}. \tag{4.2}$$

However, by assumption:

$$p_{1t}/p_{it} = p_{11}/p_{1t} \tag{4.3}$$

so that:

$$(p_{i1} - p_{it})/p_{it} = (p_{11} - p_{it})/p_{1t}. \tag{4.4}$$

Or,

$$r_i t = r_1 t. \tag{4.5}$$

Here, constancy of relative prices implies equality of own rates of return, as required. Conversely, variations in relative prices will be reflected in differences in own rates of return.

Under what circumstances is it reasonable to assume constancy of relative prices over time? We shall certainly require the assumption that the economy is stationary in some sense. Suppose for example that as time passes timber becomes more and more scarce relative to demand as forests are depleted or demand grows. Then we would expect the price of timber to rise through time relative to other goods. Similarly, technical progress, unless it be of the simplest labour-augmenting kind, will typically imply changes in relative prices. The transistor, the microchip and other innovations, to cite another example, have certainly caused electric goods to become relatively cheaper.

Consider therefore a stationary state, which may be growing economy, but which is stationary in the sense that in each period it is technically exactly the same as in every other period, except perhaps for scale. As the economy is essentially the same at every moment of time, it makes intuitive sense to suppose that relative prices might be the same at each moment of time, and this intuition is valid in so far as it can be shown that any development of the economy which is stationary, in the sense just described, may be supported by a price system which is itself stationary, in the sense that relative prices are invariant over time.

Stationarity of the real economy is sufficient for stationarity of a price system that will support production activities, but does not imply that any such price system will be stationary. Indeed it is an implication of the multiplicity of price systems and interest rates which goes under the name of 'double-switching' that prices which support stationary production will frequently be neither unique nor themselves stationary. Their non-uniqueness is an immediate implication of double-switching. The existence of non-stationary price systems for these equilibria follows when we note that the average of two systems of equilibrium prices must themselves be equilibrium prices. However the average of two price systems based on different rates of interest produces a rate of interest variable over time, and varying relative prices.

The importance of these findings may be questioned because the price system is required to support not only production (supply) but also consumption (demand). This will make the observation of non-unique prices, and in particular of a history including double-switching, much less probable than a consideration of the production side alone might suggest.

It remains to mention briefly Keynes's use of own rates of interest in his *General Theory*, if only to point out that it is not in fact particularly germane to the present discussion of equality of own rates of interest. Keynes's extraordinary argument is concerned with the comparison of money rates of return at the margin to accumulating various assets, which is something like the question of sectoral equality.

We may imagine that as the various assets are accumulated the money rates of return to further accumulation for each of them is forced down, and that the quantities accumulated are such that these marginal returns on all assets are equalized. If we could conceive of the elasticity of the money rate of return for each asset to the stock accumulated (which we may call the return–stock elasticity) as a value independent of other accumulations, which Keynes in effect does, then assets with low return–stock elasticities will accumulate rapidly relatively to assets with higher return–stock elasticities. Keynes's argument claims that money is eventually the asset with the lowest return–stock elasticity, and that this has the implication that, in an economy with a limited supply of money, the money rate of return (which of course is the own rate of interest of money) will eventually rise to a level which discourages the further accumulation of real assets.

TEMPORAL EQUALITY OF RATES OF PROFIT. We now turn to the equality, or inequality as the case may be, of the rates of profit which prevail at different moments of time. There is a long tradition among economic theorists, which goes back to the classical writers, of explaining the long-run tendency for the rate of profit to fall. This was largely a response to a supposed fall in the rate of interest which the classical economists 'took to be an indisputable fact'. Here we consider only a modern view of the problem. A justification for this division of labour may be sought in the fact that modern theories of the rate of profit are radically different from classical views.

The main source of the difference between modern and classical theories (which in this context should be taken to exclude Marx) is that the former treat technical progress as having regular and continuous effects on the economy, where the latter typically do not. Thus the characteristic classical argument for a falling rate of profit is stagnationist in nature. The decline in the rate of profit is part of the grinding to a halt of a previously progressive economy. In contrast, the modern neoclassical approach locates the explanation of a falling rate of profit in the character of a technical progress conceived as an indefinitely continuing process.

To demonstrate the theoretical issues involved we first show when a declining rate of profit would arise in a neoclassical model with aggregate capital and a constant saving propensity, and then discuss some of the shortcomings of that model as an account of capital accumulation.

Let output, Y, depend upon the input of labour, L, and a capital stock which is homogeneous with the output flow, K, according to a constant returns production function as:

$$Y = F(K, L, t). \tag{5.1}$$

Let partial derivatives be denoted by subscripts so that, for example, the marginal product of capital is denoted $F_K(K, L, t)$. We denote the rate of profit by r, so that:

$$r = F_K(K, L, t). \tag{5.2}$$

Time derivatives are shown by a dot over the variable concerned. Differentiating $F_K(K, L, t)$ totally with respect to time we obtain an expression for the time rate of change of the rate of profit as:

$$\dot{r} = F_{KK} \cdot \dot{K} + F_{KL} \cdot \dot{L} + F_{Kt}. \tag{5.3}$$

Hence for constancy of the rate of profit we must have:

$$F_{KK} \cdot \dot{K} + F_{KL} \cdot \dot{L} + F_{Kt} = 0. \tag{5.4}$$

which on rearrangement yields:

$$\frac{F_{KK} \cdot K}{F_K} \cdot k + \frac{F_{KL} \cdot L}{F_K} \cdot l + \frac{F_{Kt}}{F_K} = 0, \tag{5.5}$$

where k and l are respectively the logarithmic rates of growth of capital and labour. Now (5.5) can be expressed more simply as:

$$\sigma_K \cdot k + \sigma_L \cdot l + \gamma = 0; \tag{5.6}$$

where σ_K and σ_L are respectively the elasticity of the marginal product of capital with respect to K and L, and γ is the proportional change in the marginal product of capital due to the passage of time alone.

We know that $F_K(K, L, t)$ is homogeneous of degree zero in K and L. Hence:

$$\sigma_K + \sigma_L = 0, \tag{5.7}$$

153

and (5.6) reduces to:

$$\sigma_K \cdot (k - 1) + \gamma = 0. \tag{5.8}$$

This last expression has an intuitive interpretation. As σ_K is the elasticity of the marginal product of capital with respect to capital, it will be negative. It is weighted by $k - 1$, the rate of growth of capital per unit of labour, which will be positive under normal economic growth. Thus $\sigma_K \cdot (k - 1)$ measures the rate at which capital accumulation is pushing down the rate of profit due to the substitution of capital for labour at constant technical knowledge. The second term represents the rate at which technical progress is tending to raise the rate of profit at constant factor proportions, which must be a positive term if technical progress is beneficial. Now, unsurprisingly, (5.8) says that, for the rate of profit to remain constant, these two effects must exactly offset.

As it is known that a production function with aggregate capital cannot be derived rigorously except for simple or special production technologies, it may reasonably be asked how far the above account, of a downward pressure on the rate of profit due to accumulation being offset by an upward pressure due to technical progress, generalizes. In particular, is it generally true that accumulation with constant technical knowledge exerts a downward pressure on the rate of profit?

Given the enormous literature on the theory of capital which has been produced in recent years, it is perhaps surprising that this question remains relatively under-investigated. Many discussions of capital accumulation simply beg the question by assuming that the rate of interest would fall continuously through time. Indeed double-switching is most at variance with the traditional neoclassical view of capital accumulation when that assumption is made. However there is no guarantee of a continuous fall of the rate of profit through time, and the demand side of the economy is likely to prohibit a return to a previous and lower income state.

On the other hand, linear models of the type that have been used to illustrate simple stories of capital accumulation can lead to quite eccentric time profiles of consumption being associated with the accumulation of capital (where this is defined simply as an increase in long-term consumption). Hence there is no possibility in general of ruling out erratic developments in the rate of interest over time.

BIBLIOGRAPHY

Bliss, C.J. 1975. *Capital Theory and the Distribution of Income.* Amsterdam: North-Holland.
Harcourt, G.C. 1972. *Some Cambridge Controversies in the Theory of Capital.* Cambridge and New York: Cambridge University Press.
Hay, D.A. and Morris, D.J. 1979. *Industrial Economics: Theory and Evidence.* Oxford and New York: Oxford University Press.
Keynes, J.M. 1936. *The General Theory of Employment, Interest and Money.* London: Macmillan; New York: Harcourt, Brace.
Schumpeter, J. 1954. *History of Economic Analysis.* New York: Oxford University Press.
Sraffa, P. 1960. *Production of Commodities by Means of Commodities.* Cambridge: Cambridge University Press.

Factor price frontier

HEINZ D. KURZ

The constraint binding changes in the distributive variables, in particular the real wage rate (w) and the rate of profit (r), was discovered (though not consistently demonstrated) by Ricardo: 'The greater the portion of the result of labour that is given to the labourer, the smaller must be the rate of profits, and vice versa' (Ricardo, 1971, p. 194). He was thus able to dispel the idea, generated by Adam Smith's notion of price as a sum of wages and profits, that the wage and the rate of profit are determined *independently* of each other. Ever since, the inverse relationship between the distributive variables has played an important role in long-period analysis of both classical and neoclassical descent. In more recent times it was referred to by Samuelson (1957), who later dubbed it 'factor price frontier' (cf. Samuelson, 1962). Hicks (1965, p. 140, n.1) objected that this term is unfortunate, since it is the earnings (quasi-rents) of the (proprietors of) capital goods rather than the rate of profit which is to be considered the 'factor price' of capital (services). A comprehensive treatment of the problem under consideration within a classical framework of the analysis, including joint production proper, fixed capital and scarce natural resources, such as land, was provided by Sraffa (1960). The relationship is also known as the 'wage frontier' (Hicks, 1965), the 'optimal transformation frontier' (Bruno, 1969) and the 'efficiency curve' (Hicks, 1973). The duality of the $w-r$ relationship and the $c-g$ relationship, that is, the relationship between the level of consumption output per worker (c) and the rate of growth (g) in steady-state capital theory has been demonstrated by the latter two authors and in more general terms by Burmeister and Kuga (1970); for a detailed account, see Craven (1979).

To begin with, suppose for simplicity that there are only single-product industries with labour as the only primary input and that only one (indecomposable) system of production is known (cf. Sraffa, 1960, Part I). Then, with gross outputs of the different products all measured in physical terms and made equal to unity by choice of units and with wages paid at the end of the uniform production period, we have the price system.

$$p = (1+r)ap + wa_0, \tag{1}$$

where p is the column vector of normal prices, a is the square matrix of material outputs, which is assumed to be productive, and a_0 is the column vector of direct labour inputs. Using the consumption basket d as standard of value or *numéraire*,

$$dp = 1, \tag{2}$$

we can derive from (1) and (2) the $w-r$ relationship for system (a, a_0)

$$w = \{d[I - (1+r)a]^{-1}a_0\}^{-1} \tag{3}$$

The relationship is illustrated in Figure 1. At $r = 0$ the real wage in terms of d is at its maximum value W; it falls monotonically with increases in r, approaching zero as r approaches its maximum value R. (The $w-r$ relationship can be shown to be a straight line if Sraffa's Standard commodity s is used as *numéraire*, where s is a row vector such that $s = (1 + R)$ sa; cf. Sraffa, 1960, chap. IV.)

Let us now assume that several systems are available for the production of the different commodities and that all the production processes exhibit constant returns to scale. We call the set of all the alternative known methods (or processes) of production the *technology* of the economic system. From this set a series of alternative *techniques* can be formed by grouping together these methods of production, one for each commodity. Hence there is the question of the *choice of technique*. Under competitive conditions this choice will be exclusively grounded on cheapness, that is, the criterion of choice is that of *cost-minimization*. In the case depicted, it can be shown that the competitive tendency of entrepreneurs to adopt whichever technique is cheapest in the existing price situation, will for a given w (or, alternatively, r) lead to the technique yielding the highest $r(w)$, whereas techniques yielding the same $r(w)$ for the same $w(r)$ are equiprofitable and can co-exist (cf. Garegnani, 1970, p. 411).

What has just been said is illustrated in Figure 2. It is assumed that only three alternative techniques, α, β and γ, are available, each of which is represented by

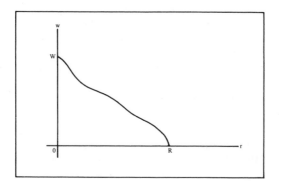

Figure 1

the associated w–r relationship; since w is always measured in terms of the consumption basket d, all three relationships can be drawn in the same diagram. Obviously, technique γ is inferior and will not be adopted. Technique α will be chosen for $0 < w < w_1$ and $w_2 < w \leqslant w_\alpha$, while technique β dominates at $w_1 < w < w_2$; there are two *switch points* (at $w = w_1$ and $w = w_2$, respectively) at which both techniques are equiprofitable. The heavy line represents the economy's w–r *frontier* (or 'factor price frontier') and is the outer envelope of the w–r relationships. At a level of the wage rate w^*, for example, technique β will be adopted giving a rate of profit r^*. (For a discussion of more general cases of single production, see Pasinetti, 1977, ch. VI; for a reformulation of some results in capital theory in terms of the so-called 'dual' cost and profit functions, see Salvadori and Steedman, 1985; on the maximum number of switch points between two production systems, see Bharadwaj, 1970.)

Figure 2 shows that the same technique (α) may be cost-minimizing at more than one level of the wage rate (rate of profit) even though other techniques (here β) dominate at wage rates in between. The implication of this possibility of the *reswitching* of techniques (and of the related possibility of *reverse capital deepening*) is that the direction of change of input proportions cannot be related unambiguously to changes in the distributive variables. This can be demonstrated by making use of the duality between the w–r and the c–g frontier. Denoting the value of net output per labour unit by y and the value of capital per labour unit by k, we have in steady-state equilibrium

$$y = w + rk = c + gk. \tag{4}$$

Solving for k we get

$$k = (c - w)/(r - g) \tag{5}$$

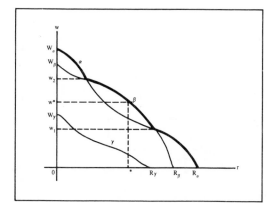

Figure 2

157

except in golden rule equilibrium ($g = r$), where k can be shown to be (minus) the slope of the golden rule $w-r$ relationship at the going level of r. In Figure 3(a) the frontier built of two techniques, α and β, is depicted. The rate of growth is fixed at the level $\bar{g}$, to which correspond c_α and c_β. For values of $r \geqslant \bar{g}$, that is, on the right side of the golden rule, Figure 3(b) gives the corresponding value of $k(r, \bar{g})$. For example, at $\tilde{w}$ technique β will be chosen, yielding a rate of profit $\tilde{r}$; the associated capital intensity is given by

$$\tan \varepsilon = (c_\beta - \tilde{w})/(\tilde{r} - \bar{g}) = \tilde{k}.$$

Figure 3(b) shows that the capital–labour ratio need not be inversely related to the rate of profit as neoclassical long-period theory maintained. In more general terms, it cannot be presumed that input uses, per unit of output, are related to the corresponding 'factor prices' in the conventional way (see Metcalfe and Steedman, 1972, and Steedman, 1985). This result calls in question the validity of the traditional demand and supply approach to the determination of quantities, prices and income distribution.

The results stated above essentially carry over to the more general case with fixed capital, pure joint production and several primary inputs, such as land and labour of different qualities, provided the formalization of the problem is appropriately adapted to the specific case under consideration. Here it suffices to point out a few additional aspects of the choice of technique problem.

With fixed capital there is always such a problem to be solved. This concerns both the choice of the system of operation of plant and equipment, that is, for example, whether a single- or a double-shift system is to be adopted; and the choice of the economic lifetimes of fixed capital goods. During the capital theory debates of the 1960s and early 1970s attention focused on the latter aspect of the use of capital. It was shown that with decreasing or changing efficiency of the durable capital good cost minimization implies that for a given level of the rate of profit premature truncation is advantageous as soon as the price (book value) of the partly worn-out item becomes negative. While the $w-r$ relationship

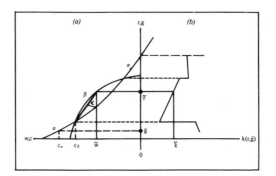

Figure 3

for a given truncation may slope upwards over some range of r, the $w-r$ frontier consists only of those parts of the $w-r$ relationships that are downward-sloping. Moreover, it was demonstrated that the frontier can display the *return of the same truncation* (cf., for example, Hagemann and Kurz, 1976). As to the other aspect of capital utilization, a similar possibility can be shown to exist: the *return of the same system of operation of plant and equipment* (cf. Kurz, 1986). Both phenomena are of course variants of the reswitching of techniques.

In systems with pure joint production a choice of technique is inherent, even where the number of processes available does not exceed the number of products. Sraffa's approach to joint production is in terms of 'square' systems of production, that is, systems where the number of processes operated is equal to the number of commodities (i.e. positively-priced products). However, as Salvadori (1982) has shown, in such a framework a cost-minimizing system does not need to exist. A way out of this impasse may be seen in a formalization of joint production that is similar to von Neumann's. In such a formalization the free disposal assumption plays a crucial role. It can be shown that the $w-r$ frontier is downward-sloping, even though individual $w-r$ relationships may have positive ranges.

BIBLIOGRAPHY

Bharadwaj, K. 1970. On the maximum number of switches between two production systems. *Schweizerische Zeitschrift für Volkswirtschaft und Statistik* 106, December, 409–29.

Bruno, M. 1969. Fundamental duality relations in the pure theory of capital and growth. *Review of Economic Studies* 36, January, 39–53.

Burmeister, E. and Kuga, K. 1970. The factor price frontier, duality and joint production. *Review of Economic Studies* 37, January, 11–19.

Craven, J. 1979. Efficiency curves in the theory of capital: a synthesis. In *The Measurement of Capital, Theory and Practice*, ed. K.D. Patterson and K. Schott, London: Macmillan.

Garegnani, P. 1970. Heterogeneous capital, the production function and the theory of distribution. *Review of Economic Studies* 37, July, 407–36.

Hagemann, H. and Kurz, H.D. 1976. The return of the same truncation period and reswitching of techniques in neo-Austrian and more general models. *Kyklos* 29, December, 678–708.

Hicks, J.R. 1965. *Capital and Growth*. Oxford and New York: Oxford University Press.

Hicks, J.R. 1973. *Capital and Time, A Neo-Austrian Theory*. Oxford: Oxford University Press.

Kurz, H.D. 1986. 'Normal' positions and capital utilisation. *Political Economy* 2, May, 37–54.

Metcalfe, J.S. and Steedman, I. 1972. Reswitching and primary input use. *Economic Journal* 82, March, 140–57.

Pasinetti, L.L. 1977. *Lectures on the Theory of Production*. London: Macmillan; New York: Columbia University Press.

Ricardo, D. 1971. *The Works and Correspondence of David Ricardo*, Vol. VIII. Edited by P. Sraffa in collaboration with M.H. Dobb, Cambridge and New York: Cambridge University Press.

Salvadori, N. 1982. Existence of cost-minimizing systems within the Sraffa framework. *Zeitschrift für Nationalökonomie* 42, September, 281–98.

Salvadori, N. and Steedman, I. 1985. Cost functions and produced means of production: duality and capital theory. *Contributions to Political Economy* 4, March, 79–90.

Samuelson, P.A. 1957. Wages and interest: a modern dissection of Marxian economic models. *American Economic Review* 47, December, 884–912.

Samuelson, P.A. 1962. Parable and realism in capital theory: the surrogate production function. *Review of Economic Studies* 29, June, 193–206.

Sraffa, P. 1960. *Production of Commodities by Means of Commodities.* Cambridge: Cambridge University Press.

Steedman, I. 1985. On input 'demand curves'. *Cambridge Journal of Economics* 9, June, 165–72.

Irving Fisher

JAMES TOBIN

Irving Fisher was born in Saugerties, New York, on 27 February 1867; he was residing in New Haven, Connecticut at the time of his death in a New York City hospital on 29 April 1947.

Fisher is widely regarded as the greatest economist America has produced. A prolific, versatile and creative scholar, he made seminal and durable contributions across a broad spectrum of economic science. Although several earlier Americans, notably Simon Newcomb, had used some mathematics in their writings, Fisher's dedication to the method and his skill in using it justify calling him America's first mathematical economist. He put his early training in mathematics and physics to work in his doctoral dissertation on the theory of general equilibrium. Throughout his career his example and his teachings advanced the application of quantitative method not only in economic theory but also in statistical inquiry. He, together with Ragnar Frisch and Charles F. Roos, founded the Econometric Society in 1930; and Fisher was its first President. He had been President of the American Economic Association in 1918.

Much of standard neoclassical theory today is Fisherian in origin, style, spirit and substance. In particular, most modern models of capital and interest are essentially variations on Fisher's theme, the conjunction of intertemporal choices and opportunities. Likewise, his theory of money and prices is the foundation for much of contemporary monetary economics.

Fisher also developed methodologies of quantitative empirical research. He was the greatest expert of all time on index numbers, on their theoretical and statistical properties and on their use in many countries throughout history. From 1923 to 1936, his own Index Number Institute manufactured and published price indexes of many kinds from data painstakingly collected from all over the world. Indefatigable and innovative in empirical research, Fisher was an early and regular user of correlations, regressions and other statistical and econometric tools that later became routine.

To this day Fisher's successors are often rediscovering, consciously or unconsciously, Fisher's ideas and building upon them. He can be credited with distributed lag regression, life cycle saving theory, the 'Phillips curve', the case for taxing consumption rather than 'income', the modern quantity theory of money, the distinction between real and nominal interest rates, and many more standard tools in economists' kits. Although Fisher was not fully appreciated by his contemporaries, today he leads other old-timers by wide and increasing margins in journal citations. In column inches in the *Social Sciences Citation Index* (1979, 1983), Fisher led his most famous contemporaries, Wesley Mitchell, J.B. Clark, and F.W. Taussig in that order, by rough ratios 5:3:1:1 in 1971–5 and 9:3:1:1 in 1976–80. Much more than the others, moreover, Fisher is cited for substance rather than for history of thought.

For all his scientific prowess and achievement, Fisher was by no means an 'ivory tower' scholar detached from the problems and policy issues of his times. He was a congenital reformer, an inveterate crusader. He was so aggressive and persistent, and so sure he was right, that many of his contemporaries regarded him as a 'crank' and discounted his scientific work accordingly. Science and reform were indeed often combined in Fisher's work. His economic findings, theoretical and empirical, would suggest to him how to better the world; or dissatisfaction with the state of the world would lead him into scientifically fruitful analysis and research. Fisher's search for conceptual clarity about 'the nature of capital and income' led him not only to lay the foundations of modern social accounting but also to argue that income taxation wrongly puts saving in double jeopardy. Fisher turned his talents to monetary theory because he suspected that economic instability was largely the fault of existing monetary institutions. His 'debt-deflation theory of depression' was motivated by the disasters the Great Depression visited upon the world.

Economics was not the only aspect of human and social life that engaged Fisher's reformist zeal. He was active and prolific in other causes: temperance and Prohibition; vegetarianism, fresh air, exercise and other aspects of personal hygiene; eugenics; and peace through international association of nations.

Fisher was an amazingly prolific and gifted writer. The bibliography compiled by his son lists some 2000 titles authored by Fisher, plus another 400 signed by his associates or written by others about him. Fisher's writings span all his interests and causes. They include scholarly books and papers, articles and popular media, textbooks, handbooks for students, tracts, pamphlets, speeches and letters to editors and statesmen. They include the weekly releases of index numbers, often supplemented by commentary on the economic outlook and policy, issued for thirteen years by Fisher and assistants from the Index Number Institute housed in his New Haven home.

Fisher was the consummate pedagogical expositor, always clear as crystal. He hardly ever wrote just for fellow experts. His mission was to educate and persuade the world. He took the trouble to lead the uninitiated through difficult material in easy stages. Whenever he was teaching or tutoring students, he wrote handbooks or texts for their benefit – in mathematics and science when he was still a student himself, in the principles of economics when he was the professor responsible for the introductory course. Fisher's economics text was published in 1910 and 1911. Its graceful exposition of sophisticated theoretical material will impress a modern connoisseur, but it was too difficult for widespread adoption. Some of it survived in a leading introductory text of the 1920s and 1930s, by the younger Yale economists Fairchild, Furniss and Buck (1926).

A BRIEF BIOGRAPHY

Irving Fisher grew up and attended school successively in Peace Dale, Rhode Island; New Haven, Connecticut; and St Louis, Missouri. His father, a Congregational minister, died of tuberculosis just when Irving had finished high school and was planning to attend Yale College, his father's *alma mater*. Irving was now the principal breadwinner for himself, his mother and his younger brother. He did have a $500 legacy from his father for his college education. The family moved to New Haven, and together managed to make ends meet. Irving tutored fellow students during term and in summers.

Fisher was a great success in Yale College, ranking first in his class and winning prizes and distinctions not only in mathematics but across the board. He was also determined to make good in the extra-curricular college culture so important in those days. His efforts won him election to the most prestigious secret senior society, Skull and Bones, the ultimate reward senior campus leaders bestowed on members of the class behind them.

Awarded a scholarship for graduate study, he stayed on at Yale. Graduate Studies were not departmentalized in those days, and Fisher ranged over mathematics, science, social science and philosophy. His most important teachers were Josiah Willard Gibbs, the mathematical physicist celebrated for his theory of thermodynamics, William Graham Sumner, famous still in sociology but at the time also important in political economy, and Arthur Twining Hadley, a leading economist specializing in what is now known as Industrial Organization.

As the time to write a dissertation approached, Fisher had still not chosen his life work. Young Fisher's interests and talents were universal. In the seven years at Yale before he finished his doctorate, he had written and published poetry, political commentary, book reviews, a geometry text together with tables of logarithms, and voluminous notes on mathematics, mechanics and astronomy for the benefit of students he was teaching or tutoring. If he had specialized in anything in six years at Yale, it was mathematics, but even in his graduate years he had spent half his time elsewhere.

Sumner put him on to mathematical economics, and in his third year of graduate study, he finished the dissertation that won him worldwide recognition in economic theory. Fisher's 1891 PhD was the first one in pure economics awarded by Yale, albeit by the faculty of mathematics. Although the university, thanks to Sumner, Hadley and Henry W. Farnum, was strong in 'political economy', there was no distinct department for the subject, let alone for 'economics'. This was generally the case in American universities. Venturing into mathematical economic theory, Fisher was very much on his own; and his route into economics was quite different from that of most American economists of his era.

The dominant tradition in American political economy was imported from the English classical economists, mainly Smith, Ricardo and John Stuart Mill; it was just beginning to be updated by Marshall. This tradition Fisher's mentors at Yale had taught him well. But the neoclassical developments on the European continent from 1870 on, the works of Walras and Menger and Böhm-Bawerk, or even those of their English counterparts Jevons and Edgeworth, had been little noticed at Yale or elsewhere in America.

At the time, the main challenge in America to classical political economy was coming from quite a different direction. The American Economic Association was founded in 1886 by young rebels against Ricardian dogma and its *laissez-faire* political and social message. They included Richard T. Ely, J.B. Clark, Edwin R.A. Seligman and other future luminaries of American economics. Many of them had pursued graduate studies in Germany. In the German emphasis on historical, institutional and empirical studies they found welcome relief from implacable classical theory, and in the German faith in the state as an instrument of socially beneficial reform they found a hopeful antidote to the fatalism of economic competition and social Darwinism. Sumner was prominent among several elders who refused to join an Association born of such heresy; he did not relent even though the AEA very soon became sufficiently neutral and catholic to attract his Yale colleagues and other initial holdouts. Fisher, a bit younger than the founding rebels and educated solely at one American university, was not involved. It was his reconstruction, rather than their revolution, that was destined eventually to replace the classical tradition in the mainstream of American economics.

Fisher stayed at Yale throughout his career. He started teaching mathematics, evidently even before he received his doctorate and was appointed Tutor in Mathematics. His first economics teaching was under the auspices of the mathematics faculty, an undergraduate course on 'The Mathematical Theory of Prices'. In 1894–5 during his Wanderjahr in Europe, this young American star was welcomed by the leading mathematically inclined theorists in every country. On his return he became Assistant Professor of Political and Social Science and began teaching economics proper. He was appointed full Professor in 1898 and retired in 1935.

Fisher was struck by tuberculosis in 1898. He spent the first three years of his professorship on leave from Yale and from science, recuperating in more salubrious climates. His lifelong crusade for hygienic living dates from this personal struggle to regain health and vigour. The experience powerfully reinforced his determination to gain 'a place among those who have helped along my science' and his ambition 'to be a *great* man', as he wrote to his wife (I.N. Fisher, 1956, pp. 87–8). After his recovery the books and articles began flowing from his pen, never to stop until his death at the age of 80.

Fisher participated actively in teaching and in university affairs until 1920. Thereafter his writings and his myriad outside activities and crusades preoccupied him. He taught only half time and had little impact on students, undergraduate or graduate. Thus Fisher had few personal disciples; there was no Fisherian School. The student to whom Fisher was closest, personally and intellectually, was James Harvey Rogers, a 1916 PhD who returned to Yale as a professor in 1930. His career was prematurely ended by his tragic death in a plane crash in 1939 at the age of 55.

Fisher was, on top of everything else, an inventor. His most successful and profitable invention was the visible card index system he patented in 1913. In 1925 Fisher's own firm, the Index Visible Company, merged with its principal competitor to form Kardex Rand Co., later Remington Rand, still later Sperry Rand. The merger made him wealthy. However, he subsequently lost a fortune his son estimated to amount to 8 or 10 million dollars, along with savings of his wife and her sister, when he borrowed money to exercise rights to buy additional Rand shares in the bull market of the late 1920s.

More than money was at risk in the market. Fisher had staked his public reputation as an economic pundit by his persistent optimism about the economy and stock prices, even after the 1929 crash. His reputation crashed too, especially among non-economists in New Haven, where the university had to buy his house and rent it to him to save him from eviction. Until the 1950s the name Irving Fisher was without honour in his own university. Except for economic theorists and econometricians, few members of the community appreciated the genius of a man who lived among them for 63 years.

Irving Fisher's marriage to Margaret Hazard in 1893 was a very happy one for 47 years. She died in 1940. They had two daughters and one son, his father's biographer. The death of their daughter Margaret in 1919 after a nervous breakdown was the greatest tragedy of her parents' lives. Their daughter Carol brought them two grandchildren.

GENERAL EQUILIBRIUM THEORY

Fisher's doctoral dissertation (1892) is a masterly exposition of Walrasian general equilibrium theory. Fisher, who was meticulous about acknowledgements throughout his career, writes in the preface that he was unaware of Walras while writing the dissertation. His personal mentors in the literature of economics were Jevons (1871) and Auspitz and Lieben (1889).

Fisher's inventive ingenuity combined with his training under Gibbs to produce a remarkable hydraulic-mechanical analogue model of a general equilibrium system, replete with cisterns, valves, levers, balances and cams. Thus could he display physically how a shock to demand or supply in one of ten interrelated markets altered prices and quantities in all markets and changed the incomes and consumption bundles of the various consumers. The model is described in detail in the book; unfortunately both the original model and a second one constructed in 1925 have been lost to posterity. Anyway Fisher was a precursor of a current Yale professor, Herbert Scarf (1973) and other practitioners of computing general equilibrium solutions. In his formal mathematical model-building too, Fisher was greatly impressed by the analogies between the thermodynamics of his mentor Gibbs and economic systems, and he was able to apply Gibbs's innovations in vector calculus.

Fisher expounds thoroughly the mathematics of utility functions and their maximization, and he is careful to allow for corner solutions. He uses independent and additive utilities of commodities in his first mathematical approximation and in his physical model; later he was to show how this assumption could be exploited to measure marginal utilities empirically (1927). But the general formulation in his dissertation makes the utility of every commodity depend on the quantities consumed of all commodities. At the same time, he states clearly that neither interpersonally comparable utility nor cardinal utility for each individual is necessary to the determination of equilibrium. Fisher's list of the limitations of his analysis is candid and complete. The supply side of Fisher's model is, as he acknowledges, primitive. Each commodity is produced at increasing marginal cost, but neither factor supplies and prices nor technologies are explicitly modelled.

Finally, Fisher shows his enthusiasm for his discovery of mathematical economics by appending to his dissertation as published an exhaustive survey and bibliography of applications of mathematical method to economics.

General equilibrium with intertemporal choices and opportunities. The distribution of income and wealth, and in particular the sources, determinants and social rationales, of interest and other returns to private property, were obsessive topics in economics, both in Europe and North America, at the turn of the century. One important reason, especially in Europe, was the Marxist challenge to the legitimacy of property income. Answering Marx was a strong motivation for the Austrian school, in particular for the capital theory of Böhm-Bawerk and his followers. Neoclassical economics was in a much better position than its classical precursor to respond to the Marxist challenge. The labour theory of value, which Marx borrowed from the great classical economists themselves, neither explains nor justifies functionally or ethically incomes other than wages.

These topics engaged the two leading American economists of the era, John Bates Clark and Fisher. Clark (1899) set forth his marginal productivity theory of distribution, arguing that a generalized factor of production, capital, the accumulation of past savings, has like labour a marginal product that explains and justifies the incomes of its owners.

Fisher attacked these problems in a more elegant, abstract, mathematical, general and ethically neutral manner than Clark, and than Böhm-Bawerk. At the same time, his approach was clearer, simpler and more insightful than that of Walras.

The general equilibrium system of Fisher's dissertation was a single-period model. No intertemporal choices entered; hence the theory was silent on the questions of capital and interest. But Fisher took up these subjects soon after.

His first contribution, one that should not be underestimated, was to set straight the concepts and the accounting. This he did in (1896) and (1906) with clarity and completeness that have scarcely been surpassed. It is all there: continuous and discrete compounding; nominal versus real rates; the distinction between high prices and rising prices, and its implications for observations of interest rates; the inevitable differences among rates computed in different *numéraires*; rates to different maturities and consistency among them; appreciation, expected and unexpected; present values of streams of in- and out-payments; and so on. Schumpeter calls this work 'the first economic theory of accounting' and says 'it is (or should be) the basis of modern income analysis' (1954, p. 872).

Perhaps the most remarkable feature is Fisher's insistence that 'income' is consumption, including of course consumption of the services of durable goods. In principle, he says, income is psychic, the subjective utility yielded by goods and services consumed. More practically, income could be measured as the money value, or value in some other *numéraire*, of the goods and services directly yielding utility, but only of those. Receipts saved and invested, for example in the purchase of new durable goods, are not 'income' for Fisher; they will yield consumption and utility later, and those yields will be income. To include both the initial investment and the later yields as income is, according to Fisher, as absurd as to count both flour and bread in reckoning net output. This view naturally led Fisher to oppose conventional income taxation as double taxing of saving, and to favour consumption taxation instead. His views on these matters are loudly echoed today.

Fisher published his theory of the determination of interest rates in *The Rate of Interest* (1907). A revised and enlarged version was published in 1930 as *The Theory of Interest*. One motivation for the revision was that Fisher's many critics apparently did not understand the 1907 version. They typically concentrated on the 'impatience' side of Fisher's theory of intertemporal allocation and missed the 'opportunities' side. It was there in 1907 already; the theory is much the same in both versions.

In 1930 Fisher is at pains to label his theory the 'impatience and opportunity' theory. 'Every essential part of it', he acknowledges, 'was at least foreshadowed by John Rae in 1834.' He does claim originality for his concept of 'investment opportunity'. This turns on 'the rate of return over cost, [where] both cost and return are differences between two optional income streams' (1930, p. ix). As Keynes acknowledged, this is the same as his own 'marginal efficiency of capital' (Keynes, 1936, p. 140).

In these books Fisher extended general equilibrium theory to intertemporal choices and relationships. This strategy was different from Walras. Walras tried to extend his multi-commodity multi-agent model of exchange to allow for production, saving and investment. This maintained his stance of full generality but was also difficult to expound and to understand. Fisher saw that intertemporal dependences were tricky enough to justify isolating them from the intercommodity complexities that had concerned him in his doctoral thesis. Therefore he proceeded as if there were just one aggregate commodity to be produced and consumed at different dates. This simplification enabled him to illuminate the subject more brightly than Walras himself.

The methodology of Fisher's capital theory is very modern. His clarifications of the concepts of capital and income lead him to formulate the problem as determination of the time paths of consumption – that is, income – both for individual agents and for the whole economy. Then he divides the problem into the two sides, tastes and technologies, that are second nature to theorists today. One need only read Böhm-Bawerk's murky mixture of the two in his list of reasons for the agio of future over present consumption to realize that Fisher's procedure was not instinctive in those times.

Fisher's theory of individual saving is basically the standard model to this day. Undergraduates learn the two-period 'Fisher diagram', where a family of indifference curves in the two commodities consumption now c_1 and consumption later c_2 confront a budget constraint $c_1 + c_2/(1 + r) = y_1 + y_2(1 + r)$, where the y's are exogenous wage incomes in the two periods and r is the (real) market interest rate. From the usual tangency can be read the consumption choices and present saving or dissaving. This is indeed a Fisher diagram, but of course he went much beyond it.

He stated clearly what we now call the 'life cycle' model, explaining why individuals will generally prefer to smooth their consumption over time, whatever the time path of their expected receipts. But he was not dogmatic, and he allowed room for bequests and for precautionary saving. Where Fisher differed from later theorists, and especially from contemporary model-builders, was in his un-willingness to impose any assumed uniformity on the preferences (or expectations of 'endowments' – the latter term was not familiar to him though the concept was) of the agents in his economies, and in his scruples against buying definite results by assuming tractable functional forms. In general, many of the advances claimed in present-day theory appear to depend on greater boldness in these respects.

On the side of technology, Fisher's approach was the natural symmetrical partner of his formulation of preferences, equally simple, abstract and general. He assumed that the 'investment opportunities' available to an individual (not necessarily the same for everybody) and to the society as a whole can be summarized in the terms on which consumption at any date can be traded, with 'nature', for consumptions at other dates. In modern language, we would say that Fisher postulated intertemporal production possibility frontiers, properly convex in their arguments, for consumptions at various dates.

All that remained for Fisher, then, was to assume complete intertemporal loan markets cleared by real interest rates, count equations, and show that in principle the equalities of saving and investment at every date determine all interest rates and the paths of consumption and production for all individuals and for the society. Like hundreds of mathematical theorists since, he set the problem up so that it conformed to a paradigm he knew, in this case the Walrasian paradigm of his own doctoral dissertation. A more rigorous proof of the existence of the equilibria Fisher was looking for came much later, from Arrow and Debreu (1954). As we know, the problems of infinity, whether agents are assumed to have infinite or finite horizons, are much more troublesome than Fisher imagined.

In any event, Fisher had an excellent vantage point from which to comment on the controversies over capital and interest raging in his day. His formulation of 'investment opportunities' seems to allow for no factor of production one could call 'capital' and enter as argument in a production function. For that matter, he doesn't explicitly model the role of labour in production either, or of land. Strangely, in Fisher's insistence that interest is *not* a cost of production, he seems to say that labour is the only cost, evidently because labour and labour alone is a source of disutility: the loss of utility from leisure being the opportunity cost of the consumption afforded by work. Proceeding in the same spirit, he postulates that, from a position of equality of present and planned future consumption a typical individual will require more extra future consumption than present consumption as compensation for extra work. The difference, the agio, is interest, whether or not it is a 'cost'. Fisher attributes the agio to 'impatience', at the same time scorning the notion that interest is the cost of securing the services of a factor of production called 'abstinence' or 'waiting'.

In the 1890s and 1900s Knut Wicksell, discovering marginal productivity independently of Clark, was modelling production as a function of labour and land inputs with the output also depending on the lags between those inputs and the harvests (Wicksell [1911], 1934, vol. I, pp. 144–66). This is an 'Austrian' formulation, akin to Böhm-Bawerk's examples of trees and wine, in which time itself appears to be productive. Fisher rightly objects to any generalization that waiting longer increases output. His own intertemporal frontiers are, to be sure, sufficiently general to encompass such technologies. They can also accommodate Leontief input–output tables and Koopmans–Dantzig activity matrices with lags. Hayekian triangular structures with inventories of intermediate goods in process, Solow technologies with durable goods and labour jointly yielding output contemporaneously or later. The only common denominator of these and other representations of technology is that they relate consumption opportunities at different dates to one another, though not necessarily always in the convex trade-off terms Fisher assumed. There does not appear to be any summary scalar measure to which the productivity of a process is generally monotonically related, whether roundaboutness, average period of production, or replacement value of existing stocks of goods.

Fisher describes himself as an advocate of 'impatience' as an explanation of interest, although he realizes there are two sides of the saving-investment market, and although he acknowledges that real interest rates can at times be zero or negative. He does appear to believe that in a stationary equilibrium with constant consumption streams, consumers will require positive interest, and that only those technologies and investment opportunities affording a 'rate of return over cost' equal to this pure time preference rate would be used. He does not face up to Schumpeter's argument in 1911 that in such a repetitive and riskless 'circular flow', rational consumers would not care whether a marginal unit of consumption occurs today or tomorrow (Schumpeter [1912], 1934, pp. 34–6). Like Böhm-Bawerk, Fisher appeals to the shortness and uncertainty of life as a reason for time preference. For life-cycle consumers, however, time preferences are entangled with age preferences, and it is hard to defend any generalization as to their net direction. Fair annuities take care of the uncertainty.

MONETARY THEORY: THE EQUATION OF EXCHANGE AND THE QUANTITY THEORY

Irving Fisher was the major American monetary economist of the early decades of this century; the subject occupied him until the end of his career. Here especially Fisher combined theorizing with empirical research, both historical and statistical. The problems he encountered led him to invent statistical and econometric methods – index numbers and distributed lags in particular – to apply for the purposes at hand to the data he and his assistants compiled. (He even studied the turnover of cash and checking accounts of a sample of Yale students, professors and employees.)

Money was a big subject in American economic literature in the 19th century, before Fisher came on the scene. The monetary events of the times – the inconvertible greenbacks issued during the Civil War, their redemption in gold in 1879, the demonetization of silver, the rapidly increasing importance of banks – stimulated research and controversy. Nevertheless, monetary theory was relatively undeveloped and unsystematized, both in Europe and in America. Fisher's treatise (1911a) was an ambitious attempt to organize with the help of theory a large body of historical and institutional information.

Yet for all its theory, statistics and index numbers, *The Purchasing Power of Money* is a tract supporting Fisher's proposal for stabilizing the value of money. This came to be known as the 'compensated dollar', the gold-exchange standard combined with a rule mandating periodic changes in the official buying and selling prices of gold inverse to changes in a designated commodity price index. In 1911 Fisher proposed that the gold price changes be uniform and synchronous in the currencies of all countries linked by fixed exchange parities, in proportional amounts related to an international price index. Later he was willing to accept as second best that the United States adopt the scheme on its own. Keynes proposed a similar but less formal rule for the United Kingdom (1923).

The proposal is an early example of a policy *rule*, another Fisherian idea ahead of its time, more likely to be popular among economists today than it was with Fisher's contemporaries. Indeed, some rules recently proposed are quite Fisherian, for example Hall (1985).

The 'compensated dollar' is but one of several proposals Fisher advanced over the years for stabilizing price levels or mitigating the effects of their unforeseen variation. In the 1911 book he also writes favourably of the 'tabular standard', which meant no more operationally than facilitating price-indexed contracts. In the 1920s he launched a crusade for 100 per cent reserves against checkable deposits, culminating in *100% Money* (1935). This idea is also beginning to resurface in the 1980s as a preventive defence against the monetary hazards of bank failures. In Schumpeter's view, Fisher's zeal for monetary reforms lost him some of the attention and respect his scientific contributions to monetary economics deserved, and made him come across as more monetarist than his own analysis and evidence justified (Schumpeter, 1954, pp. 872–3).

The Purchasing Power of Money is a monetarist book. Fisher asserts the quantity theory as earnestly and persuasively as Milton Friedman. There are two species of quantity theories. One is a simple implication of the 'classical dichotomy': since only relative prices and real endowments enter commodity and factor demand and supply functions, the solution values for real variables in a general equilibrium are independent of scalar variations of exogenous nominal quantities. While Fisher mentions this implication of general equilibrium theory, he does not dwell upon it as one might expect. Anyway, it does not quite apply to a commodity money system like the gold standard, which Fisher was analysing. Fisher's theory is mainly of the second kind, based on the demand for and supply of the particular nominal assets serving as media of exchange.

Fisher is usually given credit for the Equation of Exchange, although Simon Newcomb, a celebrated figure in American astronomy as well as an economist, had anticipated him (1885, pp. 315–47). The Equation is the identity $MV = PT$, where M is the stock of money; V its velocity, the average number of times per year a dollar of the stock changes hands; P is the average price of the considerations traded for money in such transactions; and T is the physical volume per year of those considerations. It is an identity because it is in principle true by definition. Actually Fisher, of course, recognized the heterogeneity of transactions by writing also $MV = \Sigma p_i Q_i$, where the p_i and Q_i are individual prices and quantities. His interest in index numbers was substantially a quest for aggregate indexes P and T derived from the individual p_i and Q_i in such a way that the two forms of the equation would be consistent. Much of the book (1911a), both text and technical appendices, is devoted to this quest.

Here and in later writings, particularly (1921) and (1922), Fisher was looking for the 'best' index number formula. He postulated certain criteria and evaluated a host of formulas, investigating their properties both *a priori* and from applications to data. Since the criteria inevitably conflict, there can be no formula that excels on all counts. Although Fisher was mainly interested in measuring movements of the aggregate price level, naturally he wanted a price index P and a quantity index T to have the property that $P_1 T_1 / P_0 T_0 = (\Sigma p_1 Q_1)/(\Sigma p_0 Q_0)$, where the subscripts represent two time periods at which observations of p's and Q's are available.

This and various other desirable consistency properties are not hard to meet. The difficult question is the choice of weights in the two indexes, especially when a whole series of consistent period-to-period comparisons is desired, not just one isolated comparison. For a price index, should the quantity weights be those of a fixed base year, yielding what we now call a 'Laspeyres' index $(\Sigma p_1 Q_0)/(\Sigma p_0 Q_0)$? Or should the weights be those of the ever-changing current period, yielding a 'Paasche' index $(\Sigma p_1 Q_1)/(\Sigma p_0 Q_1)$? The indicated correlate quantity indexes would be the opposites, respectively 'Paasche' and 'Laspeyres'. In 1911 Fisher opted for the Paasche price index. He also seemed to approve the idea of chain indexes, in which the period 0 of the above formulas is not fixed in calendar time but is always the prior period, even though these violate one possible desideratum, that the relative change between two periods should be independent of the base used. He also wrote favourably of the practical advantages of an entirely different procedure, namely taking the median of an expenditure-weighted distribution of percentage price changes from one period to the next.

In 1920, however, Fisher proposed as the 'Ideal Index' a candidate he had not ranked high in 1911, namely the geometric mean of the Laspeyres and Paasche formulas. This formula has the pleasant property that the correlate of an Ideal price index is an Ideal quantity index. Correa Walsh, another index number expert, on whose comprehensive treatise (1901) Fisher relied heavily from the beginning of his own investigations, reached the same conclusion independently at about the same time (Walsh, 1921).

These index number issues do not seem as important to present-day economists as they did to Fisher. Knowing that they are intrinsically insoluble, we finesse them and use uncritically the indexes that government statisticians provide. But Fisher's explorations have been important to those practitioners.

In Fisher's Equation of Exchange (1911a) the T and the Q_i are measures of all transactions involving the tender of money, intermediate goods and services as well as final goods and services, old goods as well as newly produced commodities, financial assets as well as goods. The corresponding velocity is likewise comprehensive, much more so than the 'income' or 'circuit' velocity preferred by some monetary theorists, notably Alfred Marshall and his followers in Cambridge (England), who count only transactions for final goods, for example for Gross National Product.

Fisher elaborated the equation to distinguish the quantities M and M' of the two media currency and checking deposits and their separate velocities V and V': $MV + M'V' = PT$. This was a blow to the rising importance of bank deposits relative to currency as transactions media. Previous practice counted only government-issued currency as money, in modern parlance high-powered or base money, and regarded bank operations as increasing its velocity rather than adding to a money stock.

How does the quantity theory come out of the Equation of Exchange? Fisher argues that the real volume of money-using transactions T is exogenous; that the velocities are determined by institutions and habits and are independent of the other variables in the equation; that the division of the currency supply, the monetary base in current terminology, between currency and bank reserves is stable and independent of the variables in the equation; that banks are fully 'loaned up' so that deposits M' are a stable multiple of reserves, determined by the prudence of banks and by regulation; that exogenous changes in currency supply itself are the principal source of shocks, which, given the preceding propositions, move price level P proportionately. The many qualifications for transitional adjustments are conscientiously presented, but the monetarist message is loud and clear.

The argument is familiar to modern readers, but certain features deserve notice:
(1) Fisher gives the most illuminating account available of the institutions and habits that generate the society's demand for transactions media relative to the volume of transactions. He rightly emphasizes the fact that, and the degree

to which, receipts and payments are imperfectly synchronized. He seeks the determinants of velocity in such features of social and economic structure as the frequency of wage and bill payments and the degree of vertical integration of firms. His belief that these institutions change only slowly supports his contention that velocities are exogenous constants.

(2) Much ink has been spilled on the difference between Fisher's velocity approach to money demand and the Cambridge (England) 'k' formulation. The latter, like Walras's *encaisse désiré*, directs attention to agents' portfolio decisions. To Fisher's critics that seems behavioural, while velocity is mechanical. The issue is overblown; the same phenomena can be described in either language. If the other variables in the equation are defined and measured the same way, then V and k are just reciprocals each of the other. Fisher himself discusses hoarding. Fisher's explicit attention, in discussing economy-wide demand for circulating media in distinction to other stores of value, to the fact that money 'at rest' soon takes 'wing' to fly from one agent to another seems to be a merit of his approach.

(3) As already noted, Fisher resolved a question current in his day, whether banks' creation of deposit substitutes for currency should be regarded as increasing the velocity of basic money or as enlarging the supply of money. His choice of the latter course compels attention to the structure, behaviour and regulation of banks. He could not be expected to foresee that the proliferation of future candidates for designation as 'money' would create the monetarist ambiguities we see today.

(4) For the most part later writers have not followed Fisher in his preference for a comprehensive concept and measure of transactions volume. It is hard to attach meaning to the *real* volume of financial transactions, and therefore to see why a T that includes them should be a constant or exogenous term in the equation. On the other hand, modern students of money demand tend simply to forget transactions other than those on final payments.

(5) Fisher ignores the possibility that other liquid assets can serve as imperfect substitutes for money holdings because they can be converted into means of payment as needed, though at some cost. Partly for this reason, he ignores interest rate effects on demand for transactions media. In his day there may have been more excuse for these omissions than there was later. But they are still surprising for an author who elsewhere pays so much attention to the effects of interest rates and opportunity costs on behaviour.

(6) When Fisher was writing, the United States was on the gold standard; the exchange parties of the dollar with sterling and other gold-standard currencies were fixed. Fisher discusses in detail the implications of foreign transactions for the elements of the Equation of Exchange and for the quantity theory. He recognizes that tendencies towards purchasing-power parity, even though imperfect, make money supplies in any one country endogenous, tie prices to those of other countries and enhance quantity adjustments to monetary shocks in the short run. Much of the 1911 book applies, therefore, to the gold standard economies in aggregate. Indeed, Fisher finds the increase in gold production after 1896 to be the main cause of price increases throughout the world.

MACROECONOMICS: BUSINESS FLUCTUATIONS AND THE GREAT DEPRESSION

The quantity theory by no means exhausts Fisher's ideas on macroeconomics. His views were much more subtle than straightforward monetarism, but they are scattered through his writings and not systematically integrated. Consider the following non-neutralities emphasized by Fisher:

(1) Probably Fisher's principal source of fame, especially among non-economists, is his equation connecting nominal interest i, real interest r and inflation π: $i = r + \pi$. It is frequently misused. Like the Equation of Exchange, it is first of all an identity, from which, for example, an unobservable value of r can be calculated from observations of the other two variables. More interesting, certainly to Fisher, is its use as a condition of equilibrium in financial markets; for this purpose π must be replaced by expected inflation π^e, another unobservable. In a longer run, as Fisher recognized, steady-state equilibrium would also be characterized by equality of actual and expected inflation: $\pi = \pi^e$.

The Fisher equation is frequently cited nowadays in support of complete and prompt pass-through of inflation into nominal interest rates. Fisher's view throughout his career was quite different. For one thing, neither Fisher's theory of interest nor his reading of historical experience suggested to him that equilibrium real rates of interest should be constant. Moreover, from (1896) on he believed that adjustment of nominal interest rates to inflation takes a very long time. This he confirmed by sophisticated empirical investigations, regressions in which the formation of inflation expectations was modelled by distributed lags on actual inflation. During the transition, inflation would lower real rates; nominal rates would adjust incompletely. The effect was symmetrical; he attributed the severity of the Great Depression to the high real rates resulting from price deflation.

Moreover, Fisher was quite explicit about the effects of these movements of real interest rates on real economic variables, including aggregate production and employment. In *The Purchasing Power of Money* these transitional effects are mentioned, but minimized in the author's zeal to convince readers of the importance of stabilizing money stocks. But in Fisher's writings on interest rates, the transitions turn out to be long. In his accounts of cyclical fluctuations in business activity, and especially of the Great Depression, they play the key role.

(2) An assiduous student of price data, Fisher knew that some prices were more flexible than others, that money wages were on the sticky side of the spectrum, and that the imperfect flexibility of the price level meant that the T on the right-hand side of his Equation of Exchange would absorb some of the variations of the left-hand side.

In the early 1930s he came to a very modern position. Real variables like production and employment are independent of the level of prices, once the economy has adjusted to the level. But they are not independent of the rate of change of prices; they depend positively on the rate of inflation. He even calculated a 'Phillips' correlation between employment and inflation (1926). He was just one derivative short of the accelerationist position (Friedman, 1968); in a little more time he would have made that step, aware as he was of the difference between actual and expected inflation. Anyway, his policy conclusion was that stabilizing the price level would also stabilize the real economy.

(3) During the Great Depression, observing the catastrophes of the world around him, which he shared personally, Fisher came to quite a different theory of the business cycle from the simple monetarist version he had espoused earlier. This was his 'debt-deflation theory of depression' (1932), summarized in the first volume of *Econometrica*, the organ of the international society he helped to found (1933). The essential features are that debt-financed Schumpeterian innovations fuel a boom, followed by a recession which can turn into depression via an unstable interaction between excessive real debt burdens and deflation. Note the contrast to the Pigou real balance effect, according to which price declines are the benign mechanism that restores full-employment equilibrium. The realism is all on Fisher's side. This theory of Fisher's has room for the monetary and credit cycles of which he earlier complained, and for the perversely pro-cyclical real interest rate movements mentioned above.

Fisher did not provide a formal model of his latter-day cycle theory, as he probably would have done at a younger age. The point here is that he came to recognize important non-monetary sources of disturbance. These insights contain the makings of a theory of a determination of economic activity, prices, and interest rates in short and medium runs. Moreover, in his neoclassical writings on capital and interest Fisher had laid the basis for the investment and saving equations central to modern macroeconomic models. Had Fisher pulled these strands together into a coherent theory, he could have been an American Keynes. Indeed the 'neoclassical synthesis' would not have had to wait until after World War II. Fisher would have done it all himself.

His practical message in the early 1930s was 'Reflation!' When his Yale colleagues and orthodox economists throughout the country protested against public-works spending proposals and denounced Roosevelt's gold policies, Fisher was a conspicuous dissenter. He was right. Characteristically, he crusaded vigorously for his cause – in speeches, pamphlets, letters and personal talks with President Roosevelt and other powerful policy-makers. Characteristically too, as his letters home (I.N. Fisher, 1956, p. 275) disclose, he saw clearly and unapologetically that in lobbying for what was good for the country he was also hoping to rescue the Fisher family finances.

Addressing the President of Yale shortly after Fisher's death, Joseph Schumpeter and eighteen colleagues in the Harvard economics department wrote, 'No American has contributed more to the advancement of his chosen subject ... The name of that great economist and American has a secure place in the history of his subject and of his country.' According to his son, this is the eulogy that would have pleased Irving Fisher the most (I.N. Fisher, 1956, pp. 337–8). Today, four decades later, economists can confirm the judgement and prediction of that eulogy.

Author's Note: Fortunately Fisher's son, Irving Norton Fisher, preserved the memory of his father in two indispensable publications, a biography and a comprehensive bibliography (1956, 1961). I have also relied extensively on Professor John Perry Miller's biographical essay (1967) and Professor William Barber's account (1986) of political economy at Yale before 1900. My review of Fisher's contributions to general equilibrium theory, the theory of capital and interest, monetary theory and macroeconomics draws heavily and often literally on a recent essay of my own (Tobin, 1985).

SELECTED WORKS

1892. *Mathematical Investigations in the Theory of Value and Prices.* New Haven: Connecticut Academy of Arts and Sciences, *Transactions 9*, 1892. Reprinted, New York: Augustus M. Kelley, 1961.

1896. Appreciation and interest. *AEA Publications* 3(11), August, 331–442. Reprinted, New York: Augustus M. Kelley, 1961.

1906. *The Nature of Capital and Income.* New York: Macmillan.

1907. *The Rate of Interest.* New York: Macmillan.

1910. *Introduction to Economic Science.* New York: Macmillan.

1911a. *The Purchasing Power of Money.* New York: Macmillan.

1911b. *Elementary Principles of Economics.* New York: Macmillan.

1921. The best form of index number. *American Statistical Association Quarterly* 17, March, 533–7.

1922. *The Making of Index Numbers.* Boston: Houghton Mifflin.

1926. A statistical relation between unemployment and price changes. *International Labour Review* 13, June, 785–92.

1927. A statistical method for measuring 'marginal utility' and testing the justice of a progressive income tax. In *Economic Essays Contributed in Honor of John Bates Clark*, ed. J.H. Hollander, New York: Macmillan.

1930. *The Theory of Interest.* New York: Macmillan.

1932. *Booms and Depressions.* New York: Adelphi.

1933. The debt-deflation theory of great depressions. *Econometrica* 1(4), October, 337–57.

1935. *100% Money.* New York: Adelphi.

BIBLIOGRAPHY

Arrow, K.J. and Debreu, G. 1954. Existence of an equilibrium for a competitive economy. *Econometrica* 22(3), July, 265–90.

Auspitz, R. and Lieben, R. 1889. *Untersuchungen über die Theorie des Preises.* Leipzig: Duncker & Humblot.

Barber, W.J. 1986. Yale: the fortunes of political economy in an environment of academic conservatism. In W.J. Barber, *Economists and American Higher Learning in the Nineteenth Century*, Middletown, Conn.: Wesleyan University Press.

Clark, J.B. 1899. *The Distribution of Wealth.* New York: Macmillan.

Fairchild, F.R., Furniss, E.S. and Buck, N.S. 1926. *Elementary Economics.* 2 vols, New York: Macmillan. 5th edn, 1948.

Fisher, I.N. 1956. *My Father Irving Fisher.* New York: Comet Press.

Fisher, I.N. 1961. *A Bibliography of the Writings of Irving Fisher.* New Haven: Yale University Library.

Friedman, M. 1968. The role of monetary policy. *American Economic Review* 58(1), 1–17.

Hall, R.E. 1985. Monetary policy with an elastic price standard. In *Price Stability and Public Policy.* Federal Reserve Bank of Kansas City, 137–60.

Jevons, W.S. 1871. *The Theory of Political Economy.* London: Macmillan; 5th edn, New York: Kelley & Millman, 1957.

Keynes, J.M. 1923. *A Tract on Monetary Reform.* London: Macmillan.

Keynes, J.M. 1936. *The General Theory of Employment, Interest and Money.* New York: Harcourt, Brace.

Miller, J.P. 1967. Irving Fisher of Yale. In *Ten Economic Studies in the Tradition of Irving Fisher,* ed. William Fellner et al., New York: Wiley.

Newcomb, S. 1885. *Principles of Political Economy.* New York: Harper.

Rae, J. 1834. *The Sociological Theory of Capital.* Reprinted, New York: Macmillan, 1905.

Samuelson, P.A. 1967. Irving Fisher and the theory of capital. In *Ten Economic Studies in the Tradition of Irving Fisher,* ed. William Fellner et al., New York: Wiley.

Scarf, H. (With T. Hansen.) 1973. *The Computation of Economic Equilibria.* New Haven: Yale University Press.

Schumpeter, J.A. 1912. *Theory of Economic Development.* Trans. from the 2nd German edn of 1926 by R. Opie, Cambridge, Mass.: Harvard University Press, 1934.

Schumpeter, J.A. 1954. *History of Economic Analysis.* Ed. E.B. Schumpeter, New York: Oxford University Press.

Social Sciences Citation Index. 1979, 1983. *Five Year Cumulation,* 1971–5 and 1976–80. Philadelphia: Institute for Scientific Information.

Tobin, J. 1985. Neoclassical theory in America. *American Economic Review* 75(6), December, 28–38.

Walsh, C.M. 1901. *The Measurement of General Exchange Value.* New York and London: Macmillan.

Walsh, C.M. 1921. *The Problem of Estimation.* London: King & Sons.

Wicksell, K. 1911. *Lectures on Political Economy.* Trans. E. Classen (from the 2nd Swedish edn), London: George Routledge & Sons, 1934; New York: A.M. Kelley, 1967.

Fixed capital

PAOLO VARRI

Fixed capital is the term traditionally used to indicate durable means of production, that is all those inputs of the productive process (such as tools, machines and equipment) that are not exhausted in one single period of production. Non-durable means of production, by contrast defined circulating capital, include raw materials, energy, direct labour, semi-finished goods, etc.

Of course, while circulating capital contributes entirely to the annual production of each commodity, the contribution of fixed capital to production in each period should be determined in relation to the wear and tear actually incurred during its utilization; a datum that in general is not possible to observe directly.

Fixed capital is therefore a complication in the theory of production and it is easy to understand the reason why economists, in their search for abstract simplification of very complex real phenomena, are often induced to assume that production requires only circulating capital.

But technical progress has continuously increased the relevance of machines and plant in industrial production and, as a consequence, a theory of production able to face the problem of fixed capital has become more and more necessary. The most interesting recent contribution in this direction does not belong to mainstream traditional neoclassical theory. It has been made by Sraffa (1960) going back to the classical tradition of determining the value of commodities according to their conditions of production.

HISTORICAL DEVELOPMENTS. Fixed capital is already present in the propositions of the early economists. The determination of its contribution to the annual product of a nation by the Physiocrats and Adam Smith (1766) is however only a description of the behavioural rules of the business world rather than an attempt to explain them. The first analytical discussion of the problem of fixed capital is associated with Ricardo (1821). He is concerned with two particular aspects of the problem.

First of all he noticed that, when the rate of profits is changed, the presence of fixed capital is one of the factors that may alter the proportionality between the ratio of prices and the ratio of the quantity of labour embodied in the corresponding commodities. This is the famous exception of time to the general rule of the labour theory of value that Ricardo put forward in reply to the criticisms raised by McCulloch.

The second aspect of the problem of fixed capital considered by Ricardo, is concerned with the effects of the dynamic substitution in production of machines for labour. He concludes that workers' fears of technological unemployment may be justified, even if the conclusion does not seem to follow logically from his model, that is based on Say's Law.

Marx (1867–94) analyses in detail the consequences of the introduction of fixed capital (machines) on the productivity of labour and strongly underlines the enormous reduction in the price of commodities that it implies; but apparently he does not care to determine the contribution of fixed capital to the cost of production in each period. A second deeper implication that Marx draws from the substitution in time of machines for labour is the increase in the organic composition of capital, from which he derives his controversial tendency of the rate of profits to fall.

RECENT CONTRIBUTIONS. There are two distinct contributions that, in very different ways, are relevant for the modern analysis of fixed capital: von Neumann (1937) and Leontief (1941, 1953). Von Neumann spends only few words in describing the economic meaning of his mathematical model, but he explicitly remarks that capital goods should appear in both the input and in the output matrix of his model, and should be considered as different goods for each different stage of their utilization, i.e. exactly the same method of analysis later adopted by Sraffa that, nevertheless, at the moment, did not receive any particular attention.

The second contribution, Leontief's input–output model, is relevant because it has many analogies with Sraffa's scheme of production and because Leontief explicitly tries to introduce fixed capital in his model. This is therefore a good starting point to appreciate Sraffa's solution of the problem.

Leontief's (1941) input–output model is a scheme of the flows of commodities among the various industries of the economic system initially conceived to take into account only circulating capital. It determines the quantities of the commodities produced and their prices as solutions of the following two systems of equations:

$$Aq + y = q \tag{1}$$

$$pA + v = p \tag{2}$$

where A is the input–output matrix of technical coefficients, q and y are the vectors of total production and of final demand, p is the vector of prices and v is the vector of value added.

But, as Leontief (1953) himself later recognized, a more complete description of the economic system must also involve stocks of commodities (fixed capital) in their various forms: inventories, machines, buildings, etc. He introduces therefore a second square matrix $B = b_{ij}$ that indicates the amount of commodity i required as stock to produce one unit of commodity j. Bq is then the vector of stocks of commodities required to produce the vector of commodities q. Fixed capital stocks affect the balance equation of each period only in terms of the variations of the levels of production $\dot{q} = dq/dt$. This leads Leontief to analyse the dynamic implications of the introduction of fixed capital by means of the following system of linear differential equations:

$$y = q - Aq - B\dot{q} \tag{3}$$

showing the interaction of stocks and flows as a generalization of the acceleration principle.

Whatever the interest of these dynamic extensions may be, the treatment of fixed capital is rather crude because the determination of depreciations (the fundamental problem with fixed capital) remains exogenous to the model. The amount of fixed capital consumed in each year is in fact predetermined by simplifying assumptions either as a share of the initial stock or as a fixed percentage rate of decay of the residual stock and it is included in the flow matrix A.

FIXED CAPITAL IN A GENERAL SCHEME OF FLOWS. Sraffa's (1960) approach allows a substantial analytical improvement on previous discussions of the problem of fixed capital. He does not consider machines as stocks *à la* Leontief and proposes instead to consider what remains of a machine at the end of each year of operation as a joint product together with the commodity produced. An approach that Sraffa first attributes to Torrens and that afterwards was adopted by Ricardo, Malthus and Marx and then fell into oblivion with the already mentioned exception of von Neumann.

The main interest of Sraffa is in the theory of value and distribution of income. Following the approach of the classical economists, that tried to determine prices from the conditions of production of each commodity, Sraffa formulates a scheme of the production system articulated in two stages. At the first stage of the analysis, when each industry is supposed to produce one single commodity, and the number of industries is equal to the number of commodities produced, Sraffa defines a system of equations that is usually written as follows:

$$a_n w + pA(1 + r) = p. \tag{4}$$

It shows that the structure of the production system, as described by the matrix of technical coefficients $A = a_{ij}$ and by the vector of labour coefficients a_n, together with one of the two distributive variables (e.g., the uniform rate of profits r), is sufficient to determine the structure of the vector of prices p and the second residual distributive variable (for analytical details see Newman, 1962 and Pasinetti, 1977).

The meaning of these prices has nothing to do with marginal or neoclassical theory. They represent a more fundamental concept: the exchange rates which ensure the reproduction of the economic system.

The introduction of fixed capital requires the second stage of the analysis, where each industry may produce jointly more than one single commodity. The outcome of this method of dealing with fixed capital is a general scheme of flows that avoids the hybrid interplay between stocks and flows of Leontief's solution.

Obviously a scheme of general joint production is much more complicated than single production. But it is not necessary to go into all the intricacies of joint production to analyse fixed capital. Sraffa considers fixed capital as the leading species of the genus of joint products, and this has suggested an analysis of the intermediate stage where fixed capital is the only element of joint production in a system of single product industies.

At this particular intermediate stage a new system of equations substitutes for the previous one:

$$a_n w + pA(1 + r) = pB \tag{5}$$

where $B = b_{ij}$ is a square matrix of outputs that indicates the quantity of each commodity produced and the quantity of old machines, as their joint products, and p is the price vector of the commodities produced, including the price of all old machines at their various ages.

By contrast with the case of single production it might well happen here that, for feasible levels of the rate of profits, some price comes out to be negative, but it is possible to show that, if fixed capital is the only element of joint production of the scheme, then, only the price of old machines might be negative. This has a precise economic meaning: it is a signal of productive inefficiency. It may be shown that, by correspondingly reducing the years of utilization of the machine, the (productive) efficiency of the system would increase (i.e. it would allow higher wages at the same rate of profits). This means that it is always possible, after a suitable truncation of the period of utilization of the machine, to eliminate all negative prices and to obtain a strictly positive solution. (Further analytical details may be found in the essays by Baldone, 1974; Schefold, 1974 and Varri, 1974.)

The method of joint production therefore leads to prices that are economically meaningful and at the same time makes it possible to determine the most efficient life-time of durable means of production that turns out to depend, not necessarily in a monotonic way, on the rate of profits.

The remarkable consequence of this result is that, by considering the difference of the prices of the same machine at two subsequent years, it is always possible to obtain the *correct* depreciation quota for that machine in the year considered; correct in the sense of allowing the replacement of the means of production and the payment of profits, whatever the technical conditions of use of the machine may be over its period of utilization. A solution therefore to the problem of determining the wear and tear actually occurred during the utilization of the machine that, as was noticed at the beginning, is impossible to observe directly.

FINAL REMARKS. A remarkable property of the analysis of fixed capital outlined so far is that, though avoiding the difficulties of general joint production schemes, it is rather general and comprehensive. It concerns regular systems where machines are used in their natural sequence and it is necessary to assume that at the end of their life their residual value is zero. Moreover trade of old machines among industries producing different commodities is excluded.

But the analysis does take into account two important complementary aspects of the problem of fixed capital. The first concerns the possibility of considering sets of machines jointly utilized in production, as a unique durable means of production, let us call it a plant, avoiding the indeterminacy of the price of each single component.

The second regards the valuation of obsolete machines no longer produced, but still worth using in production, that may be obtained from the computation of quasi-rents according to the same principle that applies to the rent of lands of different qualities.

More complicated schemes of fixed capital utilization are of course possible but should be analysed within the framework of general joint production.

The most important feature of Sraffa's approach to the problem of fixed capital is that, not requiring any change in the fundamental vision of production as a circular process initially adopted to analyse circulating capital, it greatly contributes to establishing it as a general approach for the analysis of modern systems of production that is alternative to marginalism and neoclassical theory.

BIBLIOGRAPHY

Baldone, S. 1974. Il capitale fisso nello schema teorico di Piero Sraffa. *Studi Economici* 29, 45–106. Trans. as: 'Fixed capital in Sraffa's theoretical scheme', in Pasinetti (1980), 88–137.

Leontief, W. 1941. *The Structure of American Economy, 1919–1929*. New York: Oxford University Press.

Leontief, W. et al. 1953. *Studies in the Structure of American Economy*. New York: Oxford University Press.

Marx, K. 1867–94. *Capital*. Moscow: Progress Publishers, 1965–7.

Neumann, J. von. 1937. A model of general economic equilibrium. *Review of Economic Studies* 13, 1945–6, 1–9.

Newman, P. 1962. Production of commodities by means of commodities. *Schweizerische Zeitschrift für Volkswirtschaft und Statistik* 98, 58–75.

Pasinetti, L. 1977. *Lectures on the Theory of Production*. London: Macmillan; New York: Columbia University Press.

Pasinetti, L. 1980. *Essays on the Theory of Joint Production*. London: Macmillan; New York: Columbia University Press.

Ricardo, D. 1821. *On the Principles of Political Economy and Taxation*. Vol. I of *The Works and Correspondence of David Ricardo*, ed. P. Sraffa, Cambridge: Cambridge University Press, 1951; New York: Cambridge University Press, 1973.

Schefold, B. 1974. Fixed capital as a joint product and the analysis of accumulation with different forms of technical progress. Mimeo, published in Pasinetti (1980), 138–217.

Smith, A. 1776. *An Inquiry into the Nature and Causes of the Wealth of Nations*. Oxford: Clarendon Press, 1976; Chicago: University of Chicago Press.

Sraffa, P. (ed.) 1951–73. *The Works and Correspondence of David Ricardo*. Cambridge and New York: Cambridge University Press.

Sraffa, P. 1960. *Production of Commodities by Means of Commodities*. Cambridge: Cambridge University Press.

Varri, P. 1974. Prezzi, saggio del profitto e durata del capitale fisso nello schema teorico di Piero Sraffa. *Studi Economici* 29, 5–44. Trans. as 'Prices, rate of profit and life of machines in Sraffa's fixed capital model', in Pasinetti (1980), 55–87.

'Hahn problem'

F.H. HAHN

Harrod (1939), who inaugurated the postwar concern with growth theory, distinguished between three growth rates: the natural, the warranted and the actual. True to his Keynesian heritage he argued that there were circumstances in which the warranted rate of growth permanently exceeds the natural rate. More importantly from the point of view of this essay he claimed that the warranted growth path was highly unstable – he called it a 'knife-edge'. By this he meant that small disturbances of the warranted growth path would lead to a cumulative divergence of actual from warranted growth. The argument was simple. Suppose, for instance, that for some exogenous reason the actual growth rate fell a little below the warranted rate. By virtue of the accelerator mechanism, savings would exceed investment (*ex ante*) and income would be given a further impulse taking it below its warranted level. This leads to further reductions in investment and to further downward displacement of the actual path. This process continues. Hicks (1950) quickly saw that this theory could easily serve as an explanation of cycles.

Many economists, however, took the view that Harrod had underestimated the prevalence of stabilizers in a market economy. In particular his theory had little to say about the behaviour of relative prices and had ruled out substitution possibilities by assuming fixed coefficients of production. Not only did he thereby overdetermine the long-run equilibrium system (the equation: natural rate = warranted rate had only exogenously given variables on both sides) but he allowed no scope to the price mechanism to stabilize the economy against small shocks. This argument found its clearest expression in a famous article by Solow (1956).

Sollow's work on Neoclassical Growth Theory is here very briefly summarized. Let y = output per man and k = capital per man and let

$$y = f(k)$$

be the production function which is concave and has the property

$$f'(0) = \infty, \quad f'(k) > 0, \quad \text{all } k \in (0, \infty).$$

Let n be the rate of population growth and s the propensity to save. For an equilibrium, saving per man must equal investment per man, write it as i. But

$$i = \dot{k} + nk$$

so we require

$$\dot{k} + nk = sy. \tag{1}$$

In steady state $\dot{k} = 0$ and we must solve

$$nk = sf(k) \quad \text{or} \quad n = s\frac{f(k)}{k}$$

which is Harrod's equation. Given the assumptions on $f(k)$ there always exists k^* which solves the equation. This then answers one of Harrod's arguments to the effect that it may not be possible to bring the natural rate (n) into equality with the warranted rate $[sf(k)/k]$.

Now divide both sides of (1) by k and rearrange to give

$$\frac{\dot{k}}{k} = s\frac{f(k)}{k} - n. \tag{2}$$

By the concavity of $f(k)$, $f(k)/k$ is a diminishing function of k. Hence starting at any $k(0) \neq k^*$ and following a path for which (a) employment grows at the rate n and (b) savings are always equal to investment (call this a 'warranted' path), the economy will be driven to the steady state k^* (where $\dot{k} = 0$). This was the gist of Solow's argument.

It will be noticed straightaway that this argument has no bearing on Harrod's knife-edge claim. Harrod had not proposed that warranted paths diverge from the steady state but that actual paths did. The latter are neither characterized by a continual equality of *ex ante* investment and savings nor by continual equilibrium in the market for labour. Thus although Solow thought that he was controverting the knife-edge argument he had only succeeded in establishing the convergence of warranted paths to the steady state.

However, even here it was not at all clear how robust *that* conclusion was to a relaxation of some of its rather strong assumptions. In particular it was widely agreed that the aggregate production function in terms of an aggregate capital input was a 'fable' (Samuelson, 1962). The question was whether this fable was instructive or misleading. An attempted answer which was closely related to the pioneering work on turnpikes by Dorfman, Samuelson and Solow (1958) was christened the 'Hahn problem', although it was not really a problem nor was Hahn's analysis of startling novelty.

Before giving a precise account it will be helpful to have a bird's-eye view.

Suppose that there are many different capital goods used in their own production as well as in the production of a single consumption good. Let $t = 0$

be the initial date at which we take the capital stock as determined by past history up to that date. (For simplicity capital goods are assumed to be infinitely durable.) Let agents have expectations concerning the change in relative prices between $t = 0$ and $t = 0 + \varepsilon$. These expectations together with the technological conditions of production will determine investment in the various capital goods. This will have the property that everyone is, at the margin, indifferent between investing in one good rather than another. Once that has been determined the economy is, as it were, on rails from which it cannot deviate if we require expectations to be correct and production to be intertemporally efficient. For the correctness of the price expectations for $t = 0 + \varepsilon$ imply what prices must be in all subsequent time periods. However, the 'rails' which the economy gets onto depend on the arbitrarily postulated expectations at $t = 0$. There are in fact an infinity of such rails depending on initial expectations. Most of these, however, lead away from the steady state and not to it (in the example of Hahn, 1966, all of them except one lead the economy away from the steady state). There are thus many warranted paths and they do not conform to the Solow proposition for the single capital good. There seems to be both indeterminacy and instability of the steady state under warranted path deviations. However, it may be that the rails which lead the economy away from the steady state are also leading it into an abyss. That is, the paths may eventually become infeasible because some capital good needed in production has disappeared. However, if we postulate some form of myopia in expectations, by which is meant no more than that agents cannot predict prices into the infinitely distant future, there is nothing to prevent the economy following such errant warranted paths for a 'long time'. However, we return to this matter below after the technical discussion.

The story which has just been told informally exemplifies the difficulties which arise in an economy which does not have a full set of Arrow–Debreu markets. Such an economy must act on the basis of price expectations and these in turn open up the possibility of 'bootstrap' warranted paths: the economy evolves the way in which it does because expectations are what they are and not for any 'real' reason. In the conclusion we return to these intuitive explanations. But first we must demonstrate the existence of many warranted paths which do not seek the steady state.

Let there be m capital goods whose quantities *per man* are denoted by the vector $k = (k_1, \ldots, k_m)$ and let $y = (y_1, \ldots, y_m)$ be the output vector (per man) of the capital goods. The output of consumption good per man is written as y_0. Let p_0 be the price of the consumption good and $p = (p_1, \ldots, p_m)$ the price vector of capital goods. All prices are reckoned in unit of account. There are constant returns to scale and one defines

$$A(k) = \{(y, y_0) | F(y_0, y \cdot k) \geqslant 0\}$$

as the production possibility set of the economy given k. In this definition $F(\cdot)$ is assumed C^2, strictly concave function with the propety:

$$\frac{\partial F}{\partial k_i} > 0, \qquad \text{for } k_i < \infty,$$

$$\frac{\partial F}{\partial k_i} < +\infty, \qquad \text{for } k_i = 0 \text{ all } i.$$

A competitive economy in equilibrium will at all dates behave as if it solved the problem:

$$\max_{A(k)} (p \cdot y + p_0 y_0).$$

Let R be this maximized sum. Then we can write

$$R = R(p_0, p, k).$$

Classical duality theory gives

$$R_i(p, p, k) = y, \qquad i = 0, \ldots, m.$$

where $R_i = \partial B/\partial p_i$. Moreover we know that R is convex in (p_0, p) and concave in k. If we suppose that population is growing at the geometric rate n then the evolution of the capital stock per man is given by the differential equation

$$R_i(p_0, p, k) - nk_i = k_i, \qquad i = 1, \ldots, m. \tag{3}$$

But if the economy has perfect foresight so that the expected rate and actual rate of all price changes coincide then it must satisfy arbitrage equations which ensure that investment in all directions is equally profitable. If we let $R_{m+i} = \partial R/\partial k_i$ this means that there is at each date a scalar, r, such that

$$R_{m+i}(p_0, p, k) + \dot{p}_i = rp_i, \qquad i = 1, \ldots, m. \tag{4}$$

Since we can choose one good as *numéraire* (say the consumption good) we need only one more equation to be able to trace the evolution of all variables from given initial conditions. That equation must refer to the common rate of return r. This will depend on the savings decisions of agents and on technology and so on (p_0, p, k, r). Write

$$\dot{r} = c(p_0, p, k)$$

In steady state: $\dot{r} = \dot{k} = \dot{p} = 0$. Let r^*, p^*, k^* be the solution of (3), (4), (5) in such a steady state. (On present assumptions such a solution exists.) To study the warranted growth path of the economy near the steady state we take a first order Taylor expansion of these three equations at (r^*, p^*, k^*). We write: $\tilde{p} = p - p^*$, $\bar{k} = k - k^*$, $\bar{r} = r - r^*$ and set p_0^* identically equal to unity. Also

$$R_{ij} = \frac{\partial R_i(p^*, k^*)}{\partial P_j}, \qquad R_{im+j} = \frac{\partial R_i(p^*, k^*)}{\partial k_j} \text{ etc.}$$

and

$$c_r = \frac{\partial c(r^*, p^*, k^*)}{\partial r}.$$

We obtain

$$\sum_j R_{im+j}\bar{k}_j - n\bar{k} + \sum_j R_{ij}\bar{p}_j = \dot{k}_i, \quad i = 1, \ldots, n \tag{6}$$

$$\bar{r}p_i^* - \sum_j R_{m+im+j}\bar{k}_j - \sum_j R_{m+ij}\bar{p}_j + r^*\bar{p}_i = \dot{p}_i, \quad i = 1, \ldots, n \tag{7}$$

$$\bar{r}c_r + \sum_j c_{m+j}\bar{k}_j + \sum_j c_p\bar{p}_j = \dot{r}. \tag{8}$$

Let R_{pk} be the $n \times n$ matrix of elements $[R_{im+j}]$, R_{pp} the $n \times n$ matrix of elements $[R_{ij}]$, R_{kk} the $n \times n$ matrix of elements $[R_{m+i,\ m+j}]$ and I the $n \times n$ identity matrix. Then the above equations can be written compactly as

$$\begin{bmatrix} c_r & \{c_{m+j}\} & \{c_j\} \\ \{0\} & R_{pk} - nI & R_{pp} \\ p^* & -R_{kk} & -R_{kp} + r^*I \end{bmatrix} \begin{bmatrix} \bar{r} \\ \bar{k} \\ \bar{p} \end{bmatrix} = \begin{bmatrix} \dot{r} \\ \dot{k} \\ \dot{p} \end{bmatrix}. \tag{9}$$

Note that $R_{pk} = R'_{kp}$.

Let us consider the unbordered matrix:

$$A = \begin{bmatrix} R_{pk} - nI & R_{pp} \\ -R_{kk} & -R_{kp} + p^*I \end{bmatrix}.$$

If we make the assumption that profits are all saved and wages are all spent then $r^* = n$. Make this assumption: Let

$$T = \begin{bmatrix} 0 & -I \\ I & 0 \end{bmatrix}$$

so that $T' = -T$. Then

$$TA = \begin{bmatrix} R_{kk} & R_{kp} - nI \\ R_{pk} - nI & R_{pp} \end{bmatrix} \det B$$

and B is a symmetric matrix. Now let $Ax = \lambda x$ be the characteristic equation for A with eigenvalue λ. Then

$$\lambda Tx = Bx = B'x. \tag{10}$$

But $TA = A'T' = B'$ and $A'T' = A'(-T)$. Let $Tx = y$. Then from (10)

$$\lambda y = -A'y \quad \text{or} \quad -\lambda y = A'y.$$

Hence if λ is a root of A so is $-\lambda$. One says that A has the saddle point property. The phase diagram for p and k in two dimensions is given in Figure 1.

If r remained constant at its steady state value r^* then Figure 1 would show all the warranted paths of the economy. It will be seen that only one of these approaches the steady state. On the other hand all the other paths may eventually become infeasible – they lead to one of the axes. Infinite perfect foresight would rule all these paths out of consideration. However, the postulate of such foresight seems farfetched.

When the whole system of equation (9) is considered matters are more complicated. One way out of the complication is to suppose that the economy behaves as if it were solving an infinite 'Ramsey problem'. The behaviour of r would then be fully determined by the Euler–Lagrange equations for this problem. But once again, in the absence of discounting, all paths but the convergent one would be ruled out and the 'Hahn problem' would disappear. But also once again the realism and relevance of such a postulate must be in doubt (see Hahn, 1968; Kurz, 1968).

The alternative is to proceed by way of a model of overlapping generations or simply by a descriptive savings function. Work along these lines (and also with more than one consumption good), has been undertaken by a number of economists. Shell and Cass (1976) have provided a good general treatment of systems such as (9). The main conclusion is that in addition to the divergent paths there is also a manifold of paths which converge. This is interesting since now even with infinite perfect foresight and convergence, there is nothing to tell

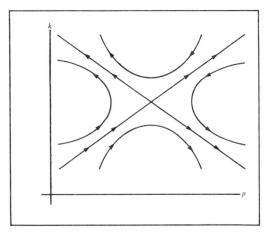

Figure 1

us which of the convergent paths the economy will choose. The same difficulty has been encountered in the overlapping generations' literature which has been very ably summarized by Woodford (1984). However in both approaches divergent warranted paths remain and some of these (in the case of overlapping generations) are viable over infinite time.

There are a number of technical matters which have not been considered in the above account – for instance the relation of the problem to turnpike theory (Samuelson, 1960) and the role of intertemporal efficiency conditions which have been encapsulated in the dual formulation here adopted. But enough has been provided to allow an intuitive summary.

The requirement of perfect foresight equilibrium is certainly too weak to determine the path of an economy if perfect foresight is not over the infinite future. Moreover there are then many paths which do not converge to the steady state. This is due to the circumstances that arbitrage, given initial expectations, imposes a particular path on the economy if expectations are to be fulfilled in the future, and if the arbitrage equations are to hold. Thus the invisible hand may for a long time provide coherence in the economy even while it is guiding it to eventual disaster. But even when there is perfect foresight over the infinite future and that future is discounted, there will be many paths that do not converge to the steady state. (Kurz, 1968, gives a case where (9) has been converted into a Ramsey problem with discounting and where all paths diverge from the steady state.) It would seem that in general the price-mechanism even with correct expectations will not bear out the rather optimistic conclusion of Solow with which this essay started.

Two matters remain to be mentioned. Warranted paths which do not converge may yet to Pareto-efficient (see Cass, 1972), provided of course they are feasible over infinite time. However this does not mean that such paths do not provide an occasion for policy since they may be associated with very undesirable inter-temporal distributions of welfare between generations. (This applies to models in which agents do not have infinite lives and in which agents do not value their descendants' utility as they do their own.)

The second matter is this: one may ask whether the steady state would not be stable if one allowed for false expectations, that is if one considered actual and not warranted paths. This question was posed by Shell and Stiglitz (1967) and is also discussed in Hahn (1969). Although Shell and Stiglitz did indeed find that with relatively inelastic expectations the steady state was stable their model was very special, particularly in the manner in which it incorporates the heterogeneity of capital goods. In a more general model Hahn (1969) found no general presumption that the steady state was stable unless expectations were completely inelastic, as was postulated by Morishima (1964). In that latter case there are no expected capital gains and losses and the arbitrage equation takes on a degenerate form. Nonetheless it remains an interesting question which set of circumstances leads to false expectations being stabilizing. No general answers are now available. But the 'Hahn problem' was concerned with correct (albeit myopic) expectations.

189

BIBLIOGRAPHY

Cass, D. 1972. On capital overaccumulation in the aggregate, neoclassical model of economic growth. *Journal of Economy Theory* 4, 200–23.

Dorfman, R., Samuelson, P.A. and Solow, R.M. 1958. *Linear Programming and Economic Analysis*. New York: McGraw-Hill.

Hahn, F.H. 1966. Equilibrium dynamics with heterogeneous capital goods. *Quarterly Journal of Economics* 80, 633–45.

Hahn, F.H. 1968. On warranted growth paths. *Review of Economic Studies* 35, 175–84.

Hahn, F.H. 1969. On some equilibrium paths. In *Models of Economic Growth*, ed. J. Mirrlees and N.H. Stern, London: Macmillan, 1973; New York: Wiley.

Harrod, R.F. 1939. An essay in dynamic theory. *Economic Journal* 49, 14–33.

Hicks, J.R. 1950. *A Contribution to the Theory of the Trade Cycle*. Oxford: Clarendon Press.

Kurz, M. 1968. The general instability of a class of competitive growth processes. *Review of Economic Studies* 35, 155–74.

Morishima, M. 1964. *Equilibrium, Stability and Growth*. Oxford: Clarendon Press.

Samuelson, P.A. 1960. Efficient paths of capital accumulation in terms of the calculus of variations. *Stanford Symposium on Mathematical Methods in the Social Sciences*, ed. K.J. Arrow, S. Karlin and P. Suppes, Stanford: Stanford University Press.

Samuelson, P.A. 1962. Parable and realism in capital theory: the surrogate production function. *Review of Economic Studies* 29, 193–206.

Shell, K. and Cass, D. 1976. The structure and stability of competitive dynamical systems. *Journal of Economic Theory* 12, 31–70.

Shell, K. and Stiglitz, J. 1967. The allocation of investment in a dynamic economy. *Quarterly Journal of Economics* 81, 592–610.

Solow, R.M. 1956. A contribution to the theory of economic growth. *Quarterly Journal of Economics* 70, 65–94.

Woodford, M. 1984. Indeterminacy of equilibrium in the overlapping generation model: a survey. Mimeo, Columbia University.

Humbug production function

ANWAR SHAIKH

Neoclassical economics has always tried to portray wages and profits as mere technical variables. At an aggregate level, this is accomplished by connecting labour and capital to output through a 'well-behaved' aggregate production function, with the marginal products of labour and capital equal to the wage rate and profit rate, respectively. Thus in competitive equilibrium each social class is pictured as receiving the equivalent of the marginal product of the factor(s) it owns (Shaikh, 1980).

The original optimism that aggregate production functions and their corresponding marginal productivity rules could be derived from more detailed general equilibrium models eventually gave way to the sobering realization that the conditions for any such a derivation were 'far too stringent to be believable' (Fisher, 1971). Yet neoclassical economists continue to use aggregate production functions, apparently because they seem to fit the data well and their estimated marginal products closely approximate the observed wage and profit rates (so-called factor prices).

This apparent empirical strength of aggregate production functions is often interpreted as support for neoclassical theory. *But there is neither theoretical nor empirical basis for this conclusion.* We already know that such functions cannot be derived theoretically, except under conditions which neoclassical theory itself rejects (e.g. the simple labour theory of value) (Garegnani, 1970). Moreover, Fisher (1971) discovered through simulation studies that the aggregate data generated by microeconomic production functions were not generally well fitted by aggregate production functions; that the functions which did best fit this data are not neoclassical in nature (this is a common finding, e.g. Walters, 1963); and that in simulation runs where the wage share happened to be roughly constant and aggregate Cobb–Douglas production functions happened to work well, this goodness of fit was puzzling because it held even when the theoretical conditions for aggregate production functions were flagrantly violated.

Shaikh (1974, 1980) has shown that this last result is simply an artifact of the constancy of the wage share. To see this, let r_t represent the rate of profit, and q_t, w_t, k_t the per worker net output, wages and capital, respectively, all at time t. Then the national accounting identity $q_t = w_t + r_t k_t$ can be differentiated to yield percentage rates of change q', w', etc., weighted by the profit share $s_t = r_t k_t / q_t$ and the labour share $1 - s_t = w_t / q_t$:

$$q'_t = B'_t + s_t k'_t, \quad \text{where} \quad B'_t = (1 - s_t)w'_t + s_t r'_t. \tag{1}$$

The preceding relation says nothing about the nature of the underlying economic processes, since it is derived from an identity. But if social forces happen to produce a stable profit (and hence wage) share, so that $s_t = s(a$ constant), we can immediately integrate both sides of (1) to get

$$q_t = A_t k_t^s, \quad \text{where} \quad A_t = C \, e^{\int B'_t \, dt}, \; C = a \text{ constants.} \tag{2}$$

Equation (2) looks like an aggregate Cobb–Douglas production function with constant returns to scale, marginal products equal to factor prices, and a technical change shift parameter A_t. It will even seemingly reflect neutral technical change if the rate of change B'_t can be expressed as a function of time. And yet *it is not a production function at all, but rather merely the algebraic expression of any social forces resulting in a constant share – even when the underlying processes are definitely not neoclassical in nature.* To illustrate this, we will now demonstrate that even a very simple 'anti-neoclassical' (Robinsonian) economy will fit such a function.

Consider an economy at time t_0, in which all possible techniques of production are dominated by a *single* linear technique (linear because capital–labour ratios are equal across all sectors). With one dominant technique, there is no neoclassical substitutability among techniques, and the linear wage–profit curve of the dominant technique is also the wage–profit frontier for the whole economy (the line $q_0 R$ in Figure 1, for the given time period). Because q, k and R (net output/capital) are all *constant* along the wage–profit frontier, the marginal products of labour and capital therefore cannot even be defined. The determination of the so-called factor prices w and r cannot possibly be tied to some corresponding marginal products. Lastly, because q and k are constant for any given frontier, a frontier such as $q_0 R$ in Figure 1 contributes only a single point q_0, k_0 to the q_t, k_t space in Figure 2.

Now consider Harrod-neutral technical change, in which both output per worker q_t and the capital–labour ratio k_t rise at the same rate, so that the output–capital ratio R remains constant:

$$q_t/q_0 = k_t/k_0 = e^{at}, \quad \text{and since} \quad q_0/k_0 = R, \; q_t/k_t = R \tag{3}$$

This is depicted in Figure 1 by the successive wage–profit frontiers and in Figure 2 by the corresponding (solid) straight line q_t of slope R.

If we were simply concerned with the best relation between inputs and output, then the *true* relation $q_t = Rk_t$ would be the correct one. But within neoclassical theory, such a fitted function would imply a constant marginal product of capital,

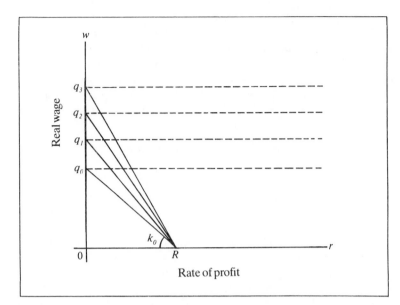

Figure 1

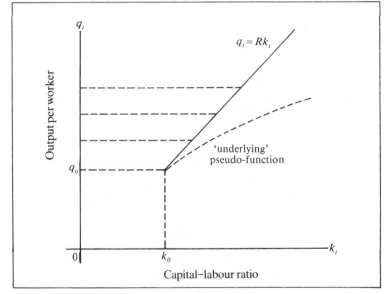

Figure 2

a zero marginal product of labour (Allen, 1967, pp. 45–6), and no technical change (since the 'shift parameter' R is constant). A good neoclassical would therefore have to reject this best (and true) fitted function in favour of some more 'appropriate' functional form (Fisher, 1971, pp. 312–13). How then might an aggregate production function fare in our anti-neoclassical world?

We have already assumed a constant profit share $r_t k_t / q_t = s$, and since the output–capital ratio $q_t / k_t = R$ is constant (equation (3)), it follows that the rate of profit $r_t = sR$ is constant. Similarly, the assumption of a constant wage share $w_t / q_t = 1 - s$ and a steadily growing output per worker $q_t = q_0 e^{at}$ (equation (3)), implies a steadily growing real wage $w_t = (1 - s)q_0 e^{at}$. All this allows us to solve explicitly for B_t' and A_t in equations (1)–(2):

$$B_t' = (1 - s)w_t' + sr_t' = (1 - s)a \tag{4}$$

$$q_t = C \, e^{(1 - s)at}k_t^s, \quad \text{since} \quad A_t = C \, e^{(1 - s)at} \tag{5}$$

Thus when the wage share is constant, *even a fixed proportion technology undergoing Harrod-neutral technical change is perfectly consistent with an aggregate pseudo-production function* (equation (5)). This is, however, a law of algebra, not a law of production. The above reasoning has been shown to have grave implications for production function studies (Shaikh, 1980). For instance, Solow's (1957) so-called seminal technique for assessing technical change amounts to decomposing the true production relation into an 'underlying' pseudo-production function and a residual A_t whose rate of change is then taken to measure technical progress (Figure 2). But this measures nothing more than distributional changes, since B_t is simply the weighted average of the rates of change of observed wage and profit rates (equations (1)–(2)). Similarly, Fisher's previously mentioned puzzle concerning the empirical strength of aggregate Cobb–Douglas production functions can be shown to be an artifact of the stability of the wage share over those particular simulation runs. Last, and perhaps most strikingly, it is interesting to note that even data points which spell out the word 'HUMBUG' can be well fitted by a Cobb–Douglas production function apparently undergoing neutral technical change and possessing marginal products equal to the corresponding 'factor prices'! Surely there is a message in this somewhere?

BIBLIOGRAPHY

Allen, R.G.D. 1967. *Macro-Economic Theory: A Mathematical Treatment*. London: Macmillan; New York: St. Martin's Press.

Fisher, F. 1971. Aggregate production functions and the explanation of wages: a simulation experiment. *Review of Economics and Statistics* 53(4), November, 305–25.

Garegnani, P. 1970. Heterogeneous capital, the production function, and the theory of distribution. *Review of Economic Studies* 37(3), 407–36.

Shaikh, A. 1974. Laws of algebra and laws of production: the humbug production function. *Review of Economics and Statistics* 51(1), 115–20.

Shaikh, A. 1980. Laws of algebra and laws of production: the humbug production function II. In *Growth, Profits and Property: Essays on the Revival of Political Economy*, ed. E.J. Nell, Cambridge: Cambridge University Press.

Solow, R. 1957. Technical change and the aggregate production function. *Review of Economics and Statistics* 39, 312–20.

Walters, A.A. 1963. Production functions and cost functions: an econometric survey. *Econometrica* 31(1), 1–66.

Internal rate of return

HARALD HAGEMANN

The internal rate of return of an investment project is that discount rate or rate of interest Y which makes the stream of net returns x_t associated with the project equal to a present value of zero. It is the solution for i in the following equation in which θ indicates the physical lifetime of the investment project.

$$C(0, \theta) = \sum_{t=0}^{\theta} x_t (1 + i)^{-t} = 0.$$

The internal rate of return is compared with the market rate of interest in order to determine whether a proposed project should be undertaken or not.

Among the criteria to be used in determining the profitability of an investment project two others are frequently considered. Whereas the payout-period criterion is a crude rule of thumb which ignores much of the time pattern of receipts, the net present value criterion is the most relevant 'rule' for optimal investment behaviour. If the present value (using the market rate of interest as the rate of discount) of a project's expected earnings is greater than its cost (including discounted future operating and maintenance costs), that is, if the net present value is positive, the investment project is potentially worth undertaking.

Whereas the net-present-value rule and the internal-rate-of-return rule lead to identical results in the two-period case and in the perpetuity case (which in essence is only a variant of the former), the two criteria may lead to different results in the multiperiod case. Figure 1 illustrates such a case in which the choice between two alternative investment options will lead to identical results for $i > i^*$ whereas the two criteria lead to different results for market rates of interest smaller than the cross-over rate i^* where the present value of I is higher while II has the higher internal rate of return. The failure of the internal rate of return criterion is the consequence of the implicit assumption that all intermediate receipts, positive or negative, are treated as if they could be compounded at the '*internal*' rate of return itself whereas the only appropriate *external* discounting rate is the market rate of interest (reinvestment problem).

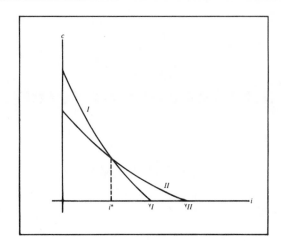

Figure 1

When the investment projects are independent and with a perfect capital market (in which the lending and borrowing rates of interest are identical) the net present value is, in general, the only universally correct criterion of appraising investment projects (see Hirshleifer, 1958 and 1970, ch. 3). For the multiperiod case the internal-rate-of-return rule is not generally correct. Furthermore, there may be *multiple rates of return* that will equate the present value of a project to zero. A necessary condition for non-uniqueness of the internal rate of return is that there be more than one change of sign in the stream of receipts over the lifetime of a project.

The controversy about the multiplicity of the internal rate of return in the late Fifties led to the development of the *truncation theorem*. This theorem turns out to be important for the general problem of choosing the optimal investment period (for a historical survey of truncation theorems see Matsuda and Okishio, 1977). In 1969 Arrow and Levhari presented a new version of the truncation theorem which contrasted sharply with the other economists' method of choosing a truncation period so as to maximize the internal rate of return. They rightly pointed out that this criterion would not be adequate for the choice of the truncation period. Instead they advocated the maximization of the present value of the investment project as the proper criterion. It was demonstrated that the possibility of truncating investment projects at any age different from their physical lifetimes and at no extra costs leads to the following results:

(1) The maximized present value of the project is a monotonically decreasing function of the rate of interest. A corollary of this is that the internal rate of return is always unique.

(2) A rise (fall) in the rate of interest will always lower (raise) the present value of the remaining future net returns at all stages of the production process.

Consequently the optimal economic lifetime, too, is a monotonically decreasing function of the rate of interest.

Flemming and Wright (1971) dropped the assumption of a constant rate of discount per unit of time and tried to generalize the theorem to the case of different interest rates over time, a case where the deficiency of the internal-rate-of-return rule is most obvious. However the 'generalization' does not take us very far because the calculation would require perfect foresight of future rates. The authors emphasize that a 'slight relaxation' of this assumption is allowed because 'a change in expectation which causes' all rates 'to be revised in the same "direction" will alter the present values of all costlessly terminable projects ... in a common direction' (Flemming and Wright, 1971, p. 262). But even this proposition holds, in general, only when the change takes place uniformly, so that there is no change in the weights of the time pattern of the stream of net returns.

More interesting is the discussion of the impact of a consequence stream, that is, costs and benefits following from truncation. Whereas a positive *scrap value* can easily be incorporated the range of validity of the truncation theorem is severely limited in the case of *shut down costs*. Shut down costs can occur before and after truncation. Sen (1975) has shown that in the general case of a consequence stream following from truncation only minimal sufficiency conditions can be formulated: non-negative consequence sums (NCS) and non-negative consequence remainders (NCR), that is, the present value of the consequence stream for each t before and after the actual point θ of truncation has to be non-negative. Neither NCS nor NCR requires the present value of the consequence stream at θ to be non-negative, that is, a negative present value of the remaining process does not endanger the monotonicity result. But the conditions are very restrictive, because NCR is violated if the last item or the discounted value of the tail of the consequence stream is negative. This may be the case because of for example, redundancy payments, environmental protection or shut down costs of a nuclear power station.

The truncation theorem was originally developed in a *partial framework*. Nevertheless, Hicks (1973) and Nuti (1973) considered it applicable in a *general framework*. However, Eatwell's (1975) criticism of these authors has clarifed that important propositions of the theorem do not carry over to the general framework (see also Hagemann and Pfister, 1978). At the partial level all prices in the economy are taken as given, that is, the individual's stream of net returns is considered not to be affected by changes in the discount rate. This assumption is impermissible when considering investment processes for society as a whole. At the general level the rate of profit is represented by the internal rate of return of the process as a whole for a given real wage. A variation of the discount factor, that is, the profit rate implies an opposite variation of the real wage rate. Because the present value of the whole process is both maximum and zero in competitive equilibrium the slope of the wage–profit curve is negative throughout. This is the only result one can draw under the conditions of the truncation theorem in the general setting. Neither the inverse relationship between the present value of the rest of the process and the rate of profit nor that between the optimal economic process length and the rate of profit invariably hold.

Furthermore, the analysis raises serious doubts as to the existence of an inverse monotonic relationship between interest and investment. The implication for Keynes's concept of the 'marginal efficiency of capital' is close at hand. As is well known, Keynes considered his concept 'identical' with Fisher's definition of the 'rate of return over cost' and stressed that there is no material difference 'between my schedule of the marginal efficiency of capital or investment demand-schedule and the demand curve for capital contemplated by some of the classical writers' (Keynes, 1936, pp. 140 and 178). To be sure, there are passages which indicate that Fisher was aware of the fact that prices and therefore not only the present values of the streams of net receipts but the net receipts themselves vary with variations in the rate of interest (see especially the 'more intricate than important' complication discussed in Fisher, 1930, pp. 170–71). However, the fixed-price assumption he commonly referred to implies a partial framework where the relationship between interest rates and prices is eliminated. It is therefore impossible to construct a demand curve for investment on the basis of a *ceteris paribus* clause for prices simply by variations of the rate of interest. An inverse macroeconomic relation between interest and investment cannot be derived from monotonicity results reached in a microeconomic framework. The difficulties encountered by Fisher and Keynes are discussed by Alchian and Garegnani from different points of view. Alchian (1955, p. 942) stresses that 'a schedule of investment demand at different market rates of interest requires that one compute the internal rates of return in terms of the prices that would prevail at each potential market rate of interest'. Garegnani (1978–9) brings into focus the problems involved in Keynes's concept of the schedule of the marginal efficiency of capital.

The return of the same truncation period and reswitching of techniques are closely linked phenomena occurring in a general framework. Some authors have tried to draw another analogy between the reswitching problem and the well-known possibility of the existence of multiple rates of return. Apparently the intention was to play down the importance of reswitching. This is reflected by the proposition that 'there is no new thing under the sun' (Bruno, Burmeister and Sheshinski, 1966, p. 553). However, multiple internal rates of return are a phenomenon related to the partial framework from which a generalization to the general level is not admissible. Truncation ensures the uniqueness of the internal rate of return but cannot rule out reswitching. Therefore, an analogy between the two phenomena does not exist.

BIBLIOGRAPHY

Alchian, A.A. 1955. The rate of interest, Fisher's rate of return over costs and Keynes' internal rate of return. *American Economic Review* 45, December, 938–43.

Arrow, K.J. and Levhari, D. 1969. Uniqueness of the internal rate of return with variable life of investment. *Economic Journal* 79, September, 560–66.

Bruno, M., Burmeister, E. and Sheshinski, E. 1966. The nature and implications of the reswitching of techniques. *Quarterly Journal of Economics* 80(4), November, 526–53.

Eatwell, J. 1975. A note on the truncation theorem. *Kyklos* 28(4), 870–75.

Fisher, I. 1930. *The Theory of Interest*. New York: Macmillan.

Flemming, J.S. and Wright, J.F. 1971. Uniqueness of the internal rate of return: a generalisation. *Economic Journal* 81, June, 256–63.

Garegnani, P. 1978–9. Notes on consumption, investment and effective demand, I and II, *Cambridge Journal of Economics*, Pt. I, 2(4), December 1978, 335–53; Pt II, 3(1), March 1979, 63–82.

Hagemann, H. and Pfister, J. 1978. Zur Relevanz des Truncation-Theorems in partialanalytischer und totalanalytischer Sicht. *Jahrbücher für Nationalökonomie und Statistik* 193(4), August, 359–79.

Hicks, J. 1973. *Capital and Time. A Neo-Austrian Theory*. Oxford: Clarendon Press.

Hirshleifer, J. 1958. On the theory of optimal investment decision. *Journal of Political Economy* 66, August, 329–52.

Hirshleifer, J. 1970. *Investment, Interest, and Capital*. Englewood Cliffs, NJ: Prentice-Hall.

Keynes, J.M. 1936. *The General Theory of Employment, Interest and Money*. London: Macmillan; New York: Harcourt, Brace.

Matsuda, K. and Okishio, N. 1977. Theorems of investment truncation. *Annals of the School of Business Administration*, Kobe Universty, 73–90.

Nuti, D.M. 1973. On the truncation of production flows. *Kyklos* 26(3), 485–96.

Sen, A. 1975. Minimal conditions for monotonicity of capital value, *Journal of Economic Theory* 11(3), December, 340–55.

Maintaining capital intact

K.H. HENNINGS

The purpose of economic activity is normally to produce a surplus which can be distributed (or appropriated) as income. But only that part of total output can be reckoned as surplus and distributed as income which is not needed to provide for the continuation of economic activity on the same level. Thus in an economy producing only corn (from abundant land and labour) an amount of total output equal to what was required to produce it has to be set aside as seed, and only the remainder can be distributed as income and is at the most available for consumption. If more is distributed, the economy cannot continue on the same level as before, that is, becomes less viable, and will ultimately become unviable so that economic activity comes to an end. To set aside as much output as is required to continue economic activity on the same level as before (or, to provide for simple reproduction) is thus a principle which may be violated in the short run, but which endangers the viability of economic activity if not adhered to in the long run. If economic activity involves stocks which are considered as 'capital', this principle requires that such capital be maintained intact. Capital is maintained intact if an amount of total output is set aside for its maintenance which ensures that the remaining output is on a level that can be kept up forever. The principle that the viability of economic activity be maintained which requires that capital be maintained intact, thus implies the Hicksian income concept (Hicks, 1939, ch. 14).

This formulation of the principle assumes that it is desirable to maintain the current level of economic activity. While it is reasonable to assume that it is not desirable to 'eat up capital' over more than a short period (despite exceptions such as wars), it is often considered desirable to consume less than the maximal possible amount, i.e. to accumulate capital and thus to increase the level of economic activity that can be permanently maintained. The principle that the viability of economic activity be maintained therefore sets a minimum standard. By comparison with propositions about the optimum accumulation of capital such as the golden rule, it is a proposition about the minimum maintenance of capital.

As here formulated the principle is empty as long as what it means to maintain capital intact is not defined. How this should be done has been the subject of long-standing debates among accountants and business economists in the guise of determining the correct principles for drawing up business accounts and calculating business income. Much the same issues have been discussed by social accountants from a macroeconomic perspective. In economic theory they have been the subject of an important debate between A.C. Pigou and F.A. Hayek in the 1930s and 1940s.

It will be useful to begin with the accountants' perspective. It has often been maintained, reasonably enough in view of the legal obligations of a firm to its creditors, that business accounts should be drawn up such that the amount of money capital invested in the firm be preserved, and that business income should be reckoned as distributable only after allowance has been made for its maintenance. This raises a host of valuation difficulties (see Parker and Harcourt, 1969), but the principle is reasonably clear: what should be preserved is the net present value of the firm, corrected for price level changes, i.e. measured in real terms. That is what matters from the point of view of someone who has invested in the firm. It is obvious that this implies that assets are valued not at historical cost, nor at replacement cost, but rather according to their most probable expected future contribution to business income. That means taking account of such factors as business risks as well as planned obsolescence when the expected physical life of an asset is longer than its expected use. Nor does preserving the net present value of a firm imply that any particular asset be preserved, or maintained intact. It may be more profitable to run down an asset deliberately, i.e. shorten its physical life (and even productivity) by neglecting to keep it in good working order, or even get rid of it altogether. For what is to be preserved is not capital in the sense of a stock of physical objects (capital goods), but net wealth. In an accountant's perspective, maintaining capital intact means preserving net wealth, and not a stock of capital. This can be done in a variety of ways, including a change in the stock of capital. Hence there is no necessary connection between preserving net wealth and maintaining a stock of capital, from the point of view of a firm. The same holds true for any other microeconomic unit, in particular households. In a microeconomic perspective, therefore, income is whatever is earned minus what is necessary to preserve, given current expectations, the net present value of the firm or household in real terms.

In a macroeconomic perspective, economic activity can without loss of generality be considered as production which involves capital goods such that at any moment there exists a stock of capital. Consider an arbitrary time period. Both at the beginning and the end of the period there will exist capital stocks which consist of different types of capital goods of different ages. Some of the capital tools existing at the beginning of the period will have been used up, or have been discarded, during the period. Others will have been used during the period, and will normally have been subject to wear and tear; whether they have been maintained in good working order or not, they are all older at the end of the period. Finally, there will be new capital goods, produced during the period.

So in general the capital stock existing at the end of the period will consist of different capital goods than those which formed the capital stock at the beginning of the period. However, if the economy is in a stationary state, the size and composition of the capital stock is the same at the beginning and the end of the period. As the age structure of all types of capital goods will be constant, replacing the oldest items of each type of capital good will ensure that all losses are replaced and all wear and tear is made good. Where that is not possible because the period is too short, and the durability of capital goods so long that none is due to be replaced, a fund can be set up to accumulate what is required for replacement. In such a stationary situation no investment decisions need to be taken. Because the structure of production is well integrated, all types of capital goods needed for replacement are produced, and can be used for the purpose for which they were produced. Similarly, all consumption goods will be used for consumption, and will together constitute the income of the economy.

Much the same will be true in an economy growing in a steady state as long as there is no technical change. There will be investment, but investment decisions will be confined to decisions to produce more of everything. The capital stock at the end of the period will be larger than that at the beginning, but its composition will be the same: all outgoing capital goods will simply be replaced by a larger amount of the same type. Income will consist of all consumption goods and the excess of new capital goods over what would have been required in a stationary situation.

In both these cases the meaning of 'maintaining capital intact' is clear. In a stationary economy it means keeping the size and the composition of the capital stock constant. In a steady state without technical change it means letting the capital stock grow while keeping its composition constant. In all other situations, i.e. if there is technical change or the economy is in a non-steady state, both the size and the composition of the capital stock will change, and maintaining capital intact can no longer be defined with respect to identical types of capital goods. Hence it was sought to specify 'maintaining capital intact' in a different manner.

Pigou (1932; 1935) proposed that 'maintaining capital intact' should be defined in such a way that a capital stock should be considered as constant if the capital goods which were used up or discarded during the period are replaced by others the production of which requires an amount of real resources equal in that period to what would have been required to reproduce the same types of capital goods as the used up or discarded ones. Because he supposed that the replacements are 'so chosen that the maximum possible addition is made to the present value of the stock of capital' (1935, p. 239), Pigou considered the capital stock as 'an entity capable of maintaining its quantity while altering its form and by its nature always drawn to those forms on which, so to speak, the sun of profits is at the time shining' (1935, p. 239). Maintaining capital intact thus meant to Pigou the replacement of outgoing items by items with the same real cost of production. It did not include provisions for making good wear and tear. Moreover, Pigou distinguished 'normal' maintenance from replacements made necessary by capital losses due to 'the act of God or the King's enemies', or acts of Parliament, which are not covered by consideration of the risks attached to the normal conduct of business (1935, p. 240). Real income, in his conception, was then total output minus what was required for 'normal' maintenance.

Hayek (1935; 1941a; 1941b) criticizes Pigou's proposals on several grounds. First of all Hayek objected to the backward-looking nature of Pigou's capital concept and pointed to the absurdities it could entail. Instead, he insisted on a forward-looking concept in which capital goods are valued (in real terms) on the basis of their prospective quasi-rents and not their costs of production. This point Pigou accepted, and later defined a capital stock to be constant if the items which replace outgoing capital goods are 'expected to yield the same income' as those they replace (1941, p. 274). Hayek also objected to Pigou's failure to include the making good of wear and tear in what was required to maintain capital intact, and argued at the same time that in a changing economy (which is subject to technical change, or in a non-steady state, or both) obsolescence is far more serious than physical wear and tear. Where obsolescence is planned, or expected, not to include allowances for it would underestimate what is required to maintain capital intact, and overestimate income. Where obsolescence is unexpected, attempts will be made to adapt as far as possible capital goods which were produced for one purpose to other uses. Not to make allowance for such attempts, or to do so only when such capital goods are finally discarded and replaced (as Pigou's proposal implies), would equally distort the calculation of both maintenance and income. Hayek also pointed out that all expected changes in the prospective quasi-rents of capital goods, say as a result of technical progress, or of unexpected price changes, represent capital gains or losses in real terms. Such windfalls should in his view affect maintenance rather than income. Hayek emphasized strongly that maintaining capital intact was not an end in itself, as Pigou seemed to imply, but a means to achieve a constant flow of income in order to avoid what D.H. Robertson (1933) had called unintended stinting or splashing, i.e. consuming either too little or too much to maintain the present level of consumption. Hence he argued that windfall gains and losses should affect income only in so far as they can be converted into permanent increases or decreases in the flow of income.

Hayek's main point was thus that in a changing economy changes in prices and expectations will lead to both real and price Wicksell effects, i.e. changes in the methods of production and in the valuation of capital goods. Both will cause entrepreneurs to adapt their investment behaviour because, aiming at a constant flow of income, they will not allow windfall capital gains and losses to affect their income beyond what can be converted into permanent increases and decreases in income. Hence precisely because entrepreneurs aim at a constant flow of income they will again and again adapt the capital stock required to produce that flow. There is thus no reason why the capital stock should in some sense be constant. Moreover, changes in capital stocks between the beginning and the end of a period reflect not so much physical wear and tear as obsolescence and adaptations due to changed circumstances and expectations. Hence maintenance cannot be distinguished from net investment, and attempts to define income by taking account of what is required to maintain capital are bound to fail. Hayek's argument thus amounts to a demonstration that in a changing economy, maintaining capital intact in the sense of keeping a stock of capital constant in some sense or another was incompatible with the Hicksian income concept, i.e. with maintaining income constant. Pigou (1941; 1946) responded to Hayek's capital theoretic critique by restating his position. Writing from the point of view of welfare theory, and dealing with what would now be called ex-post aggregates, Pigou insisted that some method, however rough and ready, of separating maintenance from new investment should be found. That is what Hicks (1942) attempted in his contribution to the debate. While accepting Hayek's critique, he doubted the appropriateness of maintaining a constant flow of income in a changing economy, and at the same time proposed a method, based on Lindahl (1933), designed to separate ex post the consequences of expected from unexpected changes in the value of capital goods, so that the former could be charged to maintenance. and the latter as windfalls to income (see also Hicks, 1958; 1969; 1973, ch. 13; and especially 1979). More recently, Scott (1984) has made a similar attempt, placing the dividing line between depreciations and appreciations due to relative price changes which should fall on income, and other changes which should fall on maintenance.

Despite some constructive efforts Hayek's critique is essentially negative. As Hicks (1974) has pointed out, Pigou's position can be associated with the attempt to provide a concept of a capital stock which corresponds to the flow of income it helped to produce. From the point of view of the construction of a production function, such an attempt is valid; but it does come up against the twin problems of technical progress and non-stationary conditions. So the problem which Pigou originally attempted to answer is still unsolved. Progress may be expected from extending recent advances in capital theory, which so far have been confined to comparative static analysis, to the analysis of a changing economy. A beginning has been made with the development (Hicks, 1973) of the concept of a 'transition' from one steady state to another, but more work needs to be done. Only when we know more about the behaviour of firms and households in an economy which is not so well integrated that all goods are used for the purpose they are produced for, and in which obsolescence and hence windfall capital gains and losses are widespread, can we decide whether it is possible to give precise meaning to the notion of maintaining capital intact. Until then the notion is useful only in the analysis of steady states which are not subject to technical change – which excludes most situations of interest to the economic theorist.

BIBLIOGRAPHY

Break, G.F. 1954. Capital maintenance and the concept of income. *Journal of Political Economy* 62, February, 48–62.

Hayek, F.A. 1935. The maintenance of capital. *Economica* 2, 241–76.

Hayek, F.A. 1941a. *The Pure Theory of Capital*. London: Routledge. Chicago: University of Chicago Press, 1950.

Hayek, F.A. 1941b. Maintaining capital intact: a reply. *Economica* 8, 276–80.

Hicks, J.R. 1939. *Value and Capital*. Oxford: Clarendon Press.

Hicks, J.R. 1942. Maintaining capital intact: a further suggestion. *Economica* 9, 174–9.

Hicks, J.R. 1958. Measurement of capital – in theory. In J.R. Hicks, *Wealth and Welfare*, Oxford: Blackwell, 1981. In *Collected Essays on Economic Theory*. Cambridge, Mass.: Harvard University Press.

Hicks, J.R. 1969. Measurement of capital – in practice. In J.R. Hicks, *Wealth and Welfare*, Oxford: Blackwell, 1981. In *Collected Essays on Economic Theory*. Cambridge, Mass.: Harvard University Press.

Hicks, J.R. 1973. *Capital and Time*. Oxford: Clarendon Press.

Hicks, J.R. 1974. Capital controversies: ancient and modern. Ch. 7 in J.R. Hicks, *Economic Perspectives*, Oxford: Clarendon Press, 1977; New York: Oxford University Press.

Hicks, J.R. 1979. The concept of business income. Ch. 14 in J.R. Hicks, *Classics and Moderns*, Oxford: Blackwell, 1983. In *Collected Essays on Economic Theory*, Cambridge, Mass.: Harvard University Press.

Lindahl, E. 1933. The concept of income. In *Economic Essays in Honour of Gustav Cassel*, London: Allen & Unwin, 399–418.

Parker, R.H. and Harcourt, G.C. (eds) 1969 *Readings in the Concept and Measurement of Income*. Cambridge: Cambridge University Press.

Pigou, A.C. 1932. *The Economics of Welfare*. 4th edn, London: Macmillan; New York: St. Martin's Press, 1956.

Pigou, A.C. 1935. Net income and capital depletion. *Economic Journal* 45, 235–41.

Pigou, A.C. 1941. Maintaining capital intact. *Economica* 8, 271–5.

Pigou, A.C. 1946. *The Economics of Welfare*. Reprint of 4th edn. with additional Prefatory Note, London: Macmillan; New York: St. Martin's Press, 1956.

Robertson, D.H. 1933. Saving and hoarding. *Economic Journal* 43, 399–413.

Scott, M.F.G. 1984. Maintaining capital intact. In *Economic Theory and Hicksian Themes*, ed. D.A. Collard et al., Oxford: Clarendon Press, 59–73.

Optimal savings

SUKHAMOY CHAKRAVARTY

How much should a nation save or, to put it differently, what is the optimal rate of growth? This question is at the heart of the extensive literature on 'optimum savings' which developed as a complement to the literature on descriptive growth models in the 1950s and 1960s. Let it be noted that the reasonableness of the question presupposes a utilitarian welfare-theoretic outlook, which locates a source of 'market failure' in the intertemporal context stemming from what A.C. Pigou (1928) had described as a defective telescopic faculty. While Böhm-Bawerk, Fisher and other economists had noted the fact the individuals show a preference for advancing the timing of future satisfaction, they refrained from making any normative statement. Instead they constructed theories of interest which utilized this crucial behavioural characteristic on the part of individual economic agents. Pigou, however, read into the fact that individuals discount future satisfaction at a positive rate, that is display impatience, 'a far reaching economic disharmony' (1928, p. 26). This made him seriously question the 'optimality' of the rate of savings thrown up by an otherwise fully competitive market even under conditions of full employment. Pigou's ideas on this question received support from the Cambridge philosopher-mathematician Frank P. Ramsey, who took the next most important step of determining a rule for determining the optimum rate of savings based on the logic of intertemporal utility maximization, one of the early exercises in economics using the technique of classical calculus of variations. Ramsey was relatively precise in laying down the normative postulates underlying his enquiry, ingenious in deriving the characteristics of the optimal path and not so much concerned with demonstrating that an optimal solution will always exist even on the premises laid out by him.

Ramsey's paper was much appreciated by John Maynard Keynes who, in his obituary note on Ramsey's untimely death, which appeared in the *Economic Journal*, called it 'one of the most remarkable contributions to mathematical economics ever made' (1930).

206

Despite Keynes, Ramsey's paper received very little attention for nearly three decades, partly, because of the 'Great Depression' where 'excessive savings' in the sense of too high a propensity to save appeared to many economists including Keynes himself, to be the problem, and the emergence of a new welfare economics, which found the cardinal approach towards utility embedded in Ramsey's formulation of the problem extremely questionable, if not unacceptable.

During the late 1950s, however, attention was redirected to the question which Ramsey had posed, especially by those who were particularly concerned with problems of development planning in relation to low income countries. Experience of sustained full employment in the advanced capitalist countries, obvious inadequacy of the stock of capital in the poorer countries from the point of view of generating employment at an adequate level of remuneration, and a back-door entry of 'cardinal utility' via the von Neumann–Morgenstern axioms, although applicable only to risky prospects, made the intellectual environment more receptive to the class of issues that Ramsey had dealt with in his 1928 paper.

Discussion was initiated by Tinbergen (1960), Goodwin (1961) and Chakravarty (1962a) from a development theoretic point of view; the motivation was to help planners arrive at optimal growth paths for labour surplus economies based on explicit parametric forms of utility and production functions.

These exercises showed that even in relatively simple cases, optimal paths do not always exist for an open-ended future. The special nature of the assumptions made by Ramsey became more evident through extensive investigations initiated by Koopmans (1960) on the axiomatization of intertemporal utility functions which were in some suitable sense continuous. While Koopmans was concerned with complete and continuous preference orderings, a different approach taken by Von Weizsäcker (1965) dealt with a partial order on the programme space defined by the principle of 'overtaking'. A consumption path C_t is said to overtake an alternative path C_t if there exists a time T^* such that $\int_0^T u(c_t)\,dt > \int_0^T U(c_t^*)\,dt$ for all $T \geqslant T^*$. The overtaking criterion, being a partial order, allows for non-comparable paths but as subsequent discussion showed this may not matter under certain economically relevant conditions, thereby providing an extension of the Ramsey criterion which deals with improper integrals of the form $\int_0^\infty u(c(t))\,dt$ with concave $U(c(t))$ functions.

While Ramsey dealt with a stationary population, during the 1960s characterization of 'optimal growth paths' in the 'overtaking sense' was extended to situations involving exogenously growing population. A reasonably complete analysis was given by Cass (1965) and Koopmans (1965) for the one good case with continuous time and twice continuously differentiable production and utility functions.

A multisectoral generalization of the original Ramsey model was carred out by Samuelson and Solow (1956) in the mid-1950s. During the 1960s, Gale (1967) and others derived multisectoral generalizations for situations involving growing populations, using once again the 'overtaking' criterion.

Aggregate models involving exogenous technical change were carried out by Mirrlees (1967), Inagaki (1970) and several others. These authors used explicit 'time discounting' and obtained for certain special cases lower bounds which a constant rate of time discounting must obey.

Most recently, Magill (1981) has provided a very thorough analysis of the existence question for optimal infinite horizon programmes involving complete orderings, and a variety of technologies. Welfare maximization over time involving exhaustible resources was first studied by Hotelling (1931), more or less contemporaneously with Ramsey. This literature has proliferated in recent years and has been exhaustively dealt with by Dasgupta and Heal (1979). A recent paper by de Grandville (1980) combines capital accumulation along with depletion of stocks and derives optimal growth paths, following the Samuelson–Solow paper.

A. Ramsey characterized the social welfare function, or more accurately, the welfare function over time, as the integral of deviations of current utility levels from a postulated finite upper bound on instantaneous utility levels, denoting it by 'Bliss' 'B', assumed zero time discounting concave utility functions, a stationary population and no technical progress. He distinguished between two types of 'bliss', one due to capital saturation and the other due to utility saturation. In compact mathematical notation, Ramsey's problem was to minimize an expression $\int_0^\infty (B - U(c(t))) \, dt$ subject to $c(t) + k'(t) = f(l, k)$ where $c(t)$ stands for consumption at time t, $k(t)$ denoted the stock of capital at 't' and 'l' for a given labour force. $k'(t) \equiv dk/dt$ represents the rate of capital formation, measured on a 'net' basis. This is a standard problem in the calculus of variations excepting for the choice of an infinite time horizon, as can be seen through substitution. The integral is of the form $\int_0^\infty F(k, k') \, dt$. Using the Euler necessary condition for a minimum value of the functional one can write down implicitly the optimal path for savings over time, provided it exists. In general, the path will not belong to a class of paths characterized by a constant saving ratio over time. Concavity of utility function $u(c)$ and diminishing returns to capital assure that the second order conditions are also satisfied. Ramsey, however, succeeded in deducing through an elegant transformation of the independent variable, namely, time, a very remarkable rule with optimal paths must necessarily satisfy. Keynes provided an intuitive explanation for the same rule. The 'Keynes–Ramsey' rule states that the optimal rate of capital accumulation at any given instant of time multiplied by the marginal utility of optimal consumption at that point of time must equal the excess of the bliss level of utility over the utility of the current optimal level of consumption. The remarkable thing about the Keynes–Ramsey rule is that it is 'altogether independent of the production function except in so far as this determines bliss, the maximum rate of utility obtainable' (Ramsey, 1928).

In the presence of time discounting, the integrand becomes $F(k, k', t)$. With this modification, the Euler differential equation which in general constitutes a second order nonlinear differential equation does not necessarily possess a first integral and hence, the optimum growth path does not lend itself to a simple characterization in terms of a decision rule which is formally independent of time ('t').

Ramsey assumes a stationary population, although he allowed for utility maximizing choice on the part of current labour. In the context of the discussion that took place in the early 1960s, population was generally assumed to be growing at an exogenously given rate. Thus $L(t)$ was put at $L_0 e^{nt}$. With this modification, the Ramsey concept of 'bliss' has to be altered.

Assuming a constant returns to scale production function and expressing all relevant variables on a per worker basis, one can derive the relationship $c(t) + k'(t) = f(k(t)) - nk$. Assuming that we are considering only steady growth paths, we have $k'(t) = 0$ and a time-independent expression $c = f(k) - nk$. The expression c is maximized for k such that $f'(k) = n$. Under some mild restriction on $f(k)$ this expression can be solved for a finite value of 'k' and the corresponding consumption level $\hat{c}$. $\hat{c}$ can be interpreted as the highest level of sustainable consumption per worker over time, that is the best among the steady states for a given technology. Instead of Ramsey's expression B, we can now write $\int_0^\infty (u(\hat{c}) - u(c)) \, dt$ as the integral, and minimize this modified functional subject to the production conditions given earlier. $u(\hat{c})$ is generally referred to in the literature as the utility of consumption attached to the 'golden rule of accumulation'.

Koopmans (1965) and Cass (1965) demonstrated that if $k(0) < \hat{k}$, the optimal paths will approach $\hat{k}$ from below over time whereas if $k(0) > \hat{k}$, it will approach it from above.

Cass included time discounting ($p > 0$), and obtained the 'modified golden rule' for which $f'(k) = n + p$ and deduced the optimal growth path.

For the case of $p = 0$, the Keynes–Ramsey rule is restored again for the same reason as noted in the Ramsey case. However, when population is growing, it is not clear whether one should use the instantaneous utility function $u(c)$ where 'c' is consumption per worker (or per capita, if the participation rate is constant) or a different social welfare functional altogether. Thus, Arrow and Kurz (1970) have argued in favour of maximizing an expression $\int_0^\infty e^{-Pt} u[c(t)] P(t) \, dt$, where $P(t)$ stands for population at time 't' on the ground that 'if more people benefit, so much the better' (Arrow and Kurz, 1970, p. 12). It is clear that in this case, a $P > 0$ is essential if an optimal solution is to exist at all.

The extension of the model to many sector cases was first attempted by Samuelson and Solow (1956). They showed that the Fisher arbitrage rule regarding prices over time could be extended to an n-good case as a necessary property of all optimal paths, no matter which specific utility function is used as it depends only on the question of intertemporal efficiency. An analogue of a 'golden rule' was obtained in situations involving no joint production, a single consumer good and the relevant convexity condition.

Linear analysis applied in the neighbourhood of the 'golden rule' solution displays a 'catenary type' behaviour in the one good case, a phenomenon noticed first by Samuelson in a multisectoral context and subsequently proved in the context of closed consumptionless systems by Radner and others. However, any general treatment of n-dimensional cases involving discounted utility functions can throw up pathologies which are not present in simpler cases, especially if joint production is allowed (Samuelson and Liviatan, 1969).

B. Revival of discussion on the optimum rate of savings in the early 1960s was motivated by policy considerations. Dissatisfaction with a politically determined rate of savings or with the market solution, especially when the capital market was considered to be subject to considerable imperfection, led economists to look more closely into the character of growth paths based on an ethically explicit criterion function over time. As time is open-ended, the discussion veered towards problems posed by an infinite planning horizon. With the discovery that optimal paths may not exist with otherwise well behaved production and utility functions, economists devoted a great deal of attention to possible modifications of the Ramsey–Pigou valuation premises to get around the non-existence problem. Koopmans, in particular, felt the need for introducing an assumption relating to time discounting to get over the problem of non-existence and so did Arrow and Kurz.

Some authors tried to explore the sensitivity of finite horizon optimal growth paths to terminal conditions, which in the nature of the case, has to be arbitrary. The idea behind these exercises was to offer an alternative to the procedure of discounting which equally violated the postulate of ethical neutrality between generations (Chakravarty, 1962b), the aim being to examine whether optimal paths will prove insensitive at least in their initial phase to terminal conditions, provided the horizon was sufficiently long. Brock (1971) subsequently generalized this type of analysis quite considerably.

Based on these discussions, Hammond and Mirrlees (1973) proposed a category of growth profiles which seemed to avoid the Scylla of 'time discounting' and the Charybdis of a given 'terminal capital stock', by suggesting a category of paths called 'agreeable paths' with the property that if an optimum path exists over an infinite time horizon, it is agreeable.

Furthermore, 'an agreeable path exists if and only if a perpetually feasible locally optimal path exists'. It is then the 'maximal locally optimal path' (Hammond and Mirrlees, 1973). Hammond subsequently extended the analysis to a multisectoral context (1976).

Agreeable paths possess an operational appeal to planners and therefore need to be pursued in greater depth. Among areas of current interest, one can also mention models which relax the assumption of additive separability, which does not seem to be sufficiently strongly grounded in ethical intuition, as well as the assumption of 'stationarity' in the sense defined first by Koopmans (1960).

Despite the existence of several unsolved problems, literature on 'optimal savings' has been of interest to economic theorists for having explored with considerable thoroughness the 'open-endedness' of the future from a national decision-theoretic point of view and for providing a convenient parametric method of generating optimal growth paths in a precise sense of the term with associated dual prices, which can be used for social benefit–cost analysis. It has also posed a philosophical issue of broader interest as to whether one can adopt ethical principles that are independent of environmental consideration in the broad sense of the term (i.e. population growth and/or technological progress).

BIBLIOGRAPHY

Arrow, K.J. and Kurz, M. 1970. *Public Investment, the Rate of Return, and Optimal Fiscal Policy*. Baltimore: Johns Hopkins Press.

Brock, W.A. 1971. Sensitivity of optimal paths with respect to a change in target stocks. *Zeitschrift für Nationalökonomie*, Supplement 1.

Cass, D. 1965. Optimal growth in an aggregative model of capital accumulation. *Review of Economic Studies* 32, July, 233–40.

Chakravarty, S. 1962a. The existence of an optimum savings program. *Econometrica* 30, January, 178–87.

Chakravarty, S. 1962b. Optimal savings with finite planning horizon. *International Economic Review* 3, September, 338–55.

Dasgupta, P.S. and Heal, G. 1979. *The Economic Theory of Exhaustible Resources*. London: Nisbet; New York: Cambridge University Press.

de Grandville, O. 1980. Capital theory, optimal growth and efficiency conditions with exhaustible resources. *Econometrica* 48(7), November, 1763–76.

Gale, D. 1967. On optimal development in a multi-sector economy. *Review of Economic Studies* 34, January, 1–18.

Goodwin, R.M. 1961. The optimal growth path for an underdeveloped economy. *Economic Journal* 71, December, 756–74.

Hammond, P.J. and Mirrlees, J.A. 1973. Agreeable plans. In *Models of Economic Growth*, ed. J.A. Mirrlees and N. Stern, London: Macmillan; New York: Wiley.

Hotelling, H. 1931. The economics of exhaustible resources. *Journal of Political Economy* 39, April, 137–75.

Inagaki, M. 1970. *Optimal Economic Growth; Finite Shifting vs Infinite Time Horizon*. Amsterdam: North-Holland.

Keynes, J.M. 1930. Ramsey, F.P.: an obituary. *Economic Journal* 40, March, 153–4.

Koopmans, T.C. 1960. Stationary ordinal utility and impatience. *Econometrica* 28, April, 287–309.

Koopmans, T.C. 1965. On the concept of optimal economic growth. In *The Econometric Approach to Development Planning*, Amsterdam: North-Holland; Chicago: Rand MacNally. (A reissue of *Pontificiae Academiae Scientarium Scripta Varia*, Vol. XXVIII, 1965.)

Koopmans, T.C. 1967. Objectives, constraints, and outcomes in optimal growth models. *Econometrica* 35, January, 1–15.

Magill, M.J.P. 1981. Infinite horizon programs. *Econometrica* 49(3), May, 679–711.

Mirrlees, J.A. 1967. Optimum growth when technology is changing. *Review of Economic Studies* 34, January, 95–124.

Pigou, A.C. 1952. *The Economics of Welfare*. London: Macmillan; New York: St. Martin's Press.

Ramsey, F.P. 1928. A mathematical theory of saving. *Economic Journal* 38, December, 543–59.

Samuelson, P.A. 1965. A catenary turnpike theorem involving consumption and the golden rule. *American Economic Review* 55, June, 486–96.

Samuelson, P.A. and Liviatan, N. 1969. Notes on 'turnpikes', stable and unstable. *Journal of Economic Theory* 1(4), December, 454–75.

Samuelson, P.A. and Solow, R.M. 1956. A complete capital model involving heterogeneous capital goods. *Quarterly Journal of Economics* 70, November, 537–62.

Tinbergen, J. 1960. Optimum savings and utility maximization over time. *Econometrica* 28, April, 481–89.

von Weizsäcker, C.C. 1965. The existence of optimal programmes of accumulation for an infinite time horizon. *Review of Economic Studies* 32, April, 85–104.

Period of production

G.O. OROSEL

The period of production is, or purports to be, a measure of aggregate capital per head. More specifically, it is a theoretical concept which tries to measure an economy's (heterogeneous) capital stock per head in (homogeneous) units of time.

Necessarily the concept of the period of production is based on an Austrian, or temporal, view of production. In this view production is conceptualized as a sequence of primary inputs on the one hand and a corresponding sequence of consumption outputs on the other. Produced means of production (capital goods) are reduced to dated primary inputs and consumption outputs. This implies that the approach is suited best for the analysis of steady states, where specific properties of capital goods are irrelevant, whereas it will be misleading, in general, if applied to problems of transition or disequilibrium. In particular, this approach is inadequate for business cycle analysis.

Although the temporal view can be traced back to Thünen, Senior, Rae and Jevons, it was Böhm-Bawerk (1889) who made it a cornerstone of his theory. This theory was directed at a fundamental problem of political economy: Why is the (net) rate of profit positive? A related problem concerns the measurement of heterogeneous capital goods in homogeneous units which are independent of distribution.

A sketch of Böhm-Bawerk's theory is as follows. According to Böhm-Bawerk the fundamental feature of an economy using capital is that there is a temporal distance, called *period of production* (or *period of investment*), between primary inputs and corresponding consumption outputs. Capital is, in its essence, a fund of means of subsistence which allows for consumption during this period. In a steady state this subsistence fund consists of different 'layers' of goods which are distinguished by their respective degree of maturity, such that each period's consumption can be provided by the layer which has just become ready for consumption. A longer period of production is equivalent, in this view, to more capital per head. Hence the per capita stock of heterogeneous capital goods can be measured in homogeneous units of time. Adding to this (a) the technological hypothesis that consumption output per head increases with the period of production, and (b) the psychological hypothesis of a positive time preference gives, in a nutshell, Böhm-Bawerk's explanation of the positivity of the rate of profit.

From the beginning, Böhm-Bawerk's theory, and in particular the concept of the period of production, has caused heated debates (involving, among others, J.B. Clark, Irving Fisher, Schumpeter, Wicksell, Hayek, Kaldor and Knight). The contributions to these debates, not all of them to the point, are not reviewed here (see, however, Kaldor, 1937; Weston, 1951). Instead, we will analyse the period of production from a fundamentalist and from a pragmatic point of view. In a *fundamentalist* view the period of production is seen as an important component of the theory sketched above and, therefore, must have properties which make it consistent with this theory. In particular, it must be a technological parameter. In a *pragmatic* view the period of production is just a conventionally measured distance between primary inputs and consumption outputs and need not have any definite properties.

In order to give a more rigorous presentation of the period of production and the problems associated with it, we make the following assumptions. Unless stated otherwise time is measured continuously and it is assumed that primary inputs and consumption outputs can each be measured in homogeneous units. A technique is assumed to be representable by a pair (a, b) of non-negative, continuous functions $a: R \rightarrow R_+$ and $b: R \rightarrow R_+$, where $a(t)$ is the amount of primary inputs expended at t and $b(t)$ is the amount of consumption outputs delivered at t (note that such a representation where (a, b) is independent of the rate of growth may not be possible for technologies with joint production; cf. the non-substitution theorem). The primary input will be called 'labour'; 'per head' (or 'per capita') will mean per unit of labour. It is assumed that

$$\lim_{t \to -\infty} a(t) = \lim_{t \to \infty} a(t) = \lim_{t \to -\infty} b(t) = \lim_{t \to \infty} b(t) = 0,$$

that a and b are not identically zero, that there are constant returns to scale (i.e. for any feasible technique (a, b) and any $\lambda > 0$ the technique $(\lambda a, \lambda b)$ is also feasible) and that there exists some real numbers $H < 0$, $G > 0$ such that the improper Riemann-integrals

$$\int_{-\infty}^{\infty} e^{-\gamma t} a(t) \, dt$$

and

$$\int_{-\infty}^{\infty} e^{-\gamma t} b(t) \, dt$$

converge for $\gamma \in (H, G)$. The analysis is restricted to steady states with technique (a, b), a rate of growth $g \in (H, G)$ and a rate of interest $r \in (H, G)$; and to conditions of zero excess profits, implying

$$w \int_{-\infty}^{\infty} e^{-rt} a(t) \, dt = \int_{-\infty}^{\infty} e^{-rt} b(t) \, dt \tag{1}$$

where w is the steady state price of the primary input, henceforth called (real) wage, and the price of the consumption good is set equal to one. Given a technique (a, b) and any point of time s, let $\lambda(s, t)$ denote the activity level, at s, of the techniques which are in 'stage' t. For a steady state $\lambda(s, t) = e^{-gt} \lambda(s, 0)$ and total labour inputs at s are

$$A(s) = \int_{-\infty}^{\infty} \lambda(s, t) a(t) \, dt = \lambda(s, 0) \int_{-\infty}^{\infty} e^{-gt} a(t) \, dt.$$

Similarly, total consumption outputs at s are

$$B(s) = \lambda(s, 0) \int_{-\infty}^{\infty} e^{-gt} b(t) \, dt.$$

This implies for per capita consumption $c := B(s)/A(s)$

$$c \int_{-\infty}^{\infty} e^{-gt} a(t) \, dt = \int_{-\infty}^{\infty} e^{-gt} b(t) \, dt \tag{2}$$

which is dual to (1). For the value of capital k per head the steady state identity $c + gk = w + rk$ implies

$$k = \begin{cases} \dfrac{c - w}{r - g} & \text{for } r \neq g \\[2ex] -\dfrac{dc}{dg} = -\dfrac{dw}{dr} & \text{for } r = g \end{cases} \tag{3}$$

THE FUNDAMENTALIST VIEW. In a fundamentalist view the period of production T must have two properties: first, it must be a technological parameter, i.e. for each technique (a, b) and rate of growth g it must be uniquely determined by the associated flows of labour inputs and consumption outputs (which are proportional to $e^{-gt} a(t)$ and $e^{-gt} b(t)$ respectively); second, as a subsistence fund for T periods with per period consumption c the steady state value of capital per head k must be given by $k = cT$. But this leads to an inconsistency: since it implies $T = k/c$ and since in general k/c varies with the rate of interest, T cannot be a technological parameter. Hence the period of production in the fundamentalist sense does not exist. An analogous inconsistency occurs if one follows Böhm-Bawerk in (wrongly) identifying consumption with wages and therefore postulates $k = wT$ rather than $k = cT$.

214

Part of the fundamentalist perspective can be rescued if one gives up the idea that the period of production is one-dimensional. This has been shown by Orosel (1979) within the context of a flow input–point output model where time is measured discretely.

The basic idea can be sketched for a stationary state. With time measured discretely a (flow input–point output) technique can be described by one consumption output $\beta(0) > 0$ and corresponding labour inputs $\alpha(t) \geq 0$, $t = 0$, -1, -2, ..., where, for some $G > 0$,

$$0 < \sum_{t=-\infty}^{0} (1 + \gamma)^{-t} \alpha(t) < \infty$$

for $\gamma \in (-1, G)$. To the sequence of labour inputs $\{\alpha(t)\}_{-\infty}^{0}$ is associated a sequence of wage payments $\{z_1(t) = w\alpha(t)\}_{-\infty}^{0}$; a sequence of simple interest payments on these, i.e.

$$\left\{ z_2(t) = r \sum_{\tau=-\infty}^{t-1} z_1(\tau) \right\}_{-\infty}^{0};$$

a sequence of simple interest payments on $z_2(t)$, i.e.

$$\left\{ z_3(t) = r \sum_{\tau=-\infty}^{t-1} z_2(\tau) \right\}_{-\infty}^{0},$$

and so on, i.e.

$$z_{i+1}(t) = r \sum_{\tau=-\infty}^{t-1} z_i(t),$$

$i = 1, 2, \ldots$. To each sequence $\{z_i(t)\}_{-\infty}^{0}$ we can define a 'period of production' T_i as the 'average distance' of $\{z_i(t)\}_{-\infty}^{0}$ from output $\beta(0)$, i.e. from $t = 0$, by

$$T_i := \frac{\displaystyle\sum_{t=-\infty}^{0} (-t) z_i(t)}{\displaystyle\sum_{t=-\infty}^{0} z_i(t)}.$$

Further, with each period of production T_i we can associate a (per capita) subsistence fund s_i which makes it possible to consume the incomes $\{z_i(t)\}_{-\infty}^{0}$ generated by the technique before the technique generates a consumption output. These funds are given by $s_1 = wT_1$ for wages, by $s_2 = (rs_1)T_2$ for simple interest on wages, and so on, i.e. $s_{i+1} = (rs_i)T_{i+1}$, $i = 1, 2, \ldots$, for simple interest on s_i during the period of production T_{i+1}, associated with these interest incomes. The total per capita subsistence fund is given by

$$s = \sum_{i=1}^{\infty} s_i = wT_1 + \sum_{i=1}^{\infty} (rs_i) T_{i+1},$$

215

which is a sum of consumption terms (w and rs_i respectively) each of which is multiplied by the associated period of production. It can be shown that for $r \in [0, G)$ all series converge and (i) all T_i are technological parameters; (ii) $k = s$, i.e. the value of capital (per head) equals the subsistence fund (per head); (iii)

$$c = w + \sum_{i=1}^{\infty} rs_i,$$

that is the consumption terms in s add up to per capita consumption. These results can be generalized to steady states with a positive rate of growth (Orosel, 1979).

The periods of production T_i are fundamentalist in the sense that they are technological parameters and that the subsistence fund corresponding to them equals the value of the capital stock. They lead to a consistent reformulation of some of Böhm-Bawerk's main ideas, but they do not give a measure of aggregate capital. In fact, in the 1960s the debates on the theory of capital have made clear that such a measure does not exist.

THE PRAGMATIC VIEW. There are three prominent proposals about how to measure the time interval between primary inputs and consumption outputs. They are associated with the names of (i) Böhm-Bawerk (1889), (ii) Hicks (1939) and von Weizsäcker (1971), and (iii) Dorfman (1959). Although only von Weizsäcker's analysis is directly applicable to steady states with a given (flow input–flow output) technique (a, b), all three proposals can be generalized accordingly. These three (generalized) concepts of the period of production, denoted by T^B, T^H and T^D respectively, are defined as follows (all integrals being improper Riemann-integrals):

$$T^B(g) := \frac{\int_{-\infty}^{\infty} t\, e^{-gt} b(t)\, dt}{\int_{-\infty}^{\infty} e^{-gt} b(t)\, dt} - \frac{\int_{-\infty}^{\infty} t\, e^{-gt} a(t)\, dt}{\int_{-\infty}^{\infty} e^{-gt} a(t)\, dt},$$

$$g \in (H, G) \tag{4}$$

$$T^H(r) := \frac{\int_{-\infty}^{\infty} t\, e^{-rt} b(t)\, dt}{\int_{-\infty}^{\infty} e^{-rt} b(t)\, dt} - \frac{\int_{-\infty}^{\infty} t\, e^{-rt} wa(t)\, dt}{\int_{-\infty}^{\infty} e^{-rt} wa(t)\, dt},$$

$$r \in (H, G) \tag{5}$$

$$T^D(g, r) := \frac{k(g, r)}{c(g)}, \quad g \in (H, G), \quad r \in (H, G) \tag{6}$$

where $k(g, r)/c(g)$ is, in value terms, the capital–consumption ratio (if, as in Dorfman's analysis, a stationary state is considered, it is also the capital–output ratio). Given our assumptions all integrals are convergent. Definitions (4) and (5) measure the difference between two points of gravity, or mean values of time, associated with outputs and inputs respectively (the densities being

$$e^{-gt}b(t)\bigg/\int_{-\infty}^{\infty} e^{-gt}b(t)$$

etc.). In (4) the densities applied are given by the respective steady state *quantities*, in (5) they are given by the steady state *values*. The justification of (6) is less obvious. Dorfman's argument is that, given g and r, k is a constant stock (of value) with a constant outflow c; therefore, the average time a unit of c remains in k is k/c ('bathtub theorem'). Alternatively, (6) can be derived from the postulate that the (per capita) subsistence fund associated with T^D, i.e. cT^D, equals k.

What are the properties of T^B, T^H and T^D, and how are the three concepts related to each other? First, it is interesting, though not shown in the literature, that T^D can also be represented as a difference between points of gravity. Without loss of generality, let the level of activity associated with t be e^{-gt}. Then to a point of time t there corresponds a technique $(e^{-gt}a, e^{-gt}b)$ and therefore wages $we^{-gt}a(t)$, profits $r\kappa(t)$ and investments $g\kappa(t)$, where

$$\kappa(t):=\int_{-\infty}^{t} e^{r(t-\tau)}[we^{-gt}a(\tau)-e^{-gt}b(\tau)]\,d\tau$$

is the accumulated value of capital, at t, associated with process $(e^{-gt}a, e^{-gt}b)$. Therefore, in a steady state with technique (a, b), growth rate g and interest rate r there is associated to each t an amount $q(t)$ of consumption claims (wages plus profits minus investments)

$$q(t):=e^{-gt}wa(t)+(r-g)\kappa(t). \tag{7}$$

It is possible to prove that these claims sum up to total consumption, i.e.

$$\int_{-\infty}^{\infty} q(t)\,dt = \int_{-\infty}^{\infty} e^{-gt}b(t)\,dt \tag{8}$$

and that T^D is the 'temporal distance' between consumption outputs and consumption claims, i.e.

$$T^D = \frac{\displaystyle\int_{-\infty}^{\infty} t\,e^{-gt}b(t)\,dt}{\displaystyle\int_{-\infty}^{\infty} e^{-gt}b(t)\,dt} - \frac{\displaystyle\int_{-\infty}^{\infty} tq(t)\,dt}{\displaystyle\int_{-\infty}^{\infty} q(t)\,dt} \tag{9}$$

In (9) T^D has a structure analogous to T^B and T^H. Because of (4), (5), (7) and (9)

$$T^B = T^H = T^D, \qquad \text{for } r = g. \tag{10}$$

217

Differentiation of (2) gives

$$T^{\mathrm{B}} = -\frac{1}{c}\frac{\mathrm{d}c}{\mathrm{d}g};$$

of (1)

$$T^{\mathrm{H}} = -\frac{1}{w}\frac{\mathrm{d}w}{\mathrm{d}r}.$$

Therefore, using (3), $k = cT^{\mathrm{B}} = wT^{\mathrm{H}} = cT^{\mathrm{D}}$ for $r = g$. For $r \neq g$ we have

$$\frac{1}{r-g}\int_{g}^{r} c(\gamma)T^{\mathrm{B}}(\gamma)\,\mathrm{d}\gamma = -\frac{1}{r-g}\int_{g}^{r}\frac{\mathrm{d}c(\gamma)}{\mathrm{d}\gamma}\,\mathrm{d}\gamma$$

$$= \frac{c(g)-w(r)}{r-g} = k(g, r)$$

since $c(r) = w(r)$. Similarly

$$\frac{1}{r-g}\int_{g}^{r} w(\rho)T^{\mathrm{H}}(\rho)\,\mathrm{d}\rho = k(g, r).$$

Hence k can be interpreted as an average of subsistence funds of the form cT^{B} and wT^{H} respectively. Finally, if for two techniques (a^1, b^1) and (a^2, b^2) *one of* the three periods of production, $T^{\mathrm{B}}(g)$, $T^{\mathrm{H}}(r)$ or $T^{\mathrm{D}}(g, r)$, is *for all* feasible g and r greater for (a^1, b^1) than for (a^2, b^2), then for these techniques no reswitching or other paradoxa can occur and (a^1, b^1) can be regarded as unambiguously more capital intensive than (a^2, b^2). However, in general the ranking of techniques according to their period(s) of production will depend on the chosen g and r. Therefore, none of the pragmatic concepts of the period of production gives an unambiguous and generally applicable measure of capital intensity. In the light of the so-called reswitching debate this result is to be expected.

CONCLUSIONS. The period of production purports to be a measure of capital intensity. Although it is a useful concept for clarifying the relation between capital and time, it is not, and cannot be, a rigorous measure of aggregate capital per head because even in a restricted model with only one primary input and one consumption output such a measure does not exist. As a *fundamentalist* concept the period of production fails because it cannot simultaneously be a technological concept and explain capital as a subsistence fund; as a *pragmatic* concept it fails because it is not possible to rank techniques according to their period of production independently of the rate of growth and the rate of interest. Hence the period of production cannot avoid the inconsistencies (pointed out in the capital controversies of the 1960s) which are associated with the concept of aggregate capital.

BIBLIOGRAPHY

Böhm-Bawerk, E. von. 1889. *Kapital und Kapitalzins*. Zweite Abteilung: *Positive Theorie des Kapitals*. Innsbruck: Wagnersche Universitäts-buchhandlung. 4th edn, Jena: Gustav Fischer, 1921. Trans. by G.D. Huncke as *Capital and Interest*, Volume II: *Positive Theory of Capital*, South Holland, Ill.: Libertarian Press, 1959.

Dorfman, R. 1959. Waiting and the period of production. *Quarterly Journal of Economics* 73, August, 351–72.

Hicks, J.R. 1939. *Value and Capital: an Inquiry into Some Fundamental Principles of Economic Theory*. 2nd edn, Oxford: Clarendon Press.

Kaldor, N. 1937. Annual survey of economic theory: the recent controversy on the theory of capital. *Econometrica* 5, July, 201–33.

Orosel, G.O. 1979. A reformulation of the Austrian theory of capital and its application to the debate on reswitching and related paradoxes. *Zeitschrift für Nationalökonomie* 29 (1–2), 1–31.

Weizsäcker, C.C. von. 1971. *Steady State Capital Theory*. Lecture Notes in Operations Research and Mathematical Systems 54, Berlin: Springer.

Weston, J.F. 1951. Some perspectives on capital theory. *American Economic Review, Papers and Proceedings* 41, May, 129–44.

Ramsey model

DAVID M. NEWBERY

Frank Plumpton Ramsey died at the age of 26 after making brilliant contributions to philosophy, mathematical logic, and, of course, economics. His two contributions to economics both appeared in the *Economic Journal*, then edited by J.M. Keynes. The first, 'A Contribution to the Theory of Taxation', published in March, 1927, laid the foundation for the modern theory of commodity taxation. The second, the subject of this entry, was 'A Mathematical Theory of Saving', published in December, 1928. Keynes, in his obituary notice published two months after Ramsey's death, in the *Economic Journal* of March, 1930, described the latter as 'one of the most remarkable contributions to mathematical economics ever made, both in respect of the intrinsic importance and difficulty of its subject, the power and elegance of the technical methods employed, and the clear purity of illumination with which the writer's mind is felt by the reader to play about its subject'.

Ramsey asked how much of its income should a nation save and derived a remarkably simple rule, usually known as the Keynes–Ramsey Rule, as Keynes provided a non-technical argument for the result. The rule states that the rate of saving, multiplied by the marginal utility of consumption, should always be equal to the amount by which the total net rate of enjoyment of utility falls short of the maximum possible rate.

Ramsey's formulation of the problem served as a model for almost all subsequent studies of optimal economic growth, and, with the critical addition of a growing population, might have created neoclassical growth theory about thirty years before Solow's (1956) contribution. He assumed a one-good world, in which labour with a stock of capital would produce a flow of output, part of which was consumed, and the balance was saved and thereby added to the stock of capital. The objective, or criterion, was to achieve the maximum level of enjoyment, summing over all time, where enjoyment was the utility of consumption, $U(C)$, less the disutility of working, $V(L)$. Ramsey made three crucial assumptions which together allowed him to solve explicitly an otherwise intractable problem. He assumed that there was no population growth, no technical progress, and no discounting of utility, 'a practice which is ethically indefensible and arises merely from the weakness of the imagination' (Ramsey, 1928, p. 543). He further supposed that there was a 'maximum *obtainable* rate of enjoyment' called *Bliss, B*, either because of capital or consumption saturation. As neither population grows nor future utilities are discounted, Ramsey then argues, rather informally, that it must be desirable to save enough to eventually reach bliss, or approximate to it indefinitely. To stop short means foregoing a finite amount of utility, which, summed over an infinite time horizon, is infinitely costly. Formally, Ramsey deals with this problem of a potentially unbounded integral of utility (summed without discounting over infinite time) by *minimizing* the amount by which enjoyment falls short of bliss integrated throughout time:

$$\min \int_0^\infty [B - U(C) + V(L)]\, dt \tag{1}$$

subject to

$$\frac{dK}{dt} + C = F(K, L). \tag{2}$$

Ramsey attacks the problem from two directions: economic and mathematical. His economic argument first solves for the relationship between consumption and the effort by equating the marginal disutility of labour to the product of the marginal product of labour and the marginal disutility of consumption. He then solves the basic arbitrage relationship equating the marginal utility of consuming a unit now with the marginal utility of consuming the product of investing the unit until the next instant of time. This key relationship implies that the marginal utility of consumption, $U'(C)$, must fall at the rate of interest, equal to the marginal product of capital, $\partial F / \partial K$. These two conditions, together with (2), the initial stock of capital, and a terminal condition as $t \to \infty$, produce a differential equation which can be integrated to give the result.

The mathematical approach observes that the calculus of variations gives the first two conditions directly, but also observes that the variable of integration in (1) can be changed from t to K by using (2) to give

$$\min \int_{K_0}^\infty \frac{B - U(C) + V(L)}{F(K, L) - C}\, dK \tag{3}$$

and since C and L are arbitrary functions of K all that is needed to minimize the integrand is to set its partial derivations to zero. Differentiating with respect to C gives

$$F(K, L) - C = \frac{B - [U(C) - V(L)]}{U'(C)}. \tag{4}$$

221

The left-hand side of (4) is the rate of investment or saving, whilst the right-hand side is equal to bliss minus the additional rate of enjoyment, divided by the marginal utility of consumption, and the whole is the Keynes–Ramsey rule.

Ramsey concluded from this rule that the optimal rate of saving should be 'greatly in excess of that which anyone would normally suggest' and gave an illustration in which the savings rate should be 60 per cent of income. One of the main themes explored by later writers was whether this was a robust conclusion, or whether the optimal rate of saving was very sensitive to the simplifying assumptions – a theme which is discussed below. Ramsey recognized that discounting utility would destroy the simple reasoning which led to (4), and was thus anxious to have an ethical reason for rejecting it. He believed that population growth would argue for higher rates of saving whilst technical progress would have ambiguous effects – as proved to be the case in later formal models.

Ramsey drew attention to two remarkable features of the rule. The first is that the level of saving does not depend on the production function. The second is that it does not depend on the rate of interest, unless this is actually zero. In fact, the first feature is only apparently the case, for in (4), C will depend on the level of output, F, and since savings, given by the right-hand side, also depends on C, it will depend on F. In his section III, Ramsey clearly pointed out that the level of saving was motivated by the demand for future comsumption, whilst the rate of interest was determined by the current stock of capital (in this one-sector model). In a concluding remark to this section he notes that 'in the accounting of a Socialist State the function of the rate of interest would be to ensure the wisest use of existing capital, not to serve in any direct way as a guide to the proportion of income which should be saved'. The second result does not survive in more general models which allow for utility discounting. Nevertheless, the arbitrage relationship does suggest a way in which the rate of interest can guide the rate of saving. If the rate of decline of the marginal utility of consumption is less than the rate of interest, taken to be the rate of return on investment, then the rate of saving is too low, and vice versa.

The main contribution of the paper was to pose a fruitful question – what should the rate of savings be? – and propose a method of analysis – that of intertemporal welfare maximization using the techniques of dynamic optimization, in this case the calculus of variations. The main result was striking – the rate of saving should apparently be rather high. In addition to this contribution, the paper also contained various remarkable extensions. It considers the choice of savings rate for an individual facing constant factor prices, who wishes to optimize his lifetime consumption pattern, and as such provides a positive theory of life-cycle savings. It shows that if utility is to be discounted, then it must be discounted at a constant rate if one is to escape the contradiction 'that successive generations are motivated by the same system of preferences'. Later, Strotz (1956) would return to this issue and the related problem of dynamic consistency. Finally, Ramsey shows that if a society consists of individuals who differ in their rate of discount, and if it is in steady state, then the equilibrium would be attained by a division of society into two classes, the thrifty enjoying bliss and the improvident at the subsistence level. In short, he characterizes the long-run general equilibrium of a society of heterogeneous individuals.

Ramsey thus laid the foundations for the study of optimal accumulation and optimal growth, as well as the positive theory of savings and the rate of interest. Space precludes a full assessment of the subsequent work his paper stimulated, though Burmeister and Dobell's (1970) textbook lists 107 references in their chapter on optimal economic growth, and much has happened since that date. Instead we shall briefly mention some of the themes of this subsequent work.

Ramsey's model represented a significant advance on the classical analysis of stationary states, since it made possible the analysis of non-stationary time paths of capital accumulation, but ultimately his model would tend towards a stationary state. With the development of growth theory the profession acquired a more appealing concept of long-run equilibrium – that of steady growth. In due course this suggested the obvious extension to Ramsey's model of incorporating these dynamic features – population growth at the steady state rate n and Harrod-neutral technical progress at a steady rate g. The instantaneous level of national welfare was variously taken as $U(C_t)$, $U(C_t/L_t)$, or, most satisfactorily, $L_t u(C_t/L_t)$, where L_t was the total population or workforce, and C_t was total consumption. Since welfare now depended on time, it made no drastic difference to include a utility discount rate, δ, and to propose a more general objective such as

$$W = \int_0^\infty U(C_t, t)\, dt = \int_0^\infty L_t u(C_t/L_t)\, e^{-\delta t}\, dt. \tag{5}$$

Steady growth now raised the question of the *existence* of an optimal savings policy in an acute form, for the integral in (5) might diverge unless δ was sufficiently large. Ramsey had faced a similar problem and avoided it by minimizing the shortfall from a reference path (or bliss). Similar devices were invoked to deal with divergent integrals, and much effort was expended on devising criteria of optimality and categorizing conditions under which an optimal savings plan existed, though many apparently reasonable problems nevertheless failed to possess an optimal savings plan, as Hammond and Mirrlees (1973) demonstrated. (They also give references to earlier discussions of the problem of non-existence.) They observe that no restrictions on the class of utility function will ensure existence, nor will any realistic restrictions on the production assumptions by themselves be enough to avoid the problem. They then argue that if we could specify a date after which events are of no significance, then the problem reduces to a finite horizon model, for which the utility integral would converge. Different people might disagree on the horizon date, but if the initial T_0 years of the plan were relatively insensitive to any horizon date later than some date T_1, then everyone would agree with the T year plan, and, in their language, the plan would be *agreeable*. Hammond and Mirrlees show that in the one-good model with a general instantaneous utility function $U(C_t, t)$ the agreeable path is unique and locally optimal, and that if an optimal path exists it is agreeable. Establishing

223

the existence of agreeable paths is, however, considerably easier than establishing the existence of optimal paths.

Whilst existence problems are important and raise intriguing philosophical problems (what if optimal growth paths do not exist?), they are not central to the economics of the problem. One of the key issues that has engaged the attention of subsequent researchers is whether the optimal savings rate is indeed as high as Ramsey argued (though, as Samuelson (1969) pointed out, Ramsey's conclusion depended on a particular choice of utility function). Certainly, Tinbergen (1956) was inclined to agree, but Mirrlees (1967) argued that Ramsey's model was seriously misleading, and that once population growth, technical progress and utility discounting were admitted, the initial value of the optimal rate of saving was typically very different from that implied by the Keynes–Ramsey rule. Once time enters the production function, it is no longer possible to obtain explicit solutions and an alternative solution strategy is required. Mirrlees argued that it was preferable to find the asymptotic form of the optimally developing economy in which output, consumption and consumption per head all grow at steady rates along a 'modified Golden Rule', and in which the savings rate is constant. The initial value of the savings rate could then be estimated by expanding around this asymptotic solution.

Mirrlees, in common with a large number of other optimal growth theorists, used a particular utility function – the iso-elastic form

$$u(c) = -c^{1-v}, \qquad v > 1,$$

$$= \log c, \qquad v = 1, \tag{6}$$

for which Ramsey's rule gives a savings rate of $1/v$ (providing an optimum exists). Mirrlees was impressed that for plausible values of the parameters of his model, the optimum savings rate was very different from the Ramsey value, and might be quite low. He also pointed out that the asymptotic solution, or the 'modified Golden Rule', would differ from the Golden Rule (according to which the rate of savings should equal the share of profit), if utilities were discounted – for the obvious reason that one would expect optimum policies to reflect the values regarding the distribution between generations.

Ramsey's model made skilful use of the classical calculus of variations, and in that vein Samuelson and Solow (1956) extended the model to deal with heterogeneous capital goods. In so doing they made possible two notable contributions to capital theory. The first was to argue that on the optimum path it was not too misleading to think in terms of an abstract quantity of capital – heterogeneity did not significantly alter the Ramsey theory. Second, the Hahn–Samuelson problem of the indeterminacy of equilibrium with capital heterogeneity disappeared on the optimal path, though the significance of this did not emerge until the paper by Hahn (1966).

As Samuelson and Solow pointed out, the classical calculus of variations could be replaced by Hamiltonian methods which would be able to deal with inequality constraints. The powerful techniques of the Pontryagin Maximum Principle and Bellman's Dynamic Programming were in due course applied to various extensions of the Ramsey problem to good effect, and their advantages and interrelationships are well discussed in the textbook of Intriligator (1971). In both approaches shadow prices or co-state variables play an important role both in characterizing the solution and demonstrating the relationships between optimality, intertemporal efficiency, and a set of intertemporal (shadow) prices (prices on futures markets) which might be used to decentralize the optimum. These shadow prices have a natural interpretation, for they value the capital stock in terms of the objective function, that is social welfare or the utility of consumption. The price guides the instantaneous allocation of output between consumption and investment, for consumption should be increased, if possible, until its value (the marginal utility of consumption) falls to the value of investment, that is of the capital stock. The evolution of the price over time then satisfies the fundamental arbitrage relationship, so that asset holders obtain a return (including capital gains) on the asset equal to the return on other assets and to the return from delaying consumption.

The strengths of these alternative approaches are best appreciated in multisector models where there are constraints on reallocating resources. If investment goods are physically different from consumption goods, and capital is immobile between sectors then savings will be constrained by the feasible output of the investment goods sector, and the planners' problem is primarily one of choosing the allocation of investment between the two sectors. In such a model the rate of return on capital will depend on the level of investment, and Ramsey's observation that in his model the two are independent is shown to be a feature of the one-good assumption. With two sectors corner solutions are quite likely (in the early stages) and the inequality constraints require the extra power of the new approaches.

The shadow prices are arguably most useful for cost–benefit analysis, rather than the more ambitious planning problems which so engaged the attentions of optimal growth theorists in the 1960s. Little and Mirrlees (1969, 1974) and Newbery (1972) and Stern (1972) were concerned to develop methods for calculating shadow or accounting prices in dual economy models of developing countries in which the level of aggregate savings was constrained. The two key accounting prices on which optimal growth models can shed light are the wage rate and the rate of discount to use in investment projects. The former emerges from the constraints on the allocation of labour and on the level of wages which must be paid, whilst the latter is again given by an arbitrage relation, or the rate of change of the shadow price of capital itself. The arbitrage equation gives a differential equation for the shadow price which, together with the equation for saving and the accumulation of capital, can be numerically integrated backwards from the asymptotic solution. Modern computers allow this to be done quickly, as illustrated in Newbery (1972).

The arbitrage equation comes into its own in exhaustible resource models where the return to the exhaustible resource must, whilst it remains in the ground, take the form of a capital gain equal to the return on other assets. This rule, due originally to Hotelling (1931), and nicely exposited by Solow (1974), has achieved prominence since the dramatic rise in the oil price of 1973–4.

Although the revival of interest in the Ramsey model in the 1960s was initially motivated by the postwar popularity of national economic planning, a popularity which waned rapidly in the 1970s, the model and its successors remain useful for the more modest aims of characterizing intertemporal competitive equilibrium in asset markets, especially for exhaustible resources like oil and gas, and for providing a more satisfactory neoclassical theory of equilibrium growth with individually rational savers. The common feature of Ramsey's two contributions to economics was that they were normative, and postulated an additive (utilitarian) social welfare function as the objective to be maximized. Several writers have taken the natural step of combining both of Ramsey's two interests and enquiring what optimal tax (and monetary) policy should be in an intertemporal model in which savings and investment are affected by these policies. Arrow and Kurz (1969) were the first to explore these issues and the closely related issues of the problem of public investment criteria systematically in a growth model in which full optimality is not achieved.

Diamond (1973) extended their work to a model with many goods, and demonstrated the desirability (under constant returns) of equal efficiency, on average, between public and private production, even though aggregate efficiency was not desired. In particular the public and private sectors should use the same discount rates. Later work (surveyed, for example, by Kotlikoff, 1984) has explored the efficiency losses involved in an economy of intertemporal optimizing individuals in the presence of distortionary taxes on capital, and have used these estimates to rank alternative capital tax reform programmes – a compromise between the optimal tax approach of Diamond, and the need to incorporate more of the complex features of particular economies.

In short, if the central question which Ramsey addressed of the right level of saving and investment has fallen from favour recently, nevertheless the spirit of the Ramsey model with its emphasis on intertemporal optimization lives on strongly, whether it be in the study of the oil market, the derivation of public investment rules, or the reform of the corporate tax system.

BIBLIOGRAPHY

Arrow, K. and Kurz, M. 1969. Optimal public investment policy and controllability with fixed private savings ratio. *Journal of Economic Theory* 1(1), 141–77.

Burmeister, E. and Dobell, A.R. 1970. *Mathematical Theories of Economic Growth*. New York: Macmillan.

Chakravarty, S. 1969. *Capital and Development Planning*. Cambridge, Mass.: MIT Press.

Diamond, P.A. 1973. Taxation and public production in a growth setting. Ch. 10 in Mirrlees and Stern (1973).

Hahn, F.H. 1966. Equilibrium dynamics with heterogeneous capital goods. *Quarterly Journal of Economics* 80(4), November, 633–46.

Hammond, P.J. and Mirrlees, J.A. 1973. Agreeable plans. Ch. 13 in *Models of Economic Growth*, ed. J.A. Mirrlees and N. Stern, London: Macmillan; New York: Wiley.

Hotelling, H. 1931. The economics of exhaustible resources. *Journal of Political Economy* 39, 137–75.

Intriligator, M.D. 1971. *Mathematical Optimization and Economic Theory.* Englewood Cliffs, NJ: Prentice-Hall.

Kotlikoff, L.J. 1984. Taxation and savings: a neoclassical perspective. *Journal of Economic Literature* 22(4), 1576–629.

Little, I.M.D. and Mirrlees, J.A. 1969. *Manual of Industrial Project Analysis for Developing Countries.* Vol. II: *Social Cost Benefit Analysis.* Paris: OECD Development Centre.

Little, I.M.D. and Mirrlees, J.A. 1974. *Project Appraisal and Planning for Developing Countries.* London: Heinemann.

Mirrlees, J.A. 1967. Optimum growth when technology is changing. *Review of Economic Studies* 34(1), 95–124.

Mirrlees, J.A. and Stern, N.H. (eds) 1973. *Models of Economic Growth.* London: Macmillan; New York: Wiley.

Newbery, D.M.G. 1972. Public policy in the dual economy. *Economic Journal* 82, June, 567–90.

Ramsey, F.P. 1927. A contribution to the theory of taxation. *Economic Journal* 37, March, 47–61.

Ramsey, F.P. 1928. A mathematical theory of saving. *Economic Journal* 38, December, 543–59.

Samuelson, P.A. 1969. Foreword to Chakravarty (1969).

Samuelson, P.A. and Solow, R. 1956. A complete capital model involving heterogeneous capital goods. *Quarterly Journal of Economics* 70(4), November, 537–62.

Solow, R.M. 1956. A contribution to the theory of economic growth. *Quarterly Journal of Economics* 70(1), February, 65–94.

Solow, R.M. 1974. The economics of resources or the resources of economics. *American Economic Review Papers and Proceedings* 64(2), May, 1–14.

Stern, N.H. 1972. Optimum development in a dual economy. *Review of Economic Studies* 39(2), April, 171–84.

Strotz, R.H. 1956. Myopia and inconsistency in dynamic utility maximization. *Review of Economic Studies* 23(3), 165–80.

Tinbergen, J. 1956. The optimal rate of savings. *Economic Journal* 66, December, 603–9.

Reverse capital deepening

ROBERTO SCAZZIERI

It has long been taken for granted that there is an inverse monotonic relationship between the rate of interest (or the rate of profit) and the quantity of capital per man. This belief was founded on the principle of substitution, whereby 'cheaper' is substituted for 'more expensive' as the relative price of two inputs is changed.

In the field of capital theory, the principle of substitution persuaded many economists, such as E. von Böhm-Bawerk (1889), J.B. Clark (1899) and F.A. von Hayek (1941), that a lower rate of interest (which is equal to the rate of profit in equilibrium) is associated with the use of more 'capital intensive' techniques, and thus with the substitution of capital for other productive factors, such as labour or land. This process is called *capital deepening*.

Recent discussions have shown that this is not necessarily true, since a lower rate of interest might be associated with *lower*, rather than higher, capital per man. This phenomenon is called *reverse capital deepening*.

This discovery was made at the same time as it was realized that it is not generally possible to order 'efficient' techniques in such a way that technical choice becomes a monotonic function of the rate of interest (and of the rate of profit).

It can be shown that both reverse capital deepening and reswitching of technique are related to the same fundamental property of the economic system: the possibility (in fact, the near generality) of non-linear wage-profit relationships. To illustrate this proposition, it is useful to begin by considering the hypothetical case of linear wage–profit relationships (see Figure 1).

The linearity of the three wage–profit relationships makes reswitching impossible as r increases between 0 and $r^*(C)$ (which is the maximum rate of profit with technology C). The reason is that no wage–profit line can ever be crossed more than once by another wage–profit line. In this special case, there is an inverse monotonic relationship between the rate of profit and the quantity of capital per man. We can read the net final output per man on the w-axis of the figure at the point at which $r = 0$. (At that point the net final output per man

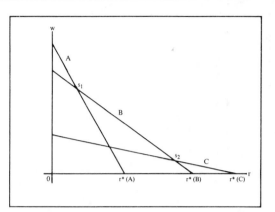

Figure 1

coincides with the maximum wage.) The net final output per man associated with technology A is higher than the net final output per man associated with technology B. The net final output per man associated with technology B is higher than the net final output per man associated with technology C. At switchpoints s_1 and s_2 the wage is the same for both technologies between which substitution takes place. It follows that, at switchpoint s_1, profit per man is higher with technology A than with technology B. Similarly, at switchpoint s_2, profit per man is higher with technology B than with technology C. Assuming that the rate of profit is uniform across technologies, we find that, at s_1, A is associated with higher capital per man than B. A higher rate of profit (or rate of interest) is thus associated with substitution of 'less capital' for 'more capital'. In this particular case, the traditional approach to capital theory would seem to be well founded.

However, these properties disappear altogether once we drop the assumption of linear wage–profit relationships. (It might be interesting to inquire into the economic meaning of straight wage–profit relationships, which are only possible in the case of a technology characterized by a uniform proportion between labour and intermediate inputs in all production processes: only in this case a change in the rate of profit leaves relative prices unaffected.)

But in general wage–profit relationships are of the non-linear type, which means that the proportion between labour and intermediate inputs is generally different from one production process to another. This feature of the wage–profit frontier makes it possible for wage-profit curves to intersect more than once thus bringing about the possibility of multiple switching. Under the same circumstances it can be shown that the relationship between the rate of profit and capital per man is no longer of the inverse monotonic type. This can be seen in the reswitching case (Figure 2), but it can also be seen in the case in which the

229

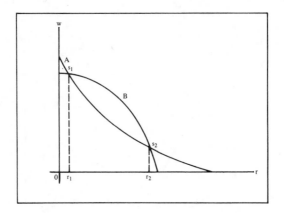

Figure 2

wage–profit curves never intersect more than once on the efficiency frontier (Figure 3). (See also Pasinetti, 1966.)

In Figure 2, reswitching is associated with reverse capital deepening. Technology A is the more profitable at levels of the rate of profit lower than r_1, it is 'overtaken' by technology B at rates of profit between r_1 and r_2, it becomes again the more profitable at rates of profit higher than r_2. At the same time, switchpoint s_1 is associated with the substitution of the technology with lower value of capital per man (B) for the technology with the higher value of capital per man (A), whereas at switchpoint s_2 the opposite happens: the technology with higher capital per man (A) is substituted for the technology with lower capital per man (B), in spite of the fact that the rate of profit is higher (reverse capital deepening).

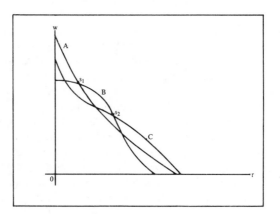

Figure 3

230

In Figure 3, there is no reswitching but we still have a reverse capital deepening. For no wage–profit curves cross one another more than once on the efficiency frontier, but at switchpoint s_2 an increasing rate of profit is associated with the substitution of a technology with higher capital per man (C) for a technology with lower capital per man (B).

Reverse capital deepening is associated with other phenomena which are not compatible with traditional beliefs about capital and capital accumulation. Simple inspection of Figure 2 or 3 shows that at a switchpoint associated with reverse capital deepening (s_2 in either figure) a technology with higher capital per man and higher net final product per man is substituted for a technology with lower capital per man and lower net final product per man. At such switchpoints a higher rate of profit (and rate of interest) could be associated with a higher ratio of capital per man to net final product per man, i.e. with a higher capital/output ratio.

Figures 2 and 3 also alert us as to the possibility that a technology adopted at a high rate of interest is associated with higher maximum consumption per head than a technology adopted at a lower rate of interest. In addition, transition to a lower rate of interest may involve the switch to a lower maximum consumption per head. (This can be seen at switchpoint s_2 in either figure, where maximum consumption per head can be read on the w-axis at point $r = 0$.) This behaviour of consumption per head in relation to the rate of interest is clearly incompatible with the view that a higher rate of interest brings about a special type of exchange, in which less consumption in the current period is substituted against higher consumption in the future. Reverse capital deepening alerts us as to the possibility that a higher rate of interest might be associated with greater current consumption per head than the consumption per head feasible with the technology adopted at a lower rate of interest (see Bruno, Burmeister and Sheshinski, 1966; Samuelson, 1966).

The relevance of reverse capital deepening is that the foundations of traditional capital theory are seriously questioned. In particular, the view that the rate of interest is the price of capital as a productive factor, and that interest may be explained by intertemporal preference, is shown to be untenable as soon as a more realistic model of productive systems is adopted.

BIBLIOGRAPHY

Böhm-Bawerk, E. von. 1889. *Kapital und Kapitalzins. Zweite Abteilung: Positive Theorie des Kapitales.* Trans. as *The Positive Theory of Capital,* London: Macmillan, 1891.
Bruno, M., Burmeister, E. and Sheshinski, E. 1966. The nature and implications of the reswitching of techniques. *Quarterly Journal of Economics* 80(4), November, 526–53.
Clark, J.B. 1899. *The Distribution of Wealth.* New York: Macmillan.
Hayek, F.A. von. 1941. *The Pure Theory of Capital.* London: Routledge; New York: University of Chicago Press, 1962.
Pasinetti, L.L. 1966. Changes in the rate of profit and switches of techniques. *Quarterly Journal of Economics* 80(4), November, 503–17.
Samuelson, P. 1966. A summing up. *Quarterly Journal of Economics* 80(4), November, 568–83.

Roundabout methods of production

K.H. HENNINGS

Methods of production are roundabout if they use produced means of production or the services of capital goods as well as those of land and labour, the latter being considered original or primary factors of production.

The concept of roundaboutness of production methods thus draws a distinction between 'rude' and more advanced methods of production, the latter using capital goods, the former not. This, however, is not a distinction of much use as even in very primitive economies man-made tools are used. But the concept has been associated with the proposition that more roundabout methods of production yield more output per unit of input, but require more time because the capital goods they use have to be produced, too. This proposition in turn has been associated with the idea that the roundaboutness of production methods depends on the division of labour as well as on the fact that production takes time. The concept therefore plays an important role in those variants of capital theory like the 'Austrian' theory of Böhm-Bawerk (1889) which emphasize the time-consuming nature of production in an economy characterized by division of labour.

The proposition that production processes take time, and that their implementation therefore requires 'advances' in the form of wage goods as well as durable capital goods was fundamental to physiocratic theory as expounded by Quesnay (1759) and Turgot (1770). It also appears in such classical writers as Ricardo (1817, ch. 1, sect. iv, v). But from Adam Smith (1776) onwards, most classical economists followed Josiah Tucker (1774, p. 24) and linked the use of capital goods to the division of labour rather than the time-consuming nature of production. This can be seen as the consequence of a shift of emphasis from agricultural to industrial production processes. Time requirements in agricultural production are given by nature, and cannot be overcome by an appropriate organization of production processes. Industrial production processes, by contrast, can be, and often are, staggered in such a way that outputs are obtained continuously and the temporal structure of production processes does not matter.

Longfield (1834) combined both aspects by arguing that production takes time on account of the division of labour. Because an increasing division of labour requires more and more different capital goods, the production processes in which they are produced lengthen the overall or composite production process which links the original factors of production to the output obtained with their help as well as the help of intermediate produced means of production. Likewise, Rae (1834) argued that increased division of labour goes with increased durability capital and hence longer periods of time required for production. Rae also emphasized that, at any time, entrepreneurs have a choice between industrial production processes of different degrees of roundaboutness, i.e. different productivity as well as associated time requirements. These ideas, however, remained outside the classical tradition, which remained wedded to the idea that the division of labour was the main reason for the use of roundabout methods of production. The time element in production was submerged in the conception of capital goods as 'stored-up' or 'congealed' labour (and land), and thus as the result of previous production processes, which had been advanced by Ricardo (1817, ch. 1, sect. iii) and James Mill (1821). On the basis of this conception Senior (1836, 57–8) introduced the distinction between land and labour as 'primary' and capital goods as 'secondary' requisites of production; this distinction was later converted into one between 'original' and 'derived' factors of production. Most authors, however, used these notions in a rather vague way in order to characterize the nature of capital goods and to assert the advantages of their accumulation.

When formulating his temporal ('Austrian') theory of capital Böhm-Bawerk (1889) built upon this tradition. He went beyond it, however, when he posited the existence of a production function in which the level of output obtained per unit of input was made a function of the degree of roundaboutness of the production method employed – a function which, he argued, was positive but subject to diminishing marginal returns. This required him to define formally the degree of roundaboutness. Considering only one original factor of production, say x, which is used in different stages x_t of the production process, and hence remains 'invested' in it for varying lengths of time s_t, Böhm-Bawerk defined the degree of roundaboutness as the average period of production S as

$$S = \sum_t x_t s_t \bigg/ \sum_t x_t$$

Here $\Sigma_t x_t s_t$ is what Jevons (1871, ch. vii) had called the 'amount of investment of capital', while $\Sigma_t x_t$ is Jevons's 'amount of capital invested'.

Böhm-Bawerk used this definition in his proposition referred to above, and erected on it a theory of the role of capital goods in production which issued in a theory of distribution. This 'Austrian' theory of capital was elaborated by Wicksell (1893) and, in modern form, by Faber (1979). The gist of the argument is that more roundabout methods of production are both more capital intensive and more productive, such that the relative availability of capital determines the method of production used, the amount of output obtained per unit of original input, and, via marginal productivity conditions, factor prices.

This theory gave rise to a lengthy debate which ran for almost half a century; for partial summaries, see Kaldor (1937), Haavelmo (1960), and Reetz (1971). Much of it centred on Böhm-Bawerk's definition of the degree of roundaboutness.

When Böhm-Bawerk turned the rather vague notion of roundaboutness into the more precise concept of an average period of production, he tied it to a linear, unidirectional view of production in which original factors of production are turned into raw materials, these with the help of further original factors into capital goods, which in turn help to produce consumer goods with the help of still further original factors. However, the attempt to 'dissolve' in the classical manner all capital goods into various amounts of original factors of production that had helped to produce them was soon seen to involve an infinite historical regress (Steindl, 1937). Similarly, if the problem is conceived, as Rae (1834) had done, as a planning problem (i.e. in a forward looking rather than a backward looking manner), taking into account all future effects on output of durable capital goods produced in the present leads to an infinite historical progress. In both cases, therefore, the time span involved is infinite. The answer to these conundrums, which stem from the fact that production processes which use capital goods are characterized by circularity as well as uni-directional linearity, was formulated as early as 1904 by Dmitriev. He demonstrated that in a well-integrated system of production processes the amount of original factors of production used directly and indirectly in the production of final outputs (i.e. consumer goods) could be calculated without resorting to the fiction of going backward or forward in time, and hence without any infinite regress or progress. Dmitriev also showed that the existence of more than one original factor of production does not pose a problem in this calculation. Yet his contribution remained unnoticed until Sraffa (1960) again drew attention to the issue of circularity and linearity in production processes.

Another major difficulty raised by the way in which Böhm-Bawerk concretized the notion of roundaboutness was that it seems superfluous for the analysis of an ongoing production process. As for example Clark (1899) argued, if production processes are appropriately staggered all one needs to observe, once the processes are in operation, are inflows of original inputs and outflows of outputs, without attempting to trace which outputs are due to which inputs, and thus without paying attention to the temporal structure of production processes. It can indeed be shown that in such circumstances Böhm-Bawerk's average period of production is equivalent to the capital–output ratio as used in modern growth theory (Dorfman, 1959). However, while correct, this argument applies to steady states only. In dynamic analyses, and particularly in transitions from one steady state to another (Hicks, 1973), or when starting more roundabout production processes, the temporal structure of production does play a role, and in these contexts the concept of a period of production may prove useful as a measure of the roundaboutness of production processes.

Yet another difficulty was pointed out by Samuelson (1966) and Steedman (1972): because Böhm-Bawerk's measure of roundaboutness has the nature of an average, there are necessarily various time profiles of original factors of production which give the same average period of production. If in addition a rate of interest is used when calculating the amount of investment of capital (as they argue one should do) before dividing by the amount of capital invested to obtain the average period of production, the latter turns into a function of the rate of interest which is not unique in the sense that it may exhibit reswitching.

Thus, if the concept of differing degrees of roundaboutness of production methods is to be given a precise meaning, it will have to be defined not as an average, but as an absolute measure relating to technical characteristics of the production processes involved. Moreover, it will have to be shown that more roundabout methods of production necessarily yield higher levels of output per unit of original input. These are the crucial assumptions. Without their validity being demonstrated, the notion of roundabout methods of production remains intuitively appealing but fruitless from an analytical point of view.

BIBLIOGRAPHY

Böhm-Bawerk, E. von. 1889. *Positive Theorie des Kapitales.* Innsbruck: Wagner. Trans. as *The Positive Theory of Capital,* London: Macmillan, 1891.

Clark, J.B. 1899. *The Distribution of Wealth.* New York: Macmillan.

Dmitriev, V.K. 1904. *Ekonomicheskie Ocherki.* Moscow: Richter. Trans. as *Economic Essays on Value, Competition and Utility,* Cambridge: Cambridge University Press, 1974.

Dorfman, R. 1959. Waiting and the period of production. *Quarterly Journal of Economics* 73, 351–72.

Faber, M. 1979. *Introduction to Modern Austrian Capital Theory.* Berlin: Springer.

Haavelmo, T. 1960. *A Study in the Theory of Investment.* Chicago: Chicago University Press.

Hicks, J.R. 1973. *Capital and Time.* Oxford: Clarendon Press.

Jevons, W.S. 1871. *The Theory of Political Economy.* London: Macmillan; New York: Kelley & Millman, 1957.

Kaldor, N. 1937. Annual survey of economic theory: the recent controversy on the theory of capital. *Econometrica* 5, 201–33.

Longfield, M. 1834. *Lectures on Political Economy.* Dublin: Milliken.

Mill, J. 1821. *Elements of Political Economy.* London: Baldwin, Craddock & Joy.

Quesnay, F. 1759. *Tableau économique.* Paris: Imprimerie Royale.

Rae, J. 1834. *Statement of Some New Principles on the Subject of Political Economy.* Boston: Hilliard Gray & Co.

Reetz, N. 1971. *Produktionsfunktion und Produktionsperiode.* Göttingen: Schwartz.

Ricardo, D. 1817. *On the Principles of Political Economy and Taxation.* London: Murray. In *The Works and Correspondence of David Ricardo,* ed. P. Sraffa, Cambridge and New York: Cambridge University Press 1951, vol 1.

Samuelson, P.A. 1966. A summing up. *Quarterly Journal of Economics* 80, November, 568–83.

Senior, N.W. 1836. *Political Economy.* London: Griffin.

Smith, A. 1776. *An Inquiry into the Nature and Causes of the Wealth of Nations.* London: Strahan & Cadell; Chicago: University of Chicago Press, 1976.

Sraffa, P. 1960. *Production of Commodities by Means of Commodities.* Cambridge: Cambridge University Press.

Steedman, I. 1972. Jevons's theory of capital and interest. *Manchester School of Economic and Social Studies* 40, March, 31–52.

Steindl, J. 1937. Der historische Regress in der Theorie der Produktionsumwege. *Jahrbücher für Nationalökonomie und Statistik* 145, 143–57.

Tucker, J. 1774. *Four Tracts Together with Two Sermons on Political and Commercial Subjects* (written 1758). Gloucester and London: Raikes & Rivington.

Turgot, A.R.J. 1770. Réflexions sur la formation et la distribution des richesses. *Ephémérides du Citoyen*. Trans. as 'Reflections on the Formation and Distribution of Wealth (1766)', in *Turgot on Progress, Sociology, and Economics*, ed. R.L. Meek, Cambridge and New York: Cambridge University Press, 1973.

Wicksell, K. 1893. *Über Wert, Kapital und Rente*. Jena: Fischer. Trans. as *Value, Capital and Rent*, London: George Allen & Unwin, 1954; New York: Kelley.

Time preference

MURRAY N. ROTHBARD

Time preference is the insight that people prefer 'present goods' (goods available for use at present) to 'future goods' (present expectations of goods becoming available at some date in the future), and that the social rate of time preference, the result of the interactions of individual time preference schedules, will determine and be equal to the pure rate of interest in a society. The economy is pervaded by a time market for present as against future goods, not only in the market for loans (in which creditors trade present money for the right to receive money in the future), but also as a 'natural rate' in all processes of production. For capitalists pay out present money to buy or rent land, capital goods, and raw materials, and to hire labour (as well as buying labour outright in a system of slavery), thereby purchasing expectations of future revenue from the eventual sales of product. Long-run profit rates and rates of return on capital are therefore forms of interest rate. As businessmen seek to gain profits and avoid losses, the economy will tend toward a general equilibrium, in which all interest rates and rates of return will be equal, and hence there will be no pure entrepreneurial profits or losses.

In centuries of wrestling with the vexed question of the justification of interest, the Catholic scholastic philosophers arrived at highly sophisticated explanations and justifications of return on capital, including risk and the opportunity cost of profit foregone. But they had extreme difficulty with the interest on a riskless loan, and hence denounced all such interest as sinful and usurious.

Some of the later scholastics, however, in their more favourable view of usury, began to approach a time preference explanation of interest. During a comprehensive demolition of the standard arguments for the prohibition of usury in his *Treatise on Contracts* (1499), Conrad Summenhart (1465–1511), theologian at the University of Tübingen, used time preference to justify the purchase of a discounted debt, even if the debt be newly created. When someone pays $100 for the right to obtain $110 at a future date, the buyer (lender) doesn't profit usuriously from the loan because both he and the seller (borrower) value the future $110 as being worth $100 at the present time (Noonan, 1957).

A half-century later, the distinguished Dominican canon lawyer and monetary theorist at the University of Salamanca, Martin de Azpilcueta Navarrus (1493–1586) clearly set forth the concept of time preference, but failed to apply it to a defence of usury. In his *Commentary on Usury* (1556), Azpilcueta pointed out that a present good, such as money, will naturally be worth more on the market than future goods, that is, claims to money in the future. As Azpilcueta put it:

> a claim on something is worth less than the thing itself, and ... it is plain that that which is not usable for a year is less valuable than something of the same quality which is usable at once (Gordon, 1975, p. 215).

At abou the same time, the Italian humanist and politician Gian Francesco Lottini da Volterra, in his handbook of advice to princes, *Avvedimenti civili* (1574), discovered time preference. Unfortunately, Lottini also inaugurated the tradition of moralistically deploring time preference as an over-estimation of a present that can be grasped immediately by the senses (Kauder, 1965, pp. 19–22).

Two centuries later, the Neapolitan abbé, Ferdinando Galiani (1728–87) revived the rudiments of time-preference in his *Della Moneta* (1751) (Monroe, 1924). Galiani pointed out that just as the exchange rate of two currencies equates the value of a present and a spatially distant money, so the rate of interest equates present with future, or temporally distant, money. What is being equated is not physical properties, but subjective values in the minds of individuals.

These scattered hints scarcely prepare one for the remarkable development of a full-scale time preference theory of interest by the French statesman, Anne Robert Jacques Turgot (1727–81), who, in a relatively few hastily written contributions, anticipated almost completely the later Austrian theory of capital and interest (Turgot, 1977). In the course of a paper defending usury, Turgot asked: why are borrowers willing to pay an interest premium for the use of money? The focus should not be on the amount of metal repaid but on the usefulness of the money to the lender and borrower. In particular, Turgot compares the 'difference in usefulness which exists at the date of borrowing between a sum currently owned and an equal sum which is to be received at a distant date', and notes the well-known motto, 'a bird in the hand is better than two in the bush'. Since the sum of money owned now 'is preferable to the assurance of receiving a similar sum in one or several years' time', returning the same principal means that the lender 'gives the money and receives only an assurance'. Therefore, interest compensates for this difference in value by a sum proportionate to the length of the delay. Turgot added that what must be compared in a loan transaction is not the value of money lent with the value repaid, but rather the 'value of the *promise* of a sum of money compared to the value of money available now' (Turgot, 1977, pp. 158–9).

In addition, Turgot was apparently the first to arrive at the concept of *capitalization*, a corollary to time preference, which holds that the present capital value of any durable good will tend to equal the sum of its expected annual rents, or returns, discounted by the market rate of time preference, or rate of interest.

Turgot also pioneered in analysing the relation between the quantity of money and interest rates. If an increased supply of money goes to low time preference people, then the increased proportion of savings to consumption lowers time preference and hence interest rates fall while prices rise. But if an increased quantity goes into the hands of high time preference people, the opposite would happen and interest rates would rise along with prices. Generally, over recent centuries, he noted, the spirit of thrift has been growing in Europe and hence time preference rates and interest rates have tended to fall.

One of the notable injustices in the historiography of economic thought was Böhm-Bawerk's brusque dismissal in 1884 of Turgot's anticipation of his own time-preference theory of interest as merely a 'land fructification theory' (Böhm-Bawerk, I, 1959). Partly this dismissal stemmed from Böhm's methodology of clearing the ground for his own positive theory of interest by demolishing, and hence sometimes doing injustice to, his own forerunners (Wicksell, 1911, p. 177). The unfairness is particularly glaring in the case of Turgot, because we now know that in 1876, only eight years before the publication of his history of theories of interest, Böhm-Bawerk wrote a glowing tribute to Turgot's theory of interest in an as yet unpublished paper in Karl Knies's seminar at the University of Heidelberg (Turgot, 1977, pp. xxix–xxx).

In the course of his demolition of the Ricardo–James Mill labour theory of value on behalf of a subjective utility theory, Samuel Bailey (1825) clearly set forth the concept of time preference. Rebutting Mill's statement that time, as a 'mere abstract word', could not add to value, Bailey declared that 'we generally prefer a present pleasure or enjoyment to a distant one', and therefore prefer present goods to waiting for goods to arrive in the future. Bailey, however, did not go on to apply his insight to interest.

In the mid-1830s, the Irish economist Samuel Mountifort Longfield worked out the later Austrian theory of capital as performing the service for workers of supplying money at present instead of waiting for the future when the product will be sold. In turn the capitalist receives from the workers a time discount from their productivity. As Longfield put it, the capitalist

> pays the wages immediately, and in return receives the value of [the worker's] labour, ... [which] is greater than the wages of that labour. The difference is the profit made by the capitalist for his advances ... as it were, the discount which the labourer pays for prompt payment (Longfield, 1834).

The 'pre-Austrian' time analysis of capital and interest was most fully worked out, in the same year 1834, by the Scottish and Canadian eccentric John Rae (1786–1872). In the course of attempting an anti-Smithian defence of the protective tariff, Rae, in his *Some New Principles on the Subject of Political Economy* (1834), developed the Böhm-Bawerkian time analysis of capital, pointing out that investment lengthens the time involved in the processes of production. Rae noted that the capitalist must weigh the greater productivity of longer production processes against waiting for them to come to fruition. Capitalists will sacrifice present money for a greater return in the future, the difference – the interest return – reflecting the social rate of time preference. Rae saw that people's time preference rates reflect their cultural and psychological willingness to take a shorter or longer view of the future. His moral preferences were clearly with the low time preference thrifty as against the high time preference people who suffer from a 'defect of the imagination'. Rae's analysis had little impact on economics until resurrected at the turn of the 20th century, whereupon it was generously hailed in the later editions of Böhm-Bawerk's history of interest theories (Böhm-Bawerk, I, 1959).

Time preference, as a concept and as a foundation for the explanation of interest, has been an outstanding feature of the Austrian School of economics. Its founder, Carl Menger (1840–1921), enunciated the concept of time preference in 1871, pointing out that satisfying the immediate needs of life and health are necessarily prerequisites for satisfying more remote future needs. In addition, Menger declared, 'all experience teaches that we humans consider a present pleasure, or one expected in the near future, more important than one of the same intensity which is not expected to occur until some more distant time' (Wicksell, 1924, p. 195; Menger, 1871, pp. 153–4). But Menger never extended time preference from his value theory to a theory of interest; and when his follower Böhm-Bawerk did so, he peevishly deleted this discussion from the second edition of his *Principles of Economics* (Wicksell, 1924, pp. 195–6).

Böhm-Bawerk's *Capital and Interest* (1884) is the *locus classicus* of the time preference theory of interest. In his first, historical volume, he demolished all other theories, in particular the productivity theory of interest; but five years later, in his *Positive Theory of Capital* (1889), Böhm brought back the productivity theory in an attempt to combine it with a time preference explanation of interest (Böhm-Bawerk, I, II, 1959). In his 'three grounds' for the explanation of interest, time preference constituted two, and the greater productivity of longer processes of production the third, Böhm ironically placing greatest importance upon the third ground. Influenced strongly by Böhm-Bawerk, Irving Fisher increasingly took the same path of stressing the marginal productivity of capital as the main determinant of interest (Fisher, 1907, 1930).

With the work of Böhm-Bawerk and Fisher, the modern theory of interest was set squarely on the path of placing time preference in a subordinate role in the explanation of interest: determining only the rate of consumer loans, and the supply of consumer savings, while the alleged productivity of capital determines the more important demand for loans and for savings. Hence, modern interest theory fails to integrate interest on consumer loans and producer's returns into a coherent explanation.

In contrast, Frank A. Fetter, building on Böhm-Bawerk, completely discarded productivity as an explanation of interest and constructed an integrated theory of value and distribution in which interest is determined solely by time preference, while marginal productivity determines the 'rental prices' of the factors of production (Fetter, 1915, 1977). In his outstanding critique of Böhm-Bawerk,

Fetter pointed out a fundamental error of the third ground in trying to explain the return on capital as 'present goods' earning a return for their productivity in the future; instead, capital goods are *future* goods, since they are only valuable in the expectation of being used to produce goods that will be sold to the consumer at a future date (Fetter, 1902). One way of seeing the fallacy of a productivity explanation of interest is to look at the typical practice of any current microeconomics text: after explaining marginal productivity as determining the demand curve for factors with wage rates on the *y*-axis, the textbook airily shifts to interest rates on the *y*-axis to illustrate the marginal productivity determination of interest. But the analog on the *y*-axis should not be interest, which is a ratio and not a price, but rather the *rental price* (price per unit time) of a capital good. Thus, interest remains totally unexplained. In short, as Fetter pointed out, marginal productivity determines rental prices, and time preference determines the rate of interest, while the capital value of a factor of production is the expected sum of future rents from a durable factor discounted by the rate of time preference or interest.

The leading economist adopting Fetter's pure time preference view of interest was Ludwig von Mises, in his *Human Action* (Mises, 1949). Mises amended the theory in two important ways. First, he rid the concept of its moralistic tone which had been continued by Böhm-Bawerk, implicitly criticizing people for 'under'-estimating the future. Mises made clear that a positive time preference rate is an essential attribute of human nature. Secondly, and as a corollary, whereas Fetter believed that people could have either positive or negative rates of time preference, Mises demonstrated that a positive rate is deducible from the fact of human action, since by the very nature of a goal or an end people wish to achieve that goal as soon as possible.

BIBLIOGRAPHY

Bailey, S. 1825. *A Critical Dissertation on the Nature, Measure, and Causes of Value*. New York: Augustus M. Kelley, 1967.

Böhm-Bawerk, E. von. 1884–9. *Kapital und Kapitalzins. Zweite Abteilung: Positive Theorie des Kapitales*. 4th edn. Trans. by G.D. Huncke as *Capital and Interest*, Vols I and II. South Holland, Ill.: Libertarian Press, 1959.

Fetter, F.A. 1902. The 'Roundabout process' in the interest theory. *Quarterly Journal of Economics* 17, November, 163–80. Reprinted in F.A. Fetter, *Capital, Interest and Rent: Essays in the Theory of Distribution*, ed. M. Rothbard, Kansas City: Sheed Andrews and McMeel, 1977.

Fetter, F.A. 1915. *Economic Principles*, Vol I. New York: The Century Co.

Fetter, F.A. 1977. *Capital, Interest, and Rent: Essays in the Theory of Distribution*. Ed. M. Rothbard, Kansas City: Sheed Andrews and McMeel.

Fisher, I. 1907. *The Rate of Interest*. New York: Macmillan.

Fisher, I. 1930. *The Theory of Interest*. New York: Kelley & Millman, 1954.

Gordon, B. 1975. *Economic Analysis Before Adam Smith: Hesiod to Lessius*. New York: Barnes & Noble.

Kauder, E. 1965. *A History of Marginal Utility Theory*. Princeton: Princeton University Press.

Longfield, S.M. 1971. *The Economic Writings of Mountifort Longfield*. Ed. R.D.C. Black, Clifton, NJ: Augustus M. Kelley.

Menger, C. 1871. *Principles of Economics*. Ed. J. Dingwall and B. Hoselitz, Glencoe, Ill.: Free Press, 1950.

Mises, L. von 1949. *Human Action: a Treatise on Economics*. 3rd revised edn, Chicago: Regnery, 1966.

Monroe, A. (ed.) 1924. *Early Economic Thought*. Cambridge, Mass.: Harvard University Press.

Noonan, J.T., Jr. 1957. *The Scholastic Analysis of Usury*. Cambridge, Mass.: Harvard University Press.

Rae, J. 1834. *Some New Principles on the Subject of Political Economy*. In *John Rae: Political Economist*, ed. R.W. James, Toronto: University of Toronto Press, 1965.

Turgot, A.R.J. 1977. *The Economics of A.R.J. Turgot*. Ed. P.D. Groenewegen, The Hague: Martinus Nijhoff.

Wicksell, K. 1911. Böhm-Bawerk's theory of interest. In K. Wicksell, *Selected Papers on Economic Theory*, ed. E. Lindahl, Cambridge, Mass.: Harvard University Press, 1958.

Wicksell, K. 1924. The new edition of Menger's *Grundsatze*. In K. Wicksell, *Selected Papers on Economic Theory*, ed. E. Lindahl, Cambridge, Mass.: Harvard University Press, 1958.

Waiting

K.H. HENNINGS

The term 'waiting' was introduced by MacVane (1887) to replace the term 'abstinence' used by earlier economists. Both terms are so closely related that they will be discussed together.

Despite some misgivings, Senior adopted the term 'abstinence' because 'there is no familiar term to express the act, the conduct, of which profit is the reward, and which bears the same relation to profit which labour does to wages' (1836, p. 89). The idea that saving implies to abstain from the use of existing goods for consumption purposes had earlier been expressed by Adam Smith ([1759] 1976, pp. 189–90), T.R. Malthus (1820, p. 314), G.P. Scrope (1833, p. 146) and especially John Rae, who had argued explicitly that men 'sacrifice a certain amount of present goods to obtain another, greater amount of goods at some future period' (1834, p. 119). Senior, however, combined saving with investing, and denoted by 'abstinence' both a form of economic activity and its result: 'By the word abstinence we wish to express the agent distinct from labour and the agency of nature the concurrence of which is necessary to the existence of capital' (1836, p. 59); or again 'abstinence expresses both the act of abstaining from the unproductive use of capital, and also the similar conduct of a man who devotes his labour to the production of remote rather than of immediate results' (1836, p. 89). Considered as an 'instrument of production', abstinence was not, however, independent: 'although human labour and the agency of nature independently of that of man are the primary productive powers, they require the concurrence of a third productive principle to give them complete efficiency' (1836, p. 58) because without it time-consuming production is not possible. Abstinence is thus associated by Senior with the idea that production takes time. As 'to abstain from the enjoyment which is in our power, or to seek distant rather than immediate results, are among the most painful exertions of the human will' (1836, p. 60), abstinence commands a price as a scarce factor of production which puts it on a par with the other, primary factors of production.

As a term denoting saving and investing, i.e. a form of economic activity which commands a reward, 'abstinence' was adopted by J.S. Mill, Cairnes and Jevons, Bastiat and Cherbuliez, Hermann and Roscher, and soon became part of established theory. Its general and rapid adoption indicates both the inadequacy and the end of a pure cost of production theory of value. Lassalle castigated and ridiculed it by comparing the sacrifices of millionaires to those of small savers (1864, pp. 110). This critique was answered by Loria (1880, pp. 610–24) and later by Macfarlane (1899) with the argument that the savings of millionaires were intramarginal, and that their rewards benefited from savers' surplus. It was probably for that reason that the term continued to be used for the act of saving and investing. Thus J.B. Clark (1899, p. 134) wrote: 'abstinence is the relinquishment, once and for all, of a certain pleasure of consumption and the acquisition of a wholly new increment of capital'. Yet more and more the term was considered unsatisfactory. Cairnes (1874, pp. 88–95) had unsuccessfully proposed the term 'postponement' in its place. By contrast, MacVane's suggestion (1887) to replace it by 'waiting' was taken up by Marshall, and later by Cassel and others, and subsequently adopted generally.

Marshall equated 'waiting' with 'postponement of enjoyment' (1920, p. 233) or 'saving' (1920, p. 830) and argued that 'the growth of wealth involves in general a deliberate waiting for pleasure which a person has ... the power of commanding in the immediate present' (1920, p. 234). In a similar way Carver (1893) associated 'abstinence' with the disutility of saving when he argued that the rate of interest is determined jointly by a falling marginal productivity of capital schedule and a rising marginal abstinence schedule. Carver showed also that abstinence is related to, but not the same as, the rate of time preference. Both Marshall and Carver thus distinguished between saving and investing, reserving the term 'waiting' (or 'abstinence') for saving.

Marshall also took up Senior's association of abstinence with time-consuming production, and extended it to consumption. Production, if it takes time, requires waiting because most outputs will appear only after most inputs have gone into the process. Similarly, durable consumer goods involve waiting because their services extend over time. The exertions, efforts and sacrifices involved in such economic behaviour in production Marshall counted among the real costs of production; where durable consumer goods are involved, they were counted among the real benefits of their use (1920, p. 339).

In this form, the 'abstinence theory' was severely criticized by Böhm-Bawerk (1921, vol. I, ch. 9 and appendix pt. 4). Based in effect on Senior's denial that capital was an independent factor of production, Böhm-Bawerk maintained that abstinence or waiting could not be counted among the real costs of production. Instead of adding the rewards for abstinence or waiting to the expenses of production the correct way was in his view to take account of the under-valuation of future benefits as reflected in such rewards and count among the (money) costs of production only the rewards of 'primary' factors.

The debate which followed this critique was obfuscated by Cassel because he changed the meaning of the term 'waiting'. Situating his discussion in the context of a price theory, Cassel identified the 'supply of waiting' with savings, thus changing the emphasis from a form of economic behaviour to its results (in money rather than in real terms). At the same time, Cassel resurrected Senior's association of saving with investing, and abstinence with a factor of production, and identified the 'demand for waiting' with the total money value of capital invested (1903, chs 3 and 4). While Cassel's procedure had the advantage of interpreting the price of waiting as the price of keeping a particular stock of capital in use, his adoption of a money value measure of capital (which was not discussed in detail) was confusing if not confused. It did, however, prepare the ground for the debates about saving and investment and their determinants which dominated macroeconomic discussions in the 1930s. In his later treatise (1918) Cassel tended to use the term 'use of capital' (*Kapitaldisposition*) in place of 'waiting'; this indicates that he discussed other issues than the microeconomic ones which had dominated the debates from Senior to Marshall and Böhm-Bawerk.

From Senior to Marshall, abstinence or waiting was associated primarily with the idea that saving involves sacrificing goods available in the present for consumption in order to invest them, and that profits can be regarded as reward for such economic activity. Yet as Rae had shown before the terms were coined, and Carver showed later, the reward for such intertemporal (re-)allocations depends not only on the characteristics of saving behaviour, but also on the productivity, or profitability, of the investment opportunities open to those willing to save. To that extent, therefore, the notion of abstinence for waiting as the activity which is rewarded by profits is misleading. Nor are such terms required to characterize economic behaviour concerned with intertemporal allocations.

From Senior to Böhm-Bawerk, abstinence or waiting was also associated with the notion that the use of durable goods in production as well as in consumption results in time-consuming economic processes, and that profit or interest is in some sense the reward for or price of the capital tied up in such processes. Yet while it is correct that time-consuming economic processes involve 'waiting' or abstinence from immediate consumption, it is not at all clear why such a characteristic of production processes should be given the status of a factor of production. Insofar as Böhm-Bawerk's critique is pertinent, see Fraser, 1937, ch. 14. Nor has it proved possible, in view of the many possible temporal structures such processes can assume, to define measures for the waiting or abstinence involved in them which are such that one can speak of profits or interest as reward or price of such a factor of production (see Haavelmo, 1960; Hicks, 1979). In spite of recent attempts to revive the notion (see Yeager, 1976), 'abstinence' or 'waiting' do not seem to be terms which are useful in economic theory beyond denoting, in a rather general manner, a characteristic feature of time-consuming economic processes.

BIBLIOGRAPHY

Bastiat, F. 1850. *Harmonies économiques*. Paris: Guillaumin. *Economic Harmonies*, London: Murray, 1860.

Böhm-Bawerk, E. von. 1921. *Kapital und Kapitalzins.* Erste Abteilung: *Geschichte und Kritik der Kapitalzins-Theorien.* 4th edn, Jena: Fisher. Trans. as *Capital and Interest,* Vol. 1: *History and Critique of Interest Theories,* South Holland, Ill.: Libertarian Press, 1959.

Cairnes, J.E. 1874. *Some Leading Principles of Political Economy Newly Expounded.* London: Macmillan.

Carver, T.N. 1893. The place of abstinence in the theory of interest. *Quarterly Journal of Economics* 8, 40–61.

Cassel, G. 1903. *The Nature and Necessity of Interest.* London: Macmillan.

Cassel, G. 1918. *Theoretische Sozialökonomie.* Leipzig: Deichert. 4th edn. 1927: *Theory of Social Economy,* London: Unwin, 1923. New edn, London, Bern, 1932.

Cherbuliez, A.-E. 1862. *Précis de la Science Economique.* Paris: Guillaumin.

Clark, J.B. 1899. *The Theory of Distribution.* New York: Macmillan.

Fraser, L.M. 1937. *Economic Thought and Language.* London: Black.

Goss, B.A. 1980. Adam Smith on Abstinence. *Australian Economic Papers* 19, 16–21.

Haavelmo, T. 1960. *A Study in the Theory of Investment.* Chicago: Chicago University Press.

Hermann, F.B.W. von. 1874. *Staatswirtschaftliche Untersuchungen.* 2nd edn, Munich: Ackermann.

Hicks, J.R. 1979. Is interest the price of a factor of production? In J.R. Hicks, *Classics and Moderns,* Collected Essays Vol. III, Oxford: Blackwell, 1983; Cambridge, Mass.: Harvard University Press.

Jevons, W.S. 1871. *The Theory of Political Economy.* London: Macmillan; New York: Kelley & Millman, 1957.

Lassalle, F. 1864. *Herr Bastiat-Schultze von Delitzsch der ökonomische Julian, oder Kapital und Arbeit.* Berlin: Schlingmann.

Loria, A. 1880. *La rendita fondiaria.* Milan: Hoepli.

Macfarlane, C.W. 1899. *Value and Distribution.* Philadelphia: Lippincott.

MacVane, S.M. 1887. Analysis of cost of production. *Quarterly Journal of Economics* 1, 481–7.

Malthus, T.R. 1820. *Principles of Political Economy.* 2nd edn, London: Murray, 1836; New York: A.M. Kelley, 1951.

Marshall, A. 1920. *Principles of Economics.* 8th edn. 9th (Variorum) edn, London and New York: Macmillan, 1961.

Mill, J.S. 1848. *Principles of Political Economy.* London: Parker; New York: A.M. Kelley, 1965.

Rae, J. 1934. *Statement of Some New Principles on the Subject of Political Economy.* Boston: Hilliard, Gray and Co.

Roscher, W. 1854. *Grundlagen der Nationalökonomie.* Stuttgart: Cotta.

Scrope, G.P. 1833. *Principles of Political Economy.* London: Longman, Rees, Orme, Brown, Green and Longman.

Senior, W.N. 1836. *Outlines of the Science of Political Economy.* London: Longman, 1850.

Smith, A. 1759. *Theory of Moral Sentiments.* Oxford: Clarendon Press, 1976.

Yeager, L.B. 1976. Toward understanding some paradoxes in capital theory. *Economic Inquiry* 14, 313–46.

Walras's theory of capital

JOHN EATWELL

The extension of Walras's (1874–7) analysis from non-capitalistic production to the case of capitalistic production involved him in the introduction of four new sets of variables: the rate of net income, i, the l prices of the capital goods, P_k, the l quantities of capital goods demanded, D_k, and the total value of saving (in terms of the numéraire), E.

The rate of net income is defined as the ratio of the rental of a unit of capital good service p_k, less charges for depreciation (μ) and insurance (v) (both of which are expressed as percentages per annum of the value of the capital good) to the value of the capital good:

$$i = \frac{p_k - (\mu + v)P_k}{P_k} \tag{1}$$

Thus the value of each capital good is equal to the *net* price of a unit of its service divided by the rate of net income. In competitive equilibrium the rate of net income is equal on all capital goods, but μ and v may differ from one capital good to another. In what follows, it will be assumed for simplicy that $\mu = v = 0$.

Walras expresses the volume of saving as the outcome of demand for an imaginary commodity (E), a unit of which yields perpetual net income at the rate i which is to be determined. In consequence the price of a unit of (E), $p_e = 1/i$. The total volume of saving derives from individuals' utility maximizing choices between units of (E) and units of other commodities.

Summing over individual demands for (E) total demand for (E) is

$$D_e = F_e(p_k', p_n', p_c', i)$$

and hence the total value of saving, E, in terms of the numéraire is

$$E = D_e p_e = G_e(p_k', p_n', p_c', i) \tag{2}$$

where p_n are rentals of non-producible factors and p_c prices of consumer goods. Thus saving is defined as a fluid homogeneous magnitude – 'savings in general'.

247

Walras regarded the market for capital as *finance* as equivalent, in the determination of net income, to the market for capital goods. But even in his examination of the latter saving is always expressed as a quantity of value (in terms of the numéraire), whilst the quantities of particular capital goods produced are expressed in terms of their peculiar physical units. The sum of the values of new capital goods demanded equals the value of saving

$$E = P'_k D_k \tag{3}$$

Although Walras labelled as capital 'all forms of social wealth which are not used up at all or used up only after a lapse of time' the determination of the rate of net income concerns only 'mobile capitals', i.e. reproducible means of production. The essential characteristic of the stock of reproducible means of production is that its composition is determined by economic forces:

> Capital assets are destroyed and vanish, like persons; and like persons they re-appear, not, however, as a result of a natural reproduction, but as a result of economic production. (p. 217)

The essence of 'economic production' is that like all other produced commodities, capital goods

> are subject to the law of cost of production. ... In equilibrium their selling prices and their cost of production are equal. (p. 171)

Thus

$$P_k = Ap_k + Mp_n \tag{4}$$

where A is the $l \times l$ matrix of input coefficients of capital goods into capital goods, and M the $l \times m$ matrix of input coefficients of non-reproducible inputs into capital goods.

Walras's complete system may be set out as follows (the lower case roman numeral identifies the equations, the preceding letter (or number) indicates the number of equations in each set):

$$D_c = F_c(p'_k, p'_n, p'_c, i) \qquad (n) \qquad \text{(i)}$$

$$D_e = F_e(p'_k, p'_n, p'_c, i)$$
$$E = D_e p_e = G_e(p'_k, p'_n, p'_c, i) \qquad (1) \qquad \text{(ii)}$$

$$O_n = N'D_c + M'D_k \qquad (m) \qquad \text{(iii)}$$

$$O_k = B'D_c + A'D_k \qquad (l) \qquad \text{(iv)}$$

$$O_n = Q_n \qquad (m) \qquad \text{(v)}$$

$$O_k = Q_k \qquad (l) \qquad \text{(vi)}$$

$$p_c = Bp_k + Np_n \qquad (n) \qquad \text{(vii)}$$

$$P_k = Ap_k + Mp_n \qquad (l) \qquad \text{(viii)}$$

$$P_k = \frac{p_k}{i} \qquad (l) \qquad \text{(ix)}$$

$$E = P'_k D_k \qquad (1) \qquad \text{(x)}$$

a total of $2n + 2m + 4l + 2$ equations to determine the similar number of unknowns, (D_c, p_c, O_n, p_n, O_k, D_k, p_k, P_k, E, i). By Walras's Law one of the equations is redundant. Similarly prices are only determined up to a multiplicative constant, and hence the price of a consumption good (A) is set equal to 1.

Walras has introduced $2l + 2$ new equations ((viii), (ix), (ii) and (x)) to determine the $2l + 2$ additional unknowns (P_k, D_k, E, i) which are required to complete his model of competitive capitalism.

Walras clearly regards the new equations and variables as an attachment to the equations of a-capitalistic production and exchange which does not disturb the solutions of those latter equations in any significant way. Thus the determination of equilibrium conditions in the theory of capital formation is expressed solely in terms of the saving function and the total value and quantities of new capital goods produced:

> With these additional data, we have all the elements necessary for the solution of our problem. New capital goods are exchanged against the excess of income over consumption: and the condition of equality between the value of the new capital goods and the value of the excess gives us the equation required for the determination of the rate of net income and consequently for the determination of the prices of capital goods. Moreover, new capital goods are products; and the condition of equality between their selling price and their cost of production gives us the equations required for the determination of the quantities manufactured. (pp. 269–70)

A peculiarity of Walras's approach to the problem of capitalistic production is that the existence of *positive* net saving plays an important role in his analysis of the determination of the rate of net income; to the extent that he even suggests that the rate of net income can only be determined in a progressive economy (pp. 269 and 479). The rationale of this odd position will become clear as we proceed.

Walras's attempt to embed the concept of 'saving in general', and an analysis of the determination of a uniform rate of net income on the value of capital goods, within the framework he had developed in the analyses of pure exchange and of a-capitalistic production was to prove unsuccessful, as was demonstrated by Garegnani (1960; see also the first chapter in this volume).

The source of the difficulty, which is examined in the next section, may be summarized as follows. The technique Walras had developed in the preceding lessons required that the stocks of means of production, expressed in their individual physical units, should be part of the (arbitrary) data of the problem. So the rentals paid for the services of these means of production will be determined by the demands for the available stocks. In the case of produced means of production the demand-prices of new capital goods will depend on the prices of their services in relation to the rate of net income (equation (ix)). And, since currently produced capital goods are *not* available for use in the period under consideration – if they were, the stock of capital would be unbounded! (pp. 282–3) – the demand price of any new good is determined solely by the demand for the stock of its services currently available. It will not be affected by changes in the output of that good except to the extent that it is used in its own production.

For any given set of prices each type of capital good has a particular rate of return over its cost of production. If the requirement of a uniform rate of net income is imposed on the model, the value (cost of production) of each capital good must be such as to yield that rate of return.

The cost of production of new capital goods may be altered by variations in the composition of the output of new capital goods if these variations lead to changes in the demands for stocks of services. The degree of variation in the cost of production will be determined by the differences in techniques which may be used for the production of the various capital goods, and the total value of savings which may be allocated between the capital goods. Thus, variation in the composition of capital good output will determine both the cost of production and the demand price of each new capital good, whilst the volume of saving will determine the range of that variation. Given the total value of saving the equality between the cost of production and the demand price of each capital good is the condition of equilibrium, and variation in the composition of the output of new capital goods is the only means whereby this condition may be satisfied. Thus this composition must not be fixed by any condition outside the system (i)–(x). For example, if demand functions for capital goods (as functions of all prices and i) were added to the system it would be *overdetermined*, for this would involve adding extra equations to the system without the addition of unknowns. Similarly, if net savings were zero, the composition of output would be determined by the requirements of replacement, and the equations are, once again, overdetermined. Walras, by confining the analysis to an economy in which net saving is positive, obscures this difficulty. Walras's system can only admit of 'saving in general' as demand for the total value of new capital goods produced. It cannot accommodate demand functions for individual capital goods. Even so, the system is generally inconsistent.

EXISTENCE OF A SOLUTION TO THE EQUATIONS OF CAPITAL FORMATION. The conditions which must be satisfied if there is to be a solution to Walras's equations of capital formation, and the rate of net income determined, will now be investigated under a simplifying – but none the less general – assumption.

The endowment of the economy is assumed to consist solely of stocks of reproducible means of production, these stocks being of arbitrary size. Only one technique of production is available to produce each commodity. Thus the equation system (i)–(x) above must be modified by the elimination of all reference to prices or quantities of non-produced means of production.

Since i is uniform, from equations (viii) and (ix) this rate must be such that

$$Ap_k i = p_k \tag{5}$$

and hence

$$0 = [I\lambda - A]p_k \tag{6}$$

where $\lambda = 1/i$. By the Frobenius theorem it is known that since A is non-negative and (we presume) indecomposable, there is only one value of the characteristic roots λ_i with which a positive eigenvector p_k is associated. All other λ_i are associated with vectors which contain negative prices and are therefore economically meaningless. Thus there can be only one value of i, and only one vector of rentals of the services of capital goods, p_k, consistent with the existence of a uniform i on all produced means of production. Once i and p_k are determined, then by equation (vii) p_c are also determined, as are D_c, E and P_k by equations (i), (ii) and (ix).

Only the demands for capital goods remain to be determined, and only the equations expressing the equality between the endowment of capital goods and the demand for new capital goods (iv) and the equation expressing equality between the value of gross saving and the value of new capital goods produced (x) remain to be satisfied. It should be noted that in equilibrium the demand for each stock of capital goods (i.e. for each stock of capital goods services) must be equal to the size of the stock, since all p_k are positive.

By Walras's Law

$$p_c'D_c + E = p_k'Q_k \tag{7}$$

i.e. the amount spent (measured in terms of the numéraire) on consumption goods, plus the amount saved, must be equal to the income earned on the endowment of means of production. Since, by equations (vii) consumption goods' prices are equal in equilibrium to their costs of production, then the total value of the output of consumption goods is equal to the value of the services used in their production.

$$p_c'D_c = p_k'Q_k^c \tag{8}$$

where Q_k^c denotes the vector of quantities of means of production used in the production of consumption goods. Hence

$$E = p_k'Q_k - p_k'Q_k^c = p_k'Q_k^a \tag{9}$$

the value of saving is equal to the total value of the services yielded by the amounts of the initial endowments *available* for the construction of new capital goods (Q_k^a), once the requirements of consumption goods production have been deducted from the original stocks.

The stock of capital good services *required* for the construction of new capital goods (Q_k^i) may be determined from the two conditions:

$$E = P_k'D_k \quad \text{and} \quad Q_k^i = A'D_k,$$

Walras's equations are consistent only if $Q_k^i = Q_k^a$; that is if there exists a vector of demands for new capital goods D_k such that this latter condition is satisfied. All elements of D_k must be non-negative, and, in turn, all input requirements are non-negative;

$$D_k = (A')^{-1}Q_k^i \geqslant 0; \qquad Q_k^i \geqslant 0 \tag{10}$$

251

However, there is nothing in the specification of the model to ensure that $Q_k^a \geqslant 0$. The original endowment Q_k must be non-negative. But the solution may imply that the amount of any one element of the endowment available for the production of new capital goods is negative, to the extent of

$$-\sum_c b_{jc} D_c,$$

the quantity of capital good j used in the production of consumption goods. Indeed, only one element of Q_k^a need be positive (this is essential if E is to be positive). Thus the set Q_k^a is bounded from below by the condition $Q_k^a \geqslant -B'D_c$. So if any element of Q_k^a is less than zero, a condition that is as likely as its converse, then the data and the equations are unequivocally inconsistent. Consistency can be attained only by chance. This is a sufficient criticism of Walras's system.

Moreover, even if Q_k^a should be non-negative, condition (10) may render the system inconsistent. The vectors Q_k^i which satisfy (10) lie in a convex cone within the positive orthant, for these vectors must be non-negative linear combinations of the columns of A'. In general, this cone will not be the entire positive orthant – this would only be the case when each productive service appeared only once as the sole input into the production of a single capital good. Hence, in general, some $Q_k^a \geqslant 0$ cannot be equated with a vector Q_k^i which satisfies (10).

This analysis is unaffected if it is assumed that there is more than one technique available for the production of each commodity. The technique which will be chosen is that which yields the highest rate of net income. This technique will be used whatever may be the composition of demand or of the endowment.

The rationale of this result is that there is no reason to suppose that prices paid for the services of the stocks of reproducible means of production will correspond to those prices which would result in a uniform rate of net income, the condition of long-run equilibrium.

Including non-produced means of production in the analysis will not render the model consistent. The vector of rentals which clears the markets for non-produced factors will have associated with it a vector of rentals for capital goods which would be compatible with a uniform rate of net income. Except by a fluke, this vector of capital goods rentals will not be market clearing.

AN ALTERNATIVE SOLUTION. Walras himself became aware, in the 4th, definitive, edition of the *Elements*, that his equations of capital formation might not admit of a solution:

> If we suppose that all fixed capital goods proper ... are already found in the economy in quantities Q_k ... and that their gross and net incomes are paid for at prices determined by the system of production equations and by the rates of depreciation and insurance, it is not at all certain that the amount of savings E will be adequate for the manufacture of new fixed capital goods proper in just such quantities as will satisfy the last l equations of the above system (p. 308).

His solution was, however, an evasion of the real problem:

> On the other hand, in an economy in normal operation which has only to maintain itself in equilibrium, we may suppose the last equations to be satisfied (p. 308).

i.e. being in equilibrium we may hope for the attainment of equilibrium!

But Walras also recommended a way out of the dilemma:

> All we could be sure of, under these circumstances of insufficient savings to ensure equilibrium is (1) that the utility of new capital goods would be maximized if the first new capital goods to be manufactured were those yielding the highest rate of net income, and (2) that this is precisely the order in which new capital goods would be manufactured under a system of free competition (p. 308).

If we take up this proposal the equations (viii) in Walras's system should be modified, the equality between cost of production and demand price being replaced by the inequality:

$$P_k \leqslant Ap_k + Mp_n \tag{viii}'$$

i.e. demand price is less than or equal to cost of production – with the proviso that in the cases of those capital goods for which the inequality holds output will be zero.

The important role which the replacement of equalities by inequalities plays in the establishment of an economically meaningful solution to the equations of exchange and of acapitalistic production and exchange is well known. In the case of consumption goods a demand price which is less than the cost of production for any positive output means that output of that good must be zero. In the case of non-producible inputs an endowment which is greater than the quantity demanded at any positive price results in the price of that input being zero. Both these circumstances have a clear economic meaning. Reproducible means of production share characteristics of both and the economic meaning of the use of the inequality is less clear. The services of the stock of a reproducible input may command a positive price and yet new units will not be produced if the demand price of that commodity is less than its cost of production. The rate of net income earned in the production of such a commodity, calculated at the ruling prices, will be less than the ruling rate. But a situation in which the rate of net income is not the same on all produced means of production does not conform to the conventional notion of long-run equilibrium. An 'equilibrium' defined with inequalities between demand price and cost of production of some capital goods is a curious hybrid, for although the prices of all non-produced means of production are uniform throughout the economy (a long-run equilibrium condition), the rate of net income is not uniform (a short-run condition). This hybridization cannot be justified by considerations affecting the relative mobility of resources in the two classifications, since mobility of non-reproducible inputs between uses is customarily attained by changes in the structure of the stock of producible inputs with which they are combined. This situation arises not from any particular view of the actual operation of a capitalistic economy but is dictated by the necessity, in Walras's theory, of expressing the stock of reproducible means of production as a set of arbitrary (physical) magnitudes.

In a Note to Chapter III of his *Equilibrium, Stability and Growth*, Michio Morishima has adopted Walras's strategem and demonstrated (with the aid of some additional assumptions) that a solution to the modified system exists. His proof follows the mathematical procedures developed by Wald, and Arrow and Debreu, adapted to the case of capital formation. The technique developed above in the analysis of Walras's equations of capital formation will be used to investigate Morishima's analysis.

The investigation will be conducted under the assumption that all means of production are reproducible, and that only one technique is available for the production of each produced commodity (consumption goods and capital goods). At least one input coefficient is positive for any output. These assumptions are made solely in the interests of simplicity. It will be evident from what follows that the argument could readily be extended to include non-reproducible means of production and many possible techniques.

Suppose that all capital goods are produced and that the price system is that which corresponds to a uniform rate of net income. Then, for the reasons outlined above there will in general be a discrepancy between the stocks of capital goods' services available for the production of new capital goods, and the set of possible combinations of stocks required if all saving is to be absorbed and the outputs of new machines are to be non-negative. Some elements of the difference $Q_k^a - Q_k^i$ (for any Q_k^i selected from the set of possible alternatives) will be positive and others negative. Those elements which are positive relate to an endowment which is greater than that which is absorbed in the production of both consumption goods and capital goods at existing prices. Those elements which are negative relate to an endowment smaller than demand for its services at existing prices.

To attempt to remove the discrepancies select the good for which the ratio $(q_j^a - q_j^i)/q_j$ is greatest, and set the output of the good at zero. The price of its services (which will be denoted by π_j) may now be set anywhere in the range between zero and its price when produced (p_j). The inequality in (viii)' will therefore hold for good j. Since there was previously an excess supply of this good then it might be expected that π_j set lower than p_j would tend to reduce that excess by encouraging substitution in consumption toward j intensive goods. Such changes may also supplement the available stocks of those services for which there was previously an excess demand. Any value of $\pi_j < p_j$ will result in a higher rate of net income implicit in the price equations of those capital goods which are produced; this may, in turn, tend to increase saving and hence available stocks of all capital goods for capital good production. As good j is not produced it acquires the role in the price system of a non-producible means of production, and the analysis may be pursued once more in the manner outlined above; i.e. by relating the intersection of the set $Q_k^i(k \neq j)$, which for all possible pairs

$i, \pi_j \, (\pi_j < p_j)$ results in the absorption of saving, with the set of Q_k^i which satisfy the condition

$$q_j^a \geqslant q_j^i$$

(if the inequality holds $\pi_j = 0$), to the set Q_k^a defined by

$$E - \pi_j q_j^a = p_k' Q_k^a \qquad (k \neq j)$$

There is no reason to believe that the discrepancy will disappear, and so the procedure may be repeated; the production of the capital good for which the value of $(q_k^a - q_k^i)/q_k$ is the greatest should be set equal to zero, and π_k set below p_k. The analysis is then conducted as if there were two non-produced inputs.

The quantity available for capital good production of a capital good previously eliminated from production may fall below zero for all $\pi_j < p_j$ as the structure of production changes with successive eliminations (p_j being calculated as the cost of production of good j at the prices ruling at the stage of the analysis under consideration, not at the stage at which it was eliminated). In such circumstances the price of j must be raised to p_j, which means that it is reintroduced into production, a different good is selected for elimination, and the process continues in the same manner as before.

At each stage of the process of elimination it may happen that there is a set of Q_k^a (of those capital goods still in production), appropriate to the prices associated with a uniform rate of net income on the goods produced. But this event is similar to the attainment of a uniform rate of net income when all capital goods are produced, that is, a configuration of the endowment which happens to result in a Q_k^a which falls in the subset Q_k^i. Since the initial endowment is arbitrary it cannot be claimed that in such a case the existence of an equilibrium to the equations has been proven – since in general, for all circumstances, it has not. A configuration of the endowment can always be found which would result in the elimination being taken a stage further. Each stage of the elimination merely recreates this situation, and thus there is no reason to believe that the process will cease.

The process of elimination may thus continue until only two capital goods remain in production, and $l - 2$ capital goods are consigned to the category of non-produced means of production. There is still no necessity that Q_k^a should equal a feasible Q_k^i (k not including the $l - 2$ eliminated goods). That good which is in excess supply should be eliminated. The system now only contains *one* produced means of production, and the savings function (ii) is, in effect, the demand function for that good alone. No constraints are now imposed on the configuration of prices by the condition that the rate of net income on the produced means should be uniform – for since only one capital good is produced there can only be one value of the rate of net income.

The only case in which there must necessarily be a solution to the system is that in which only one capital good is produced. Condition (viii)′ will hold with just one equality.

Thus, apart from the chance case in which the elimination process is halted with more than one capital-good in production, a maximum uniform rate of net income is attained only when just one capital good is produced. The rate of net income defined in the production of the single good produced is used to capitalize the value of non-produced capital goods and hence these 'earn' the rate of net income by definition. Morishima's model is thus yet another example of the use in neoclassical models of the 'one-produced input world' assumption, which input is to be the one produced is endogenous to the model.

Walras's analysis of capital formation and credit, far from being the triumphant confirmation of his theory of pure economics, is a failure which brings his whole system into question. He is unable to overcome the contradiction between saving in general as a homogeneous fluid magnitude and the heterogeneity of capital goods. This contradiction could be overcome by expressing the endowment of capital goods as a single magnitude – their value. But the value of the endowment cannot be part of the data of the problem without engendering circular reasoning. Walras, in avoiding this circularity, constructed a system in which, whilst the method of specifying the data is logically sound, the equations are inconsistent.

BIBLIOGRAPHY

Garegnani, P. 1960. *Il capitale nelle teorie della distribuzione.* Milan: Giuffrè.

Morishima, M. 1964. *Equilibrium, Stability and Growth.* Oxford: Clarendon Press.

Walras, L. 1874–7. *Eléments d'économie politique pure.* Trans. and ed. W. Jaffé as *Elements of Pure Economics.* London: Allen & Unwin, 1954; Homewood, Ill.: R.D. Irwin.

Wicksell effects

EDWIN BURMEISTER

In realistic economic models with n different types of capital goods, the value of the capital stock is

$$V = \sum_{i=1}^{n} P_i K_i \tag{1}$$

where P_i is the price of the ith capital good in terms of some *numéraire*. The value of capital, however, is not an appropriate measure of the 'aggregate capital stock' as a factor of production except under extremely restrictive conditions. Wicksell (1893, 1934) originally recognized this fact, which subsequently was emphasized by Robinson (1956).

If attention is restricted to alternative steady-state comparisons, in constant-returns-to-scale economies without joint production V is a function of the interest rate, r; see, for example, Burmeister and Dobell (1970). The *Wicksell effect* is the change in the value of the capital stock from one steady state to another, namely

$$\frac{dV}{dr}. \tag{2}$$

The term 'Wicksell effect' was introduced by Uhr (1951), but its importance was not widely recognized until the writings of Robinson (1956) and Swan (1956).

The Wicksell effect is the sum of the *price Wicksell effect* (which is the revaluation of the inventory of capital goods due to new prices) and the *real Wicksell effect* (which is the price-weighted sum of the changes in the physical quantities of different capital goods):

$$\frac{dV}{dr} = \sum_{i=1}^{n} \frac{dP_i}{dr} K_i + \sum_{i=1}^{n} P_i \frac{dK_i}{dr}. \tag{3}$$

257

Numerical examples show that the price Wicksell effect can be negative, i.e.,

$$\sum_{i=1}^{n} P_i \frac{dK_i}{dr} < 0 \tag{4}$$

is possible, even when (i) the total Wicksell effect is positive $[dV/dr > 0]$, or (ii) particular capital stocks are increasing with $dK_i/dr > 0$ for some but not all i; see Burmeister and Dobell (1970, pp. 289–93). In neoclassical models with only one capital good ($n = 1$), the real Wicksell effect is always negative. Moreover, the sign of the price Wicksell effect depends upon the choice of *numéraire*, and hence so does the total Wicksell effect given by (3). The sign of the real Wicksell effect, however, is independent of the choice of *numéraire*.

One central issue of the Cambridge controversies in capital theory involves Wicksell effects. Does a decrease (increase) in the steady-state interest rate always imply a rise (fall) in per capita steady-state consumption provided the rate of interest is greater (less) than the rate of growth of labour? In one-capital good models, the answer to this question is, 'Yes'. In general, the answer is, 'Yes', if and only if the real Wicksell effect is negative; see Burmeister and Turnovsky (1972) and Burmeister (1976).

To establish this relationship between the behaviour of per capita consumption and the real Wicksell effect, consider a technology which can be represented by a *production possibility frontier*

$$Y_1 = T(Y_2, \ldots, Y_n; L, K_1, \ldots, K_n) \tag{5}$$

where Y_i is the output of commodity i, L is the labour which grows at the exogenous rate g, and K_i is the stock of commodity i used as a capital input.

It is assumed further that $T(\cdot)$ is twice continuously differentiable, exhibits constant returns to scale, and has a Hessian matrix $[T_{ij}]$ that is negative semi-definite and whose rank varies with the degree of joint production in the economy; see Samuelson (1966), Burmeister and Turnovsky (1971), and Kuga (1973). The analysis which follows can be generalized to non-differentiable technologies as in Burmeister (1976), but for simplicity only differentiable technologies are considered here.

In steady-state equilibria all quantities grow at the rate g, implying that the output of every commodity must satisfy

$$Y_i \equiv C_i + K_i = C_i + gK_i, \qquad i = 1, \ldots, n, \tag{6}$$

where C_i denotes the consumption of commodity i. Substituting these steady-state restrictions into (5) and using lower-case letters to denote per capita quantities, we have

$$c_1 + gk_1 = T(c_2 + gk_2, \ldots, c_n + gk_n; 1, k_1, \ldots, k_n). \tag{7}$$

Let the prices of commodities and the rental rates for capital goods, both in terms of the wage rate as *numéraire*, be denoted by p_i and w_i, respectively,

$i = 1, \ldots, n$; also let r denote the interest or profit rate. It is well-known that intertemporal profit maximization and/or efficiency necessitates that

$$\frac{\dot{p}_i}{p_i} + \frac{w_i}{p_i} = r, \qquad i = 1, \ldots, n. \tag{8}$$

Imposing the steady-state requirement that relative prices remain constant, (8) implies that

$$w_i = rp_i, \qquad i = 1, \ldots, n. \tag{9}$$

Using the well-known marginal conditions

$$\frac{\partial T}{\partial(c_i + gk_i)} = -\frac{p_i}{p_1} \quad \text{and} \quad \frac{\partial T}{\partial k_i} = \frac{w_i}{p_1}, \qquad i = 1, \ldots, n, \tag{10}$$

we see that a vector

$$(c^*, k^*; r^*, p^*) = (c_1^*, \ldots, c_n^*; r^*, p_1^*, \ldots, p_n^*) \geqslant 0 \tag{11}$$

satisfying (7) and (10) represents a steady-state solution at the growth rate g. It thus follows immediately from differentiation of (7) that almost everywhere

$$\sum_{i=1}^{n} p_i \left(\frac{dc_i}{dr} \right) \Bigg|_{(r^*, p^*)} = (r - g) \sum_{i=1}^{n} p_i \left(\frac{dk_i}{dr} \right) \Bigg|_{(r^*, p^*)}; \tag{12}$$

see Burmeister (1976) for details.

Now let v denote the per capita value of capital in terms of the wage rate as *numéraire*:

$$v = \sum_{i=1}^{n} p_i k_i. \tag{13}$$

The change in the per capita value of capital across alternative steady-state equilibria is obtained by differentiating (13); thus almost everywhere the per capita Wicksell effect is

$$\frac{dv}{dr} \Bigg|_{(r^*, p^*)} = \sum_{i=1}^{n} \left(\frac{dp_i}{dr} \right) \Bigg|_{(r^*, p^*)} \cdot k_i + \sum_{i=1}^{n} p_i \cdot \left(\frac{dk_i}{dr} \right) \Bigg|_{(r^*, p^*)} \tag{14}$$

Comparing (14) and (12), it is seen that it is the real Wicksell effect which determines whether or not 'consumption' is well-behaved across steady-state equilibria. That is, if the real Wicksell effect is negative and

$$\sum_{i=1}^{n} p_i \cdot \left(\frac{dk_i}{dr} \right) \Bigg|_{(r^*, p^*)} < 0, \tag{15}$$

259

then almost everywhere

$$\sum_{i=1}^{n} p_i \left(\frac{dc_i}{dr}\right)\bigg|_{(r^*,\, p^*)} \gtreqless 0 \quad \text{as} \quad r \gtreqless g. \tag{16}$$

In particular, when $c_2 = c_3 = \cdots = c_n$ and only commodity 1 is consumed, consumption as measured by c_1 rises (falls) as r is increased from r^* to $r^* + \Delta r^*$ when r^* is greater (less) than g. (The familiar Golden Rule condition giving maximum per capita steady-state consumption holds at $r^* = g$.)

It follows, then, that a negative real Wicksell effect is the appropriate concept of 'capital deepening' in a model with many heterogeneous capital goods. That is, when (15) and hence (16) hold, an economy with a low interest rate (but exceeding g) has 'more capital' than one with a higher interest rate in the sense that it is capable of providing more steady-state per capita consumption. Although (15) and (16) always hold in a neighbourhood of $r^* = g$, examples show that they do not generally hold everywhere. This possibility – that (16) does not hold everywhere – is perhaps the most interesting conclusion to emerge from the Cambridge controversies and has been termed a 'paradox'. However, the 'paradox' involves comparisons of alternative steady-states rather than comparisons of alternative feasible paths; Bliss (1975) provides a lucid explanation of why such 'paradoxes' are in fact not surprising or damaging to the neoclassical paradigm.

Imposing some set of conditions on the technology $T(\cdot)$ should be sufficient to assure that the real Wicksell effect is always negative. Such conditions would be of interest – especially if they could be empirically tested – since they would validate the qualitative conclusions derived from the one-good models often used in macroeconomics without any theoretical justification for ignoring aggregation problems. Moreover, Burmeister (1977, 1979) has proved that a negative real Wicksell effect is a necessary and sufficient condition for the existence of an index of capital, κ, and a neoclassical aggregate production function $F(\kappa)$ defined across steady-state equilibria such that (i) $c = F(\kappa)$, (ii) $r = F'(\kappa)$, and (iii) $F''(\kappa) < 0$. Unfortunately, no set of such sufficient conditions is known, but the literature on capital aggregation suggests that they would impose severe restrictions on the technology.

BIBLIOGRAPHY

Bliss, C. 1975. *Capital Theory and the Distribution of Income*. Amsterdam: North-Holland.

Burmeister, E. 1976. Real Wicksell effects and regular economies. In *Essays in Modern Capital Theory*, ed. M. Brown, K. Sato and P. Zarembka. Amsterdam: North-Holland.

Burmeister, E. 1977. On the social significance of the reswitching controversy. *Revue d'économie politique* 87(2), March–April, 330–50.

Burmeister, E. 1979. Professor Pasinetti's 'unobtrusive postulate', regular economies, and the existence of a well-behaved aggregate production function. *Revue d'économie politique* 89(5), September–October, 644–52.

Burmeister, E. and Dobell, A.R. 1970. *Mathematical Theories of Economic Growth*. New York: Macmillan.

Burmeister, E. and Turnovsky, S.J. 1971. The degree of joint production. *International Economic Review* 12, February, 99–105.

Burmeister, E. and Turnovsky, S.J. 1972. Capital deepening response in an economy with heterogeneous capital goods. *American Economic Review* 62, December, 842–53.

Kuga, K. 1973. More about joint production, *International Economic Review* 14(1), February, 196–210.

Robinson, J. 1956. *The Accumulation of Capital.* London: Macmillan; Homewood, Ill.: R.D. Irwin.

Samuelson, P.A. 1966. The fundamental singularity theorem for non-joint production. *International Economic Review* 7, January, 34–41.

Swan, T. 1956. Economic growth and capital accumulation. *Economic Record* 32, November, 334–61.

Uhr, C.G. 1951. Knut Wicksell, a centennial evaluation. *American Economic Review* 41, December, 829–60.

Wicksell, K. 1893. *Value, Capital and Rent.* Reprinted New York: Augustus M. Kelley, 1970.

Wicksell, K. 1934. *Lectures on Political Economy.* 3rd edn, London: George Routledge and Sons Limited, 1938; New York: A.M. Kelley, 1967.

Wicksell's theory of capital

MASSIMO PIVETTI

Wicksell first developed his real theory of capital on 'the purely imaginary assumption' that the phenomena of capital and interest could take place without the intervention of money or credit; he then endeavoured to bring to light the modifications that are called for by the appearance of money, and by so doing he laid the foundation of this century's dominant approach to money and real magnitudes. Wicksell's theory can actually be said to have established the basis of mainstream long-period analysis of the economy, with its explanation in real terms of the equilibrium rate of interest and the conception of money as a factor that may be important to the gravitation of the economy towards its equilibrium position but not as a determinant of that position.

Wicksell's general equilibrium – what he calls 'The Theory of Exchange Value in its Final Form' (1901, p. 196) – consists of a system of equations by which relative prices are determined simultaneously with normal outputs, factor uses and the equilibrium prices of factor services (that is, distribution), on the basis of given consumer tastes, technical conditions of production and factor endowments. 'Capital' enters *twice* into the picture: first, when the quantity produced in the economy of each final article is expressed as a function of all the quantities of factors employed, according to given 'production functions' reflecting the given technical conditions; secondly, in the relations expressing the condition that the supply of each factor of production annually available in the economy must be equal to the quantity of it annually employed (i.e. demanded). On the basis of these conditions, the equilibrium prices of factor services depend on their relative scarcities; the equilibrium rate of interest, in particular, depends on the relative scarcity of the whole available capital and is the same on all capital (Wicksell, 1901, pp. 144–6). Wicksell's system thus depicts a 'long-run' equilibrium, which ultimately reflects the idea, common to the original versions of the marginal theory, that the competitive tendency towards a uniform rate of interest (profit) would deprive of any significance, as centres of gravitation of the economy, quantities and prices determined for situations in which each particular capital-good gave a different rate of return over its cost. (The same idea explains Wicksell's attention being focused throughout his main writings on *circulating* capital, for which the equilibrium condition represented by a uniform rate of return tends rapidly to impose itself through changes in the proportion amongst the different kinds of capital-goods annually employed in the economy. As for the treatment of durable or fixed capital, see Wicksell, 1923.)

The important point to be noticed about Wicksell's 'production functions' is that the capitalist element is expressed in them not by means of *value* magnitudes but in 'technical units'. He was fully aware that the partial derivatives of any such function in which 'capital' appears in value terms can be of no use for determining the 'productive contribution' of the different productive factors, and hence distribution. (An increase in the value of capital may simply reflect a rise of wages and rent, possibly without causing any change in the magnitude of the return; the additional product of the new capital may thus be nil, but this would give no information at all about the new level of the rate of interest: see Wicksell, 1893, pp. 25, 115–19; 1901, p. 148.)

In *Value, Capital and Rent* Wicksell used Böhm-Bawerk's 'average period of production' (Böhm-Bawerk, 1889, vol. II, bk. II, ch. II) so that the role of capital was seen as making possible the introduction of a longer period of time between the beginning and the conclusion of the process of production 'and consequently the adoption of a more roundabout method of production than would be possible if production were less strong in capital or totally devoid of capital'. He maintained, accordingly, that the greater the amount of capital employed, 'that is to say, the lengthier the average period of production that can be applied, the greater will be the annual production of finished consumption goods, provided the same number of workers and the same area of the country are involved' (1893, p. 116).

Wicksell realized, however, that the average period of production made it necessary to have recourse to calculation with simple interest (1893, pp. 125–6; 1901, p. 205 and Preface to the 2nd edn); so in the *Lectures* (1901), while still adhering to Böhm-Bawerk's view of the role of capital, Wicksell moved to a conception of capital in the production functions as a *complex* of variables: dated quantities of labour and land (or 'saved-up labour and saved-up land' as he called them to indicate that instead of being quantities of current labour and land *directly* employed in the production of consumption goods, they are employed in the production of capital goods). Wages and rents actually paid to those quantities of labour and land remain 'invested' in production from the moment they are paid until the conclusion of the process of production of the consumption good concerned; on the other hand, their marginal productivities are greater than those of current labour and land directly employed in production – the idea being that the productivity of original factors becomes greater if they are employed for distant ends than if they are employed in the immediate production of consumption goods: this difference in productivity constitutes the very source of interest (1901, p. 154).

Now, for the *rate* of interest to be same on all kinds of investment (in labour–capital or in land–capital, for a single year or for a period of years), the marginal productivities of the dated quantities of original factors – that is, the partial derivatives of the production function with respect to each of the variables included in it – must stand in a certain relation to each other, 'corresponding to that which exists in a calculation with compound interest' (p. 160). Full equilibrium determination then entails that the dated quantities of labour and land appearing in the production functions cannot be taken as given, but must be included amongst the unknowns of the system (pp. 203–5).

We can sum up the above by saying that the notion of marginal productivity is never applied by Wicksell directly to capital or capital goods; it is applied (in his chief work) to dated quantities of the two original 'factors of production'. Each commodity is seen as ultimately resolving itself into labour and land employed in different years – current labour and land, and 'saved-up' labour and land; they are remunerated according to their marginal productivities and are employed in the proportions demanded by the equilibrium condition of a uniform rate of interest. The equilibrium level of the rate of interest ultimately reflects the relative scarcity of saved-up original factors:

> the marginal productivity of the latter is greater, simply because current labour and land exist in relative abundance for the purposes for which they can be employed, whilst saved-up labour and land are not adequate in the same degree for the many purposes in which they have an advantage. This again is to be explained by the circumstances which limit the accumulation of capital (p. 155).

The explanation of the equilibrium rate of interest by the scarcity of capital, and as the reward for 'waiting', is one and the same thing as the conception of the rate of interest as the variable that brings to equality the supply of and the demand for capital. To this equality we now turn our attention.

In the relations expressing the equality between the supply of and the demand for each factor of production, together with the total quantities of labour and land, the total quantity of capital annually available in the economy is taken as given; it is a single magnitude, so that what Wicksell actually takes as given to solve the system is the total *exchange value* (measured in terms of one of the final products) of the capital available in the economy (pp. 204–5). A value magnitude is thus included amongst the determinants of distribution and prices. In criticizing Walras for having taken the physical quantities of the different kinds of capital goods as given, Wicksell argued that we need 'a unified treatment of the role of capital in production ... in order to calculate the rate of interest, which in equilibrium is the same on all capital' (p. 149). Accordingly, the quantity of capital available in the economy is conceived in his system as a single magnitude, a value magnitude taken as given, whilst, as we saw above, its physical composition, the relative quantities of its different technical constituents, is left free to change during the process of adjustment to equilibrium in order to satisfy the condition of a uniform rate of interest.

If the quantity of capital available in the economy is increased by 'real, productive, saving' (i.e. 'by restricting or postponing consumption'), then, *ceteris paribus*, the equilibrium rate of interest must fall. At the old rate the supply of capital now exceeds the quantity of it annually employed in the various industries; competition amongst capitalists presses the rate of interest downwards, thereby causing more roundabout processes, which were previously unremunerative, to become profitable. In Wicksell's view, not only does the process of production of each consumption good tend to become more 'capitalistic', through increases in 'saved-up' labour and land relative to current labour and land used in the course of a year and the introduction of 'longer-dated' investments, but also the composition of final demand and output tends to change in favour of more 'capitalistic' consumption goods, through the relative cheapening of such goods brought about by the fall in the rate of interest. Following, therefore, an increase in the supply of capital, substitution amongst alternative methods of production and amongst alternative consumption goods would ensure a new equality between supply of and demand for capital at a new lower level of the rate of interest. It may conveniently be added that if only circulating capital is taken into consideration – as Wicksell actually did by centring his theory of capital upon the case of capital goods that last only one year in an economy where production takes place in yearly cycles – then there is no need to distinguish, in the determination of interest, between supply of and demand for capital as a stock and as an annual flow; one may simply refer to the equilibrium rate of interest as being determined by supply and demand for gross saving.

This explanation of the 'real capital rate', with the essential role played in it by the interest elasticity of demand for saving, constitutes the basis of Wicksell's theory of money and prices (1898a, 1898b, 1906). We shall here refer to its more mature version, contained in volume II of the *Lectures* (1906).

In Wicksell's opinion, 'any theory of money worthy of the name must be able to show how and why the monetary or pecuniary demand for goods exceeds or falls short of the supply of goods in given conditions'. He contended that the advocates of the Quantity Theory, in postulating the price-level as an increasing function of the quantity of money, failed to show 'why such a change of price must always follow a change in the quantity of money and to describe what happens' (1906, p. 160). In the solution he put forward, the primary cause of price fluctuations is singled out as the difference between the actual money or loan rate and the normal or natural real rate of interest, determined by the scarcity of capital (saving).

As we saw above, *ceteris paribus* a lowering of the real rate unconditionally demands increased saving. The same applies to a lowering of the loan rate in the case of 'simple credit between man and man'; the loan market would directly reflect in such a case the supply of and demand for saving, so that there would be an immediate connection between the money rate and the real capital rate. Changes in the loan rate would take place simultaneously and uniformly with corresponding changes in the real rate, with the result that no change in the level of commodity prices could occur. Things are different when the activity of the banks is taken into consideration: banks 'possess a fund for loans which is always elastic and, on certain assumptions [i.e. with a pure credit system], inexhaustible', with the consequence that the immediate connection between the money rate and the real natural rate disappears. 'In our complex monetary system', says Wicksell. 'there exists no other connection between the two than the *variations in commodity prices* caused by the difference between them' (1906, pp. 194, 206).

Thus, starting from an equilibrium situation and no changes occurring in the circumstances upon which the real natural rate depends, a reduction of the rate of interest on the part of the banks will lead to an increase in monetary demand: owing to the increased demand for loan capital and the expansion of credit, on the one hand, and to a reduced supply of saving, on the other, an excess of investment spending over saving decisions will arise. Since the normal or equilibrium situation of the economy is characterized by the full employment of all productive factors, the increased monetary spending will result in a rise in prices, both of production and of consumption goods. As the parallel rise in money prices and incomes tends to leave the real capital rate unaffected, at the new higher price level an excess of investment spending over saving decisions will present itself again – so that the inflationary process is bound to continue as long as the money rate is kept below the real rate. The opposite would occur if banks maintained the rate of interest above its natural level. In both cases, in order to re-establish monetary equilibrium – the stability of the price level – banks would have to bring the money rate of interest back to the level of the 'real natural rate'. The conclusion then is that by virtue of the 'connecting link' of price-movements, the money rate will gravitate towards the real rate, even if such a gravitation process will not be of an automatic-spontaneous nature. (We may add that persistent full employment does not seem to be essential to the Wicksellian notion of a non-automatic gravitation of the actual money rate towards the normal natural rate. If, in the face of a money rate of interest that is higher than the natural rate, rigid money wages are assumed, then the role of 'connecting link' between the two rates might be played not only by reductions in prices but also by the fall in employment.)

So, in this picture it is maintained that a low rate of interest causes prices to rise, and vice versa. But Wicksell recognizes that in actual experience rising prices very rarely coincide with low or falling interest rates, and that the opposite is the general rule. He argues that this 'apparently crushing objection' to his theory ('an objection which the members of the Tooke School have triumphantly produced at every opportunity as a support for their theory') is indeed perfectly consistent with his view of the influence of the rate of interest on prices: instead of assuming a lowering of the rate of interest by the banks, other things being equal, one has simply to make the more realistic assumption that the difference between the two rates arises because the natural rate rises or falls whilst the money rate remains unchanged and only tardily follows it. The *primum movens*, that is to say, generally consists in changes in the natural real rate of interest: a rise (fall) in the natural rate will result in a rise (fall) in prices which, in its turn, will sooner or later force up (down) the money rate (1906, pp. 202–8; see Keynes's identical explanation in *A Treatise on Money*, 1930, vol. I, p. 196n. and vol. II, pp. 198, 203).

The critique of the marginalist notion of capital which was stimulated by the work of Piero Sraffa (1960) applies also to Wicksell's theory. Amongst the numerous relevant contributions, we shall recall here the careful critical analysis of Wicksell's theory of capital contributed by Garegnani (1960, chs 4–6, see also Garegnani, 1970), and the symposium on capital theory in the *Quarterly Journal of Economics* (1966) with the contributions by Pasinetti, Samuelson, Morishima, Burmeister and others.

As we saw above, in Wicksell's system the quantity of capital annually available in the economy is taken as given in terms of a single magnitude, which is thus included amongst the determinants of general equilibrium. At the same time, a decreasing demand function for capital (saving) is postulated, based on the 'substitution' principle – the principle according to which a fall in the rate of interest cheapens the more capital-intensive processes of production relative to the others, thereby raising the proportion of capital to the other productive factors in the economy. Such a demand function is essential to the idea that, *ceteris paribus*, increased saving will result in a reduced natural rate of interest, hence to the explanation of interest by the scarcity of capital.

Both these aspects of the marginalist analysis of capital have been found faulty on logical grounds, the main ingredients of the critique having been provided by Sraffa (1960). By studying the movement of relative prices consequent upon changes in distribution, he found that, in the face of unchanged methods of production, *reversals* in the direction of that movement may occur – a phenomenon which 'cannot be reconciled with *any* notion of capital as a measurable quantity independent of distribution and prices' (1960, p. 38); that is, of the very unknowns that the quantity of capital available in the economy should contribute to determine. (No such reversals could possibly occur if a single magnitude existed which was both independent of distribution and prices *and* representative of capital. Böhm-Bawerk's average period of production, for example, is independent of distribution and prices, but is not representative of the quantity of capital: if it were, then, assuming an average period of production of commodity A greater than that of commodity B, p_a would *continuously* rise relative to p_b with the rising of the rate of interest, contrary to what is shown by Sraffa (para. 48).) Moreover, the reversals in the direction of the movement of relative prices and the analogous phenomenon of 'reswitching' of methods of production (ch. XII) entail that no demand function for capital (saving) can be deduced from the existence of alternative methods of production and alternative consumption goods, except in very restrictive hypotheses.

We pointed out above the crucial role played in Wicksell's theory by the concept of a natural real rate of interest. The same concept plays a significant role also in Keynes's writings. This is clearly so in the *Treatise*; but also in the *General Theory*, notwithstanding the author's statement that he no longer regards the concept as 'a most promising idea' (Keynes, 1936, p. 243), yet the 'natural rate' is still there, as the rate of interest that would ensure equality between full employment saving and investment decisions. Keynes's underemployment equilibrium is ultimately the result of the presence in the economic system of factors that hinder the possibility of bringing the actual rate of interest down to its 'natural' or full employment level – it is the result, in other words, of a limited flexibility of the money rate of interest. If one takes into account that also in Wicksell there is no automatic gravitation of the money rate towards the level of the natural real rate (banking policy having to perform the task; see above), then the difference between the two authors will not appear so marked: they both share, in particular, the idea of an inverse relation between the rate of interest and investment decisions, whilst the contrast of opinion is essentially centred upon the degree of (non-automatic) flexibility of the rate of interest in the face of discrepancies between full employment saving and investment decisions. We believe that largely in the light of such a comparison the thesis was successfully laid down that, far from constituting *the* general theory, 'The General Theory of Employment is the Economics of Depression' (Hicks, 1937, p. 154). So our point here is that a better knowledge of Wicksell's work would have greatly facilitated the singling out of the traditional premises in *The General Theory* that aided the subsequent 'neoclassical synthesis', thereby helping to realize the importance of the critique of the marginal theory of capital and interest for establishing Keynes's principle of effective demand on firmer ground.

BIBLIOGRAPHY
Böhm-Bawerk, E. von. 1889. *Capital and Interest: a Critical History of Economic Theory.* Trans. W. Smart, New York: Stechert, 1932.
Burmeister, E. 1976. Real Wicksell effects and regular economies. In *Essays in Modern Capital Theory*, ed. M. Brown, K. Sato and P. Zarembka, Amsterdam: North-Holland.
Garegnani, P. 1960. *Il capitale nelle teorie della distribuzione.* Milan: Giuffrè.
Garegnani, P. 1970. Heterogeneous capital, the production function and the theory of distribution. *Review of Economic Studies* 37(3), 407–36.
Hicks, J.R. 1937. Mr. Keynes and the 'classics': a suggested interpretation. *Econometrica* 5(2), 157–9.
Keynes, J.M. 1930. *A Treatise on Money.* London: Macmillan. In *The Collected Writings of John Maynard Keynes*, New York: St. Martin's Press, 1971.
Keynes, J.M. 1936. *The General Theory of Employment, Interest and Money.* London: Macmillan; New York: Harcourt Brace.
Pasinetti, L., Levhari, D., Samuelson, P.A., Morishima, M., Bruno, M., Burmeister, E., Sheshinski, E. and Garegnani, P. 1966. Paradoxes in capital theory: a symposium. *Quarterly Journal of Economics* 80(4), November, 503–83.
Sraffa, P. 1960. *Production of Commodities by Means of Commodities: Prelude to a Critique of Economic Theory.* Cambridge: Cambridge University Press.
Wicksell, K. 1893. *Über Wert, Kapital und Rente.* Jena: G. Fisher. Trans. by S.H. Frowein as *Value, Capital and Rent.* London: Allen & Unwin, 1954; reprinted, New York: Kelley, 1970.
Wicksell, K. 1898a. *Geldzins und Güterpreise bestimmenden Ursachen.* Jena: G Fischer. Trans. by R.F. Kahn as *Interest and Prices: A Study of the Causes Regulating the Value of Money*, London: Macmillan, 1936; New York: A.M. Kelley, 1965.
Wicksell, K. 1898b. The influence of the rate of interest on commodity prices. In K. Wicksell, *Selected Papers on Economic Theory*, London: Allen & Unwin, 1958. Cambridge, Mass.: Harvard University Press.

Wicksell, K. 1901. *Föreläsningar i nationalekonomi. Häft I.* Stockholm, Lund: Fritzes, Berlingska. The 3rd Swedish edn (1928) of this volume trans. by E. Classen, ed. L. Robbins, as *Lectures on Political Economy,* Volume I: *General Theory,* London: Routledge & Kegan Paul, 1934; New York: Kelley, 1967.

Wicksell, K. 1906. *Föreläsningar i nationalekonomi. Häft II: Om penningar och kredit.* Stockholm, Lund: Fritzes, Berlingska. The 3rd Swedish edn (1929) trans. by E. Classen, ed. L. Robbins, as *Lectures on Political Economy,* Volume II: Money, London: Routledge & Kegan Paul, 1935; New York: Kelley, 1967.

Wicksell, K. 1923. Realkapital och kapitalränta. *Economisk Tidskrift* 21, 45–80. Trans. by S. Adler as *Real Capital and Interest* as Appendix 2 to Volume I of the *Lectures,* London: Routledge & Kegan Paul, 1934.

Contributors

Christopher Bliss Nuffield Reader in International Economics, Fellow, Nuffield College, Oxford. Fellow, Econometric Society; Fellow, British Academy. 'On putty-clay', *Review of Economic Studies* 35 (1968); *Capital Theory and the Distribution of Income* (1975); *Palanpur: the economy of an Indian village* (with N.H. Stern, 1975); 'The economic theory of retailing', *Journal of Industrial Economics* (June 1988); 'Trade and development', *Handbook of Development Economics* (ed. H. Chenery and T.N. Srinivasan, forthcoming).

Edwin Burmeister Commonwealth Professor of Economics, University of Virginia. Fellow, Econometric Society; Guggenheim Fellow (1974–5). 'The "Saddlepoint property" and the structure of dynamic heterogeneous capital good models', *Econometrica* (January 1973); 'Synthesizing the neo-Austrian and alternative approaches to capital theory: a survey', *Journal of Economic Literature* (June 1974); *Capital Theory and Dynamics* (1980); 'Sraffa, labor theories of value, and the economics of real wage rate determination', *Journal of Political Economy* (July 1984); 'Arbitrage pricing theory as a restricted multivariate regression model: ITNLSUR estimates', *Journal of Business and Economic Statistics* (January 1988); 'Joint estimation of factor sensitivities and risk premia for the arbitrage pricing theory', *Journal of Finance* (July 1988).

Sukhamoy Chakravarty Professor of Economics, Delhi School of Economics, Delhi University. Chairman, Indian Council of Social Science Research, New Delhi. Fellow, Econometric Society; President, Indian Econometric Society (1983–7); President, Indian Economic Association (1986); Honorary, International Economic Association (1987). 'The logic of investment planning', *Contributions of Economic Analysis* (1959); *Capital and Development Planning* (1969); *Contributions to Indian Economic Analysis – a survey* (with J.N. Bhagwati, 1971); *Alternative Approaches to a Theory of Economic Growth: Marx, Marshall,*

270

Schumpeter (1982); *Development, Planning: the Indian Experience* (1987); 'The state of development economics', *Journal of the Manchester School of Economics* (1987).

John Eatwell Fellow, Trinity College, Cambridge. Editor, *Contributions to Political Economy* (series). *An Introduction to Modern Economics* (with Joan Robinson, 1973). *Keynes's Economics and the Theory of Value and Distribution* (ed. with Murray Milgate, 1983); *Whatever Happened to Britain?* (1984).

Pierangelo Garegnani Professor, Facoltà di Economia e Commercio, University of Rome. *Il capitale nelle teorie della distribuzione* (1960); 'Heterogeneous capital, the production function and the theory of distribution', *Review of Economic Studies* 37(3), (1970); 'On a change in the notion of equilibrium in recent work on value: a comment on Samuelson', *Essays in Modern Capital Theory* (ed. M. Brown, K. Sato and P. Zarembka, 1976); 'Notes on consumption, investment and effective demand', *Cambridge Journal of Economics* (1978, 1979); 'Value and distribution in the classical economists and Marx', *Oxford Economic Papers* 35 (1984); 'On some illusory instances of "marginal products"', *Metroeconomica* (June–October 1984).

Harald Hagemann Professor of Economics, University of Hohenheim, Stuttgart. Fulbright Visiting Professor, New School for Social Research, New York (1986). *Rate of Return und Profitrate* (1977); *Technischer Fortschritt und Arbeitslogiskeit* (with P. Kalmbach, 1983); 'Nicholas Johannsen's early analysis of the saving–investment process and the multiplier', *Studi Economici* 42 (with C. Ruhl, 1987); *Keynes' General Theory nach funfzig Jahren* (1988); 'A Kaldorian saving function in a two sectoral linear model', *Nicholas Kaldor and Mainstream Economics* (ed. E.J. Nell and W. Semmler, 1989); 'The structural theory of economic growth', *Structure, Change and Economic Theory* (ed. M. Baranzini and R. Scazzieri, 1989).

Frank Hahn Professor of Economics, University of Cambridge; Fellow of Churchill College, Cambridge; Fellow, British Academy; Foreign Honorary Member, American Academy of Arts and Sciences; Honorary Doctorate, University of Birmingham, University of London; President, Econometric Society (1968); President, Royal Econometric Society (1986). 'On the foundations of monetary theory', *Essays in Modern Economics* (ed. M. Parkin and A.R. Nobay, 1973); *Money and Inflation* (1982); *In Praise of Economic Theory* (1984); *Equilibrium and Macroeconomics* (1984); *Money, Growth and Stability* (1985); 'On involuntary unemployment', *Economic Journal* (1987).

Tatsuo Hatta Professor, Institute of Social and Economic Research, Osaka University. 'The paradox in capital theory and complementarity of inputs', *Review of Economic Studies* 63 (1976); 'A theory of piecemeal policy recommendations',

Review of Economic Studies 64 (1977); 'A recommendation for a better tariff structure', *Econometrica* 45 (1977); 'Structure of the correspondence principle at an extremum point', *Review of Economic Studies* 47 (1980); 'Competition and nationally optimum resource allocation under the presence of urban tariff congestion', *Journal of Urban Economics* 14 (1983); 'The global correspondence principle: a generalization' (with J.N. Bhagwati and R.A. Brecher), *American Economic Review* 77 (1987).

K.H. Hennings Professor, Technische Universitat Hannover. *Böhm-Bawerk on the Rate of Interest: a re-interpretation* (1973); 'The exchange paradigm and the theory of production and distribution', in *Foundations of Economics* (ed. M. Baranzini and R. Scazzieri, 1985).

Charles R. Hulten The Urban Institute, Washington. 'Divisia index numbers', *Econometrica* (1973); *Depreciation, Inflation and the Taxation of Income from Capital* (ed., 1981); *The Legacy of Reaganomics: prospects for long-term growth* (ed. with Isabel V. Sawhill, 1984).

Heinz D. Kurz Professor of Economics, Department of Economics, University of Graz, Austria. *Zur neoricardianischen Theorie des Allgemeinen Gleichgewichts der Produktion und Zirkulation* (1977); 'Rent theory in a multisectoral model', *Oxford Economic Papers* (1978); 'Effective demand and employment in a "classical" model of value and distribution', *Manchester School* (1985); 'Classical and early neoclassical economists on joint production', *Metroeconomica* (1986); 'Burmeister on Sraffa and the labor theory of value', *Journal of Political Economy* (1987); *Capital, Income Distribution and Effective Demand* (1989).

David M. Newbery Director, Department of Applied Economics, Cambridge University. 'Risk sharing, sharecropping and uncertain labour markets', *Review of Economic Studies* (1977); *The Theory of Commodity Price Stabilization* (with J. Stiglitz, 1981); 'Oil prices, cartels and the problem of dynamic inconsistency', *Economic Journal* (September 1981); 'Commodity price stabilization in imperfect or cartelized markets', *Econometrica* (May 1984); *The Theory of Taxation for Developing Countries* (with N.H. Stern, 1987); 'Road damage externalities and road user charges', *Econometrica* (March 1988).

Gerhard O. Orosel Professor of Economics, University of Vienna. 'A paradoxon of the market mechanism', *Journal of Political Economy* 82 (1974); 'Unbalanced growth and fixed capital in a lagged Leontief model', *International Economic Review* 18 (1977); 'A reformulation of the Austrian theory of capital and its application to the debate on reswitching and related paradoxa', *Zeitschrift für Nationalökonomie* 39 (1979); 'Profitable speculation and price stability', *Jahrbucher für Nationalökonomie und Statistik* 199 (1984); 'Infinite horizon rational expectations equilibrium in a competitive model for an exhaustible resource', *International Economic Review* 26 (1985); 'Tentative notes on prestige seeking and Pareto-efficiency', in 'Welfare Economics of the Second Best' (ed. D. Bos and C. Seidl), *Journal of Economics/Zeitschrift für Nationalökonomie* Supplementum 5 (1986).

Luigi L. Pasinetti Professor, Università Cattolica S. Cuore, Milan. *Essays in the Theory of Joint Production* (ed., 1980); *Structural Change and Economic Growth* (1981); *Leçons sur le théorie de la production* (1985); *Structural Change, Economic Interdependence and World Development* (ed., with Peter Lloyd, 1987).

Massimo Pivetti Professor of Political Economy, Dipartimento di Scienze Economiche e Sociali, University of Naples. *Armamenti ed Economia: gli effetti della spesa militare e della produzione di armamenti nell'economia americana* (1969); 'Edwin Cannan e la Teoria Classica', Introduction to the Italian edition of E. Cannan's *History of the Theories of Production and Distribution* (1975); 'International integration and the balance of payments constraint: the case of Italy', *Cambridge Journal of Economics* 4 (1980); 'On the monetary explanation of distribution', *Political Economy – Studies in the Surplus Approach* 1(2), (1985).

Lionello F. Punzo Professor of Economics, University of Pisa; Lecturer of Mathematical Economics, Department of Political Economy, University of Siena. 'Multisectoral models and joint production' (with K. Velupillai), *Mathematical Models in Economics* (ed. F. van der Ploeg, 1984); 'La matematica di Sraffa', *Tra teoria economica e grande cultura europea: Piero Sraffa* (ed. by R. Bellofiore, 1986); 'Harrodian macrodynamics in generalized coordinates', *Growth, Cycles and Multisectoral Economics* (ed. G. Ricci and K. Velupillai, 1988); *The Dynamics of a Capitalist Economy. A Multi-Sectoral Approach* (with R.M. Goodwin); 'Von Neumann and K. Menger's mathematical colloquium', *John Von Neumann and Modern Economics* (ed. by M.H. Dore, S. Chakravarty and R.M. Goodwin, forthcoming); 'Generalized diagonal coordinates in dynamical analysis and capital and distribution theory', *Festschrift in Honour of Richard M. Goodwin* (ed. K. Velupillai, forthcoming).

Murray N. Rothbard S.J. Hall Distinguished Professor of Economics, University of Nevada. Vice President for Academic Affairs, Ludwig von Mises Institute. *Man, Economy and State: a treatise on economic principles* (1970); *Power and Market: government and the economy* (1977); *America's Great Depression* (1983); *The Ethics of Liberty* (1983); *For a New Liberty* (1985); *Conceived in Liberty* (1986).

Roberto Scazzieri Professor of Economics, Univ.... ,f Padua. Saint Vincent Prize for Economics (1984). *Efficienza produttiva e livelli di attivita'. Un contributo*

273

di teoria economica (1981); *Protagonisti del pensiero economico* (Vols 1–5, ed. with A. Quadrio-Curzio, 1977–83); 'The production process: general characteristics and taxonomy', *Rivista Internazionale di Scienze Economiche e Commerciali* 30(7), (1983); *Foundations of Economics. Structures of Inquiry and Economic Theory* (ed. with M. Baranzini, 1986); 'Ziber on Ricardo', *Contributions to Political Economy* 6 (1987); *Structure, Change and Economic Theory* (ed. with M. Baranzini, 1989).

Anwar Shaikh Professor, Department of Economics, New School for Social Research, New York. Research Grant, Jerome Levy Economics Institute of Bard College (1989); Distinguished Scholar, American Scholars to China, National Academy of Sciences (1985). 'Laws of algebra and laws of production: humbug II', *Growth, Profits and Property: essays in the revival of political economy* (ed. E.J. Nell, 1980); 'The transformation from Marx to Sraffa: prelude to a critique of the neo-Ricardians', *Marx, Ricardo, Sraffa* (ed. Ernest Mandel, 1984); 'The welfare state and the myth of the social wage' (with E. Ahmet Tonak), *The Imperiled Economy* (ed. Robert Cherry et al., 1987); 'The falling rate of profit and the economic crisis in the US', *The Imperiled Economy* (ed. Robert Cherry et al., 1987); 'Accumulation, finance, and effective demand in Marx, Keynes and Kalecki', *Financial Dynamics and Business Cycles: new prospects* (ed. Willi Semmler, 1988); 'A simple solution to Harrod's knife-edge problem', *Kaldor and Mainstream Economics: confrontation or convergence* (*Festschrift for Nicholas Kaldor*) (ed. E.J. Nell and Willi Semmler, 1989).

James Tobin Professor Emeritus, Department of Economics, Yale University. Nobel Prize in Economics (1981); Fellow, National Academy of Arts and Sciences; Fellow, Econometric Society; Fellow, British Academy; President, American Economic Association (1971). *Essays in Economics* (3 Vols, 1971/75/82); *Asset Accumulation and Economic Activity* (1980); *Policies for Prosperity* (1987); *Two Revolutions in Economic Policy* (with Murray Weidenbaum, 1988).

Paolo Varri Professor of Economics, University of Brescia. *Variazioni di produttivita nella economia italiana: 1959–67. Una applicazione dello schema di Sraffa* (with G. Marzi, 1977); 'Basic and non-basic commodities in Mr. Sraffa's price system', *Metroeconomica* 1 (1979); 'Prices, rate of profit and life of machines in Sraffa's fixed capital mode', *Essays on the Theory of Joint Production* (ed. L.L. Pasinetti, 1980); 'Il valore dei residui negli schemi di produzione congiunta', *Giornale degli Economisti ed Annali di Economia* (July/August 1981); 'Impostazioni alternative nella analisi dei problemi teorici della produzione congiunta', *I prodotti congiunti/Aspetti controversi di teoria della produzione* (ed. 1982).